Edward D. G. Prime

**Around the World**

Sketches of travel through many lands and over many seas

Edward D. G. Prime

**Around the World**
*Sketches of travel through many lands and over many seas*

ISBN/EAN: 9783337212599

Printed in Europe, USA, Canada, Australia, Japan

Cover: Foto ©Andreas Hilbeck / pixelio.de

More available books at **www.hansebooks.com**

# AROUND THE WORLD:

## SKETCHES OF TRAVEL

THROUGH MANY LANDS AND OVER MANY SEAS.

By E. D. G. PRIME, D.D.

WITH NUMEROUS ILLUSTRATIONS.

*NEW YORK:*
HARPER & BROTHERS, PUBLISHERS,
FRANKLIN SQUARE.
1872.
G

Entered according to Act of Congress, in the year 1872, by
HARPER & BROTHERS,
In the Office of the Librarian of Congress, at Washington.

TO

MY BELOVED AND VENERABLE

MOTHER,

WHO, BEYOND THE GATE OF FOURSCORE, GAVE ME HER PARTING
BLESSING, AND WATCHED FOR MY RETURN;

WHO NOW CALMLY AWAITS HER SUMMONS TO THE BETTER
COUNTRY,

THIS VOLUME

IS AFFECTIONATELY INSCRIBED.

# PREFACE.

THE journey of which the following pages contain a running account was undertaken by the writer mainly for the recovery of health, but also for the general purposes of travel and observation. The volume was designed, not in any measure as an exhaustive account of what is to be seen, and learned, and enjoyed in such a tour (a score of volumes would not contain the record), but to give to the intelligent reader suggestive glimpses of the world of interest which such a journey affords. The time devoted to it, a single year, may seem short when the great extent of land and sea is taken into account, but the facilities of travel are so great at the present day that more may now be compressed into a year than formerly into two or three.

Nor was the tour made so rapidly as might be supposed. The actual traveling time in going round the world has been reduced to seventy-five days, distributed as follows: From New York to San Francisco, by rail, six days; from San Francisco to Yokohama and Hong Kong, by steamship, twenty-seven days (this voyage might be made with perfect ease, at a little more expense of coal, in twenty-two days); from Hong Kong to Calcutta, by steam-ship, twelve days; from Calcutta to Bombay, *viâ* Allahabad, by continuous rail, a journey of 1450 miles through the heart of India, three days; from Bombay to Suez, by steam-ship, eleven days; from Suez to Paris or London, by steam-ship and rail, six days; from London to New York, ten days. This is taking the most direct route, and does not include excursions in various directions to and through different countries on the way, but it leaves between nine and ten months of the year to be spent where and in what way the inclination of the traveler may suggest. Having previously become familiar, by travel, with many of the countries of Europe, the writer devoted the greater part of his time to more eastern lands, spending two months in Japan and China, the same in India, and a portion of the remainder in Egypt and Western Asia. Taking a single year, and starting at the right time, enables the traveler to be in each country, and on every sea, at the most favorable season; whereas a longer period would inevitably bring him into some Oriental region in midsummer, when the heat is almost intolerable even for residents, or among the typhoons and cyclones of the tropical seas.

For the same reason he must needs travel westward, or he will as inevitably find himself in some part of the world at the season when he would wish to be any where else. The natural order, with the sun, is the only practicable course, excepting at great expense of comfort, and no little exposure of health and life.

The journey detailed in this volume was arranged, with regard to these contingencies, so accurately, that the highest range of the thermometer occurring in its whole extent was in crossing our own continent at starting, and in landing at New York on the return; and yet, in different parts of Asia that were visited, the degree of heat during a large part of the year varies from 100° to 130° Fahrenheit in the shade. In India, the thermometer often stands in summer at 120° and 130° during the day, and does not fall below 100° at night; but we neither saw frost during the entire year, nor a higher degree than 89 of the thermometer.

The precision with which such a journey can be arranged beforehand, with the present facilities and regularity of travel, may be gathered from the writer's experience. He had planned his entire excursion several months before setting out, with the times of arrival and departure for each country that he expected to visit; and until reaching Europe, where his plans were intentionally left uncertain, he was scarcely a day out of time at any stage of the journey. He had arranged to be at Calcutta on the 1st of December, to spend that month and the following (the only two months suitable for traveling) in India, and was there on the 3d, having accomplished his plans of travel in Japan and China with equal precision. Nearly six months before leaving home he had appointed to spend the first week of January, 1870, in the north of India, to be present at the religious anniversary of the Week of Prayer. He crossed the first range of the Himalaya Mountains the last day of the old year, and about an hour before the new year commenced alighted at the home of a friend in the beautiful valley of the Dehra Doon. He had engaged to meet at Cairo, on the 15th of February, his brother, William C. Prime, who had started eastward the week before he started west, and was there at the appointed time. His brother was detained by head winds up the Nile, and they did not meet; but on reaching home and comparing notes, they had the satisfaction of learning that they had spent two days together in Venice at different hotels, a few squares apart, without knowing it. He had arranged to be in Paris on the 1st of June, and was there on that day, and at home again punctually at the end of the year, the last of July.

The pleasure of the excursion was greatly enhanced to the writer by the presence of the one who is making with him the voyage of life, without whom it would not have been undertaken. Although an invalid, she accomplished the journey with far less fatigue than was anticipated. They enjoyed, during the greater part of the time, the very pleasant company of B. B. Atterbury, Esq., his daughter and son, Miss Mary Parsons, and Mr. Kilian Van Rensselaer, all of New York, who also made the entire circuit. Many agreeable traveling companions, of numerous nationalities, were met with by the way. To speak of all the pleasures and courtesies received from friends resident in the countries visited would require a separate volume. It is already written in our hearts—but not to be published.

For the encouragement of future travelers around the world, it is well to state that the journey was made without accident of any kind; without the occurrence of serious illness to any of the party; without missing a steamer or a train; without detention for a single day, scarcely for an hour; and without the loss of the most trifling article of baggage. More than once were we in peril on the land and on the sea, but under the care of a kind and watchful Providence we made the circuit of the earth and returned to our home in safety, all the objects of our journey attained—health, pleasure, instruction—and a world of information concerning many lands and people gathered, which will be a life-long source of enjoyment.

# CONTENTS.

## I.
NEW YORK TO SALT LAKE .................................................. 17-24
    Early Voyages around the World.—Magellan, Drake.—Pacific Railroad.—Palace Cars.—The Mississippi.—The Missouri.—Omaha.—Meeting a Train.—Indians.—Prairie-dog Villages.—Cheyenne.—Laramie City.—Sabbath on the Plain.—Rocky Mountains.—Echo and Weber Cañons.—Devil's Gate.
    ILLUSTRATION: Prairie-dog Village, 22.

## II.
THE MORMONS.................................................................. 25-35
    Uintah Station.—Stage Ride.—Salt Lake Valley.—Wonderful Fertility.—Irrigation.—Salt Lake City.—Brigham Young.—Mormon System.—The People.—Condition of the Women.—Joe Smith's Sons.—United States Troops.—Tabernacle.—Temple.—Fugitives.
    ILLUSTRATION: View on Salt Lake, 25.

## III.
CALIFORNIA..................................................................... 35-45
    Sierra Nevada Mountains.—Union Pacific Railroad.—Cape Horn.—Importance of Pacific Railroad.—Darien Canal.—Reaching San Francisco on Time.—Review of Journey.—A magnificent City.—Furs in August.—Seal Rock.—Climate of California.—No Rain in Summer.—Fruits: Grapes, Figs, and Pomegranates.
    ILLUSTRATION: On the Sierra Nevadas, 36.

## IV.
THE YOSEMITE VALLEY AND THE BIG TREES .................... 46-68
    Few Visitors from California.—Severe Journey.—How to go.—San Joaquin Valley.—Garrote.—Horseback Ride.—Mrs. Gobin.—Descent into the Yosemite Valley.—Mr. Colfax.—Hutchings's Hotel.—Yosemite Fall.—Sentinel Rock.—Domes.—Bridal Veil.—Mirror Lake.—Vernal and Nevada Falls.—Trout Fishing.—Inspiration Point.—The Big Trees.—Fruit-ranches.
    ILLUSTRATIONS: View of the Yosemite, 46.—Yosemite Fall, 53.—Fall of the Bridal Veil, 55.—Cathedral Rocks, 56.—Mirror Lake, 57.—Vernal Fall, 58.

## V.
ON THE PACIFIC ............................................................... 69-85
    Steam-ship Japan.—Sabbath Services.—Not meeting the Steamer.—Flying Fish.—Lunar Rainbow.—"The Ocean Wave" Newspaper.—Chinese Concert.—Trial of the Purser.—Dropping a Day.—Where does the Day begin?
    ILLUSTRATION: Flying Fish, 72.

## VI.

**EXCURSIONS IN JAPAN**...................................................85–109

First View of Japan.—Gulf of Yeddo.—Typhoon.—Yokohama.—Coolies.—Excursion to Daiboots.—Kanagawa.—The Bamboo.—Japanese Ponies.—Beautiful Scenery.—Statue at Daiboots.—Going to Yeddo.—The Yakonins.—Bettoes.—The Tokaido.—Yeddo.—Niphon Hotel.—Japanese Guard.—Temples.—Rev. Mr. Verbeck.—Book-stores.—Atangoreama.—Tycoon's Palace.—Shiba.

ILLUSTRATIONS: Entrance to the Gulf of Yeddo, 86.—Japanese Temple, 91.—Village Life in Japan, 93.—Statue at Daiboots, 95.—Bettoes, 99.—Japanese Kango, 101.—Japanese Resting, 102.—Tea-garden near Yeddo, 103.—Belfry in Courtyard of Temple, 106.

## VII.

**JAPAN AND THE JAPANESE**...................................................110–125

Territory.—Mikado.—Daimios.—Kinsats and Niboos.—Foreign Intercourse.—Character of the People.—Politeness.—Ladies' Dress.—Obi.—Dyeing Teeth black.—Shaving Heads.—Sandals.—Peculiar Customs.—Painting and Drawing.—Porcelain and Lacquer-ware.—Inlaying of Metals.—Beggars.—Saki.—Executions.—Burial.—Religions.—Shintooism.—Buddhism.—Confucianism.—Christianity.—Prospects.

ILLUSTRATIONS: Japanese Saluting, 115.—Female Hair-dresser, 116.—Japanese Horse-shoe and Saddle, 119.—Group of Horses, 119.—Athletes, 120.—Beheading, 122.

## VIII.

**INLAND SEA OF JAPAN**...................................................126–132

Suwonada.—Three Thousand Islands.—Cones.—Hiogo.—Osaka.—Tokaido.—Straits of Simoni-saki.—Panorama of Islands.—Pappenberg.—Nagasaki.—Gale in Eastern China Sea.—Yanktse-kiang River.

ILLUSTRATIONS: View in the Inland Sea, 126.—Entering the Inland Sea, 128.—Pappenberg Island, 130.

## IX.

**SHANGHAI TO HONG KONG**...................................................132–144

Approaching Shanghai.—Woosung River.—Chinese Forts.—War-junks.—City of Shanghai.—Taeping Rebels.—Foreign Town.—Wheelbarrows.—Chinese City.—Filth and Smells.—Chinese Criminals.—Modes of Punishment.—Duke of Edinburg.—International Boat-race; Americans victorious.—Pekin.—Nankin.—Suwonada Steamer.—Hong Kong.—Happy Valley.—Victoria Peak.—Schools.—Pigeon English.—Colonial Prison.—Motto on Post-office.

ILLUSTRATIONS: Chinese Trading-junk, 133.—Chinese Punishment, 137.—Chinese Temple, 139.—Hong Kong, 141.

## X.

**CANTON AND ITS SIGHTS**...................................................144–159

Early Commerce.—Steamer.—Bogue Forts.—Pearl River.—Villages.—Pawn-brokers.—Pagodas.—Whampoa.—River-population.—Boats.—Streets.—Shah-Min.—Streets of Canton.—Fan-kwai.—Puntinqua Garden.—Temples.—Mermaid.—Five Hundred Gods.—Priests.—Honam.—Chinese Dress.—Processions.—Funeral.

ILLUSTRATIONS: Chinese Pagoda, 146.—Fort near Canton, 149.—Sedan Chair, 150.

## XI.

**CHINESE MANNERS AND CUSTOMS**...................................................160–172

What they eat.—Birds' Nests.—Dog-markets.—Rats.—Porkers.—Fruits.—Small Feet.—Tea; Growth.—Black and Green, how prepared.—Contrarieties of the

*CONTENTS.*   xiii

Chinese.—Dress.—Language.—Coffins.—Competitive Examinations a Key to Chinese Character.

ILLUSTRATION: Chinese Small Foot, 163.

## XII.
RELIGIONS OF CHINA............................................................173–183

Confucianism. — Buddhism. — Tauism. — Superstition. — Ancestral Worship. — Cheating the Gods.—Inferior Gods.—Christianity in China.—Effect of Opium War.—Example of irreligious Foreigners.—Difficulty of acquiring the Language. —What Christian Missionaries have accomplished.—Medical Missionaries.—Dr. Kerr.—Oliphant & Co.

ILLUSTRATIONS: Casting Lots before a God, 175.—Prince Kung, 177.

## XIII.
MACAO, SINGAPORE, AND PENANG.......................................183–203

Stories of Pirates.—Portuguese at Macao.—Assassination of Amiral.—Churches. —Our Lady of Sorrow.—Camoens's Garden.—Captain Endicott.—Hon. Caleb Cushing.—Leaving for Calcutta.—Steamers.—The Hindostan.—Captain, Crew, and Passengers.—The Monsoon.—A Storm.—Walter M. Lowrie.—180th Degree. —Singapore a Paradise.—Cocoanuts, Nutmeg, Cinnamon, etc.—Gardens.—Mr. P. Yoakim.—Rev. Mr. Keasbury.—Rev. Mr. Grant.—Major Malan.—Straits of Malacca. — Penang. — Rev. Mr. Macdonald. — Chinese. — Mahomet Noordin. — Tropical Vegetation.—Boa Constrictors.—Bay of Bengal.—Turtles.—Snakes.— East Indiamen.

ILLUSTRATIONS: Macao, 185.—Coolie Barracoons at Macao, 187.

## XIV.
CALCUTTA............................................................203–221

Hoogly River.—Lady seized by Tiger.—Palms and Acacias.—Banyan Tree.— Palace of ex-King of Oude.—Scene at Landing.—Spence's Hotel.—Hindoo Servants.—Aroused by Jackals.—Crows, Kites, and Adjutants.—"City of Palaces." —Maidan.—Gay Scene.—Residences.—Public Buildings.—Tanks.—Watering Streets.—Institutions.—Colleges.—Asiatic Society.—American Zenana Mission. Serampore.—Carey, Ward, Marshman, Judson, Henry Martyn, Dr. George Smith. —Hindoo Festival.

ILLUSTRATION: Entrance to the Hoogly, 204.

## XV.
GOVERNMENT OF INDIA; EUROPEANS, ETC..........................221–234

Antiquity of the Nation.—Alexander the Great.—East India Company.—Present Rulers.—Viceroy.—Education.—University, Colleges, and Schools.—Complicity with Idolatry.—European Population.—Eurasians.—Heat.—Punkas.—Living. —Rainfall.—Sand-storms.—American Ice.

ILLUSTRATION: A Sand-storm, 233.

## XVI.
PUBLIC WORKS, PRODUCTIONS, ETC...................................234–243

Roads.—Canals.—Telegraph.—Railways.—Opium.—The Poppy.—Preparing the Drug.—Opium Market.

## XVII.
THE NATIVES OF INDIA; CASTE, ETC..................................244–254

Native Society. — Hindoos. — Mohammedans. — Sikhs. — Parsees. — Costumes. — Jewels. — Women of India. — Native Wealth. — Food. — Caste. — Brahmins. — Kshatryas.—Vaishyas.—Sudras.—Breaking Caste.—Pariahs.

xiv                    *CONTENTS.*

## XVIII.

CALCUTTA TO BENARES .................................................254–270

Leaving Calcutta.—Grand Durbar.—Howrah.—East India Railway.—Cold Nights.—Scenery.—Plain of India.—Mogul-Serai.—The Hindoo Holy City.—Monkey Temple.—The Ganges.—Man Mandil.—Grand Mosque.—Ghauts.—Brahminy Bulls.—Burning the Dead.—Rajah of Benares.—Elephant Ride.—Golden Temple.—The Ancient City.

ILLUSTRATIONS: The Grand Mosque, 262.—Burning the Dead, 263.—A Hindoo Temple, 268.—Ruins near Benares, 270.

## XIX.

BENARES TO ALLAHABAD ...............................................271–281

Crossing the Ganges by Moonlight.—Chunar.—Goddess Kali.—Thugs.—Discovery and Suppression.—Major Sleeman's Narrative.—The Jumna at Allahabad.—Railroad Bridge.—Rev. Mr. Walsh.—The City of God.—Fortress.—Great Mela.—Pilgrims.—Faquirs.—Government Connection with Idolatry.

## XX.

THE MUTINY; CAWNPORE AND LUCKNOW..........................281–296

Diversity of Opinions.—Anniversary of Battle of Plassey.—Greased Cartridges.—Chupatties.—Outbreak at Dundum.—Meerut.—Delhi.—Allahabad.—Agra.—Cawnpore.—Nana Sahib.—General Wheeler.—Massacre of Soldiers.—Massacre of Women and Children.—Well at Cawnpore.—Memorial Garden.—Monument.—Massacre of Missionaries.—Suttee Chowra Ghaut.—Lucknow.—King of Oude.—Residency.—The Siege.—Havelock.—Sir Henry Lawrence.—Persian Newspaper.—"Voyage round the World."

## XXI.

AGRA AND THE TAJ ......................................................296–310

Only Rain in India.—East Indian Hotel.—Bed and Bedding.—Fort and Palace.—Heavy Cannon.—Pearl Mosque.—The Taj.—Gateway.—Park.—Shah Jehan.—Noor Mahal.—Mosque and Jowab.—Cost of Building.—Terraces.—Minarets.—Description.—Interior.—Sarcophagi.—Inscriptions.—Song and Echo.—Christian Village at Secundra.—Tomb of Akbar.—His Palaces and Wealth.—Arrested for Stealing.

ILLUSTRATION: The Taj (*Frontispiece*), 301.

## XXII.

DELHI..........................................................................311–320

Old Delhi.—Shah Jehan.—Gates.—Chandnee Chowk.—Fortress.—Diwan-a-im.—Diwan-i-khas.—Peacock Throne.—The Palace.—Jumma Musjid.—Kootub-Minar.—Iron Pillar.—Divers.—Ruins.—Rev. James Smith.—Blowing up the Magazine.—Post-office at Delhi.

## XXIII.

AMONG THE HIMALAYAS................................................320–328

Saharunpur.—Presbyterian Mission.—Government Stud.—Omnibuckus.—Horses.—Road over Sewalic Range.—Drawn by Coolies.—Leopards.—Tiger-hunting.—Doctor Fayrer.—Duke of Edinburg.—Wild Elephants.—Snakes.—Valley of Dehra Doon.—Rev. Mr. Woodside.

## XXIV.

ON THE HIMALAYAS......................................................328–336

Ascending the Mountain.—Jhanpan.—Monkeys.—Wild Peacocks.—Mussoorie.—

CONTENTS. XV

Landour.—View from the Summit.—Thibet and Cashmere.—Dr. Kellett.—The Sabbath.—Meneely's Bell.—Tea Plantations.—Praying Machine.—Pacific Railroad.—Week of Prayer.—Amballa.—Rev. Dr. Morrison.—Lodiana.—Cabool Princes.—The Koh-i-noor Diamond: its History.
ILLUSTRATIONS: A Gorge in the Himalayas, 320.—A Praying Machine, 333.

## XXV.
LODIANA TO BOMBAY ................................................... 336–343

Suttee at Cawnpore.—Jubbulpore.—Colony of Thugs.—Journey by Dak-gharry.—The Nerbudda.—Wild Horses.—Night Journey.—The Jungle.—Tigers.—Loading Revolver.—An Accident.—Dak-bungalows.—Nagpore.—Mahratta Country.—Cotton.—Egutpoora.—Tunnels.

## XXVI.
BOMBAY ................................................... 343–350

Island of Bombay.—Portuguese Colony.—Harbor.—Population.—Varieties of Races.—Buildings.—Parsees.—Towers of Silence.—Malabar Hill.—Burning the Dead.—Caves of Elephanta.—Mr. Kittredge.—Buddhist Monastery at Kenhari.—Dr. Bhau Daji.—Indian Jugglers.—Cocoanut Grove.—Hospital for Animals.
ILLUSTRATION: A Bullock Carriage, 345.

## XXVII.
BOMBAY TO CAIRO ................................................... 350–361

Leaving India.—British Rule.—Fearful Scene at Sea: two Men overboard.—Aden.—Broad-tail Sheep.—Red Sea.—Straits of Bab-el-Mandeh.—Constellation of the Southern Cross.—Mocha.—Abyssinian Hero.—Djiddah, Port of Mecca.—Gale.—Suez.—Crossing of the Israelites.—Dr. Robinson.—The Suez Canal.—Chartering a Steamer.—Ismailia.—Reaching Cairo.—Shepheard's Hotel.—Strange Chambermaid.
ILLUSTRATIONS: Suez, 355.—Night on the Canal, 359.

## XXVIII.
CAIRO TO JERUSALEM ................................................... 362–375

The Citadel.—Caliphs and Mamelukes.—Old Cairo.—Memphis.—The Nile.—Pyramids and Sphinx.—Backshish.—Leaving Cairo.—Meeting Friends.—Alexandria.—Catacombs.—Pompey's Pillar.—Alexandrian Library.—Light-house of Pharos.—Bound for the Holy Land.—Port Said.—Englishmen.—Experience in London.—Americans abroad.—Effects of our War.—Reaching Jaffa.—Orange Groves.—Russian Convent at Ramleh.—Muezzin's Call to Prayer.—The Sabbath.—Going up to Jerusalem.—Mediterranean Hotel.
ILLUSTRATIONS: The Pyramids, 364.—A Street in Cairo, 365.

## XXIX.
THE HOLY CITY ................................................... 375–388

The Road to Calvary.—Pilate's House.—Via Dolorosa.—Chapel of the Flagellation.—Arch of Ecce Homo.—Houses of Dives and Lazarus.—Church of Holy Sepulchre.—Stone of Unction.—The Sepulchre.—Hill of Calvary.—Chapel of St. Helena.—Invention of the Cross.—Latin Chapel.—Vesper Service.—Father Antonio.—Mount Zion.—Bishop Gobat.—Jews' Wailing Place.—Mosque of Omar.—Temple of Solomon.—Gate called Beautiful.—Gethsemane.—Mount of Olives.—King David's Flight.—Bethlehem.—Bethany.—Valley of the Jordan.—Attacked by Bedouins.—Sabbath in Jerusalem.
ILLUSTRATIONS: Via Dolorosa, 376.—Church of the Holy Sepulchre, 377.—The Beautiful Gate, 383.—Jerusalem and Gethsemane, 384.

## XXX.

**TO DAMASCUS AND CONSTANTINOPLE**..................................389–401

Desolation of the Holy Land.—Leaving Jerusalem.—Robberies.—Ramleh.—Jaffa.—Mount Carmel.—Beyrout.—Messrs. Goodell and Bird.—Druses.—Army expected from China.—Massacre of 1860.—Grandeur of Lebanon.—Leaving for Damascus.—Diligence.—French Road.—Valley of Cœlo-Syria.—River Abana.—Damascus.—Street called Straight.—Rev. Mr. Crawford.—Abd-el-Kader.—Khans.—Mohammed.—Mount Hermon.—Sturza.—Cloud of Locusts.—Leaving Beyrout.—Cyprus.—Rhodes.—Patmos.—Smyrna.—Polycarp.—Mytilene.—Tenedos.—Dardanelles.—Gallipoli.—Stamboul.

ILLUSTRATIONS: Beyrout, 392.—Damascus, 398.—Patmos, 400.

## XXXI.

**STAMBOUL TO NAPLES**..................................................402–417

Storms at Constantinople; Snow, Rain, Mud.—Political State of Turkey.—Progress among the People.—Armenians.—Bibles.—Dr. Hamlin.—Robert College.—Leaving Stamboul.—Sea of Marmora.—Turkish Naval Officers.—Landing at Night.—The Piræus.—Athens.—The Acropolis.—Mars Hill.—The Pnyx.—Marathon.—Party murdered by Brigands.—Syra.—Cape Matapan.—Navarino.—Cephalonia.—Zante.—Gulf of Corfu.—Brindisi.—Banditti.—Entering Naples.—Beggars.—Bay of Naples; Vesuvius, Sorrento, Pozzuoli, Baiæ, Cumæ, Lake Avernus, River Styx, Elysian Fields.—Herculaneum and Pompeii.—National Museum.—Cemeteries of Naples.

ILLUSTRATION: Frieze of the Parthenon, 407.

## XXXII.

**ROME TO FLORENCE**....................................................418–436

Old Route to Rome.—Terracina.—Roman Frontier.—Passports.—Illumination at Rome.—Present at two Councils.—Pius IX. and Herod.—Arch of Titus.—Sacred Vessels of the Jewish Temple.—The Pantheon.—Anecdote of Charles V.—Barberini.—Raphael's Skull.—The Tiber.—Overflow.—Catacombs: Origin; St. Sebastian and St. Agnese; Bodies; Inscriptions.—Sun shining on Rome.—Florence.—View from San Miniato.—Uffizi and Pitti Palaces.—Pisa, Leaning Tower, Galileo.—Chandelier.—Victor Emanuel.—Waldenses.—Religious Liberty.

ILLUSTRATIONS: Ground-plan of the Catacombs, 428.—Florence, from San Miniato, 434.

## XXXIII.

**VENICE HOMEWARD**....................................................436–455

Piercing the Apennines.—City of the Sea.—How to enjoy Venice.—Moonlight and Midnight.—Bell of San Marco.—Vienna.—Change in Government.—Mausoleum of Capucin Church.—Duke of Reichstadt.—Maximilian.—Prague.—"The Bohemian Fashion."—Tycho Brahe.—Huss.—Jerome.—Dresden.—Berlin.—Charlottenberg.—Wittenberg.—Luther and Melancthon.—Ninety-five Theses.—Potsdam.—Frederick the Great.—Cologne.—Cathedral.—The Rhine.—Worms.—Weissenberg.—Strasbourg.—The Siege.—The War.—Nancy, Bar le Duc, etc.—Paris.—London.—Isle of Wight.—England.—Scotland.—Ireland.—Atlantic Ocean.—Home again.

ILLUSTRATION: Bingen on the Rhine, 448.

# AROUND THE WORLD.

## I.

### NEW YORK TO SALT LAKE.

A JOURNEY around the world is a very different undertaking to-day from what it was when Magellan set his prow toward the setting sun, and sailed onward—onward—until, with the rising sun, his ships returned to the harbor of Seville. It does not appear to have been well established, even among scientific men of that day, that the earth was round, and those who admitted the truth seem to have had a strong apprehension that it would not be safe for navigators to venture too far over the other side; they might not be able to make their way up again. The ships, too, in which these early voyagers ventured out into unknown seas were mere shallops compared with those which now traverse every ocean. The vessels in which Columbus first crossed the Atlantic are said to have been not more than a hundred tons burden—less than half the tonnage of the pleasure yachts whose safe passage over the same ocean within a few years has been accounted a great nautical exploit. The ships of Magellan, which were the first to compass the globe, were two of 130 tons, two of 90, and one of 60. When, nearly half a century later, Sir Francis Drake left the shores of England to sail around the world, the five ships that composed his fleet numbered respectively 100, 80, 50, 30, and 15 tons. To attempt to cross any ocean at the present day in such vessels, much more to brave all the perils of the Eastern Seas, would be accounted a piece of reckless hardihood. The heroism of those early navigators of unexplored seas is beyond all praise.

For two centuries after it was first accomplished, the voyage around the world was not made within less than three years. This was the time consumed by the ships of Magellan. He, unfortunately, did not live to share in the final glory of the achievement due to his genius and heroism, having fallen in a conflict with the natives of the Philippine Islands the second year out. Sir Francis Drake was three years in sailing round. Captain Cook was three years in making each of his voyages; and the last, in which he also fell by the hands of savages, extended to four years. Now the circuit is a mere holiday excursion, and may be made in less than three months.

It was to me a coincidence of some interest that the day (August 1, 1869) on which I had completed all my arrangements for the journey of which some account is given in the pages following was precisely three hundred and fifty years from that on which the first circumnavigator of the globe left the harbor of Seville. My plans for the journey had been definitely made several months before, and a complete programme of the entire tour prepared, including every country that I expected to visit, and almost every day of the year. I was desirous to leave immediately on the opening of the Pacific Railroad, but I delayed in order to reach the Japan and China Seas at a period of the year when they are free from the typhoons which sweep over them with destructive violence during the summer months, and also to reach India just at the beginning of winter, the only season in which a stranger can travel there with comfort or safety. The appointed time having arrived, we left New York by the New Jersey Central Railroad, and on the evening of the following day were in Chicago, where we spent the night. I had telegraphed in advance for accommodations in the Pullman Pacific cars, which at that time were running regularly no farther east than Chicago. On reaching the station of the Northwestern Road the next morning, I was most agreeably surprised to find that Mr. Pullman had set apart for the exclusive use of our party one of his finest palace cars—the " Promontory," then entirely new; and that, to add still farther to the pleasure of the excursion, the secretary of the company, Mr. Charles W. Angell, in whom I recognized a former friend, had made his arrangements to accompany us as far as Omaha, five hundred miles on the way, to see us safely across the Missouri River and out on the broad prairie. These moving palaces have now become familiar to the traveling world, but at the time we entered the " Promontory" it was an event to find on wheels and to take with us a luxurious home—a parlor by day, and ample staterooms by night, in which we lived and slept with as much comfort as in a hotel. And I may here add that in no other part of the world did we find, either on land or on sea, such luxurious accommodations, or travel in so much ease. We would gladly have taken the same mode of conveyance all the way round.

We crossed the Mississippi by the high bridge at Fulton, and entered what then appeared to be the granary of the West. The summer of 1869 had been so wet that from the time of leaving New Jersey we did not see one fine field of Indian corn until we entered Iowa, and the wheat crop had also been severely affected; but almost immediately after we crossed the Mississippi the corn-fields of the West assumed their traditional grandeur, and the whole country had a new face. In the evening we had an illumination of our car, which was abundantly supplied with lamps, concealed in the day by mirrors. Two Harvard students, bound westward on a hunting expedition upon the prairies, called, and spent the evening with us, and it passed away as rapidly as the train. Our first night on the palace car was one of quiet repose, and the morning brought us to Council Bluffs, on the Missouri, where we were ferried over to Omaha, the bridge at this point being then in course of erection. Here we bade farewell to our escort, and struck out into the wide regions of the West, speeding onward and onward—one hundred miles after another—never ascending a perceptible elevation, and scarcely ever deviating from a straight line.

At North Bend, on the Platte River, we spoke a train from San Francisco bound east. It was like meeting a ship in mid-ocean. There was no little excitement as we descried each other in the distance across the prairie; and when we halted at the station I displayed the Stars and Stripes, which I carried not so much for protection as for dear remembrance in the many and far-distant lands that we were to visit. We had a few moments of hasty conversation and inquiry for the news from either direction, and when the passengers by the other train learned that we also were bound for New York, but by way of the setting sun, they sent up three hearty cheers for the old flag and for the party that was to bear it around the world. Amid our answering cheers the trains moved off, east and west, and were soon lost to each other in the distance.

Late in the day, after dining at Grand Island, I went out on the engine to enjoy the excitement of scudding over the wide ocean of land. We were then beyond the sight of homes, and the stations on the road were few and far between. We overtook a troop of horses that were roaming wild over the prairie. As they saw the train approaching they selected the track for a race-course, and started for the Pacific Ocean at the top of their speed. But the iron horse was too much for them. Every now and then we overhauled the coursers, when the shrill whistle of the engine, instead of driving them from the track, only inspired them with new vigor, and imparted fresh speed. A stern chase is usually a long chase, but we ran them down, and they struck out into the prairie right and left. Then we came upon a flock of prairie birds, which seemed possessed with the idea that they could not escape from the lines of telegraph poles and wires on either side of the railroad track, and for a long time we kept them company; but at length they also disappeared, and we had the course all to ourselves, and improved it well. The ride was exciting, without fear of danger on the level plain, and as we hauled up at the next station, the engineer took out his watch, and, turning to me, said, "One hour and five minutes." On my asking how many miles we had run between the two stations, he said " Forty." And yet, so perfectly level, and straight, and smooth was the road, that I had sat upon the engine with as much ease as in the car.

At Plum Creek, where we were detained half an hour by a heated axle, we found 150 United States soldiers stationed to guard the road against the Indians. I called on the commanding officer at his tent near by, and learned from him that a band of hostile Indians had crossed the track a few nights before, about four miles below. Of course I communicated the pleasing intelligence to the ladies, whose chief terror in undertaking the journey had been the wild Indians on the Pacific Railroad. But, to reassure them (as none of us had any extra hair that we wished to lose), I got out my revolver, and, lest some one should be hurt, took the precaution not to load the dangerous weapon, and no hostile savages made their appearance that night.

The next morning broke upon us nearly 500 miles west from Omaha. We were then ascending the Black Hills, the highest elevation on the Pacific Road, the station at Sherman being 8264 feet above the sea level. The country was beginning to assume the air of desolation which marks the Great American Desert. On all sides were rolling hills, to which the antelopes that we scared up in great numbers bounded off with the fleetness of the wind, after pausing for a moment to examine the cars. They were frequently within rifle-shot. Whole counties of prairie-dog villages skirted the road, the curious little animals usually sitting bolt upright on their haunches, like statues, on the tops of their houses, or scampering away as we passed their towns.

PRAIRIE-DOG VILLAGE.

Cheyenne was at that time the most populous city on the line of the road west of Omaha, although it was less than two years old. On account of its relative importance, we had selected it as the most desirable place for stopping to spend the Sabbath. After breakfasting, I asked one of the oldest inhabitants, an intelligent-looking youth, what was the population of their city. He replied very seriously that about a year ago it was 12,000, but they had shot, and hung, and killed so many it now numbered only 4000. We congratulated ourselves that we had concluded to go farther on, and accordingly, about noon on Saturday, we left the train, and found comfortable quarters at the hotel at Laramie City.

This place is situated on the table-land known as Laramie Plains—an immense plateau 7134 feet above the level of the sea, without a mountain or hill in sight, looking north or south, but with the Black Hills on the east, and the Rocky Mountains, with their perpetual snow, on the west. From our windows we looked across the vast plain directly out into the deep ether, just as one looks across the ocean into the sky, the rotundity of the earth being as distinct in the one case as the other. The view of the Rocky Mountains, on the west, was grand beyond description. They seemed to come almost to our feet, although they were in reality some 60 miles distant, and in that perfectly clear atmosphere it was a calm delight just to sit and gaze upon the mighty chain with which the Almighty had bound together this vast continent. I had heard it said on the way that it never rains on Laramie Plains, but we had not been there more than two hours before the rain commenced pouring in torrents, and it continued to come down as abundantly for at least an hour, giving us a supply of wholesome water, which can not be found for a thousand miles on the Pacific Railroad.

The Sabbath passed pleasantly. In the morning we attended the service of the Rev. Mr. Cornell, an Episcopal missionary, and in the evening I addressed an assembly of residents and miners, who filled the largest public room in the town. At the close of the evening service, many whom we had met as perfect strangers gathered round us, and we were detained long by our mutual expressions of interest in finding that we had common sympathies and hopes, though belonging to many different branches of the Christian family. The place, we were assured, was not what it was a year before. It had been thinned out by the process resorted to in the neighboring city of Cheyenne. We heard accounts of summary executions having taken place in the streets, but a more orderly or quiet town of two thousand inhabitants on a Sunday I have never seen in any part of the country.

Taking the train again at noon on Monday, we crossed the Plains, and commenced the ascent of the Rocky Mountains, if ascent it could be called when we passed up and over them so gradually that we did not know it. We had been in sight of the distant peaks for two days while stopping at Laramie City; but there were no lofty ranges to cross, and no mountains towering above us, until long after we began the descent on the other side. It was simply a scene of wild desolation—utter barrenness, as if the soil had been cursed that it should not bring forth. There was only an occasional bunch of wild sage, almost as dreary looking as the barren soil. One who has not seen this portion of the Pacific Railroad, and other portions of the Great American Desert for nearly a thousand miles in extent, can form no idea of the dreary waste that stretches on and on, until the eye longs to rest on something fresh and green, or even upon a rock; for, contrary to all our ideas of the Rocky Mountains, not a rock was to be seen in this portion of the route.

It was not until we entered the Echo Cañon that the mountains assumed any grandeur; but here, and in the Weber Cañon, a scene of wonderful magnificence opened upon us. On one hand (the left in passing westward) all is smooth—not a rock to be seen, although the mountains rise to a sublime height from the bed of the Weber River; but the opposite side of the narrow defile is composed of towering rocks, assuming all forms of magnificent proportions, sometimes towering up in vast precipices toward the skies, and at others stretching out over the road, or assuming grotesque shapes. It was in the Echo Cañon that Brigham Young threatened to destroy the army of General Sidney Johnston by rolling rocks down upon them as they marched through the narrow causeway, when the army was sent to look after the Mormons. The passage of the river and the railroad out of this weird region into the Salt Lake Valley is called the Devil's Gate. The name was given on account of the fearful wildness of the scenery to which it leads, but it is equally appropriate as leading to the moral scene to which it introduces the traveler as he enters the Salt Lake Valley. Echo City is the border town of the Mormon Territory of Utah.

VIEW ON SALT LAKE.

## II.

### THE MORMONS.

At Uintah Station, about a mile from the "Devil's Gate," we left the cars and took stage for Salt Lake City, thirty-five miles distant. The branch railroad was not then completed. The stage-road was rough and stony for a few miles, but the greatest inconvenience arose from the innumerable little streams which crossed it, as the means of irrigating the whole eastern portion of the valley. Many of these water-courses are natural, but others have been made by divisions and subdivisions, in order to carry the water to parts which could not otherwise be irrigated. The streams are seldom bridged, and the gullies made in the loose soil were a great source of discomfort to the stage traveler, to whom they prove too decidedly anti-dyspeptic for a pleasure excursion. But the stages and horses were good, and the ride, which was accomplished within about five hours, I would not have lost, even at the cost of a more severe shaking than we received. It gave us a fine opportunity for seeing the marvelous transformation of a desert into fruitful fields. Compared with what it was when the Mormons entered it twenty-one years before, the valley was more like a creation than the result of human skill and labor, and yet the change has been wrought almost exclusively by irrigation. The vast mountain barrier which stretches along the eastern portion of the valley is an immense fountain, streams of the purest water issuing from its sides at every point, and furnishing the means by which this once arid desert has been converted into one of the most fertile plains to be found on the face of the continent. When the Mormons entered this valley, it was like the desolate mountains over which we had passed for hundreds of miles — a perfect waste of sand and wild sage, or devil's bush; but, within a little more than twenty years from their first immigration, they had extended a line of farms along the eastern shore of the lake, sixty miles in extent — farms that equal in fertility the finest prairies in the East.

We traversed thirty-five miles of these cultivated fields, and every mile only increased our admiration of the results of this system of utilizing pure mountain water. The most beautiful crops of wheat formed the staple production — beautiful not alone because they were abundant, but because ripened and harvested, so far as they had been gathered, without a drop of rain, the straw and the ear so bright that they shone like silver in the sun. The fields of Indian corn and sorghum were standing up more luxuriant and taller than any we had seen east of the Mississippi, and equal to any we had seen in Iowa. The orchards on every farm were loaded with fruit, some of it ripening, but the most in about the same stage as at the East in the same latitude. The roadside, for the greater part of the way from Uintah to Salt Lake City, was a succession of apple, and plum, and peach orchards; the fruit, especially the apples, of large size, and the trees literally bending to the ground with their burdens.

At Salt Lake City, Governor Durkee, in speaking of the wonderful fertility of the valley under Mormon tillage, said he could point out to me a lot of ten acres which had produced 900 bushels of wheat at a single crop; and Mr. Hooper, the delegate to Congress from Utah, also stated to me that there were in the agricultural bureau of the Territory records of the production of wheat at the rate of 93 bushels to the acre. These, of course, were exceptional cases, and were the result of manuring as well as irrigation, and the most careful cultivation. By the same system of irrigation, Salt Lake City, which had not a tree or shrub when it was first settled by the Mormons, is now a park of locust and cottonwood-trees, the former raised entirely from the seed, and the latter transplanted from the cañons in the mountains. Every street has its stream of water, and every garden in its turn is regularly watered under the direction of commissioners. This is certainly a wonderful change for a score of years. One can not but admire the enterprise which has created a garden out of a vast desert, but the amount of labor expended in preparing the soil for cultivation has been small compared with the toil of the early pioneers at the East, who had dreary forests to clear away before they could go to work upon the soil itself. Here the settlers had only to turn the water upon the soil, and the work was almost done.

This is the outside of Mormonism, and fair enough it is. The plague-spot, the corrupt system of imposture and delusion, is in the homes of the Salt Lake City and Valley. I went to Salt Lake City to learn upon the spot what Mormonism is; and having had the best opportunities for acquiring the information desired, I came away thoroughly convinced that it is a system of the grossest iniquity, and, on the part of the leaders, an arrant imposture upon a poor deluded people. There is much to admire in the material prosperity of the Territory, in the industry, order, and public spirit of the people, and even in the administration of affairs by the Mormon leaders; but one needs only to examine with a careful eye, and to reflect upon what he learns, in order to be convinced that the spirit and purposes of the whole thing are selfish and wicked. I have never met with any person, man or woman, who, having been at Salt Lake City, wishes to go there again. The feeling of disgust which comes over a stranger on entering the place increases every hour; and when once the city is left behind, a sense of relief springs up as if a load were taken off the shoulders. The very atmosphere seems loaded with a moral pestilence, and an indescribable feeling of shame comes over the mind as we walk the streets and meet with men and women who are living lives which ought to be lives of shame to them. I did not call to pay my respects to Brigham Young simply because I had no respects to pay to such a man, in such a house as he keeps. Immediately upon reaching Salt Lake City I received from a Mormon high in position a polite invitation to call upon "the President," which I as politely declined. I could learn nothing from him that I could not learn more satisfactorily and more reliably elsewhere, and I had no mawkish curiosity to gratify. I became satisfied, from what I heard while there, that great injury has been done to the Mormons themselves, and that there has been much compromise of dignity, if not of principle, by visitors of all ranks, and among them Christians and Christian ministers, who have shown an eagerness to be presented to the arch-leader of Mormonism. The inference which the Mormon people draw is, that he must be a great and good man when the great and the good wish to pay him reverence; and Brigham Young himself is puffed up by the attentions which are shown him by persons from the outer world.

The Mormon people generally are sincere, devout believers in the system of religion which they have adopted, and in the men who rule over them. They are an ignorant class, gathered from the lowest walks of life, and have no means of acquiring knowledge but through Mormon sources. The schools which they sustain do not afford the means of real education, although one or two of them have been greatly improved of late. The sale of books and of all sorts of literature, standard and periodical, at the bookstores in the city, is made almost exclusively to "Gentiles," and it would be very difficult to diffuse light among the Mormons. They have, almost without exception, implicit confidence in their spiritual rulers, who, they are taught to believe, are divinely commissioned to exercise authority over them, and whose integrity it would be a sin to call in question. The leaders, on the other hand, I believe to be as unscrupulous a set of men as can be found. There doubtless are some exceptions, but these exceptional cases are not among those who are admitted to the councils of the actual rulers of the community. The system of Mormonism, as now administered, has three foundation stones —*Love of Power, Avarice, and Lust:* on these it rests, and it has no better basis, as facts patent to every intelligent visitor will show.

The system, to begin with, was an arrant imposture, not having even the redeeming feature of fanaticism to excuse those who concocted it. It has been kept up by impostors, who pretend to have received divine revelations to carry out their plans. And what are their purposes? Here is a large community, gathered from all parts of the world, living under an absolute despotism. The people have no share in the government, although living under the protection of a republic. The form of voting is a mere sham, as the rulers know just how every man votes, and he must needs vote one way. The acts of the rulers, especially in their financial affairs, are sometimes submitted to the approval of the people in public assembly, but in such a manner that they can form no judgment, and they are all virtually compelled to hold up their hands together. Every thing is under the control of a few men who pretend to a divine commission to rule the people. No ideas of republican freedom, of personal responsibility and rights, are permitted to enter the minds of the community; and the whole police system is so perfect that it is next to impossible for them to acquire such ideas. The leaders, too, are perfectly unscrupulous in the exercise of their power. I could give instances, which I have received on the best authority, in which they have not hesitated to instigate crime and to authorize acts which no man would dare to execute on his own responsibility, but in the performance of which the willing tools are found in an obedient people, who are taught that the voice of the tyrants is the voice of God. Can any one doubt that these men, the rulers, are keeping up this delusion for the sake of perpetuating their own power?

Again, we find a large, industrious, frugal community toiling on their farms, paying into the public treasury one tenth of all their productions, often called upon to contribute to public improvements, and, besides this, heavily mortgaged in person and property to pay off all the expenses of emigration and settlement. I have heard a great deal said about the benevolence of the Mormon authorities in bringing these poor people from distant parts of the world and settling them upon comfortable farms, but liberality is one of the last ideas that have been entertained in connection with the matter. Every cent is charged to the emigrant, and must be paid with enormous interest, so that it is, in reality, a grand money-making system. This is proved from the fact that the rulers of this people are rolling up large fortunes. A great portion of the people's money goes into the public treasury, but not one of the people knows what becomes of it after that. There are pretended financial reports, but no auditors. Brigham Young snaps his fingers in the face of his inferior officers, and asks them if they have confidence in him; and when they reply, as they must, that they have confidence, he tells them that is enough. Faith is all that is necessary. Brigham Young is immensely wealthy, and lives like a prince, and the rulers, as a general thing, are rapidly acquiring wealth. While these men are preaching to the people self-denial and devotion to the public interest, and calling for their money without stint, no one can doubt that they themselves are governed by the greed of gold.

There is another foundation stone to the system. Almost every man who is able to support more than one wife has more, but any person who visits the Territory, and learns what every one can learn, and yet imagines that religion, or any thing but the basest passions of man's animal nature had or has any thing to do with this part of the system, must be very credulous. For instance, I saw and conversed with one man, now more than seventy years of age, who formerly lived in a New England town, and married, in his early life, a New England woman. He joined the Mormons with his wife, and when she was getting somewhat in years he took another wife, of course a young one; and now that the second is getting older, he has just taken a young girl of eighteen. Can any one doubt his motives? Brigham Young's wives are differently enumerated from thirty-five to forty. Heber Kimball had fourteen when he died a short time since. The pretense that a woman can not be saved, in the highest sense, without being married, and other like impostures connected with this part of the system, only add a darker, fouler stain to the character of these men, who are living to fulfill the lusts of the flesh.

The condition of the women is deplorable. They have adopted the system of Mormonism as a religion; they confide in their rulers, believing them to be honest, but they regard polygamy as a cross, and speak of it as such; a cross which they are bound to bear, while, with scarcely an exception, every woman would prefer to be an only wife. Many wear this cross in deep sorrow, such as the circumstances would naturally produce. From extensive inquiry of those who had every opportunity to be well informed, I became satisfied that the women of the Mormon community are far from being satisfied with their state, whatever representations to the contrary may have been made. I was told by a gentleman who had conversed with some of Brigham Young's daughters, who are comparatively well educated, that they declared positively they would never marry a man who had another wife.

The future of Mormonism—what is to come of it, and what is to come out of it—are questions of no little moment to the American people. We have among us a community aspiring to be a sovereign state; until the opening of the Pacific Railroad, isolated by its position from the rest of our country, but now brought into direct communication with all parts of the land; a thriving people, constantly increasing by emigration from other countries; with social institutions not only opposed, but abhorrent to the great mass of the nation; the leaders, and the people with them, contemning the authority of the general government, and resisting it when they dare; and all this disloyalty sustained and intensified by fanaticism. What is to come of it?

After studying the subject upon the ground, my apprehensions of any real difficulty in dealing with the matter, either by moral means or by governmental authority, have subsided. There are no signs of relenting or of voluntary submission on the part of the rulers, nor will there be while they can in security retain power and make money out of the people as they are now doing, and living in the unrestrained indulgence of their lusts. There are no signs of any extensive disaffection on the part of the people. They are an ignorant class, have little opportunity of becoming better informed; they have adopted the system from religious motives, and have given themselves up to it with blind devotion.

But there are elements at work which I have no doubt will, ere long, lead to an explosion, so that the whole thing shall go to pieces of itself, even without the employment of military or extra-judicial force. Were there no other ground of discord, it is not to be expected that the people, who are now getting into communication with the rest of the world by means of the Pacific Railroad, will long remain blind to the character of the despotism that is exercised over them, or that they will continue to pour their money into the coffers of a few rapacious men who are rolling up wealth. Some of the more successful have already declined paying their tithes, and have been cut off from the Church. There were pointed out to me at Salt Lake City the elegant residences of four brothers, together worth half a million of dollars or more, who came some time since to the point at which, in their opinion, compliance with the increasing demands of Brigham Young and his apostles ceased to be a virtue. One of them sent five hundred dollars in payment of tithes. Brigham sent it back, saying it was not enough. The man coolly put the money into his pocket, telling the avaricious rulers that he would henceforward do his own tithing and administer his own charities. They are all now independent of the Church. Some men must acquire intelligence; this will extend, and it is not in the nature of man, especially in this age of the world, to submit to such absolute tyranny as is exercised by the Mormon rulers.

Then, again, these rulers, governed alike by selfish motives, are likely to fall out among themselves. There is already more or less jealousy of Brigham's power and increasing wealth, and the world will ere long have another illustration of the adage, "When rogues fall out, honest men will get their dues." At the time of my visit at Salt Lake a cloud was rising which threatened no good to Brigham Young and his fellows. Two of Joe Smith's sons had appeared on the stage, and were preaching a reformation to crowded houses. Where a corrupt hierarchy depend on divine revelations for their authority, it is easy to get up counter-revelations. The legend which these young Smiths had just brought to Salt Lake was that, previous to his death, Joe Smith, the original prophet and leader of the

Mormons, had predicted the birth of a son by a favorite wife, who should be his successor in the Church. This he had by revelation. Five months after the death of Joseph the son was born, was named David, and now, at the age of twenty-three, he comes, with his brother Alexander, to claim the headship of the Church and the leadership of the people. He denounces polygamy, as opposed to the principles and revelations of his father, inculcates loyalty to the government of the United States, and does not hesitate to reflect upon the despotism and avarice of the present rulers. He could not stay in Salt Lake City a day but for the protection of the United States authorities and arms, especially the latter (nor, indeed, would any Gentile's life be worth insuring for a single night were it not for the big guns of the United States troops on the hill overlooking Salt Lake City); but he was fearlessly holding forth to crowded assemblies on the abuses of Mormonism, and the apostles and elders were replying to his statements and strictures. There are so many indications of dissension in the Mormon community that I feel confident it will go to pieces by its own rottenness, and I trust that its dissolution is not very far distant.

I do not attempt any description of Salt Lake City; of its remarkable growth in the desert from nothing to a well-built town of twenty or twenty-five thousand inhabitants; of the Tabernacle (which is complete), and of its great organ, one of the largest in the world, which has been years in building; of the Temple, the foundations of which only were laid. These were not what I went to see so much as Mormonism itself. I studied it to my satisfaction, and hailed the morning on which I took my leave of the place, even though the daylight had not dawned when I took my seat in the stage. When it came light I noticed among our fellow-passengers a lady and gentleman whom I had seen alight from the stage only the evening before. I afterward learned that they had come with the expectation of spending a week, but the lady was so disgusted with all she saw and heard that she entreated her husband to take her away at once, and before daylight they were outward bound.

Soon after daylight, when we were a few miles out of Salt Lake City, we picked up two passengers who were on foot. I was seated on the top of the coach, and, as one of them took a seat below me, something heavy in his coat-flap fell upon my toes. I thought I recognized a revolver, and said to him, "I perceive that you are prepared to take care of yourself." He turned, and looked me in the face in order to scan my motive in speaking to him, and then gave me his history. He had been in business in Salt Lake City, and, becoming obnoxious to the Mormons, learned that his life was in danger, and fearing assassination, had left in the night, prepared to sell his life dear if attacked. At a safe distance from the City of the Saints he mounted the coach, with the intention of looking out for a part of the country more conducive to longevity than he had reason to fear Salt Lake City or Valley would prove.

## III.

### CALIFORNIA.

AFTER this episode at Salt Lake City we resumed our journey by the Pacific Railroad at Uintah, and soon reached the western half of the great thoroughfare, the Central Pacific; not the half in distance, but much more than half in the boldness of the undertaking and in the grandeur of achievement. Leading over the abrupt heights of the Sierra Nevada Mountains (which might, with great propriety, exchange names with the Rocky Mountains, for rocky elevations and precipices abound far more in the former than in the latter), the work to be accomplished on the Central Pacific was far more forbidding than any thing upon the

Union Pacific. By the force of a mighty engine, and occasionally with a double team of iron horses, we climbed the dizzy heights, and wormed our way along the sides of the mountains. At different points we could look from the car window down the precipitous rocks into the ravine, more than fifteen hundred feet below. Cape Horn, a bold promontory, around which the road makes a sharp curve at this elevation, is as famous among Pacific Railroad travelers, and almost as much of a terror, as the cape from which it takes its name is to navigators. The twenty-five miles of close snow-sheds through which we passed (since increased, I believe, to thirty or forty), were a more curious

ON THE SIERRA NEVADAS.

than pleasing portion of the passage. We could only now and then, through the interstices of the sheds, catch a glimpse of the wild and grand scenery which marks this part of the road. Before we commenced the ascent of the Sierra Nevadas the thermometer which I carried with me stood at 89 degrees in the Salt Lake Valley. When we reached the summit, early the next morning, the same thermometer indicated 34 degrees. We were then at an elevation of 7000 feet, and it was August 14th. When we reached the California plain in the afternoon of the same day the mercury was again at 88.

My views of the importance of the Pacific Railroad to the country and to the world have been greatly enlarged, not only by passing over it, but still more by observing in foreign countries, and even in the very heart of Asia, the influence which it is already exerting upon the intercourse and the ideas of the world at large. There was no enterprise connected with our country that awakened such interest in the East as this. All over India it was the theme of earnest inquiry; and, when I had crossed the Sewalic range of the Himalaya Mountains, and reached the beautiful and fertile valley of Dehra Doon, I was earnestly entreated by the English and American residents to deliver a public lecture on the Pacific Railroad, of which they had heard much, and wished to hear still more. On my return south from the Himalayas I met at Allahabad the report of the commission appointed by the East India government to visit this country and examine our railroads, and especially the Pacific Road. Their report was quite as enthusiastic and laudatory as one emanating from the companies themselves could be. In my opinion, the value of the road as an immediate channel of commerce has been overestimated. No railroad—not all the railroads in the world can carry on the commerce of the world. They are limited in capacity, and a great passenger route can never become a great channel for the transportation of freight. This is especially true of a single track road, and more especially true of a road of such immense length as the Pacific, on which passenger trains are liable to be detained, and must have the precedence over freight. It will be as impossible to carry on the commerce of the world over one or more railroad tracks as to carry on the entire correspondence of the world over a single telegraph wire. The passenger business of the Pacific Road must nearly, if not altogether, absorb its capacity of locomotion; but its vast importance, even in a commercial point of view, will be enhanced rather than diminished by this result. It is to be the great medium of communication between the different parts of the world; and while actual commerce—the transportation of the products of the earth, and of the skill of different nations—must have a channel of greater capacity, the commercial intercourse of the world will receive from the completion of this and similar works a stimulus which has never been fully estimated, and the value of the road to its enterprising proprietors, as well as to the world at large, will be increased instead of being diminished by this very restriction.

The grand enterprise of the century is to be the ship canal across the Isthmus of Darien. Commerce must have water for its channel; it must have a channel of such capacity that there will be no occasion for breaking up cargoes; and the nearest approach to a natural union of the two oceans will be a canal of sufficient depth and breadth to allow the largest ordinary steamers and sailing vessels to pass through without transshipment of goods. It has been a matter of surprise that our government and our capitalists have not taken hold of this great scheme with more determination to have it carried through to completion. I know many of the difficulties which lie in the way, international and economical, but it is an enterprise of such vast importance to the country and to the world that it ought to be begun at once, and completed as soon as it can be done, if a practical route can be found.

It was late Saturday evening when we reached San Francisco. More than two weeks before I had written to the proprietor of the Lick House engaging rooms for 10 o'clock of that evening, and I note it as one of the many indications of precision in modern travel that, although I was nearly a fortnight on the way from New York to the Pacific, including different pauses of a day or two at a time, I was never an hour behind time on the Pacific Railroad, and I reached the hotel at San Francisco within an hour of the time I had named some weeks before. The entire journey around the world was marked by nearly the same exactness, of which I may have occasion to speak from time to time.

A week passed in the city of the Golden Gate, and I found myself still in a maze. I did not lose my consciousness during the long journey from the Atlantic to the Pacific. It was all a reality when, after spending two or three days in traversing the older states, we crossed the Missouri and swept out upon the broad prairies of Nebraska, and over the Black Hills, and then over the Rocky Mountains, and through the Great Salt Lake Basin, and over the Sierra Nevadas. All this was real. Neither the time nor the way seemed long, although it was not difficult to comprehend that we were actually spanning the continent.

Seven days and seven nights of steady travel upon a smooth road, behind a locomotive, will tell upon any distance; and when, early on the morning of the seventh day of actual journeying, we crossed the summit of the Sierra Nevada Mountains, we strained our eyes to catch a glimpse of the broad Pacific, although it lay a long day's journey out of sight. As we descended the magnificent slope we felt sure that we were coming into the Golden State, and when we saw the wheat-fields, and vineyards, and the abundance of luscious fruits at the railway stations greeted our eyes and then our palates, we became more and more pleasantly assured that we were within the borders of California, the cornucopia of the country.

Darkness had gathered over us before we crossed the bay and entered San Francisco, so that we could form little conception of the city. But when, the next morning, on going out into the streets on our way to church, instead of a mushroom city of twenty years, made up of rough boards and canvas, like the new cities through which we had passed along the line of the Pacific Road, we found ourselves in an old established town, with broad streets and magnificent stone buildings, as substantial and imposing in appearance as those of cities which have been built for centuries, I could not make it real that this was San Francisco, a city not yet twenty-one years of age. It was more like one of the creations of Aladdin's Lamp. The oldest inhabitants were those that came in 1849, and it was not a little curious to find in so large a city so many who came *anno urbis conditæ*. To the inquiry, "How long have you been in California?" the answer seemed almost invariably "Twenty years; I came in 1849." These old settlers have a sort of pre-emption right, of which they are not a little proud, as well they may be.

San Francisco is something to be proud of, but of one thing I should never boast, and that is of its climate. During the month of August we had not one day of genial or even moderately comfortable weather. Cold fogs in the morning, and cold winds during nearly all of the twenty-four hours, made up our experience. With the winds from the ocean, which sweep over the sand-hills, come storms of sand and dust that are excessively annoying, and from which there is no escape. The weather at that season of the year is so cold that ladies wear their furs, and gentlemen go clad or armed with heavy overcoats. Winter is said to be the real summer of San Francisco, and I would fain believe it is so; yet Californians speak in terms of admiration of the very weather that penetrated our bones. But the old proverb, *de gustibus etc.*, I presume, is as applicable to the gusts of San Francisco as to any others. A few miles from the coast the weather is mild and delightful; farther inland it becomes intensely hot, and again upon the high lands it becomes delightfully cool.

Of the sights and scenes in and around San Francisco I mention but one. Between the city and the ocean there is a neck of land, a high promontory of sand six or seven miles wide. The great drive of the town is across this promontory to the shore, where the waves come rolling in to rest after their long journey from Japan and China. About three hundred yards from the land two rugged rocks rise abruptly out of the water to the height of seventy-five feet, covering an area of perhaps an acre each. These rocks are the property and the habitations of an immense colony of sea-lions, as they are called, or seals, who hold undisturbed possession, and who are protected in their right of property and from all injury by statute law. Some of these sea-lions are of enormous size; and it is an amusing sight, which never loses its interest, to watch them in their clumsy efforts to climb to the very pinnacles of the rocks by means of their fins and tails. They often come in conflict struggling for the high places, and then we are sure to hear the loud disputation, unlike any controversy which I have ever heard before, their fierce growls and barks being heard above the noise of old Ocean, whose waves are constantly breaking on the shore. There are seals of all sizes, from the tiny cubs to the strong old settlers, who look as if they might have been masters of the rock for a hundred years. I doubt if there is another such scene to be witnessed any where upon the earth or sea; and the great curiosity is, that these undomesticated denizens of two elements are living in a community of their own, almost within stone's throw of a frequented shore, in as wild a state as when the continent was discovered, constantly within the sound of human voices, and yet as apparently unconscious of the vicinity of man as if they were a thousand miles from land.

California is a great state. I have been informed of that fact repeatedly, and by those who have lived in it long enough to know whereof they affirm; but it is, in truth, a great state. In territory it is equal to all New England, New York, New Jersey, Pennsylvania, Maryland, and a part of Delaware. It is not only large enough, north and south, to constitute several climes, but it has a remarkable variety of climate within a narrow compass. If variety is the spice of life, California is the spiciest country to live in that I have found in all my wanderings. I have never before been where chills and fever were so prevalent. I do not mean the terrible disease bearing that name, of which I have a greater dread than of the yellow fever, but the alternate shakings and warmings which one gets in passing from one part of the state to another. The morning that I came into it (August 15th, at 5 o'clock) the thermometer, as I have already stated, stood in the car window on the Pacific Railroad at 34°, only two degrees above freezing. At 2 o'clock the same day, farther west, the same thermometer stood at 88. This, it is true, was on different planes; but one may "shiver and shake" day after day at San Francisco, and an hour's sail will take him into the blandest atmosphere. In going up to Stockton, we left San Francisco August 23d, at 3 o'clock P.M., wrapped up in our warmest winter cloaks and overcoats, and stopping at Benicia, only thirty miles distant and on the same plane, we cast off our wraps and stepped into the most delightful summer weather, and saw the sun go down in a sea of gold —a sensation and a sight which we had not enjoyed since our arrival. During the same journey the weather would be intensely warm during the day, and, in the same locality, by midnight we would find ourselves searching, half awake, for all the stray clothes within reach, and in the morning the thermometer would indicate frost. The same diversity and variations of temperature prevail in almost every portion of the state, and in some places that I have visited I have been informed that the thermometer rises frequently as high as 110, and even 120 in the shade.

One of the wonders of this great state is that every

thing does not die out utterly in the summer, and leave the valleys ever after as barren as the granite rocks of the walls of the Yosemite. Not a drop of rain falls in the summer in the great valleys which are the agricultural regions of the state. In passing through these valleys in the month of August, they do not give the slightest signs of vegetation, excepting the trees, which are sparse. The ground is apparently as dry as an ash-heap fresh from the burning. You may travel all day long and never see a blade of grass, nor even a green weed; but, as soon as the fall rains commence, the hills and valleys are clothed with the richest verdure, another year's crop of grass and grain comes on, and the once arid slopes and plains are burdened with the harvest. Vegetation must have some strange power of lying dormant and then springing into life, or there must be latent moisture in the soil which preserves it from perishing, for, while the surface of the earth is without the least evidence of vegetable life, the fruit and ornamental trees, whose roots strike deeper into the soil, are as luxuriant in their growth and in their foliage as if rain had fallen every day in the year. It is no uncommon thing to see a vineyard or plantation of fruit-trees in full and green leaf, and loaded with the richest fruit, standing in the midst of a perfectly arid tract of country, and this, too, without irrigation. My partial examination of California has satisfied me that agriculture in all its branches is to be the great interest of the state, and, indeed, it is so now.

The fruits of California have not equaled my expectations. It is true, the rage for mammoth productions, mammoth vegetables and fruits, of which we heard so much in the early settlement of the state, has given place to a more sensible attention to quality; but, even with this improvement, the fruits generally are not equal in flavor to those of the Eastern States. They grow in a profusion that is without any parallel within the range of my observation, and with so little cultivation that they seem almost to be spontaneous; they have a smoothness and perfection of form which gives them the beauty of flowers; I have seen trees loaded with fruits of the largest size on which an imperfect specimen could scarcely be found, and yet, when they come to be eaten, they do not fulfill their bright promise. The first, and, as it was said, the finest of the peaches had disappeared before we arrived; but those which we have eaten, although magnificent in appearance and rich in color, have been without the flavor that the peaches at the East preserve throughout the season. It is, perhaps, too early to form a judgment of the apples; but I have tried many varieties, and, while they are fair to look upon—exceeding in size and smoothness all the productions of the Eastern States, so that, to judge merely from their external appearance, one might suppose that this fruit, as well as many others, had taken a new lease of life for the Pacific coast, and had entered upon an entirely new career—I have not tasted a good apple in California. This fruit, even more than others, is without flavor and without juice. Such quinces as I have seen growing in various parts of the state, among the mountains as well as in the valleys and on the plains, I never even imagined before. They grow to an enormous size, and are as smooth as an orange—quite different, taking a whole tree together, from any thing with which I have been familiar, and there can be little fear that this fruit is not sufficiently highly flavored.

But the glory of California fruit is its pears and grapes. The former grow with a luxuriance and rapidity, and with such abundance of large and luscious-looking fruit bending the trees to the earth, that, on entering any of the fruit-orchards, a stranger is compelled to break out continually in astonishment. All varieties of pears, if not actually indigenous to the soil, have found in California their true home, and many of them, at least, are as delicious as they are finely developed. Some specimens of this fruit, in years past, have been a wonder at the East; but there are a few more left. Pears have become so abundant—even the choicest varieties—that they have actually become a drug in the market; and Bartletts which will weigh a pound, and which blush when you simply look at them, will scarcely pay for sending them to market. I was at a ranch not an hour's distance from San Francisco, containing all kinds of fruit and pears of every variety, hundreds of bushels of such fruit as was never seen in any other country, the owner of which said he should leave it all to rot upon the trees, as it would not pay for the picking.

Grapes grow every where in the state with the greatest luxuriance, and spontaneously. They require no sort of training; they are trimmed annually almost to the level of the soil, leaving a small stump, and, before the season is over, such a burden of the finest of fruit is seen, and in clusters like the grapes of Eshcol, as can now scarcely be found any where else on earth. The choicest of foreign grapes, which at the East are matured only in graperies by artificial heat, here revel in the open air. I believe all visitors in California, if not the citizens, unite in pronouncing the grapes the finest of its fruit, and they grow in such profusion that all classes may have them at this season as an article of daily diet. Figs and pomegranates grow with the same luxuriance; the former, as in Oriental countries, producing three crops in a season. The fig-tree grows with astonishing rapidity. I have seen, even among the mountains, and still more in the broad valleys, fig-trees twenty or twenty-five feet in height, that could not be more than ten or twelve years old, and covered with the second crop of the largest and finest figs. It is surprising to see so little account made of this fruit, which, in other countries, is an important article of food, and which is more nourishing than any of our native fruits. But the taste for it must be acquired, and it is evident that it has not been extensively acquired in California.

VIEW OF THE YOSEMITE.

## IV.

### THE YOSEMITE VALLEY AND THE BIG TREES.

I was surprised, on reaching the Pacific coast, to learn how few Californians have ever been to the Yosemite Valley. On making inquiry of one and another of the old residents, who would be most likely to give me information in regard to the most desirable route to the valley, I could scarcely find one who had been there. It was not because "a prophet is not without honor save in his own country," for the Californians generally have a very high appreciation of the attractions of the wonderful cleft, as indeed they have of every thing included within the wide-stretching borders of their magnificent state. Scarcely five thousand persons have visited the Valley since it was first discovered and brought to notice, and of these a large proportion, if not the largest, have been persons from other states and countries. There are several reasons for this practical indifference, on the part of the neighbors, to this wonder of the world. One is, that the Californians are a practical people; and though they do not seem to have a very strong attachment to their gold, they are very fond of making it, whether in the mines, or on Montgomery and California Streets of San Francisco. The trip also requires time—a longer time than I had supposed—and time is money in California as well as elsewhere. But the chief reason I presume is, that the Californians know more of the difficulties of the journey than strangers who come, often with this as the main attraction, and who, having come so far, will not be deterred by the terrors of the way. It is, in truth, about the most severe expedition that I have ever accomplished, and, at this dry season of the year, beyond all comparison the dirtiest. Dust does not express the idea, although for days, in going and returning, you are enveloped in clouds, the dirt covering and penetrating every thing that you have on, entering your eyes and ears, and all the avenues to your throat, and so begriming every thing that, when one gets back into the region of baths and clean clothes, he will be sure to cast behind him all that he has had on, and never look back to see what becomes of it, only too thankful that it is his no longer. We met some travelers just returned from the Valley, who, like the spies on the way out of the Promised Land, attempted to dissuade us from going in, but we concluded that "what has been done can be done," and determined to see it for ourselves. And, in very truth, no other excursion that I have ever made, in any other part of the world, has been so remunerative in interest. Nowhere else have I seen so much of grandeur and beauty in natural scenery combined.

Two weeks are required for a satisfactory visit, including the journey to and from the Valley. It may be accomplished in ten days, but the excursion will be hurried and more fatiguing. There are three routes from Stockton, one by Bear Valley and Mariposa, another by Centreville, and a third by Big Oak Flat. The last has become the easiest route by the extension of the stage-road, and we chose it on going into the Valley for the saving of time and fatigue. Leaving San Francisco in the afternoon by boat, we reached Stockton—117 miles—in the course of the night. We were roused early the next morning to take the stage at six o'clock. The road, on the first day, was smooth and perfectly level the greater part of the way, but fearfully dusty. No rain had fallen, not a drop for many months, as is the case every summer; but all day long our route lay through a succession of wheat-fields, covering what is called the Valley of the San Joaquin (pronounced San Waukeen), which is an extended plain, once regarded as waste land, but in reality one of the most fertile wheat regions in the world. The grain had been put in sacks and stacked on the ground, where it was threshed, and where it is suffered to lie for weeks without fear of injury from the weather.

The first day's staging brought us to Garrote at 10 o'clock in the evening, weary enough to lie down and rest until noon of the next day, but at 3 o'clock in the morning we were roused to resume our journey by stage. The name of the place was not at all pleasantly suggestive, and although we did not meet with the fate of some of the early settlers, from which the name was derived, we were most unpleasantly reminded in the morning of a comparison of Dickens, that being called up before daylight to go off in a stage is very much like being called up to be hanged. But we were in for the war, and, stiff and still weary, we again took our seats and rode through the woods to Hardin's Ranch, which we reached at 10 o'clock in the day. Here we were to take horses, and, after a hasty lunch, were in the saddle. Two of our horses were donkeys, of no magnificent proportions, which fell to the lot of those of our party who were not least in stature, and altogether we formed a cavalcade that the Knight of La Mancha might have been proud to lead. Our guide, who, with the care of horses, and saddles, and riders, had no mean responsibility, was William Bourne, a name somewhat ominous. Before committing ourselves to his direction, however, I distinctly inquired if he were that *bourne* of which I had read "from which no traveler returns." He assured me he was not; that scores of travelers had fallen into his hands, and had come out safe and sound; and I desire to add my testimony to his faithfulness, and my belief that there is not a more trusty guide in all the Valley.

The ride of that day and evening—for we were ten hours in the saddle—was one which made its impress upon our memories in more ways than one. All unused as we were to the exercise, we carried with us for many days the most tender recollections of its severity, but we shall carry with us while we live the most pleasing recollections of its romantic and sublime interest. Hour after hour we wound our way through the magnificent forest, its grand old trees growing upon us as we passed along, from those of ordinary proportions to sugar-pines of ten and twelve feet in diameter, and then to the Big Trees, of which l shall speak hereafter.

About 3 o'clock we reached the hospitable mansion of Mrs. Gobin, at Crane's Flat, which I desire to commend to the special regard of all travelers toward the Yosemite. Mrs. G. is a native of the Emerald Isle, but she is proud to speak of New York as "her adopted city," and New York may well be proud to count her among its numerous adopted daughters. She occupies a little shanty on the

D

flat, and while her liege lord looks after his sheep on the surrounding mountains and green flats, she entertains travelers to and from the Valley in a truly magnificent style. Nowhere after leaving San Francisco did we find such fare, such delicious bread and butter, coffee and rich cream, canned fruits of all kinds, mutton, ham, etc. She made many apologies for being taken unawares, and not having a dinner in readiness for us; when we rode up she was just in the midst of the blanc mange which she was preparing for Mr. Colfax's party, who were then in the Valley, and who were to pass her ranch the next day; she would have a good dinner ready for us on our return from the Valley, etc., etc., which promise she fulfilled to our perfect satisfaction a few days after. But we were in special need of a good lunch just at that time, and on my assuring her that I would make it all right with Mr. Colfax, whom I expected to meet in the evening, she spread for us, there in the wilderness, on rough boards, a repast the memory of which will long linger in our thoughts, and which was all the more grateful, in our hunger and fatigue, because it was so unexpected. Mrs. Gobin deserves this tribute for her genial manners and her generous fare. Her native modesty is such a striking trait in her character that I have no doubt her ruddy face will assume a deeper blush should she chance to see her name in print; but she is one of those public benefactors that can by no means escape a measure of immortality, and I take pleasure in handing her down to the notice of coming generations.

Before descending, let us take a bird's-eye view of the Valley. It is a cleft in the Sierra Nevada Mountains, varying from half a mile to a mile in width, six miles in length, with two branches at the head of the Valley running one or two miles farther in opposite directions, the walls on both sides and throughout its whole extent being nearly perpendicular, and from three to six thousand feet in height. The brow of El Capitan, the guardian promontory, actually projects over the Valley, which lies three thousand feet below. The River Merced, a large stream of the purest water, flows through it, connecting it in a way with the outer world, although the course of the stream as it enters or leaves the Valley affords no ingress or egress for the traveler. It enters by two successive perpendicular falls of six hundred and four hundred feet, and leaves the Valley by such a rugged channel, between such lofty walls, that no foot can follow it. The Valley throughout its whole extent is a plain, with only sufficient descent for the flow of the river, the bottom having an elevation of four thousand feet above the level of the sea, and its sides from half a mile to more than a mile additional height. Whether it was formed when the world was made, or by some great throe of nature long afterward; whether the Valley itself was made by the sinking of the bottom several thousand feet, or by the slow action of ordinary causes; whether it was once the bed of a glacier or of a seething caldron, geologists will probably discuss as long as geology remains such an uncertain science. But the solution of such questions is not at all material to the appreciation of the wonders and beauties of this remarkable place; and I prefer, as most travelers will, to take the Valley just as it is now, rather than as it might have been in remote ages of the past; nor shall I attempt to solve the problems connected with this wonderful phenomenon.

There are only two practicable routes into or out of the Valley. They are both near the lower extremity and on opposite sides, and lead by narrow, zigzag pathways down the precipitous sides. There are numerous places in the descent where the turning of a saddle, or the misstep of a horse, or the sliding of the horse's foot on the rock might hurl the rider a thousand feet upon the rocks. Knowing some of the difficulties, not to say dangers, of the passage, I had all day added my exertions to those of the guide in urging the party onward, that we might have daylight for descending, but it was near sunset when we reached the brow of the mountain.

Our guide, having adjusted and secured every saddle, took the lead, the ladies taking position next, and in solemn silence we followed, single file. I would not, for all the gold in California, have made the descent an hour later on a moonless night, although it has been done in the dark. As it was, the sun had actually set before we had taken one hasty look up and down the Valley and commenced the passage. Committing ourselves, step by step, to the care of the great Guide, who has said, "He shall give his angels charge over thee, to keep thee in all thy ways; they shall bear thee up in their hands, lest thou dash thy foot against a stone," we rode on, the curtains of night gathering closer and closer about us, until before we reached the plain the last rays of daylight had vanished, and we could only look up to the night-lamps of heaven for the glimmer that guided us. But the skies were perfectly clear, and the hosts of heaven came out in unwonted numbers to watch us as we slowly wound our way down the mountain.

The descent occupied considerably more than an hour, and on reaching the foot we were still five miles from the hotel, which was higher up the Valley. After a few moments' rest and a refreshing draught from a brook, we resumed our ride. Four miles on we forded the Merced, where, getting some idea of the locality of the hotel from the guide, and leaving the rest to follow on under his care at a walking gait, I gave the reins to my horse, and, trusting altogether to his knowledge of the trail, dashed off at full gallop through the wood. About half a mile from Hutchings's, as I came out upon a clearing, an immense bonfire almost blinded me. A large company was assembled at Leidig's to give a sort of barbacue to Mr. Colfax, who, with a large party, including Lieutenant Governor Bross, of Illinois, and Mr. Bowles, of the *Springfield Republican*, was at Hutchings's. Reining in my horse merely to ask for the trail, I dashed again into the thicket, and after another half mile dismounted at the celebrated but not very splendid house of Mr. J. M. Hutchings, the genius of the Valley, who first brought it into public notice. Never was a place of rest more welcome to weary travelers than was this rude hotel.

Awakened early in the morning by the noise of departing guests, and by the conversation of those who remained, which, as the house is a mere shell, could be heard by all in common, we came out to take our first look by daylight at the Valley, its gigantic walls and lofty waterfalls. Directly in front of the hotel the Yosemite Fall meets the eye,

YOSEMITE FALL.

the water dropping gently over the brow of the opposite cliff 1500 feet, then striking the rock, and flowing on in a cascade 620 feet farther, when it makes a final leap of 400 feet, and is gathered up in the basin below. In the course of the morning we walked to the foot of the fall, half a mile distant, and sat and listened to the story of the stream which had fallen from the dizzy height, and drank of the pure water as it flowed quietly away toward the Merced. The volume of water at this season of the year is not large, but no accumulation could add to the gracefulness of this highest of the falls. The height is so great that the stream is sometimes turned aside from the perpendicular by the wind swaying it to and fro like a sheet of gauze, and occasionally it is almost lost in mist in making the long descent in air.

From the hotel, or its immediate vicinity, may be seen several other points of interest. Almost overhanging it is Sentinel Rock, 3043 feet high, on which a flag is still flying that was long ago fastened there by some adventurous youth. On the opposite side of the Valley, and about a mile farther up, is the North Dome, a perfectly bald mountain of gray granite, the side presented to the Valley glistening in the sunlight as if it had been polished by hand. This is 3568 feet above the Valley. A much finer view of it may be had from the trail leading to the Vernal Falls, from which point the dome is as perfect as that of St. Peter's at Rome. Directly across one of the branches of the Valley is another rock of much greater height, being 4737 feet above the Valley, the Half Dome, having the appearance of being cleft from another half, but without any corresponding portion to complement it. These mountains of rock, which have been hewn into their present state with consummate skill, are composed of the adamantine granite, which has left but few marks of the passage of time in any thing like débris at their base. The small amount of débris at the foot of the cliffs, in some cases its entire absence, is one of the most remarkable characteristics of these rocky walls. I noticed one spot where the rock was 3000 feet in perpendicular height, and the greensward came square up to its base.

After the ride of yesterday we were content to spend the greater part of the day in the quiet study of what could be seen from our quarters, but at 4 o'clock we mounted our horses for a ride down the Valley to El Capitan and the Fall of the Bridal Veil, about five miles distant. The aft-

FALL OF THE BRIDAL VEIL.

ernoon was beautiful; the golden light of the descending sun was streaming up the Valley, gilding the mountain sides and rocky peaks, and when we reached the fall lighting it up as for a bridal. This is the most delicate of all the falls, the line of water in its clear descent being woven by the wind into thin lace. After fastening our horses we took our seats upon the rocks, and sat, and gazed, and talked of its wondrous beauty until our guide reminded us that night was coming on. A little higher up the Valley are the Ca-

CATHEDRAL ROCKS.

thedral Rocks, the most varied group of the Valley, while just opposite stands the guardian, El Capitan, one mighty mass or shaft, rising up from the river's edge 3300 feet, until its brow appears to lean over its base.

Another morning found us early in the saddle, and on our way to Mirror Lake, which lies ever slumbering between the North and Half Dome. The reflection from its surface is not only perfect, but absolutely surprising. In Watkins's photographic gallery at San Francisco (a collection, by the way, which every one who goes to the Valley should see) are several views of this remarkable lake, and no one could distinguish in the photographs the reflection from the mountains themselves by any difference in the distinctness of the pictures, and the views above and below are equally extensive. The famed upright reflection, presenting the trees on one side of the mountain in their natural position, I satisfied myself, was a mere delusion caused by the shape of the trees, and not any remarkable phenomenon.

The grand feature in our visit to the lake was the sunrise above, or rather below, the brow of the Half Dome, 4700 feet down in the depths of the water. We watched for it half an hour or more; at length the edge of the cliff, reflected almost directly beneath our feet, was touched with gold—in a moment more the brilliant edge of the sun fell below the cliff, and all the glory of a sunrise in the mountains, inverted and beneath the waters of an apparently fathomless lake, burst upon us. The sun sailed down into

MIRROR LAKE.

the deep ether, instead of rising as it was wont. The effect was so singular and striking that I fear my description will give no idea of it as it appeared to our wondering eyes.

The sun now being fairly up, or rather down in the lake, we remounted, and galloped over the rough trail and up the other branch of the Valley to the Vernal and the Nevada Falls. These are both upon the same stream, which is one of the main branches of the Merced, and a stream of large volume. Access to the falls is not without difficulty, nor altogether without danger, owing to the rudeness of the pathway which lies along the rocky chasm. One lady in our company, though not of our own party, actually gave out and was left behind, while we pressed forward. We were a thousandfold repaid for all our toil, and forgot all

VERNAL FALL.

danger as we stood in the spray, first of the Vernal Fall, 400 feet in height, and without a break. The rainbow which covered it like a promise was as perfect and brilliant as the sun itself; in some directions of the wind, blowing the spray toward the spectator, it becomes a circular bow, and sometimes a double circle. Ascending the dizzy height by the ladders which were placed against the wall, and which were by no means an inviting pathway, we found a rocky parapet directly over the fall, and the sight from above was equal to that from below, although the reverse of it. The river seemed a mass of falling crystals instead of a stream of water.

Following the stream half a mile farther up, along a succession of cascades and race-courses not unlike the rapids at Niagara, although more picturesque, we took our seats on the rocks near the foot of the Nevada Fall, by many considered the most striking, if not the most beautiful of all the falls. It is 600 feet in height. We could have spent the day at this spot watching the stream as it fell in vast masses over the brow of the cataract, occasionally holding back as if to gather courage for the terrific plunge, and then with accumulated force falling into the deep basin at its foot. There was a constant vibration, a pulsation of one or two seconds' interval in the falling mass, which was now less, and now greater.

Near the upper or Nevada Fall rises the loftiest peak about the Valley, called the Cap of Liberty, from its close resemblance in shape to this ancient emblem of our nationality, and also known as Mt. Broderick. It is a lofty rock of granite rising 4600 feet above the Valley, smooth as a helmet, and yet quite accessible. The view from its summit of the whole region which it overtops is said to be magnificent, and I should have made the expedition but for the want of another day to devote to it. The ascent can be made with ease in a day, in connection with a visit to the Vernal and Nevada Falls, by taking an early start in the morning, and omitting for the day the visit to Mirror Lake, but no one who has not strong powers of endurance should undertake it.

After dinner, the last day of my visit, mine host proposed to me to go out and persuade some of the beautiful denizens of the Merced, whom I had seen disporting themselves in its crystal waters, to join us at breakfast the next morning. I had been from boyhood on intimate terms with their speckled cousins east of the Rocky Mountains, and, nothing loth, accepted the invitation. In a little more than an hour we returned with a string of trout, many of them half a pound each, which together weighed precisely ten pounds. Deponent did his full share in hooking them, but Emanuel, a Mexican muleteer boy, who had gone with us to carry our fish, and who had provided himself with a line and a rude pole, was the hero of the hour. Hearing a violent struggle going on a short distance from us, and running to see what the fight might be, I found he had just landed a trout that weighed at the hotel two pounds and five ounces. The trout of the Western slope are very similar to our own, with the exception of the gold and vermilion spots, which are entirely wanting. How they have lost them, or whether they ever had any, I am not informed.

In the course of the evening, when my hook and line went by the board, I gave myself up to the admiration of the heavens, the glory of which, in the perfect clearness of the atmosphere, was indescribable. There was no moon, but the stars seemed multiplied, if not magnified, tenfold, and shone with a splendor which I have never seen equaled elsewhere. Looking up into the bright heavens from out the deep valley, whose walls on both sides were more than half a mile in perpendicular height, was like looking at them through a telescope, and there was a strange fascination in the scene. Recalling the impressions which the long vision made upon my mind, I can scarcely tell which transfixed me most with admiration, the perfect, positive purity of the air, or the intense brilliancy of the myriad lamps of the skies.

The Yosemite Valley, being a part of the public lands of the United States, was ceded to the State of California by act of Congress in 1864, "upon the express condition that the premises shall be held for public use, resort, and recreation, and shall be inalienable for all time." It is in the hands of commissioners appointed by the state, but nothing is done to make it more accessible, or to make the routes to the various parts of the Valley more practicable and less dangerous. There are some private claimants to lands in the Valley which ought in some way to be disposed of, and then a liberal annual appropriation should be made by the State of California, or by the United States, for the improvement of the trails to and through and around the Valley. It is a shame that this wonder in the world's scenery, having such a proprietor as the Golden State, should be suffered to lie in such a condition, when a few thousand dollars a year would make it comparatively easy of access, and greatly facilitate the approach to its various objects of interest and of wonder.

I have been often asked since visiting the Valley whether it equaled my expectations, and my answer is that of every one whom I have met who has made the pilgrimage: it is far grander and more wonderful than any thing I had conceived. Pictures and photographs give the outlines, but convey no idea of the lofty sublimity of those walls of granite which inclose you on every side, and which reach far up into the blue ether by day and toward the stars by night. So complete is the isolation, and so perfect this inclosure, that many persons on getting into the Valley are seized with a kind of apprehension that they shall never be able to get out, as if they had been let down from the clouds into some deep chasm far remote from human abodes.

Bright and beautiful was the morning that we were to take our leave of the Valley of Wonders, as, indeed, was every morning. Only once during the days and nights of our sojourn had we seen a cloud against the sky, and this was in keeping with the rest of the scene. It was while we were seated at the foot of the Nevada Falls, looking up at its summit, that a bank of cloud, whiter than the driven snow, rolled over the brow of the mountain and hung there for a long time, as if it belonged to the mountain instead of the air.

We rose early to leave the Valley. The trout were waiting for us at the breakfast table, and, these dispatched, our train of prancing steeds (diminutive mustangs and donkeys) were brought up to the door. The process of arranging and rearranging the saddles over, no momentary prelude to the journey, we mounted, and presently were galloping single file down the Valley. In the morning sunlight we passed the Cathedral Rocks and El Capitan, stretching our eyes once more to reach their tops and comprehend the dizzy height. We paused once again before the Bridal Veil to see it woven afresh into fleecy lace, and then wafted into thin mist, and then dissipated into thin air. We reached, at length, the foot of the mountain, and prepared for the ascent. It appeared by no means as perilous as when, in the gathering darkness, we had slowly wound our way down its precipitous sides. Slowly we wound our way up again, often pausing to suffer our faithful and patient animals to gather breath, and at length reaching the top and taking our stand together upon the bald summit which looks into and far up the Valley, the perils and the chief fatigue of the excursion over, we joined in singing, to the tune of Old Hundred,

"Praise God from whom all blessings flow."

The sound of our voices died away long before it reached the deep valley above which we were standing, but it went up, we trust, into the ear of Him who shaped this wonderful Valley, and set these mountains fast by the word of his power.

Inspiration Point, which is on the Mariposa route, just before making the descent into the Valley, affords the finest comprehensive view of the whole scene to be had from any point. This route should be taken either in going into or in leaving the Valley, not merely on account of the commanding view which the point affords, but to vary the route, and to afford an opportunity for visiting the several groves of the gigantic trees of the Sierra Nevada range, among the greatest wonders of California, which all lie in the vicinity of the Yosemite Valley.

The first strong desire to visit the California coast that I ever felt was excited by reading the accounts of the Big Trees, as they are usually called, the great marvel of the vegetable world, and the longing to behold them with my own eyes never subsided until, tape in hand, I took their proportions. I am satisfied, but disappointed. They are just as large as they have been represented, the same number of feet in diameter and in circumference. I made my measurement with an accurate line, and found every thing right, but, on comparing my anticipations with what I saw, I find that I was expecting to see each tree covering about an acre of ground with the area of its trunk, to say nothing of its top extending slightly above the clouds. The truth is, no one at first sight can appreciate, or even comprehend the greatness of these giants of the forest, and this for several reasons. Our conceptions of magnitudes, or heights and distances, are seldom accurate. Very few persons ever found the Falls of Niagara one half as high as they expected. These trees, too, are so symmetrical in shape, so perfectly well-proportioned, and so like other trees in their general aspect, that it is difficult to take into one's mind the simple element of greatness by itself. But I imagine that the main reason why they do not at first impress the beholder with their immensity is, that they stand in the midst of giants. To visit the groves where they are found, the traveler passes through a regular gradation, from a treeless plain and small oaks, to firs and pines which swell out into larger dimensions, until trees of ordinary size become the exceptions, and great trees the general rule. For miles before reaching the giants themselves I saw scores and then hundreds, and then, I may say, thousands of sugar-pines that would measure thirty or forty feet in circumference; trees of this size shooting up 150 feet in a shaft as straight as an arrow, and with scarcely any perceptible diminution in size, and then branching out and rising 100 feet higher. One man, who had long occupied a ranch in the vicinity, told me he had measured sugar-pines that were fifteen feet in diameter, or forty-five feet in circumference. After traveling through such a forest for half a day, one is really not in the best state to judge of big trees, and when he comes upon those that are a little larger, he may be excused if he can not open his eyes much wider, and exclaim Oh!

These wonders of the forest were discovered in 1852 by a hunter, whose story met with no credence until others had penetrated the same wilds and had seen for themselves. They have now a name and celebrity throughout the wide world; and although they are not indigenous in any other country, or any part of this country excepting the small tract in which they were first found, they are now growing in almost every land, propagated from seeds taken in the cone from California. The tree grows rapidly and vigorously in almost any climate, and although few will live to see the result of their experiments in the production of trees of equal size with the parent stems, yet its character may be studied now in almost every country. The generic name of the tree—*Sequoia*—perpetuates the memory of George Guess, the ingenious Cherokee half-breed who invented an alphabet that was for a long time in use among that nation. His Indian name—Sequoyah—was given to the newly-discovered Redwood of California by the learned botanist Endlicher, who first defined the genus, calling the tree *Sequoia Sempervirens*. The leaf of the Redwood is flat, like that of the *Arbor Vitæ*.

When the great trees were discovered, the classification became the subject of much discussion in different countries, and different names were given; but it has at length been established that they are of the same genus, and another honor is attached to the memory of the Cherokee genius whose name is now associated with the grandest production of the vegetable kingdom. It is called *Sequoia Gigantea*. It is very similar in form and in the general appearance of the trunk to the Redwood. One not familiar with both would scarcely distinguish them as they stand in the forest; but the leaf of the *Gigantea* is branching, like the cedar of the Eastern States, although much longer and stronger, and not flat, like the *Sempervirens* and the *Arbor Vitæ*. The Redwood, which is the common tree of the Pacific slope, furnishing a large portion of its timber, also attains to gigantic size, trees having been found, according to authentic reports, of little less circumference than the Big Trees themselves. Professor Whitney, in his scientific report of the state, speaks of Redwood trees having been found all the way from twenty to thirty feet in diameter, and great numbers are now standing in the forest of fifteen or twenty feet in diameter. The wood of the two species is the same—dark red, much darker than any cedar that I have seen, and almost as light as cork. From one of the prostrate monarchs, quite removed from the rest, and giving evidence of having been among the largest of its tribe, I took a sliver and had it made into a flagstaff. It is as dark in color as old mahogany.

There are several groves of the *Sequoia Gigantea*, but they are all in the vicinity or the direction of the Yosemite Valley, the principal trails to the Valley leading through the groves. The Mariposa Grove, although not the first discovered, is perhaps the most celebrated, and will afford the most satisfaction to those who have not time to visit all. This is the grove which was ceded, in connection with the Yosemite Valley, by act of Congress, to the State of California for preservation. It is situated about fifteen miles south of the Valley, is 5500 feet above the level of the sea, and has 125 trees which are more than forty feet in circumference. They run down to this diminutive size from ninety-two, ninety-one, eighty-seven, eighty-two feet. One tree in this grove, now partially burned at the base, was originally more than 100 feet in circumference. Since I was in the Valley I have received an account of a tree more recently discovered that measures forty feet four inches in diameter, or 121 feet in circumference. It is melancholy to see how many of the larger trees have been felled by the fire, and in a great measure consumed. Before seeing them I imagined their destruction to have been the result of mere vandalism, but a ride through the forest afforded a more satisfactory explanation of the disasters which had befallen the giants. Every dense forest that is visited by man, either civilized or savage, is liable to the ravages of fire, and this is peculiarly the case in this part of the country, where no rains fall during several months of the year. The embers of a camp-fire or the wad of a hunter's gun may kindle a fire which will spread over a wide tract, and burn for weeks or months. On our return from the Valley we passed through one of these conflagrations for more than a mile, at times almost suffocated by the smoke, and not without apprehension that the immense pines which were blazing at their base, and for fifty feet up the trunk, might chance to fall very inconveniently at the moment of our passing. The *Sequoia* is peculiarly exposed to the ravages of fire. The bark of the large trees is some eighteen inches thick, is as fibrous in its texture as a bale of cotton, and, being perfectly dry, invites the raging element to a contest of strength. Some of the trees have conquered, coming out of the contest with diminished proportions, but others, and these apparently the proudest monarchs of the grove, have bowed their lofty heads and measured their length upon the soil. It is to be hoped that those which have been placed under the protection of the State of California will be guarded against the approach of fire, as well as against all mutilation from any other cause.

The Calaveras Grove, situated in another county, was the one first discovered. It is composed of about 100 trees of large size, one of which, twenty-seven feet in diameter, was felled several years since by boring at its base, and the stump, smoothed off about six feet from the ground, has been made the scene of festivities in which a large company has taken part. It was then sheltered by the erection of a building over it. A friend has given me a statement of the amount of house-room which is afforded upon the surface of the stump of one of the trees. A circle of thirty feet diameter contains 707 square feet. If this could be had in squares, it would give for a single floor a parlor sixteen feet by twelve; a dining-room fifteen feet by ten; a kitchen twelve feet by ten; two bedrooms, each ten feet by ten; a pantry eight feet by four; and a closet four feet by two. Quite a roomy house for a small family might thus be constructed on a single stump. This will give a good idea of the magnitude of the trees; or, if any one wishes to know what space the tree would cover on the ground, let him strike a circle with a radius of fifteen feet, and he will have it before him. The tree in the Calaveras group which was felled was carefully examined some distance from the ground to ascertain its age, and 1255 concentric circles, indicating as many years, were counted. There was, of course, a gradual increase in the thickness of the circles. The first hundred measured only three inches, the second hundred nearly four inches, the tenth hundred nearly eight inches, and the twelfth hundred thirteen inches, showing great rapidity of growth, and the comparative youth of the trees considering their size. Another tree, of seventy-six feet circumference, was carefully sawed, and the rings counted to the number of 1935. Whether others will yet be found of still more gigantic size is doubtful, as the forests have already been extensively explored; but it is not at all impossible. The height of these trees is not so great as has sometimes been represented, but 300 or 325 feet, which some of them attain, is no mean height. There are taller trees in Australia, where the *Eucalyptus* has been known to reach the height of 480 feet; but, taking them all in all, there are no vegetable wonders elsewhere that equal the Big Trees of California.

On the return to San Francisco we stopped for half an hour at Keith's gardens, near Garrote, an extensive plantation of fruit on the edge of the mountain, and in the very midst of a region which, being dug over and over for gold, is now the picture of desolation. The fruits raised in the mountain region—peaches, grapes, pears, etc.—are considered finer than those produced in the low country. I visited also the extensive fruit-ranch of Dr. Strentzel, at Martinez, directly opposite Benicia, which is considered one of the finest in the state. He has nearly a hundred acres of the choicest trees and vines, which were loaded with the fairest and finest fruits—pears and apples, peaches and plums, figs and pomegranates, etc.—such as no other clime can excel. It was the finest exhibition of fruit that I have ever seen. Dr. S. has exhibited in its cultivation a discrimination and taste which was too much neglected in the early days of the state.

While waiting on the wharf at Benicia for a steamer, my attention was attracted to a placard painted on a board and placed on a high post, as if containing important directions for travelers. The same is posted all over the state, and the following story respecting it was related to me by a Californian. Out among the mountains, a miner, traveling alone, came to a fork in the road, and, doubtful which course to take, saw, to his great delight, what he took to be a guide-board. It was too dark for him to read it from the ground, and with great difficulty and many slides he at length succeeded in reaching the top. Holding on with one hand, he struck a match with the other, and by the dim light read the following important announcement: "Fifty-five miles to Sacramento, eighty miles to Stockton, and 175 miles to the wholesale and retail store of H. H. & Co., —— Street, San Francisco." They evidently understand the art of advertising in California.

## V.

### ON THE PACIFIC.

On the 4th of September we took our traps on board the Japan, one of the large, splendid ships of the Pacific Mail Steam-ship Company which ply between San Francisco and Japan and China. We were booked for a long voyage, not being allowed to see land for twenty-two days, the allotted time which, by the rules of the Company, the captain is required to fill out before reaching the port of Yokohama. Should he, by the aid of favoring gales, or by any miscalculation in regard to the amount of coal consumed, reach the coast of Japan before the time, he must sail up and down the coast until the twenty-two days have expired, and may then run into the Gulf of Yeddo and land his passengers. He may be longer in making the voyage, but he must by no means accomplish it in less time, although it could easily be made, without crowding the ship, in eighteen days.

The Japan is one of the finest ships of the fleet to which she belongs. She measures 4351 tons, is 370 feet in length, 79 in breadth; her depth of hold is $31\frac{1}{2}$ feet, and, as we are sailing, she is 20 feet out of the water. Her cylinder is 105 inches in diameter, and her smoke-pipe 36 feet in circumference—not a very small chimney, reminding us of the big trees in California. She is registered to carry 1450 passengers, of which number we had only about 500, nearly all of these Chinamen returning to their former homes. The ship carries thirteen large life-boats all ready for launching, each one capable of floating some fifty persons or more, but it adds very little to my sense of security to see this array of life-boats. In those sudden emergencies which constitute one of the chief dangers of the sea, it is seldom that they are successfully launched, or prove of any essential service to the mass of the passengers.

The crew were all Chinese, as well as the servants in the cabin and the waiters at the table, but they were admirably trained, were perfectly quiet, and ready at every call and for every emergency. The fire alarm was sounded soon after leaving port, merely to accustom the men to the warning, the passengers having been duly notified, and every man was at his post. Another day the life-raft, a large India-rubber float, was got out, put in perfect order, and made ready for a launch. The Chinese sailors are born and brought up on the water, many of the families of populous cities living in boats, so that they may be considered a sort of amphibious animal, and they would probably be as strange on land as a fish out of water.

We found in Captain Freeman a gentlemanly, polite officer, not only looking well to his ship—the first duty of a seaman—but attending as well to the comfort and pleasure of his passengers, which can not be said of all captains on the sea. I had but one complaint to make of the regulations of the ship, which in the main were admirable and rigidly carried out, and this complaint lies more against the Company than the master of the ship, although in a subsequent voyage, in another vessel of the same line, I found that the rule of which I complain could be and was relaxed by the captain voluntarily asking me to perform a service in which no clergyman on board the Japan was allowed to officiate.

We passed through the Golden Gate on Saturday, the 4th, and, getting out to sea, I met on board Bishop Kingsley, of the Methodist Episcopal Church, who was on his way to visit the missions and conferences of that Church in Asia and Europe, and who died suddenly at Beyrout the following spring. I consulted with several of the passengers, and finding them all desirous to have religious services on the following day, and obtaining Bishop Kingsley's consent to officiate, provided it were allowed by the officers of the ship, I went to Captain Freeman, not supposing for a moment that it would be forbidden. But I was informed that it was a rule of the Company that the Episcopal service only should be read at the usual hour of public worship, eleven o'clock on Sunday. He stated that if we would conform to the Episcopal Church by reading the service we could do so, otherwise it would be read by the surgeon of the ship, and that would be the only religious exercise of the morning. As we were neither competent nor inclined to comply with this condition, we all attended and heard the service, or a part of it, read by a young man who seemed to feel, as he was in reality, out of his place, and who curtailed the whole service to less than twenty minutes. As clergymen, we were quite willing to be led in our devotions and to be instructed by any competent person, and so were the passengers generally, while we could not but regard it as an indignity to all on board that, when ministers of the Gospel were present, and the passengers, one and all, desired to enjoy their ministrations, they should be deprived of the privilege, and delivered over into the hands of a surgeon—a youth who made no pretensions to religious character—as the only proper person to minister to them in holy things.

We were very differently treated on the voyage from Yokohama to Shanghai, the captain alluding to the rule, but very sensibly remarking that he thought it more desirable to have religious service properly conducted by a clergyman than to have it administered in the manner mentioned above. I hope, ere this, the Company has modified its standing order.

So far as the sea itself and its sights were concerned; we had a tame voyage. We did not have even the variety of first "seeing a ship and then shipping a sea," which one may have at any time on the Atlantic. We saw one ship. On the seventh day out, just at dusk, a sail was descried on the horizon, ten or twelve miles distant, quite out of our course, and standing toward the northeast. The usual discussion ensued as to what she was, where from and where bound, but we are all profoundly ignorant to this day on this important point. One ship that we expected to see we did not see. On leaving San Francisco we were informed that we should meet the homeward-bound steamer in mid-ocean and exchange mails, and accordingly we waited day after day, with our packages of letters ready. On this hangs a tale which I shall presently relate.

One evening word came to the saloon that the lights of the coming steamer were in sight, and we were all on deck in time to see a beautiful little star sink below the horizon. When we had given up the steamer we watched for whales, and some of these sea-monsters made their appearance near the ship; and then we took to watching the flying-fish as they came out of their native element on short excursions in the upper air. With their silver bodies and transparent

FLYING FISH.

wings, they are as beautiful as a bird, and their flight is by no means ungraceful. Some of them flew from one to two hundred feet before going below to moisten their wings. The sea-birds never left us, even when more than a thousand miles from any land, and I could not help feeling a deep sympathy for them, living so far away from the rest of the world. But if they prefer such a life, I have nothing to say against it. I know they did not ask for any sympathy, or seem to need it.

One evening we had a brilliant lunar rainbow, exhibiting the prismatic colors very distinctly, but in its indefiniteness of outline it bore the same relation to the solar rainbow that moonlight does to sunlight. Though unusually bright, it had a dreamy, mysterious look that was fascinating rather than satisfying. We have had little opportunity to study the sea in its various moods; it was almost an unbroken calm.

The first day after leaving San Francisco, while we were in the vicinity of the land, we had one of those long ground swells which are so apt to turn the thoughts inward, and many of our passengers seemed to feel in duty bound to conform to the custom of the sea. Their meditations, if I were to judge from their visages, became by no means sweet; but when we were once fairly on the bosom of the deep, they all smiled again, and our voyage was as pleasant as one could desire. We had one little episode, which only helped us to appreciate fair weather and a smooth sea. On the seventeenth day out, as we were seated at the lunch-table, a heavy gale struck us broadside, and the grand old ship made a graceful bow sideways. For several hours the wind blew a pretty stiff gale, lashing up the sea and spreading the whitecaps profusely over its surface. At dinner we found the racks upon the table to hold our soup and other eatables fast and prevent their reaching our laps too summarily instead of going down the natural way. For some reason unexplained, several of the passengers concluded they would not take dinner that day, but matters became more quiet in the course of the night, and all went on smoothly again.

But whatever of variety was wanting in the sea and its changes was abundantly supplied by our occupations and diversions on shipboard. It does not require much to amuse a child, and not much more to entertain grown-up men and women at sea. In a long voyage, every incident, however trifling, is invested with an importance which would be incomprehensible to those on shore. This is not because we become children in going to sea, but because, in some circumstances, we must make the most of every thing.

It took us two or three days to get used to the sea and to one another, and to learn each other's histories (it is wonderful what an amount of information, good and bad, in regard to one another, we do gather up in the course of two or three days), and then little groups began to form and to pass an occasional hour on deck, or in the upper saloon, in singing home songs, all of them sacred, but not all religions. Then we had afternoon lectures, and in the evenings literary readings, and sometimes there were games in which the large children joined with as much zest as any of the small children. And then we had puzzles of various kinds, and charades, and the whole portfolio of amusements laid up in the past was overhauled, and all that was available was brought out and brought into requisition. Our good Captain Freeman and others of the ship's officers were as big boys and as good boys as any on board, and all seemed ready to perform their parts.

We had been but a few days at sea when some of the passengers determined to get up a newspaper, and accordingly issued a Prospectus, giving the reasons for such an undertaking, the chief of which was that no American can live without his newspaper, and that it is as essential in the midst of this wide ocean as upon any narrow strip of land. One of the objects to be advocated by the paper was the obtaining from the powers that be eight instead of four meals a day, and an unlimited increase in the speed of the ship. The first number of the paper, which was semi-weekly, and was called "THE OCEAN WAVE," was issued on Saturday, September 11th, and was received with great favor by its numerous subscribers. I make some extracts from the opening number:

"Passengers on board the steam-ship 'Japan,' who lie awake by night and sleep by day, must have noticed that the steamer regularly lays to at about 4 o'clock in the morning. The officers of the steamer, with a disingenuousness that merits the severest reprobation, have endeavored to convey the impression that this is done to enable the steward to go a fishing, and that he thus catches a daily supply of codfish balls, potted sardines, and stuffed crabs; also that some of the crew are at the same time sent ashore for fresh cabbage and turnips. The reporters of 'The Ocean Wave' (Long may it wave!), with their well-known vigilance, have been on the alert, and have made the discovery that the P. M. S. S. Co. have a telegraph wire laid across the Pacific Ocean, with stations at regular intervals, and that the steamer is stopped every morning to communicate with either shore to learn the price of pork and beans, that the quantity allowed for lunch may be regulated accordingly. The conductors of 'The Ocean Wave' (Long may it wave!), after a protracted negotiation with the Company at New York, carried on through the Pacific Cable at incredible expense, such as none but a well-established journal like our own could incur, have made arrangements to receive the news from all parts of the world up to the hour of our going to press. We are thus enabled to present to our readers the following interesting and important intelligence from both continents."

Then follows a list of head-lines, among which are the following:

"Highly important intelligence from all parts of the World." "Earthquake at San Francisco: Great loss of life and destruction of Property." "Sanguinary Battle between the Bulls and Bears in New York City." "Brilliant Reception of the President at Communipaw." "Diabolical Conspiracy against the Emperor of France," etc., etc.

I give below a specimen of the dispatches:

"*San Francisco*, 9 *o'clock P.M.*, *Sept.* 10, 1869. Our ancient and venerable city has again been visited by one of those terrible calamities to which tropical countries are liable. Early this afternoon portentous signs of the coming visitation awakened intense apprehension among our citizens, who are proverbial for their calmness on all occasions. The wind suddenly died away to a stiff gale; ladies were seen in some instances in their cloaks, but without furs; gentlemen were content to wear a single overcoat, carrying the other on the arm: one could walk the entire distance from the post-office to the Occidental without swallowing more than his peck of dirt. Such indications as these could not fail to produce intense excitement. About an hour after sunset a low rumbling sound was heard, coming apparently from the direction of Monte Diablo, and soon there was a heavy shaking of the earth. Some of the curb-stone brokers who were enjoying themselves at a restaurant on Montgomery Street, supposing the end of the world had come, and wishing to stave it off until they had secured the payment of notes due the next day, rushed into the street and gave the alarm. The fire-bells instantly sounded the preconcerted signal, and the citizens generally, after throwing their chinaware out of the windows to save as much as possible from the general wreck, attempted to save their lives by making for public squares, which happily abound in San Francisco. The crowd became so great at the intersection of Montgomery and Market Streets —a narrow pass—that they trampled one upon another in wild confusion, and a fearful loss of life ensued. Some say as many as three hundred persons—men, women, and children—perished; others put the estimate as low as two women and one boy.

"In the general consternation that prevails, it is impossible to obtain accurate information in regard to the destruction of property, but it is reported that many of our finest buildings are demolished. The magnificent and costly adobe structures that once adorned our city are nearly all prostrate. A messenger just in from the Mission Dolores states that great seams have opened in the walls of that venerable pile. The new hotel, on Montgomery and Market Streets, appears to have suffered most severely; as we passed it a few moments since, it was nearly level with the pavement. Scarcely a church in the city has a steeple standing. We shall collect farther information and send another dispatch in an hour or two.

"*Later:* 11 *o'clock P.M.* The first reports of the earthquake were greatly exaggerated. It is ascertained that the rumbling noise and the jar were produced by the passage of a heavy dray with a ponderous casting from the Union Iron Works through Mission Street. No lives were lost. The steeples of the church which were supposed to have fallen had never been erected. The new hotel had been built only as far as the basement. The splendid pile of the Mission Dolores still stands in magnificent proportions, though rather the worse for years. The alarm has subsided.

"*Paris, Sept.* 10, 1869. For some days past the French capital has been full of rumors of a foul conspiracy against the government and the emperor. Intense excitement was produced on Monday morning by the following placard, which was found posted in various parts of the city, and some daring miscreant had fastened one to the entrance gate of the Louvre.

"'*What is the difference between the Emperor Napoleon and a Neapolitan beggar?*'

"Every morning the placards were found replaced by mysterious hands. It was evident that an attempt upon the life of the emperor was intended, or a conspiracy to reduce him to the abject condition of the lazzaroni of Italy. The police set themselves at work to ferret out the conspiracy, but without success. A meeting of the Supreme Council is to be held this morning to deliberate upon the alarming crisis.

"*Evening.* The Council assembled at 9 o'clock this morning. The emperor and empress were both present, bearing the marks of having spent a sleepless night, but their anxiety was relieved by a distinguished member, who gave the following solution to the placard:

"'The one issues manifestoes, the other manifests toes without his shoes.'

"Paris is again tranquil."

The following was among the literary contributions:

### THE KNOT OF BLUE AND GRAY.

"Upon my bosom lies
  A knot of blue and gray;
You ask me why; tears fill my eyes
  As low to you I say

"I had two brothers once,
  Warm-hearted, bold, and gay;
They left my side—one wore the blue,
  The other wore the gray.

"*One* rode with Stonewall and his men,
  And joined his fate to Lee;
The other followed Sherman's march
  Triumphant to the sea.

"Both fought for what they deemed the right,
  And died with sword in hand;
One sleeps amid Virginia's hills,
  And one in Georgia's sand.

"The same sun shines upon their graves,
  My love unchanged must stay;
And so upon my bosom lies
  This knot of blue and gray."

One of our entertainments was a Chinese concert. There were 450 Chinamen on board, returning to their native land, all in the steerage. Even the wealthy Chinese prefer the steerage, where they have their cooking according to their national taste. On being told that there were some good musicians among them, a gentleman of our party, with the captain's permission, invited them aft into the saloon to give us a musical entertainment. There were three Chinese instruments—a sort of banjo, a kind of violin, and one indescribable; another Chinaman did the vocal part, chiefly on one note, and this through his nose. They were in harmony, and kept perfect time, the movement being very rapid, but the instruments had a range of only about half an octave, and after two or three tunes it became excessively tedious, and at length unendurable. We were to have another entertainment the same evening, but they held on their way with increasing vigor and spirit, until we all began to be filled with consternation lest they should never stop. We could not inform them that enough was enough, and one piece after another followed without any interval. The gentleman who had got up the entertainment was the picture of distress, considering himself responsible for the hopeless condition into which he had brought us. A collection was proposed and taken up, and presented to them, with the idea that this would end the matter, but it was indignantly refused, one of them saying in broken English they had "plenty money"—they played "for fun," and would play "plenty more," and at it they went again with fresh vigor. He produced a gold watch to prove to us that he was able financially to hold out much longer. At last an interpreter was called in, a truce was obtained, and the other entertainment followed.

But our most entertaining diversion on the long voyage was found in a trial which grew out of our failure to speak the returning ship. The two steamers which leave the opposite shores of the Pacific are in the habit of meeting somewhere in mid-ocean to exchange mails. The science of navigation is now reduced to such a nicety of calculation that in clear weather, when an observation can be taken, a skillful seaman can tell within a quarter of a mile the precise point on the globe on which he is sailing, and can make an appointment to meet another vessel on any mile of the sea at any given time, and keep his appointment with unerring certainty.

On leaving San Francisco we were informed that we should meet the homeward-bound steamer about the ninth day out, as both would be sailing on the same parallel of latitude. Accordingly, we had a large number of letters written to surprise the friends at home. They were duly mailed, postage paid, but the returning steamer never made her appearance. When all hope of seeing her had gone by, the purser of the ship, who was mail-agent, was heard to say he never expected we should meet the ship, but that it was all the same to him, inasmuch as he had made his percentage on the sale of post-stamps, which he had bought for currency and sold for coin.

Such an aggravated case of swindling coming upon the heels of our disappointment could not be suffered to pass without official investigation. A warrant for his arrest was issued by the proper authority, and he was brought before the judge of the United States Court of the Middle District of the Pacific Ocean, in charge of the United States Marshal. He gave bail for his appearance on the following day, when the trial commenced. A jury was impanneled, composed of equal numbers of ladies and gentlemen, and the trial proceeded according to the formalities of law, and continued through two days. Able counsel appeared for the prosecution, and also for the prisoner. A number of witnesses were examined and cross-examined, and, in accordance with the precedents established by courts on land, a vast amount of interesting information was elicited having no reference to the case before the court.

At the opening of the court on the second day the district attorney rose, and with great solemnity objected to the farther trial of the case on the ground that one of the jurors had been heard to express an opinion favorable to the prisoner. The court inquired whether the juror objected to was a lady or a gentleman, and on being informed that it was a lady, decided that in such case it was no disqualification, inasmuch as from time immemorial ladies had enjoyed the privilege of expressing their minds as freely as they chose. When the testimony was all in, the case was argued with great ability, and, after a charge from the court, was submitted to the jury, who brought in a verdict of "Not guilty, but recommended to mercy."

This trial was the most entertaining incident of the voyage, and to record all the amusing and witty things that were said and done, and which often baffled all the efforts of the judge and marshal to preserve order in the court, would require a volume in law sheep. But it was worthy of being reported and preserved among the *causes celebres*.

On the voyage we passed through one experience which was novel to most of us, and which occurs only on the Pacific Ocean. It was the dropping a day out of the calendar. We retired to our state-rooms and fell asleep on Friday night, the 17th of September, leaving every thing correct according to the almanac. When we awoke the next morning we found that it was Sunday, the 19th, and we had not overslept ourselves. I went to the room of the first officer, whose duty it is to keep the log of the ship, in which every thing important is entered, and found he had made the following record:

"*Sunday*, 19*th day of September*. Note. Having crossed the prime meridian, 180°, bound westward, Saturday, the 18th, is discarded, being called by name and date next following, as above."

We were not without warning on the subject—indeed, it had been a matter of speculation for several days, as we were approaching the 180th degree of longitude west and east of Greenwich, and all the more interest attached to it from the uncertainty as to what day we should cross that meridian. Had it been one day later, a Sunday would have been blotted out, and we should have gone to bed on Saturday and got up on Monday. As it was, we were called to adjust our feelings to what seemed an arbitrary change of the holy Sabbath from its proper place to one day earlier in the calendar. We did so, and kept the day as the Sabbath with clear consciences. Occasionally, during the morning, the thought would come into our minds that those whom we had left behind us were in the midst of Saturday, and that during our sleep we had made an extraordinary leap to get into Sunday, but, so far as my own feelings were concerned, the Sabbath was as holy as any that I have spent on sea or land.

Every one knows that in traveling around the world from east to west a day is lost, for the same reason that if one could go round the world in twenty-four hours in the same direction, he would retain the same relative position to the sun, he would travel with the sun, and there would be no succession of day and night. So, in traveling more leisurely westward, a certain amount of time is added to each day, which, in making the circuit of the earth, would amount to an entire day. In order, therefore, to adjust his reckoning to the calendar of the place which he left, he must, at some point in the journey, pass over one day of that calendar as if he had not lived it, while, in reality, he has lived the whole time by lengthening every day in his journey. Where shall he make this change in his reckoning? where shall he drop the day? Navigators have answered this question by making the change on the 180th degree of longitude west or east of Greenwich (or London, which is practically the same thing). When they reach this meridian sailing westward, they drop a day; when they reach it sailing eastward, they repeat a day. If it comes on Saturday, eastward bound, they have two Saturdays in succession; if on Sunday, two Sundays; and so of any other day.

This matter of dropping a day derives its chief interest

from its relation to the Christian Sabbath, and in this respect it has an importance which I have not seen attributed to it. It actually solves some questions which have been the theme of distracting controversy.

The shape of our world, and its revolution on its axis, make it an absolute impossibility that its inhabitants should all commence keeping the Sabbath at the same time. As the sun rises earlier upon one land than another, so must the inhabitants of those lands enter upon sacred time at different periods. There is no more actual correspondence between New York and London in regard to the Sabbath than there is between San Francisco and Japan, although in traveling between the two former places no change of reckoning is made, while the change of a day is made in passing to and fro between the two latter. There is a difference of one hour for every fifteen degrees of longitude in the commencement and close of each day, so that in reality the whole world are keeping different periods for the Sabbath, according to their localities. This divests the question as to the precise time that we shall observe as the Sabbath of its moral character, provided we are keeping as near as possible to an observance of the command to keep holy every seventh day. It becomes, in some circumstances, a question of longitude rather than of morals. If I leave San Francisco (as I did) on Saturday, the 4th of September, and should reach Yokohama on the morning of the 21st—which would be Saturday according to my reckoning —I should find Christian people keeping the Sabbath day; it would be Sunday, although there are only ninety-five degrees of longitude, or six and one third hours of time, between the two places. Am I bound in conscience to continue to keep my day as the Sabbath, and thus be at variance with all the Christian people whom I may meet? If so, I must continue to do it the rest of my journey in Asia and Europe, and when I reach America, and during the whole of my future life, unless I should chance to make a journey round the world the other way, from west to east, which would bring me right again. It is evident that perfect uniformity in this respect is impracticable, and that the common consent of Christians around me becomes a duty, as long as it is impossible to keep the same hours which I have observed at home. If I were to attempt to do the latter, I must needs commence my Sabbath at ten o'clock A.M. on reaching Yokohama, going west, and at twelve o'clock at noon on reaching Singapore.

There is no other point or line on the world's surface so favorable for making the change in reckoning, for dropping or adding a day, as that which has been taken by English and American navigators, the 180th degree of longitude, at which the reckoning from east to west longitude, or the reverse, commences. This line falls in the middle of the Pacific Ocean, where there are no inhabitants to be affected by the change excepting on the scattered islands of the sea, and, in sailing east or west, there is a vast expanse of water to cross before coming to Christian settlements. I felt no scruple, therefore, in conforming to a conventional rule, though it has not the force of a moral law, in dropping one day out of my diary, or in stepping at once out of Friday night into Sunday morning, because I must at some point in my journey round the world make my calendar agree with the world in which I expect to live, and this is altogether the most suitable point at which to do it.

I have alluded to the bearings of this subject on some of the controversies which divide the Christian Church. There is in the United States a sect of Christians called the Seventh-day Baptists, numbering several thousands, whose name indicates that they are cut off, or have cut themselves off from their brethren by their conscientious convictions that the seventh day of the week, or our Saturday, ought to be observed as the Christian Sabbath. Now, if one of the members of that Church would accompany me around the world, having passed the prime meridian we should be in harmony on this point—we should both be keeping the same day as the Sabbath, for he, of course, would be conscientiously opposed to making any change. He would be in harmony with the mass of Christians as we pass along westward, but when we reach the United States he would be one day in advance of the Church to which he belongs. He would then be a regular first-day Baptist. So of the Jews, who strictly observe the seventh day as the Sabbath. A voyage around the world would convert them, whether they were willing or not. Might it not be a legitimate course for seventh-day-Sabbath Christians and for Jews to appoint a delegation to go around the world from east to west, agreeing to abide by their experience when they should return and make their report, just as we adopt the reports of committees on other matters when we are satisfied as to their correctness? This would bring the whole Christian and the Jewish world into the harmonious observance of one day as the Sabbath, and it would involve no more sacrifice of principle on the part of any members of these denominations than it would for any one of them to make the change in his reckoning in going around the world, which every one would probably do who should accomplish the circuit of the earth.

There are in the Pacific Ocean two groups of islands not far from each other, on nearly the same degree of longitude, although both of them east of the prime meridian, the inhabitants of which observe different days as the Sabbath. These are the Sandwich and the Society Islands. The reason of this diversity is to be found in the fact that the missionaries who carried the institutions of the Bible with them sailed from different lands and in different directions, meeting, as it were, midway in the journey around the world. The missionaries to the Sandwich Islands sailed from the United States, going westward by Cape Horn. The missionaries to the Society Islands sailed from England, going eastward around the Cape of Good Hope, but, as they crossed the 180th degree of east longitude, they should have made a change in the day, which would have brought them into accord with the inhabitants of the Sandwich Islands.

If there is any answer to the old problem, Where does the day begin, it is this: At the 180th degree of longitude, east or west. This is the only line on which there is an arbitrary change or commencement of a day, but, as a practical thing, the day begins all around the world, not at the same moment of time, but just as the sun visits different parts of the earth at successive periods in the twenty-four hours. The time will never come when the day will begin all over the world at the same moment, or when the whole world will be keeping the same hours as the holy Sabbath, until the earth is flattened out and becomes a plane instead of a globe. With the present shape of our world it would be as much an impossibility as for the sun to rise upon every part of the globe at the same instant of time.

## VI.

### EXCURSIONS IN JAPAN.

Sunday, the 26th of September (according to our reckoning, after dropping a day into the ocean), was the twenty-first day out from San Francisco. Toward evening I was on deck with Captain Freeman, when he remarked that about two o'clock the next morning we should have a sight of a point of one of the Japanese islands; a pretty close calculation, I thought, even for an old sailor, after being three weeks without a glimpse of any thing earthly. Accordingly, I was on the lookout soon after midnight, and sure enough, within an hour of the time indicated, the dim outline of the shore became visible.

I have been at sea when the sight of land was far more welcome, for this voyage was upon a summer sea, and under sunny skies nearly all the way, and the time had passed pleasantly on shipboard; but it was a joy again to see the solid earth, and the green shores of Japan are among the most beautiful of any that skirt the seas. When the morning dawned, and we drew near the shores, covered profusely with verdure and foliage, the hills and the valleys had all the brilliancy of color of the Irish coast, with an endless variety of contour, and an originality of surface that made the whole scene one of great beauty without the element of grandeur. The sacred mountain of fire, Fusiyama, the glory of Japan, which the Japanese, as by a sense of religious duty, put into every picture and on every article that they manufacture, rose up about sixty miles distant. The volcano, though not active, forms a lively feature in the landscape. In clear weather it may be seen more than a hundred miles out at sea.

ENTRANCE TO THE GULF OF YEDDO.

As we steamed up the Gulf of Yeddo, the scene became more and more animated and Japanese in its aspect. Great numbers of fishing-boats, with their square sails rudely hung against the masts, were putting out from the shore on their daily errand, and shoals of smaller boats, sculled by native Japanese, were plying around. Occasionally a palm-tree would show itself on the shore, but the pine and the fir, and other evergreens for which Japan is celebrated, abounded all along the shore. Now and then a bamboo grove, with its light bluish-green and feathery foliage, not only one of the most beautiful, but really the most useful vegetable growth in the world, would diversify the velvety landscape. The narrow valleys running back from the water were green with rice-fields, and the terraced hills with different crops.

In the Gulf of Yeddo we met a steamer bearing the familiar flag, outward bound. We afterward learned that she was going out to the relief of the United States ship of war Idaho, which had sailed the week before for home, *viâ* Cape Horn, in perfect trim. She had only fairly got to sea when she was overtaken by a typhoon and reduced to a mere wreck. One of the officers whom I met at Yokohama told me that for an hour and a half the ship lay in the centre of this circular gale in a dead calm, waiting for the circumference to strike them. When the shock came she was dismasted and so shaken as to be utterly unseaworthy, and I learned afterward that she was sold for an old hulk. So accurately had we timed it in reaching the coast of Japan the week after the equinox.

We were soon entering the harbor of Yokohama, the principal port of Japan, in which vessels of all nations, men-of-war and merchantmen, were lying at anchor, and giving the bay a familiar look. The Stars and Stripes were displayed from a number of ships. The firing of our gun and the dropping of the anchor brought around us a swarm of native boats, all propelled with sculls by Japanese men and women almost as innocent of clothing as when they were born. Some of them brought residents on board to look after friends, and others came to take ashore the passengers, most of whom were to land at Yokohama, to remain, or be transferred, like ourselves, to the steamer for Shanghae.

In the course of the morning our luggage was piled into one of the boats, and ourselves into another propelled by five lusty natives, who at every stroke of their sculls sent forth a groan or wail which would now and then break into a scream more novel than pleasing. We landed in the midst of a crowd of coolies absolutely naked, with the exception of two or three inches of cotton cloth about their loins, and then came the strife for the baggage. But it was a far better-mannered crowd than one will find in any civilized country in which I ever landed. After the formality of opening one of our numerous trunks by a Japanese custom-house official, who politely bowed that it was all right and did not wait for any fee, the crowd of naked coolies divided off into separate squads. All remained quiet while two or three of their number were making some arrangement in regard to our luggage, I could not tell what. I soon found that they were preparing to draw lots to see which squad should have the porterage. The lots were little ropes of straw, curiously intertwined, and bound together by a band of straw. The band was severed, and with a shout the coolies all lifted their hands. Four of the strands were found to be tied by another band, indicating the four fortunate coolies, the rest submitting without a sign of dissatisfaction. I could not avoid the inward exclamation, "Oh that coolies, and carmen, and hackmen in some other lands that I have seen would cast lots for their passengers instead of tearing them to pieces!" The whole carrying business of Yokohama is done by these coolies, four of them—two in front and two behind the cart—sometimes taking a ton and a half at a load. In drawing and pushing their rude carts they seem to be greatly assisted by a monotonous groan or shout emitted at every step, more piercing than that of the boatmen.

That part of Yokohama which we enter on landing is not a Japanese town, but built and occupied by foreigners, and has none of the characteristics of a native city. There is no wharf, a wide bund or street extending nearly a mile along the water, on the shore-side of which the foreign merchants have their bungalows and offices. Some of these are surrounded with walls, the yards being ornamented with Oriental shrubbery and plants, including the beautiful evergreens. Many of the foreign merchants reside on the high bluff overlooking the town and the bay, which affords a fine view of the country as it stretches out toward Fusiyama. Kanagawa, about three miles across a small bay, was first selected as the foreign port for Yeddo, but Yokohama was substituted, and it has now a foreign population of about 2000. It has become the principal foreign port of the empire, and is a place of much activity in business, especially on the arrival or departure of a steamer. These events infuse new energy into the whole population, from the merchants, who just then are overwhelmed with their correspondence, down to the coolies and boatmen, to whom steamer-days are harvests. During the intervals all classes take things more quietly.

Yokohama is likewise the residence of the foreign ministers. For a time they were located at Yeddo, but the hostility of the Yakonins made it unsafe. The British embassy was attacked, the inmates put to the sword, and the residence burned. After passing through many perils the foreign representatives concluded to try a location that was more salubrious.

We remained at Yokohama over one steamer in order to visit Yeddo and to make some excursions into the country. One of the most interesting of these was to the statue of Daiboots, fifteen or twenty miles distant, and near the ancient capital of the Tycoons, the extinct city of Kamakura. The whole region of country is strikingly beautiful, and indeed the whole island, and, so far as I have seen it, the whole empire of Japan. The common roads or paths, with a single exception, are not wide enough to allow the passage of wheels, and ordinarily one must choose between riding Japanese ponies (the most vicious domestic brutes that I have met), being carried by coolies in a sedan chair, or going on foot. We made a sort of compromise, sending our horses forward twelve miles to meet us on the way, while we made the first part of the excursion by water.

We left Yokohama in the morning in a covered sail-boat

manned by six Japanese sailors, who, in their rude way, are expert seamen, and sailed through a part of the Gulf of Yeddo that was thoroughly explored by the Perry Expedition. It was so unfortunate as to receive a quantity of Yankee names in place of those, far more appropriate and musical, that they had worn for centuries. We passed in sight of *Perry* and *Webster* Islands, through *Mississippi* Bay, and moored our bark in *Goldsborough* Inlet. I have not the Japanese originals at command, but, from the general beauty of the names with which I am familiar, I am sure that all these places "would smell as sweet" if they had been left to wear those they had worn from time immemorial. The Japanese names of towns, and rivers, and seas are singularly beautiful. The language itself, as spoken by the people, is musical, a decided contrast to the Chinese. It is not unlike the Italian in this respect.

Kanagawa is the residence of one of the Daimios, a place of some importance, and a charming spot. We landed at a romantic tea-house, a great resort for excursionists, and the arrival of our party with an order for *tiffin* produced no little stir among the occupants. One was off with a net to the tank near by; in a few moments some of the excellent fish with which the waters of Japan abound were on the coals, and it was but a short time until they were before us. Another was busied in preparing the universal beverage, which in Japan, as in China, is a simple infusion of tea, without milk or sugar, and almost without taste. But our own capacious lunch-basket supplied all deficiencies. The whole thing was made ready with wonderful celerity, and we were served with an ease and an air of politeness that I have not seen excelled in New York or Paris. While our horses were made ready I walked to an old Shintoo temple near the tea-house, and then to one of the beautiful groves of bamboo which abound in the islands; the reeds, which were only three or four inches in diameter, shooting up to the height of sixty or seventy feet, and the graceful branches spreading out at the top like plumes, forming a

JAPANESE TEMPLE.

perfect canopy. There is no vegetable production in the East—none in all the world that is applied to more uses than the bamboo, which is a species of grass. Not even the palm, in all its varieties, is more useful. The roots are made into preserves, and the young shoots are eaten. The Japanese often build their houses entirely of bamboo—beams, posts, rafters, siding, and thatch; while the scaffolding, ropes, and ladders which they employ in building are made of the same. Nearly every article of furniture in the house is bamboo—chairs (so far as they have any), bedsteads and beds, stools, tables, and stands. Their most common utensils are made exclusively or in part of bamboo—tools, brooms, buckets and dippers, measures, and boxes of all kinds; the chop-sticks with which they eat, baskets, and trays. Ornaments of all kinds, musical instruments, umbrellas, cloth, paper, books, and pens, come from the same source. Boats are built and rigged throughout of bamboo. Scarcely any thing, indeed, in the whole economy of Japanese life can be named that is not made in whole or in part from this invaluable production of nature. In China, too, it is an important element in government, occupying a more indispensable place than birch in America. It is said that China could not be governed without the bamboo. A catalogue of its various uses would fill many pages.

Every thing being in readiness for our ride, I selected a sober-looking animal from among the ponies that were brought up, but I was no sooner in the saddle than he plunged his heels into the side of one of his neighbors, just missing the leg of the rider. His next move was to rear and strike the shoulders of the same horse with his fore feet, as if challenging him to single combat. Often during the ride of twelve miles, when he found another horse gaining upon him, he would suddenly stop and let fly his heels, regardless of where they hit. I kept my seat with difficulty; but afterward, while riding another of the same delightful animals, I was thrown completely over his head, striking upon my shoulder, and escaping without any material

VILLAGE LIFE IN JAPAN.

injury other than bruises. Some fared worse. One gentleman whom we met on the way was thrown from his horse three times, after which he concluded to make use of his own legs. These were a fair specimen of the Japanese horses—a wild, unmanageable race of animals.

The route from Kanagawa to Daiboots lay through a succession of narrow, beautiful valleys, every inch of which seemed to be under cultivation, one tier of rice-fields rising above another by a very slight gradation. We crossed a range of hills and struck into a ravine, through which ran a rapid stream, breaking frequently into beautiful cascades. The stream was skirted on either side with large camellia-trees, a variety of evergreens, and the ever-beautiful bamboo. Passing through several small villages, we were constantly greeted with the cry from men, women, and children, "O-ha-yo"—equivalent to our "Good-morning," or "How are you?" which it resembles in sound. Hostility to foreigners is confined almost exclusively to the cities, and even there to the Yakonins. At the end of a two-hours' ride we were on the site of the ancient capital, Kamakura.

All that remains of a city, which must have been one of great magnificence, is a cluster of large temples, in which are preserved numerous relics of the Tycoons of other ages. A grand avenue, nearly two hundred feet wide, leads down to the sea, two miles distant. The site of the city, which was destroyed in a war long, long ago, is now a fertile field. Two miles farther on is the statue of Buddha, known as the statue of Daiboots. It is a lonely relic of a past age, having been erected, according to the best accounts, about 600 years ago. It is colossal in size, of the finest bronze, and executed with wonderful skill, the joints between the several plates being so completely formed as scarcely to show a seam. The countenance is strikingly expressive of profound contemplation, completely fulfilling the traditional ideas of Buddha. The height of the statue, which is in a sitting posture, is about forty feet. Considering the

STATUE AT DAIBOOTS.

remote age in which it was produced, and the simplicity of the people at that period, it is a remarkable work of art. The lofty temple, which must have inclosed, or at least covered it, has long since disappeared, and for centuries, in a lonely nook among the hills, this statue has sat in silent meditation, exposed to the storms which come in from the neighboring sea, but as fresh and uninjured as when it was erected. There is no greater curiosity in Japan than this statue, of which there is no authentic record, excepting that it has stood in the wilderness for centuries, having once been surrounded by the teeming population of a splendid capital.

The day being far spent, we were not able to reach the island of Inosima, which, with the intervening country, was described to us as more beautiful than any thing we had seen. As it was, the darkness had gathered round us before we reached Kanagawa and regained our boat, and neither wind nor tide favoring us, it was near midnight when we landed at Yokohama. But the night was mild and beautiful, and the brilliant stars shone down upon us as we lay upon the deck quietly enjoying the sail. The sea itself was like a sea of fire, the phosphorescence lighting up the scene as by submarine lights.

There are many other excursions to be made from Yokohama, the country in all directions being romantic and inviting. There is much sameness, but it is the sameness of beauty, which does not weary. The valleys are a striking feature in Japanese scenery, never stretching out into wide plains, but exquisite gems exquisitely set in the cultivated, terraced hills which inclose them. They wind like streams among the hills, constantly opening up some new scene of beauty at every vista.

A visit to Yeddo, which the geographers in our youthful days assured us was the most populous city on the globe, was one of the chief attractions of a journey to Japan, but on landing in the country it became a matter of doubt whether we should see this great and mysterious city at all. The hostility of the Yakonins, the two-sworded men of the empire, always most marked at the capital, had become more pronounced than usual. Only the week previous, Sir Harry Parkes, the English minister, was attacked in the usual style, while riding in the streets of Yeddo, attended by his own servants and the Japanese guard. He escaped without personal injury, but the horse of one of his attendants received a sabre blow which was aimed at the rider.

The traditional aversion of the Japanese to all intercourse with the outer world is by no means so strong as that of the Chinese, nor so general, but even in Japan there are certain classes whose interest it is to keep alive this exclusiveness and hatred to foreigners. The government, from time immemorial, has used every art to keep out foreign ideas and foreign influence, and within the last few years has resorted to all the devices of Oriental diplomacy, of which duplicity is the chief, to delay the inevitable result; and if it has not instigated the violence which has been fatal to many foreigners, those who are in the interest of the government have done the deeds.

The *Samourai*, or *Yakonins*, compose a considerable portion of the population, and form the dangerous element of society, dangerous at least to foreigners. They are the retainers and fighting-men of the Daimios, and one of their characteristics is that they never appear in the streets unless armed with two swords, a long and a short one. The long sword is heavy, of the finest tempered steel, and kept always as sharp as a razor. This sword, which is worn constantly by the Yakonins, is the instrument used for decapitation in capital punishment, one blow from a strong hand completely severing the head from the body. It would readily cleave through a man's skull or take a limb from his body. These two-sworded men—the gentry of the country, as they consider themselves—have the strongest reason to oppose any change that would deprive them of their position and living. Having little or nothing to

G

do, they indulge freely in the intoxicating cup, and when drunk on the streets are very ready to express their dislike to foreigners by trying the temper of their swords upon them. As in some civilized regions, drunkenness is the immediate instigating cause of nearly all the assaults that are made. The chief peril of the traveler arises from the suddenness with which the assailants make their attack. The blow comes like a flash of lightning out of a clear sky, and the assailants disappear as suddenly.

After much deliberation on the subject, we came to the conclusion that we might as well not have come to Japan at all as not to go to Yeddo; and we went. The city is at the head of the bay on which Yokohama is situated, and a little more than twenty miles distant. There was at that time no regular communication between the two places, and intercourse, excepting among the Japanese, was not encouraged by the government. For our party of eight we had two carriages, driven by colored men, natives of the United States, who had been several years in Japan. The carriages, as well as the drivers, were importations.

Our baggage was sent on before us by coolies, who make nearly as good time on the road as the native horses. Each carriage had a *bettoe*, who is literally a footman. Every one who keeps a horse in Japan has a *bettoe*, who is inseparable from the horse at home and on the road. In riding or driving he runs with the horse, and is always ready to take him by the head and guide him, especially in turning a corner, the horses having little regard for the bit. The *bettoes* are as fleet of foot as the North American Indians, and will travel as fast and as far in a day as the horse. They are naked, with the exception of the little strip of cloth around the loins; but, in lieu of clothing, they are often tattooed from the shoulders to the knees in colors, red, and blue, and other dark shades, which gives them a picturesque appearance. When we arrived at Yeddo our *bettoes* were as fresh as when we started from Yokohama, showing far less signs of weariness than the horses themselves.

BETTOES.

The Tokaido, or imperial highway, the only road in Japan that can be traveled by carriage, extends from one end of the island of Niphon to the other, about three hundred miles, passing directly through the capital, and connecting it with Yokohama or Kanagawa. The drive between the two cities is one of the most interesting in the world. Little of nature is to be seen, but from first to last it is like a drive through a museum, a grand curiosity-shop; the Tokaido, the whole twenty-two miles, being a succession of the same beautiful little shops, with neatly-arranged wares, useful and ornamental, which line the streets of all the cities of Japan. These shops are small, but the fronts are open to the street, and every thing they contain can be seen at a glance. Once or twice there was a slight break in the succession of shops and tea-houses, where the ground was low and occupied by rice-fields, but art soon resumed its sway.

Nor was this apparently endless, but ever-changing panorama of art, though exclusively Japanese and novel in its character, the most interesting of the sights to be seen on the way. The living panorama was by far the most striking and entertaining. The Japanese are a migratory people in their tastes, always on the move, either for business or pleasure; and from Yokohama to the capital we passed through a living swarm of people, representing all the phases of this peculiar race.

I scarcely know where to begin in describing the throng that was moving to and fro, or stationary by the roadside, within and in front of the shops. I may as well begin at the lowest element—the naked coolies, who were carrying burdens of every sort on their shoulders, or more generally swung upon a pole that rested on the shoulders of two or four men, as the burden might require; or who were carrying travelers in *norimons* or *kangos*, the carriages of the country, answering to the sedan chair of China and India. So numerous was this class of travelers that it often seemed as if two thirds of the whole population were carrying the

JAPANESE KANGO.

other third on their shoulders. About the same proportion of the people and the same variety of classes travel in this way in Japan as in the omnibus or car in one of our cities. Then would come passengers of all sorts on foot, and their feet on high clogs or straw sandals, going on errands we knew not what; men and women, the latter with children lashed to their backs, the universal method of carrying children in this country, and one which does not seem to interfere with any of the occupations of the people, either in the house or the field; then would come traveling merchants, with their wares carried by attendants; and every now and then we would come upon some haughty-looking, two-sworded official on horseback, with attendants, and receive from him a sinister look as he passed, saying as much as "What business have you pantalooned and petticoated foreigners in this country, and on this Tokaido?"

And now we would meet some jolly crowd, or find them assembled at the tea-houses by the way, and receive from them the pleasant salutation *O-ha-yo* (good morning), or a smile and a graceful bow; and then we would jostle one of the pack-horses of the country bearing towering loads, the heels of the vicious beasts scattering the people right and left; here would come a Buddhist priest, with his head completely shaved, and looking in the upper story

JAPANESE RESTING.

very much like a new-born baby, and there a professor of the healing art, equally guiltless of hair, and having an equally sage appearance. Often we came upon groups and single persons sitting upon their haunches in a curious attitude, which we found was the way the people rest themselves when fatigued. All over Japan we noticed the same peculiar custom.

An open space on the way was devoted to a miserable race of beggars, some of them diseased and others deformed, who were importunate in their cries for a tempo, one of the smallest coins. At frequent intervals an opening in the shops revealed a beautiful grove or square, with a Shintoo or Buddhist temple, although few, if any, worshipers were to be seen. The tea-houses occurred frequently; and, as we stopped at any one of them to rest our horses, or for a relay, or to conform to the general custom of travelers on the Tokaido to take a cup of tea, a damsel would come out to the carriage, and with a respectful, easy bow, and a *O-ha-yo*, hand up a tray of tiny cups of tea, which it was our duty to drink as often as it was handed, although it was such a weak infusion of the leaf as to make it more like medicine than a beverage. The Japanese know nothing of the delicious decoction, well creamed and sweetened, which cheers the hearts of the housewives, and house-husbands too, in other and distant lands.

As we approached Yeddo, the shops, which are almost invariably fronts of houses, became wider and more imposing, though never rising above a second, and seldom above a first story, being spread out upon the ground. Through the openings we could look back into the most exquisite

TEA-GARDEN NEAR YEDDO.

little yards or gardens, ornamented with flowers and the dwarfed evergreens, of which there is a great variety all over Japan.

And now we are entering the suburbs of Yeddo, and now the city itself. The crowd increases, and becomes more and more curious, the ladies of our party (as do the ladies every where) attracting the most attention. The people all along the street, as if out on a holiday, stand and stare and laugh as we pass, as if we were the first of our kind ever seen in Yeddo. Passing through one of the many gates within the city, which seem designed for police purposes and not for defense, we meet a Japanese regiment of soldiers, and give them a wide berth, while laughing most heartily in our sleeves at the grotesque, tatterdemalion appearance they make. They reminded us strongly of the fantasticals of our own city. The bass-drummer was a real Falstaff, the sight of whom would have thrown Hogarth into an ecstasy of delight.

On reaching Yeddo we were driven to the Niphon Hotel, the finest hotel in the empire, and one which would not discredit any city in the world. No passports and no passes were demanded, although, in crossing a river ten or twelve miles below, we showed written passes obtained from the American consul at Yokohama, for which he charged us one dollar each, while the Japanese officials just across the street countersigned them without any fee. The hotel—occupying, with its grounds beautifully laid out, about four acres—was built by a Japanese stock company, not so much for a speculation, I imagine, as to confine the foreigners who might visit Yeddo. It is situated immediately on the bay, next to what is known as "the Concession"—the land appropriated to foreigners for purposes of trade.

On the sea front of the grounds were thirteen flag-staffs, in readiness for the flags of as many foreign representatives. When the treaty was signed, and Japan was opened to foreign trade, it was expected that the foreign merchants would come to Yeddo to transact business. A concession of land on the shore of the bay was made for the erection of warehouses, and the hotel was built to confine the foreigners in the same quarter. But Yeddo can not be approached by large vessels, and those engaged in the foreign trade found that they could do their business better at Yokohama, and the hotel has consequently been a failure. There were only four or five, besides ourselves, staying there, and, as a general thing, it is quite empty. It is a magnificent building for this country. The rooms, public and private, are large and airy, and are quite well furnished. The broad piazzas, extending along the entire front of about 200 feet, command a fine view of the bay, and from the cupola there is an extensive view of the city. An acre or more between the hotel and the bay is laid out in Japanese style—with miniature hills and lawns, and lakes and bridges, and ornamented with flowers and trees trimmed in fancy shapes. It is a beautiful picture in itself.

The grounds of the hotel are surrounded by a high wall, and in the city front is an arched gateway, along which are barracks for the Japanese guards, without whom we were not expected to go into the city. Whether they went out with us as spies on our purposes or to protect us was to us a matter of no consequence, inasmuch as they proved a protection from the crowds which every where surrounded us.

As soon as we had got ourselves and our traps arranged, we intimated at the office our desire to take a walk and visit a large temple near by. Presently eight men, each armed with the inevitable two swords, were ready to attend us, one man for each one of our party, and, thus escorted, we sallied forth into the street. We had not gone a block before a large crowd of men, women, and children began to surround us, pressing close to us, especially curious to examine the ladies of our party, and to take hold of their dresses. It was a very good-natured crowd, and even our guards smiled at their curiosity, and said as much by their looks as that they were quite harmless. When we reached the temple they all cast off their sandals, and rushed in be-

BELFRY IN COURT-YARD OF TEMPLE.

fore us to get a better view while we were standing. One might suppose we were the first visitors of the sort they had ever seen, and that they imagined we had just come down from the stars.

The temples of Yeddo tower above all the other buildings of the city. The houses and shops (and every house seems to be a shop) are all of a single story or a story and a half, built low, so that they may not have far to fall in case of an earthquake, one of the every-day occurrences. The temple that we first visited was a structure about fifty feet in height, of which the four-sided high roof formed a chief part. The architecture was Oriental and really imposing, and the interior far more magnificent and in every respect in better taste than I expected to find it from the weather-beaten appearance of the exterior. The people of the place are not allowed to enter without taking off their sandals, and an exception was made of our party only in the case of the ladies; but this custom seems to arise from a regard to cleanliness, and not from reverence. No Japanese ever enters a house or shop without taking off his shoes and leaving them at the threshold.

We had arranged to drive the next morning to Asaxa, a distant suburb of Yeddo, which is devoted in a great measure to the games and sports of the people, where jugglers and experts of all kinds give their performances in the open air. There is a celebrated temple in this quarter, which we were desirous to visit, but the morning being rainy, we were obliged to abandon our purpose, and it was, perhaps, well that we did, for there is more lawlessness in this quarter of the city than in any other, and we should have been more exposed. Some friends whom I afterward met were stopped on their way and advised to return on account of exciting demonstrations which were taking place on that day.

In company with the Rev. Mr. Verbeck, the American missionary who was called to the head of the English Department of the Imperial University, I visited several of the book-stores to see and inquire into their literature. The Japanese are a reading people. I often found the servants, when not on duty, engaged in reading; and on one occasion I took the book from the hand of one of them, and found it a profusely illustrated volume. Their reading is chiefly sensational novels, arranged after the most approved style of French or English fiction—with a pair of lovers, who pass through all sorts of adventures, in which the sun, moon, and stars conspire against them, but the lover at length, with his heavy sword, cuts through all opposition, performing miracles of valor, carrying off his prize, and they live and die the happiest of mortals. Their literature is not more free from grossness and immorality than that of civilized nations.

The second morning we drove to a high bluff in the centre of the city called Atangoreama, which is reached by a long flight of stone steps, about a hundred in all. We were attended this time by a mounted guard of nine *Yakonin* soldiers, who surrounded our carriage when we rode, and dismounted to accompany and protect us whenever we had occasion to walk. Every where we attracted the same attention and the same crowd. The heights of Atangoreama afford the finest view of the city, and overlook the castle or palace of the Tycoon, which, since the Tycoonate was abolished, is used for the purposes of the new government. The castle stands upon high ground, and is strongly fortified after the Japanese fashion, with walled terraces and deep, wide moats, making it almost impregnable to native attacks, although comparatively weak to those skilled in the more modern arts of war. A drive along the castle walls and moats is one of the great attractions of Yeddo.

The city, which stretches out for miles in every direction, abounds in beautiful spots and interesting scenes, in which Japanese art has combined with nature to produce the finest effect. Gen. Van Valkenburg, the American minister, who resided at Yeddo while the foreign legations were located at the capital, in speaking to me of its beauties, said one might take a new walk or a new ride every day in the year and find some charming scene. We were compelled to leave the most of these unseen, but we were advised not to fail of visiting the ancient cemetery of the Tycoons, with its splendid temples. These sacred grounds must have been laid out many centuries ago, and successive rulers have spent immense sums in adorning them and keeping them in order. The place is called Shiba (pronounced *Siba* at Yeddo and *Shiba* in the provinces, the precise difference between Shibboleth and Sibboleth). It covers a vast extent of ground—a hundred or perhaps hundreds of acres, we could not tell how many, for there was nothing to bound the vision when we were once within the inclosure.

Entering by a massive gateway, we drove a long distance on a broad avenue shaded by magnificent old trees. The avenue itself, and the grounds on both sides, ornamented with trees and shrubbery, are kept with that scrupulous neatness which is characteristic of the Japanese. We came at length to another arched gateway, where we left our carriages and passed into a square court of some acres, in which stands a temple exceeding in grandeur and splendor all that we had imagined of Japanese architecture. The exterior is heavily ornamented with carving, and the interior literally shone with burnished gold.

Leaving this temple, we passed to another part of the cemetery, and were conducted through a succession of courts and temples not so large as the first, but far more elaborately and beautifully ornamented. I was surprised by the refined taste in the combinations of colors and in the other ornaments with which they were loaded. Some of the wide court-yards, inclosing temples, were surrounded with porticoes, or *loggia*, the roofs of which were exquisitely frescoed with a beauty and modesty of coloring that I have never seen surpassed in any country. The paneling contained carvings of birds in endless variety, painted as if from life.

From Shiba we returned to Yokohama, passing through

the same living and moving museum as on the way up. It was a curious scene, and in passing through it I was often reminded of the remark of a gentleman whom I met just as we were starting for Yeddo, " You will need a hundred eyes to see all that you will meet with on the way."

## VII.

### JAPAN AND THE JAPANESE.

The territory of Japan comprises four large islands and nearly 4000 smaller ones. There are seven grand divisions, which are subdivided into sixty-eight provinces, and these again into smaller districts and towns. It has an area of 190,000 square miles, and a population of about 20,000,000. For the last 600 hundred years there have been both a civil and a religious ruler, although the latter was scarcely any thing more than a nominal officer. The former, known under the name of Taikun or Tycoon, had the reins of government in his own hands; but the Mikado was recognized as the religious head of the country, and was indeed superior in rank to the Tycoon, although he had little to do with public affairs, and his existence was almost regarded as a myth. In the year 1868 a revolution was inaugurated, and at length became successful, by which the power of the Tycoon was overthrown. He was reduced to the position of prince of the empire, the Mikado was duly installed as supreme ruler, and is now recognized as such throughout the empire. Below him there are 260 Daimios, of whom eighteen are the great chiefs of the empire—feudal lords with supreme authority in their own provinces, and having under them thousands of retainers, the two-sworded men of the country, a class who live upon the Daimios, supposed to be ready to do their fighting for them, and who are sometimes quite as ready to fight on their own account. Each of the more powerful Daimios has many thousands of these retainers, who regard themselves, and are regarded by the rest of the people, as the gentry of the country, entitled to live without labor. Before the late change in the government the Daimios were required to reside at the capital half the year, and to leave their families there the whole of the year as hostages or pledges of their adherence to and support of the reigning power. Their residence, with an immense number of their retainers, added greatly to the population of Yeddo. Since the change they are allowed to reside in their own provinces, and Yeddo is now a city of deserted palaces, the population having been decreased by the removal of the Daimios and their retinues to the extent of more than half a million, some say more than a million.

The Mikado, who is now the supreme and only acknowledged head of the government, formerly had his palace at Miako, the religious capital of the empire; but since he has been acknowledged as emperor, he has taken up his residence at Yeddo, or is supposed to have done so, for he is seldom, if ever, seen by the people, and even the receptions which he has given to the representatives of foreign powers are said to have been given by proxy. Such is the mystery thrown by the Japanese officials around every thing pertaining to their government, that it would not be strange if the Mikado, in giving audience to foreign embassadors, had deputed some one to represent him without allowing it to be known that he had not appeared in person. The duplicity of Oriental courts, and their utter incomprehensibility are so well known, that scarcely any thing of this nature should awaken surprise. All who have to deal with them will be taken by surprise only when they shall be found acting on open ground and upon fair principles.

The present government of Japan gives no promise of being stable. The Mikado has been placed in power, not by his own ability or energies, but by some of the more influential Daimios, and is now in the hands of a clique who will see that he does nothing prejudicial to their plans and interests. Indeed, his authority is merely nominal; he has but the semblance of imperial power, the Daimios being supreme within their respective territories. For the sake of presenting a united front against foreign nations, and of keeping up the traditional forms of royalty before the people, the central organization is maintained; but it is more than ever exposed to revolution, and may speedily fall through its own weakness. It has no resources of any kind. It is financially bankrupt, and is resorting to every temporary expedient to obtain the means of existence. Crime of almost any nature may be condoned by the payment of sufficient sums. Just before I was in Yeddo, a woman was convicted of the murder of her husband, and was sentenced to be crucified, but she escaped the cross by the payment of a sum amounting to about $1000.

While I was at Yokohama, an official order, which had been sent to the Japanese merchants, was made public, to the great disgust of the authorities, who wished to keep it secret from foreigners, requiring all native merchants and traders, who might receive either cash or checks from foreigners, to present the same to the government officers and receive in exchange Japanese money, half *kinsats* and half *niboos*—the former almost worthless paper bonds which are irredeemable, and the latter a depreciated coin, and one which is counterfeited to an unlimited extent. The object of the order was to enable the government to raise funds by substituting poor money for good, and making a large percentage; and also by obtaining the cash for Japanese *promises to pay*—a mode of raising the wind which, by the way, is not confined to Japan.

The establishment of any thing like a republican form of government, which some have predicted, with the present elements, is out of the question. The only people in Japan who are allowed to bear arms, and who, from this cause alone, represent the physical force of the nation, are the *Yakonins*, numbered by hundreds of thousands, who are supported in idleness, and who would be deadly hostile to any reorganization of the government, or of society, which would degrade them to a level with the common people, and make it a necessity for them to obtain a living by working for it. The people of Japan can not rise and organize for themselves. They have neither the intelligence, nor the means, nor the disposition to make a demonstration toward such an end. It appears more probable that Japan, for some time to come, will be the scene of successive revolutions; that it will not settle down into any thing like stability of government. There is nothing out of which to make, or on which to found, such a government as some of its sanguine friends have been predicting. There are intelligent men among the higher classes of the Japanese—men who have looked into the condition of other nations, and who are not wanting in admiration of what they see that is good in them—but they are not men who are enlightened according to our standard, or who would be qualified to lead such a people out of their present condition into that of more enlightened nations. Nor would the conflicting interests of so many petty sovereigns as Japan contains—with which are closely united the interests of so many who are dependent on them—allow of such a radical change as the country must undergo before it can enjoy the blessings of a free or even of a good government.

Foreign commerce and foreign intercourse have not been a blessing thus far to the Japanese. Foreign communications and trade have broken in upon the quiet habits of a people that were living in almost Arcadian simplicity; they have excited avaricious and grasping desires among those who were content before with moderate returns for their industry; they have made the cost of living far greater to the people themselves, and as yet have given them little in return that has been a benefit. Much must be done in the future to promote the welfare and advancement of the people as a compensation for compelling

H

them to open their beautiful islands to the world, and for the injury that has been already done, or all this foreign intercourse will have proved only a curse. The Christian world owes a heavy debt to these heathen nations which have suffered so much at the hands of Christian governments.

The Japanese, although far more agreeable in their manners than the Chinese, are both intellectually and physically inferior. They are quicker in apprehension, perhaps; more imitative and more willing to learn from others; they possess, or at least exhibit, more curiosity; they are decidedly ingenious, but are wanting in mental vigor as compared with their neighbors. Neither do they have that overweening sense of their importance in the scale of being and of superior knowledge which belongs to the Chinese. Their bearing toward each other and toward the outside world is regulated accordingly. The government treats foreigners, and especially foreign officials, with sufficient superciliousness, but the people themselves are open-hearted, and exceedingly easy and polite in all their intercourse. Take the nation together, they are the most polite and graceful of all the people of the East. I should call them the Frenchmen of Asia; but this would be doing injustice to the Japanese; for, while the peasantry of France, like those of other nations, are often coarse and rude in their manners, the Japanese, even in the rural and more retired districts, have a grace and even a courtliness of manner, and are as polite in their intercourse as those who dwell in the cities. I have seen the people meeting in the most ordinary circumstances, and bowing with the most profound respect to each other, as if they were embassadors instead of the ordinary working men and women of the country. I have wished a hundred times since coming to Japan that we could import into our own and some other civilized countries a measure of this "want of civilization," or "barbarism," or whatever any one may choose to call it.

In their houses and shops, and in many of their industrial

JAPANESE SALUTING.

and domestic arrangements, they are patterns of neatness and good taste. One may walk for miles through their streets, looking into their dwellings or places of business, which are all open by day, and he will never tire in his admiration of the cleanliness which prevails, and of the regard to order and general effect in the arrangement of their various wares and varying colors. They are like the shops of Paris in this respect. The little gardens attached to their dwellings or places of business are gems, and as neat as their houses. I have several times seen a house divided (without a partition or wall of any kind) between a shop and a dwelling; and while the blacksmith, or carpenter, or cooper would be plying his occupation in one half, the other, raised but a foot or two, would be covered with matting so cleanly that no one would think of stepping on it without taking off his shoes. I can not say as much for the personal habits of the people; for, while they bathe regularly once or twice a day (men, women, and children going through the operation vigorously together in a common bath-house), they put on the same clothes, and wear them until they are worn out.

The style of dress in Japan is even more varied than it is on Broadway in New York. It reaches from nothing up to an elaborate toilet. The women, I am happy to say, never appear in public without some sort of clothing (which is more than can be said of the men), and the former show that superiority of talent in this department which is characteristic of the sex in other parts of the world. A Japanese lady thoroughly arrayed is really an elaborate work of art. A large amount of attention, and no little expense, to begin with, is devoted to the arrangement of the hair, even the common people regularly employing a hairdresser. If they can not afford the luxury every day, they will make it last for two days by sleeping on a wooden pillow placed under the neck. The item of next importance in a Japanese lady's toilet is her *obi*, or girdle, which is usually of some bright colors, and arranged behind with great care, so as to form the camel's hump so popular among other uncivilized nations, especially New Yorkers. The Grecian bend is an old institution in Japan, and to see one of these dark-skinned ladies, with her extensive head-dress, a hump upon her back, an extremely narrow skirt, high wooden pattens, her body thrown forward as she minces her steps, you would

FEMALE HAIR-DRESSER.

imagine that she was caricaturing the brainless votaries of fashion in other lands; but she is only dressing as her people have dressed, and walking as they have walked for centuries. The *obi* serves a purpose in Japan which I have not heard attributed to it elsewhere. When a woman becomes a widow, she makes no change unless she wishes to announce her purpose never to marry again, in which case she ties her *obi* in front. How effectual it is to ward off all proposals I do not know; but, as it is always and every where the privilege of a woman to change her mind, it is said the girdle occasionally works its way around to its normal position behind.

One of the customs of married life is absolutely hideous. The Japanese generally have fine teeth, but when a woman marries she is compelled by the laws of society to dye her teeth black, and this process is renewed every three or four days. In city or country, wherever you go, you meet the grim smile of the women who have fallen into the bonds of matrimony, and they look more like hybrid monsters, with their black teeth, than like the lovely beings that they ought to be. What was the origin of this custom I do not know, but there are only two things which have led me to desire temporary imperial authority in Japan—one is to establish some sort of costume for the men, and the other to abolish the custom of married women dyeing their teeth.

In Japan men shave their heads just where the Chinese do not, making a bald spot upon the crown, which likens them to Jesuit priests, while they leave a broad circle of hair around the head. Men and women shave the eyebrows off smooth, and have the hair carefully plucked out of the ears and nose. The barber is an important functionary in this part of the world, every person of high or low degree calling his services into requisition almost daily. Economically, it might be regarded as a great expense to the nation, but, on the other hand, it affords employment and support for a large class.

The shoeing of the Japanese is as simple as are their understandings. They are strictly Oriental in their habits in this respect, wearing only sandals or pattens in muddy weather (which, by the way, is the general rule and not the exception in Japan, more than 100 inches of water having fallen thus far during the present year, and 125 inches last year). The sandals and pattens are held to the foot by a cord passing between the first and second toes, so that they can be slipped on or off without effort. Some persons allege that the Japanese are born with a wide space between the toes for this very purpose, but it is quite as likely that the cord has made or increased the space which is natural to every man. They wear no stockings, and yet they seem as much afraid as chickens of stepping into the water, while their dread of the fluid, except in the form of a regular bath, is displayed in the universal habit of carrying an umbrella, even when it sprinkles never so little. I have seen scores of people, almost entirely naked, walking on high pattens, with umbrellas spread over their heads, as if the rain of heaven or the moisture of the ground would prove fatal.

Many of their habits are the very opposites of those of other nations. The carpenter, in using the plane, always draws it toward him instead of pushing it. It is the same with the saw, which he draws when he wishes to cut, the teeth being set accordingly. One of their customs struck me as an improvement upon the mode of doing things in civilized countries, especially after I had acquired some knowledge of the heels of their vicious ponies. In stabling their horses they tie them with the heads to the door or front of the stable, so that they can approach them in front instead of behind, thus reducing to every-day practice the trick of the showman who made a handsome sum by admitting visitors to see a horse whose head was where his tail ought to be. Their horses, by the way, are generally shod with straw instead of iron. A straw mat is fastened upon the foot with cords of the same material, and so slightly that the streets in which horses are used, especially the Tokaido, are strewn with the cast-off sandals of the ponies.

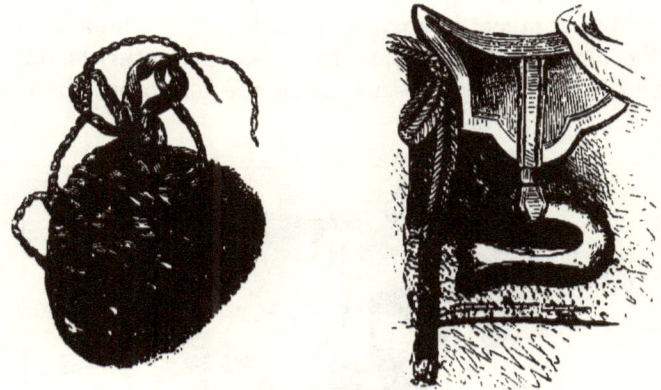

JAPANESE HORSE-SHOE AND SADDLE.

The Japanese have a great fondness for painting and drawing, as almost every article that is manufactured in the country will show. Their books are profusely illustrated, often with plates highly colored, and, excepting that

GROUP OF HORSES.

they seem to have no idea of perspective, they excel in poetical representation. Their drawings of animals are in the highest degree spirited and graceful, and it is a perfect marvel how much they will express by a few simple strokes of the pencil. They are, withal, great caricaturists, but in their drawings they present rather the humorous than the unpleasantly grotesque.

ATHLETES.

In some of the arts the Japanese are in advance of all other nations. The porcelain of Japan, notwithstanding it takes its name from the Celestial Empire, is rarely rivaled in China. The lacquer-ware is beyond comparison with the productions of any other country. The finest specimens are rarely exported, being held at prices that strike a stranger as enormous. They excel in working in metals, especially in bronzes and in all inlaying work. I saw in their shops exquisite vases of bronze that were valued at $1200 the pair, the work of which could not be equaled in Paris. The inlaying of metals, as of steel with gold and silver, is carried to the highest perfection, almost making it an art peculiar to Japan. In tempering and fashioning steel blades the ancient fame of Damascus has been revived among this simple people. We entertain altogether too high an opinion of our modern perfection in art as compared with some people whom we have been wont to place on the borders of barbarism.

The beggars in Japan, as in many other countries, form a distinct profession, though not so numerous or so imperious in their demands as in Europe, and their moderation and apparent honesty are a model for the beggars of all nations. Seeing some forty or fifty coppers hanging on as many nails at the front of a shop (the copper coin has a hole in the centre), I inquired what they were for, and was told they were placed there by the shopkeeper to save time and trouble in answering the calls of the mendicants. When one came along he simply took a copper and passed on, never abusing the charity of the shopkeeper by taking two. The device by which their calls are attended to might be worth imitating in other parts, if equally honest beggars could be found.

The people are not without some of the habits of civilized nations, and drunkenness among others. This is a common vice, a cheap form of highly intoxicating liquor called *saki*, distilled from rice, affording the means of getting drunk at little expense.

Capital crimes are punished either by decapitation with the sword or crucifixion. Several executions by the former mode took place while I was in Japan. The latter has been common until within a few years, and it is still practiced. Each city has its execution-ground, which is often upon the high road. We passed those of Yokohama and Yeddo in going to the latter city.

Their mode of disposing of the dead is both by burial and burning, the wishes of the dying being considered by the friends imperative as to the mode in which the body shall be disposed of. In some parts of Japan burning is always practiced. A large furnace is connected with the

BEHEADING.

cemetery, in which the body is speedily consumed, the ashes being carefully preserved, and buried with as much sacredness as the entire remains in other countries. Some of the cemeteries are very beautiful, covering a large extent of the hill-sides. The large cemetery at Nagasaki, as seen from the harbor, presents a very striking appearance, tiers of tombs rising one above another in graceful terraces.

The Japanese are not what we should call a religious people. The two prevailing forms of religion are Shintooism and Buddhism, but neither of these has a strong hold upon the people, or awakens deep religious feeling. Nowhere have I seen the manifestations of reverence, or any thing approaching profound worship. Even their temples are far from being accounted sacred. They are often made places of entertainment and of continued residence for strangers. The first Protestant missionaries, on coming to Japan, had a temple assigned them as their home, and occupied it for a long period. When we entered the temples at Yeddo we were invariably followed by a curious crowd, but no one made a sign of prostration, or engaged in any act of worship, or exhibited any respect for the place more than for an ordinary building.

Shintooism (called also *Sinsyuism*) was the ancient faith of the country. Its hierarchy consists of the Mikado, two ecclesiastical judges, and the priesthood, which comprises also the monks. The temples are usually on elevated places, or surrounded with trees (the "high places" and "green trees" of idolatry mentioned in the ancient Scriptures). They have no idols in the temples; on the altar stands a mirror, which is regarded as an emblem of the purity required in the worshipers, and as requiring sincerity of worship. The form of worship is simple: first, washing in the sacred font; then praying before the mirror to the great Sun-goddess, making an offering of money or rice, or its equivalent; and last, striking the bell, to signify to the goddess that the worship is over. The bells connected with the temples are large, and are usually hung near the ground, where they can be easily struck. The precepts of the Shintoo religion are summed up as follows: 1. Inward purity of heart; 2. Abstinence from whatever makes one impure; 3. Observance of the festivals and holy days; 4. Pilgrimages to holy places, which are often on high mountains. The Mikado being the head of this religion, it has become the established form since the revolution, and the government has even undertaken a sort of crusade against the idols which are in use in other temples and worship.

Buddhism was introduced in the sixth century, and made great progress, running an almost equal race with the old form, but it has been greatly modified both as to faith and the forms of worship. In Japan, as in China, Buddhism in many of its forms of worship is strikingly similar to Romanism, and in looking at the monks or priests in their processional march around the temple, and in listening to their monotonous chants, I could almost believe myself in a Roman Catholic church.

Confucianism, an importation from China, is very prevalent, but it scarcely exists as a distinct form of religion. It is a sort of fashionable or refined infidelity, rather exerting a silent influence over the minds of the higher classes than having a place as an organized faith or form of worship.

Nominal Christianity in Japan had its origin in the Roman Catholic missions of the sixteenth century. The tragic sequel to its introduction and its spread by the Jesuits is a chapter in the history of the country of the deepest interest. Like all the propagandism of Rome, the history is as much political as religious. Popery has ever had more of the worldly than of the spiritual element—more love of power than of souls, and this was, and still is, manifested in Japan as elsewhere. The Jesuits are still at work, and here as elsewhere they stir up the hostility of the government against them. They are chiefly responsible for the opposition of the government to Christianity. One of the most interesting and encouraging facts connected with the religious prospects of Japan is that the government has invited nearly every Protestant missionary in the islands to enter its service for the education of the young men of the country. Immediately after the accomplishment of the late revolution, the new government of the Mikado established a department of public instruction, placing at the head of the department one of the princes of the empire, who ranks with the ministers of Foreign Affairs, of War, Finance, etc. An appropriation of 50,000 kokus of rice (about $250,000) a year is made to meet the expenses, which is distributed among several institutions located in different cities. The principal college (known as the Reforming or Progressive College) is at Yeddo, with 450 pupils, and the Rev. G. F. Verbeck, the American missionary, has been called to the direction of English instruction, more than half the pupils being under his care. He resides at Yeddo, in a house provided by the government, has a liberal salary, and is provided with a guard of soldiers, who attend him wherever he goes, in or out of the city. Dr. Brown, Dr. Hepburn, and others have been urged to engage in the same service.

Every thing connected with Japan, and especially with

the government, partakes more or less of mystery, and nothing more than the attitude of the government toward Christianity—issuing edicts forbidding the people to embrace it, posting these edicts all over the country, and at the same time calling into its service, for the education of the youth of the higher classes, Christian missionaries who have come to the country with the avowed object of laboring for the conversion of the Japanese to Christ, and at the same time leaving them wholly untrammeled as to what they shall teach. But, with all that is mysterious or unfavorable, there is much to encourage hope in regard to the future of the country. The growing disposition to conform the administration of the government to the American model, and to introduce American science and arts; the increasing intercourse, official and social, with the United States; the sending of so many youth to be educated in the United States under the influence of our Christian institutions, and the calling into the public service at home of so many Protestant Christian teachers, are remarkable signs which may well inspire hope.

VIEW IN THE INLAND SEA.

## VIII.

### INLAND SEA OF JAPAN.

The most beautiful sea-voyage in the world is the passage of the Inland Sea of Japan. Between three of the four largest islands—Niphon, Kiusiu, and Sikoke—there is an expanse of water five hundred miles in extent from east to west, and varying greatly in breadth, connected at different points with the ocean, but forming a great landlocked sea. The name, like most Japanese names, is singularly beautiful—Suwonada. Into this wide expanse have been sprinkled more than three thousand islands, which, by volcanic action, have been moulded into all the forms of beauty imaginable. Some of them are lofty cones, rising directly from the water to the height of several hundred feet. One of these cones I found, by referring to the ship's chart as we were passing it, is nine hundred feet high. Others are rounded off with more variety of outline, and stretch away for miles with constantly changing profiles, and with shores, and hill-sides, and valleys as green as an emerald. I have found nothing to compare with it in any other sea, and this is the testimony of every traveler that I have met who has made the passage. We were two days and one night—a bright, beautiful, moonlight night—in steaming through the sea, and, as I recall the voyage, the scene rises up before me like the vision of some fairy scene. During the whole passage the water had scarcely a ripple upon its surface, and an ever-changing panorama of green islands, and narrowing straits, and expanding bays, and picturesque landscapes, hills and valleys, with cities scattered along the shore, rolled by us with constantly varying beauty.

This sea lies in the direct route from Yokohama to the north of China, whither we were bound. Passengers for Hong Kong go by the steamer we had left, which, after touching at Yokohama, lays its course south of the large islands. A corresponding steamer takes the passengers who are bound for Shanghai, and passes through the Inland Sea, stopping for a day at each of the ports of Hiogo and Nagasaki, and so arranging the time of leaving these ports as to have the finest parts of the voyage by daylight. After we had completed our stay of two weeks at Yokohama, we took the steamer Costa Rica, bound for Shanghai. Sailing down the Gulf of Yeddo, out into the open sea, we coasted for a day along the green shores of Niphon, and the second evening entered the Inland Sea by the south, the rolling billows at once subsiding and leaving us to enjoy a night's repose. Early the next morning we anchored in the harbor of Hiogo, one of the open ports, and the most beautifully situated town in Japan. Osaka, of which Hiogo is in reality the port, is fifteen miles distant, and is the site of the fortified castle of the Tycoons, destroyed by fire when the Tycoon left it in the late revolution. It is a city of great wealth, its silk-houses surpassing those of any other city of the empire. The morning was rainy, and we did not go to Osaka to spend the day, as we had intended; but

ENTERING THE INLAND SEA.

the clouds soon cleared off, and we went ashore at Hiogo to enjoy the hospitality of Colonel Stewart, the United States consul, and to make an excursion to a cascade in a cleft far up the mountain. Colonel Stewart was occupying the residence and grounds which formerly belonged to the governor of the place, and it was enough to verify the visions of the Arabian Nights just to enter the grounds. It is in the heart of the Japanese town, but so arranged that, on entering the gate, "*Presto, agramento, change*," and you find yourself apparently a thousand miles from any other habitation, in some new creation. Bamboo and plantain groves surround you; a lotus pond, covered with magnificent leaves, and alive with large goldfish; grottoes and shaded walks invite you to forget the outer world, which is excluded by a high wall and by dense shade.

Leaving this beautiful spot, we mounted the horses and made the ascent of the mountain, having a view not only of the falls, but of the extended rice plains before us, of the magnificent harbor, and of Osaka, with the fine surrounding country in the distance. Hiogo gives promise of becoming an important place in the commerce of Japan. It certainly has great attractions as a residence.

At four o'clock the next morning the ship's gun resounded through the harbor, reverberating among the mountains which overlook the town, and at five we weighed anchor and were soon steaming through the beautiful sea. All day long our course lay through islands succeeding islands, all of which seemed as smooth as if shapen by hand, rounded off or carved in graceful shapes, and clothed with the velvety green of Japan, making the passage one of unbroken beauty. In the afternoon we sailed along a shore on which the Tokaido—the imperial highway—lined with double rows of trees, wound along, over hill and dale, as far as the eye could reach. The day was clear and calm, and as it drew near its close the sun poured a flood of rosy and purple light over islands and sea—such a light as painters put upon canvas when they are thought to exaggerate. The evening, with a bright moon, was equally beautiful, but we had to fill out the landscapes in imagination, and when we retired we had passed again into the open sea.

We rose next morning at six, in time to see the gates of the East opened, the same flood of purple light pouring over the mountains as we were entering the Straits of Simoni-saki, the most beautiful passage of the two days' sail. Islands, with charming little bays, were around us, the country under more perfect cultivation than any portion of the coast that we had seen, the terraces running far up the hill-sides, and trees and shrubbery indicating the taste of the inhabitants. On either side of this strait was a large city, well fortified. Two war-steamers, officered, engineered, and manned by Japanese, lay at anchor in the harbor, while great numbers of sailing vessels were bound hither and thither. All that day we had the same calm sea and fine weather, with the constantly-shifting panorama of islands, many of them not more than an acre in extent, but stretching themselves up in all sorts of beautiful shapes. The shores were so bold that a vessel can almost sail along and touch the sides without touching bottom. The Inland

Sea of Japan is said, I know not on what authority, to have the deepest soundings of any water on the globe. Just at dusk we came upon the arched rock, a small island jutting out from the sea, united at the top, but with a wide arch some thirty or forty feet in height, under which boats can sail with ease. As the last rays of daylight were vanishing, we entered the harbor of Nagasaki, on the extreme west of Japan, which is completely concealed from the sea, running back around high headlands. At the mouth of the harbor lies an island called by the Japanese Takaboko, and by the Dutch Pappenberg, which has a melancholy

PAPPENBERG ISLAND.

history. At the close of the sixteenth century, when the introduction of Christianity by the Jesuits excited the apprehension of the Japanese government, and the order was given to exterminate the foreign religion by a bloody persecution, many thousands of Christians fled to this island for a last refuge. They were pursued by the authorities, and those who escaped the sword were driven into the sea and perished in the waters. The precipice over which they were driven is still pointed out. These were the martyrs who were recently canonized, *en masse*, at Rome, whose fate forms one of the fearful chapters of Japanese history.

Our ship lay for two nights and a day in the harbor of Nagasaki, affording us an opportunity to visit the town, and to enjoy the beautiful scenery, which, were it not on such a limited scale, would rival the grandeur of Hiogo. The harbor, and the mountains which inclose it on all sides save the narrow entrance, form a perfect amphitheatre, the sides rising gradually, and, as it were, by tiers of seats or steps, to a great height, the beauty of the sight being diversified by the Japanese town, the foreign settlement, the temples, and other edifices. Notwithstanding the multiplied charming features of the scene, we fancied that those who continued to reside here must, ere long, feel secluded from the rest of the world by the very walls of green which, to a stranger, are so lovely.

About midnight the last night of our stay, I heard a whistling in the rigging of our ship, which assured me that the calm we had enjoyed for so many days preceded, if it did not presage, a storm; and I was not disappointed. Soon after daylight we steamed out of the quiet and well-protected harbor into the Eastern China Sea, only to meet the northeast monsoon, which for eighteen hours blew with fearful violence. Our ship was not a small one (some 2000 tons), but she was tossed upon the uneasy sea as a thing of no account. We prepared ourselves as well as we could to withstand the blast, but we could not long keep the deck, and were forced to go below. The ladies were compelled to take their berths, and even there they were not safe. One of them, for whom I can testify, by a lurch of the ship, which threatened to roll entirely over, was tossed from her berth to the opposite side of a wide state-room, when I sent for the ship's carpenter and had her boarded up to prevent her being dashed to pieces. At short intervals, all day long, one crash after another was heard as a table broke loose or the steward's crockery went into a heap. I was lying on the locker in the main cabin when a heavy swell tossed the ship upon her side, throwing the large marble slab of the heater from its fastenings. It struck near me on the floor, and was dashed into a dozen pieces. Though in a stanch and mighty ship, we felt, as we had not had occasion to feel before, how weak are the proudest works of man in contending with the breath of the Almighty. We could only commit ourselves to His care during the long, dark night, while the tempest raged and the great waves tossed us up and down. With the morning came a change. Early in the day we entered the broad mouth of the Yanktse-kiang River, and quietly steamed toward Shanghai, thankful that we had reached another continent in safety, and that for a little while our tossings upon the deep were over. A more perfect contrast than our experience upon the Inland Sea of Japan and that upon the Eastern China Sea could not well be imagined.

## IX.

### SHANGHAI TO HONG KONG.

We entered the Yanktse River, as the Amazon is crossed, far out at sea. Long before we were in sight of the low shores the water became as yellow as that of the Tiber, taking its color from the soil of the country, which is constantly washing down the river, filling up the wide mouth, and making the navigation more and more difficult. One shore only was visible at first, and then the low sand-banks of the opposite shore appeared, but nowhere was any elevation in sight. The whole region is upon a level with the sea, and is protected against an occasional overflow by embankments. The country far up the Yanktse was under water, the river spreading itself out in immense lakes. Thousands of lives had been lost by drowning, and by the loss of food which such a calamity always occasions in this densely populated country.

We soon entered the Woosung, a small river on which Shanghai is situated, about twelve miles from its mouth. At the entrance is a long range of earthworks—one of the supposed impregnable forts which the Chinese, in their self-sufficiency and contempt of foreigners, erected at various points, and which have proved equally efficient with the paper fortifications recommended in Salmagundi. They were easily battered to pieces by the English fleet in the war of 1841. Near these fortifications was a large fleet of Chinese war-junks, built, doubtless, after the model that was most approved a thousand years ago. The prow of each vessel was provided with two large eyes, one on each side, to enable the ship to see its course in a dark night. Without these eyes a vessel is considered as unsafe as a blind man walking the streets of a strange city. The vessels have great high poops, ornamented with carvings and

CHINESE TRADING JUNK.

other fixtures, making them a curiosity to a stranger just coming into the empire. The junk which visited the harbor of New York many years ago was a fair type of the swarms which fill the rivers of China, although not so highly ornamented as many I have seen. These junks are no mean sea-boats. They are exceedingly clumsy looking above water, but their keels are often beautiful models, and they ride out a storm in safety when many a fine yacht would go down.

Shanghai is one of the four ports first opened by the treaty of 1842. It was little visited by foreigners previous to that time, but, being admirably situated to secure the commerce of the great valley of the Yanktse and of the whole of the north of China, it sprang at once into importance, and has become the chief foreign commercial city of the empire. Canton has lost its former pre-eminence, and Hong Kong alone rivals this city of the north. The old Chinese city of Shanghai, which is near the foreign settlement, one of the large towns of China, is inclosed within a high wall, which in the growth of the place proved insufficient to contain the population, and they have spread themselves over the surrounding plain. It was captured by the Taeping rebels in 1853, and held until 1855, when they retreated from this part of the country. During several subsequent years, while the rebels were overrunning the surrounding region, there was a large influx of people, who came to this city for protection and residence, and it enjoyed great prosperity in consequence. Foreigners who held the land in the vicinity of the new town made immense fortunes on paper; but after the rebellion was quelled, and the Chinese who had come to Shanghai returned to their homes, a great and disastrous revolution occurred, and the fortunes which had been made in haste vanished still more rapidly. The city has not entirely recovered from this shock, and, in common with the other ports, it is suffering from the general depression of the China trade.

The foreign settlement makes a fine appearance as we

approach it by water. It stretches along the river nearly two miles, being divided into what are called the American, English, and French settlements, the two former being under one municipality, and the latter under French rule. A wide "bund" or quay, which serves equally as a place of commerce, promenade, and drive, occupies the river front, the finest buildings of the city—the hongs of merchants and public buildings—being situated on the bund, and giving a very imposing appearance to the place. Several streets run back from the river, and contain numerous fine residences and business houses. The climate is very trying in winter. The malaria of the low country was formerly productive of fevers, but at great expense a system of drainage and of street construction was carried out, by which the health of the place has been improved. The cost of these improvements was so great that the Chinese say Shanghai is paved with dollars.

The first thing that arrests a traveler's attention on landing is the novel mode of conveyance peculiar to Shanghai. The popular carriage is a wheelbarrow. The streets of the old city are narrow and rough, and so much broken up by bridges that this vehicle can not be used; but in the foreign settlement you find the Chinese men and women every where riding on wheelbarrows. The wheel is much larger than those in use in our country, and the passengers are seated one on each side of it. When two are riding, if they are of equal weight, the carriage is evenly balanced; but when two persons of unequal weight are carried, or only one, the wheel is turned up at an angle, so that the weight shall come upon the point in its circumference that strikes the ground. This, I think, must be a modern invention or adaptation, for no real Chinese city that I have seen will admit of its being used, and the roads leading into the country are not favorable for such a mode of conveyance, especially in wet weather.

The Chinese part of the town has a population of nearly a million, including that portion built around the walls for want of room within. During the rebellion the number was almost twice as great. The city proper is entered by several gates, which are narrow passages, admitting only what goes on foot. Every thing in the shape of merchandise, and every stone and timber for building, is carried in on the shoulders of coolies, as in most parts of the East. The burdens which these coolies carry suspended between them by a bamboo pole are sometimes enormous, but they stand up manfully under them, and shout continually as they go through the throng to those ahead to make way for them. All classes in the crowded city show the utmost consideration for each other. The streets of the city are never more than six or seven feet wide, and yet through these narrow passages a crowd is constantly surging, without ever coming in contact or interfering with each other's burden or business.

The city within the walls is exceedingly filthy, so much so that I would not think of taking a lady into it, not even in a sedan chair, the ordinary mode of conveyance for foreigners; for, although she might be protected from coming in contact with its filth, few have the strength of constitution to endure the smells of the place. I have more than once tested the "two-and-seventy stenches" in the streets of Cologne which Coleridge enumerates, but they are outnumbered and overpowered in the streets of almost any Chinese city. The little canals which run through the town are the most disgusting of all, and it is a mystery how human beings can swarm in such a place and human life continue. I should imagine that the heat of every summer would bring a pestilence, and the place be depopulated. But the Chinese not only live, they multiply and thrive amid these elements of disease and death.

One will not be inclined to linger long in his walks through the native city, although he may see much at any step that is both novel and interesting. The Chinese costumes, the Chinese shops, the Chinese sights and smells of all kinds, are perfectly new, and the most of them, as he has never met with them before, he will never wish to meet again.

At several points as I was passing along I came upon police-stations, where criminals of different grades were undergoing different degrees of punishment. Some were simply confined in large cages, the sport of the passers-by. Others wore immense collars made of two wide boards brought together at their edges, with a hole large enough for the neck. The collar is so wide that the prisoner can not reach his head with his hands, and is dependent upon his friends or upon charity not only for his food, but for getting it to his mouth. Others had their heads jutting out of the tops of cages which were so high that they could not sit down, and so low that they could not stand up, or in which they stood on tip-toe, and they were condemned to pass days and nights in this uncomfortable and even torturing position.

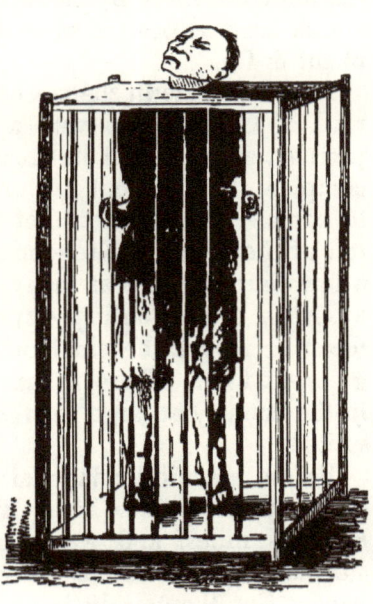

CHINESE PUNISHMENT.

A short time before, several criminals who had been guilty of a capital offense were condemned to death, and placed in these cages, where they died from starvation before the eyes of the people, no one being allowed to furnish them with food. Torture, as I subsequently learned by witnessing it at Canton, enters largely into the idea of punishment among the Chinese, and is freely resorted to for the purpose of extorting confession from the accused.

There is very little to detain an ordinary traveler in

Shanghai. Its sights, if there are any, are soon seen. No one will wish to make more than a passing visit to the Chinese city, and the foreign part derives its only importance from its commerce. The town was all agog while I was there with the visit of the Duke of Edinburg, Prince Alfred of England. One of the entertainments was an international boat-race between four-oared boats—American, English, Scotch, and German. It was no little gratification to us, as Americans, to join in the rousing cheers which welcomed the Stars and Stripes as they came in four lengths ahead of all competitors, and our pleasure was all the more enhanced by the fact that the victors were friends whose hospitalities we were enjoying at the house of Oliphant & Co.

It was too late in the season to visit Pekin and the great wall of China. We were advised not to undertake the journey, as we might be frozen up, which would make a complete derangement of our plans of travel for the year to come. We regretted not being able to reach the capital of the Flowery Kingdom, but it is just as well to see a few Chinese cities as many. With the exception of Pekin, they are all built pretty much after the same uninteresting model, the chief difference consisting in the degrees of filth. There is less of the beautiful in scenery in the country at large than in almost any country I have visited.

Before reaching Shanghai we had thought seriously of going up the Yanktse-kiang River as far as Kang-kow, six hundred miles, and we found splendid American-built steamers, with luxurious accommodations, making regular trips. But there is little to be seen. The country, the whole distance, is flat and uninteresting, and much of it at that time was overflowed with water.

Nankin, which has always been famous in the geographical, if not the historical records of China, is about two hundred miles above Shanghai, but we were assured that we should have great difficulty in landing and reaching the city, and that when we got there we should find it a heap of ruins, very much as it was left by the Taeping rebels. Not a tile of the famous Porcelain Tower remains excepting those which are manufactured for sale as relics. Many of the great cities of the empire were almost wholly destroyed during the rebellion. When the rebel army occupied a town they used it for fuel, the country generally being destitute of timber, and in this way the light wooden houses disappeared, as by a general conflagration, in the hands of such an immense host. Some of the cities are rebuilt, but others remain a desolation.

CHINESE TEMPLE.

To any traveler who is not able to devote much time to this country, I would recommend a trip from Shanghai to Ningpo, a hundred miles distant, which is reached daily or nightly by steamer, and then to Hang-chow, farther in the interior, which will afford an opportunity of seeing some of the finest scenery in this part of China, and of visiting two of its most interesting cities. He can then take the steamer down the coast, either stopping at Foo-chow and Amoy, or going directly to Hong Kong and Canton. The approaches to Foo-chow up the River Min, on which it is situated, are very picturesque, but the city itself has the reputation of being the filthiest in the empire.

Finding the Suwonada, the swiftest and finest steamer on the coast, ready to leave for Hong Kong, and having an invalid in my company, I took passage for Hong Kong direct, intending to return to Amoy. We found the Suwonada every thing that could be desired in navigating this turbulent China Sea, excepting that she would never lie still, and when afloat, so tempestuous did we always find these waters that I almost fancied the rocky islands, if not the continent itself, must be tossing up and down with the waves. The commander of the ship, Captain Clark, is a graduate of Harvard College, a thorough seaman, and a perfect gentleman. Another pleasure in sailing in her was that she floated the Stars and Stripes — ever a welcome sight, and most so when farthest from home.

We reached Hong Kong, 820 miles, at the end of the third day. Hong Kong is an island about twenty-five miles in circumference, an English possession, taken as indemnity in one of the wars, and ceded to Great Britain in 1841, from which time it grew rapidly in commercial importance, until its rival, Shanghai, diverted a large part of the China trade. Victoria is the name of the town, although abroad it is almost invariably spoken of as Hong Kong. It is still one of the two chief foreign cities on the coast, and is visited, probably, by more ships than any other. It is a sort of posting station for the whole Eastern world, ships without cargo and ships without orders coming here to await orders from their owners. Having an English governor, and all the paraphernalia of an English colony, it is a place of no little court ceremony, and the social distinctions which attach even to the most petty governmental dependencies of Great Britain are peculiarly rife.

HONG KONG.

There is scarcely a level acre upon the whole island. Indeed, the only spot that I remember to have seen is a charming little valley about a mile from the town, which has been appropriated to a race-course—the several cemeteries, English, Roman Catholic, and Parsee, occupying the rising ground around the race-course, and forming a very incongruous combination of grave-yards and sporting-grounds. This beautiful spot is called Happy Valley: whether named before its present occupation, or for what one of these different purposes it was first occupied, I have not learned. The island is made up of lofty peaks, one of which, Victoria Peak, overhanging the town, and from which you could almost throw a stone into the streets, is 1825 feet high. The view from the peak is as perfect a panorama as that from the Righi; and although by no means so extensive nor in any measure so magnificent, wanting the elements of grandeur which abound among the Alps, yet it is a splendid view. We ascended in sedan chairs, each chair carried by four coolies, and, walking and riding by turns, were an hour and five minutes in reaching the summit. The view of the town below; of the harbor with its shipping, looking like miniature craft; of the surrounding waters and islands, abundantly repays for the exertion and expense. The city is built along the harbor, in terraces rising one above another, until the upper tier is some three or four hundred feet in height. The governor's residence is a fine mansion, with large and well-kept grounds. Many of the hongs of the merchants are palaces, and the public buildings would do honor to any city. The City Hall, just completed and inaugurated by Prince Alfred, who arrived two or three days after we reached Hong Kong, is a splendid structure situated on the bund.

The governor has established a system of schools of different grades for the Chinese, who compose by far the largest part of the population, and it is well administered. At the invitation of a member of the governor's council, I spent a morning in the high school, and witnessed, with great interest and pleasure, the evidences given, by an *extempore* examination, of the progress made by the more advanced Chinese, not only in the elements of an English education, but in the sciences. I saw and heard enough to satisfy me that the excuse given for the universal custom among foreign residents of talking with the Chinese in the miserable "Pigeon" English, namely, that there are many vocal sounds in English which they can not utter, is without foundation. There is not a letter or combination which these youth had not mastered, although, of course, with some foreign accent. The Pigeon English is a mongrel dialect, probably first invented by the Chinese as a substitute for English, very much as young children invent a language for themselves before learning to speak in the dialect of older persons. It has been perpetuated by foreigners for the sake of holding conversation with the

Chinese who have adopted it. *Pigeon* is said to be the nearest approximation that the Chinese make to the word *business;* hence Pigeon English means business English. It is an unnecessary accommodation to the natives, who are just as able as other nations to acquire the sounds of our language.

The following version of "My name is Norval" is a fair specimen of the Pigeon English. It needs a glossary almost as much as real Chinese.

My name b'long Norbal, topside that Glampian hillee
My fader, you sabee my fader, makee pay chow-chow he sheepoo
He smallo heartee man, too muchee take care that dolloo, gola?
So fashion he wantchee keepee my, counta one piecee chilo, stop he own side.
My no wantchee, wantchee long that largee mandali, go knockee alla man :
Littee teem, Joss pay my what thing my fader no likee pay.
That moom last nightee teem get up loune, alla same my hat,
No got full up, no got square ; plenty piecie
That lobbel man, too muchee qui-si, alla same that tiger,
Chop-chop come down side that hillee, catchie that sheepoo, long that cow ;
That man, custom take care, too muchee quick lun way.
My one piecie owne spie eye, look see that lallee-loon man what side he walkee.
Hi-yah! No good chancie, findie he, lun catchie my flen :
Two piecie loon-choon lun catchie that lobbel man! he
No can walkee welly quick, he pocket too muchee full up.
So fashion knockee he largee.
   He head man no got shutte far
My knockie he head. Hi-yah! My No. 1 stlong man.
Catchie he jacket, long he t'lousa, gola : You likee look see?
My go puttee on just now. My go home, largie heart just now
My no likee take care that sheepoo. So fashion my hear you hah got fightee this side
My take one piecee coolie, come you countlee, come helpie you.
He heart all same cow, too muchie fear, lun away.
Masquie, Joss take care pay my come you housee.

I visited the Colonial Prison, where more than four hundred criminals of all nations were confined, and have never seen a penitentiary more neatly kept, or apparently under better management. Among the prisoners were several Chinese women who had been convicted of child-stealing, a very common crime. The boys are stolen and sold for boatmen, and the girls either for boat-hands or for the brothels, to be educated for a life of infamy. I inquired of the superintendent if any form of oath was administered to the Chinese when they were called to testify in the courts, and was informed that none was used in cases of small importance, but that in graver cases they swore by a cock's head. The cock is taken to a joss-house or temple, the head cut off with some ceremony, and on this, as the basis of the most solemn oath that is administered, a Chinaman gives his testimony in an English court.

I can not refrain from copying just here the beautiful motto, which every one will recognize as taken from the book of sacred wisdom, and which I found engraved on the stone arch in front of the post-office at Hong Kong, than which nothing could be more appropriate in this distant part of the world: "As cold waters to a thirsty soul, so is good news from a far country."

## X.

### CANTON AND ITS SIGHTS.

It is not long since Canton was all of China to the outside world. For two centuries before the opening of the treaty ports it was the only city at which any amount of foreign commerce was carried on. The East India Company established a factory (the name for a place of business) at this point as early as 1689, and the representatives of various countries followed their example; planted themselves alongside the city and carried on traffic with the people, without being permitted to enter the city itself. The foreign factories, so celebrated in Eastern commerce, occupied a wide space along the river, just under the walls of the city, and to this space all "outside barbarians" were limited, and within it they were, at one time, actually confined as prisoners, living in no little terror of their lives. It is only within the last twenty-five or thirty years that the gates of the city have been opened to foreigners. So recently as 1856, the Chinese, becoming exasperated against all foreigners, in the incipiency of one of the wars, attacked the factories, pillaged and burnt them, making the once beautiful collection of palaces a mere heap of ruins. The whole city was soon after taken possession of by the British army and held for several years, since which time the gates have been open to all from every country who choose to enter.

Canton is situated on the Pearl River, ninety miles from Hong Kong, which is now the port of Canton, for scarcely a vessel goes up the river. The business of the place and the foreign commerce is nearly all transacted at Hong Kong. An American river steamer leaves the latter place every morning at eight o'clock, and another returns each day at the same hour. The first half of the distance, in going up, is through a wide bay interspersed with islands, but with nothing striking in its scenery.

At length we reach what are called the Bogue forts, famous in the China wars. They are extensive fortifications, and by the Chinese were considered impregnable, and a perfect protection against all vessels that might attempt to pass up the river. But they stood no chance before the guns of the British fleet, and are now extensive lines of ruined fortifications. They form a picturesque feature of the landscape, as we pass between them through the Tiger's Mouth (Boca Tigre), from which the forts took their name.

At this point commences all that is attractive on the voyage up. The banks of the Pearl River are flat, but they are in a high state of cultivation, covered with rice-fields and plantations of bananas, which were looking green and fresh, and added much to the beauty of the shores. Farther inland were rows of lychen-trees, and occasionally clusters of a species of the banian, which is common in this part of China. Numerous villages could be seen at a distance from the shore, the piratical tendencies of the Chinese forbidding the people to build near the water, except

K

n large and walled cities. In every village one or more large square stone buildings towered up far above all the ordinary houses, which are only one story in height. These buildings, a striking feature in all southern Chinese towns, are pawnbrokers' establishments, and are also used as places of deposit for valuable articles that are not in constant use. The owners of these establishments become responsible for the safe keeping of all goods and valuables intrusted to them, the people having generally no safe place in which to keep them at home. Scores of these square towers may be seen looming up above the rest of the city all over Canton. Now and then we came upon a five or seven-story tower, a prominent feature in the scene, which afforded us

CHINESE PAGODA.

our first view of the Chinese pagodas. They are usually fast going to decay, and most of them are considered too insecure to be ascended.

Twelve miles below Canton we reached Whampoa, once a place of some commercial importance, and soon after came upon the outskirts of the wilderness of boats which forms one of the most remarkable sights of the great city. It is estimated that 300,000 of the people belonging to Canton live on the water in boats, not merely to obtain a livelihood from the water, but chiefly for the sake of a residence. The people are born, spend their days, and die in these boats, the only homes and the only shelter that they have from the time of their birth until they are committed to the grave, and yet a happier-looking class of people I have not seen any where in China. One morning I saw under my window, which was on the shore, a family of ten persons—father, mother, and eight young children—taking their breakfast of rice, and fish, and a few greens in one end of their boat, and apparently as well contented as if they owned a palace. These boats are of all sizes and of all sorts, the most of them small sampans, about the size of an ordinary row-boat, with a simple mat or bamboo covering over one half, while others are large and elaborately ornamented with carvings in wood, and gold and paint. Some of them are occupied as restaurants and places of amusement, the large boats being usually moored alongside of each other, with long water-streets running between the blocks. Besides these there are innumerable craft, junks of all sizes, sailing or rowing up and down and across the river, making it exceedingly difficult at times to find an opening through which to steer a boat. The men who live on the boats go ashore for employment during the day, and the women ply the oars, and capital boatmen they are. I give them a decided preference over men, for they are not only equally handy with the oar or the scull, but they are far more polite, and, I may add, more honest than their other halves who are on shore at work during the day.

One would imagine that a boat must be a dangerous place to bring up a family of children, but the mothers tie a joint of bamboo to each of their little ones, and if they tumble overboard it serves as a float, and they are recovered. They do not grieve much if the child never turns up, especially if it be a girl.

There have been some fearful scenes among this floating population. The typhoons which sweep over the China Seas and along the coast, and which are so destructive to shipping, seldom come so far inland as Canton, but four or five years since one of the most severe ever known passed over the city, and it is comparatively easy to imagine the havoc made with these floating homes of the poorer people, but impossible to describe, or even to conceive, the scenes which followed. This wilderness of river craft, which at ordinary times is so quiet, and only sways hither and thither with the tide, was like a heap of chaff before the tempest. The house-boats, many of which were of large size, became as dust to the wind, and were carried away no one knew where; the heavier boats were sunk in great numbers, the occupants were hurled into the water as their homes were torn to pieces, and when the storm had passed, and an estimate could be made of the loss of life, it was found that 60,000 persons had perished. For a long time the river was strewn with the dead bodies.

Just before reaching the city we came upon a small island fortified in the Chinese style, and having a picturesque appearance.

Canton is regarded as the first city in the empire for wealth and elegance. It is the best built, and, what is no mean praise for a Chinese city, it is the cleanest. There is no external magnificence in any of the buildings. The houses, generally combining both shop and residence, are usually of one story, never more than two, and there is scarcely such a thing to be imagined here as architectural taste. It would be wasted if there were such an element in the composition of the people, for the city, like all others, is so compact that nothing could be seen to advantage. Many of the streets are covered with matting to shut out the rays of the sun, giving them a sombre, indoor appearance. Indeed, when one enters the gates of this or any other city that I have seen in China, he bids adieu to the outer world, and even to the heavens, and wanders on in a shaded labyrinth until he leaves the city itself.

FORT NEAR CANTON.

There are no prominent buildings, with the exception of the pawnbrokers' towers; even the temples are low, scarcely rising above the surrounding houses, and altogether the view of the town from without has nothing that is striking or interesting. There is one beautiful spot, but not a part of Canton. When the occupation of the city by the foreign powers was given up in 1861, the old factory site was a desolation. In place of this, a low, sandy island, directly on the river bank half a mile higher up, was appropriated to foreigners, and at great expense was raised some ten or twelve feet above high-water mark, and surrounded by a granite wall of hewn stone. The lots were then sold, and the foreign residences and hongs built upon it. It is now a small city of palaces, and forms the only beautiful feature in the view of Canton as one passes it by the river. There are three longitudinal and several cross streets set with trees, the compounds being ornamented with plantains, shrubbery, and flowers, a public garden or square adding to the attractions of the place. The island is called Shah-Min. It is connected with the city by an iron bridge 100 feet long, which no Chinese is allowed to cross.

In enumerating the sights of Canton I should begin with the streets themselves, which, notwithstanding their contracted dimensions and great irregularity, are as varying and entertaining in their aspect as a kaleidoscope. They are never more than eight or ten feet wide; not a street in the city will admit of the passage of any kind of wheeled carriage, the only mode of conveyance for passengers being the sedan chair, which is carried on the shoulders of coolies,

SEDAN CHAIR.

suspended on poles. All merchandise and every thing else is carried by coolies in the same way.

The streets do not answer to their high-sounding names such as "Pure Pearl Street" (not referring to the perfumes that abound more or less every where), "Street of Benevolence and Love," "Couchant Dragon Street," "Court of Unblemished Rectitude," etc.; but some of them are perfect bazars, the shops on either side being filled with costly articles well arranged for effect, rich jewelry, silks of all kinds, curiosities in ivory, and all sorts of ornamental and fancy work.

The principal streets are hung with gay banners suspended from the tops of the houses and from the fronts of the shops. The signs, which are gaudy, stand upon the end, and, with their bright colors, give a showy aspect to the fronts of the buildings; while the great variety of curious articles exposed to public view by the open doors; the noisy tide of human beings, which is all the while surging through these narrow avenues on foot and in chairs, with the coolies carrying burdens of all sorts; the processions which one often meets, and which take up the whole street as they pass along, all together make up such a scene as can be found in no other city in China, and the like to which is not to be found in any other part of the world. We were never molested in our peregrinations through Canton, but were occasionally greeted with the salutation which the Chinese are fond of bestowing upon foreigners, *Fan-kwai, Fan-kwai* (foreign devils, foreign devils). Even the little children caught up the sound and shouted it after us.

The silk weaving, which is largely carried on at Canton, is accounted among its curiosities; but it is chiefly interesting, as showing how the most beautiful fabrics can be wrought in small and dirty hovels and retain their purity. All the silks of China, for which Canton is most celebrated, are woven by hand on the rudest of looms, frequently by mere girls and boys. I watched with no little surprise the growth of a fine brocade, a little boy managing the harness, and a girl sitting at the loom and casting the shuttle. Every figure came out of their hands perfect, the whole piece looking as if it just came from the fuller, without spot.

We made an excursion one afternoon about two miles up the river to the celebrated Puntinqua Aquatic Garden, the only specimen of Chinese gardening that I saw that exhibited real taste, or that had real beauty. The Chinese style is exceedingly stiff, and consists, in great measure, in training plants, and shrubs, and trees in grotesque shapes, distorting the vegetable kingdom into a supposed resemblance to the animal. The Puntinqua Garden is laid out on a magnificent scale, is chiefly devoted to the cultivation of aquatic plants in picturesque lakes, with beautiful summer-houses and palaces scattered among them, and is provided with all the requisites for elegant entertainments. The furniture is of the most costly description. It was planned, and for years kept in order, by a high officer of government, who made an immense fortune out of his office, chiefly by peculation, as it is asserted. His estate of several millions of dollars had been confiscated, and this extensive and beautiful monument to his taste was rapidly going to ruin. No one would probably be found having either the fancy or the means to invest in such an expensive toy.

The temples of Canton, as of China generally, are very inferior to those of Japan. There is nothing I have seen that will bear comparison with the grand old temples of Shiba at Yeddo. The latter are kept with scrupulous neatness, the surroundings as well as the interiors showing perfect taste, while the temples at Canton are simply curious places, the approaches to them being often obstructed with rubbish and dirt. One of the most celebrated is that of the patron god of the city, better known as the "Temple of Horrors," from a series of rude representations of the torment of purgatory and perdition which occupy, but do not ornament, the square in front of the temple. They are wooden or clay images, one group representing the several stages of transmigration through which a human being passes before he reaches the condition of the lower animals. They rival the pictures on the walls of the Church of San Lorenzo, outside of the walls of Rome. One man is represented as undergoing the process of boiling in a caldron of oil; another is ground between two millstones, his head and body having gone through the purifying process, the lower part of his legs only projecting from the mill; another is placed between two planks, which are closely pressed together, and sawed longitudinally, the blood oozing out at the sides. But it is all done in such a rude style as to make the representation ludicrous instead of horrible. At the side of a large open square in front of this temple I saw a small inclosure, with a placard in front, which read as follows, in plain English: "Mermaid; ten cents to go in and see it." We went in, and found one of those curious Japanese manufactures which are known the world over, a monkey's head so cleverly affixed to the body of a fish as to conceal the line of junction. I asked the man who had it in charge if it came from Japan, and he simply replied "Humbug." I made several inquiries in regard to it, and the only answer I got was "humbug." He had evidently got hold of a term the meaning of which he did not understand, supposing it to be complimentary. The same square was crowded with groups of persons gambling, consulting astrologers and necromancers, and having a good time generally, while the thoughts of religious worship were among the last that could have entered their heads. The temple itself is more resorted to by the people of the city than any other, but there is very little of the form of worship at any. Every man has his shrine at the door of his house or shop, at which he burns his joss-sticks, and with this vicarious devotion he is probably satisfied.

Another celebrated joss-house is known as the Temple of the Five Hundred Gods. The Chinese deify their ancestors, and it is thus easy to make a large collection of gods. These five hundred are carved and gilded life-size images of as many sages, real or imaginary, arranged in long rows up and down the temple. They are a curious sight, especially in the great variety of faces and forms which they present, all classes of features and all nationalities being represented, sometimes with very good effect. Among the gods was one in European dress, tight-bodied coat and pantaloons; but how he came to be deified in China I did not learn.

As we approached this temple we saw half a dozen priests standing in front of a sort of altar, with their books open, ready to commence the service, which we afterward heard them intoning in true ritualistic style. One of them, happening to turn his head, saw us approaching, and the whole group immediately left their altar and prayer-books and gathered around us, the lady who was with me, as usual, attracting the chief attention. They at once, as I judged from their looks, fell to criticising her dress. They assumed that we could not understand their conversation, but a gentleman was with me who had been ten years in China, and was perfectly familiar with their language, and he informed us in English that they were discussing the material of which the lady's dress was composed. One said it was gauze, another maintained it was worsted, and another silk. One of them spoke with commendation of her wearing a veil, which they all thought was eminently proper for a lady. After they had discussed these points to their satisfaction, they returned to their prayer-books, and as we walked on through the temple we heard them drawling out the service.

The most imposing temple, and that which seems most strictly devoted to purposes of worship, although few of the people are seen in it, is the Buddhist temple at Honam, directly across the river. It is reached by a long avenue of stately trees, with a large archway about half the distance from the entrance to the grounds. It has some claims, though not great, to magnificence of structure. It is well endowed, and supports a large number of lazy priests with closely-shaven heads, and a considerable number of that sacred animal known at home as the hog. The animals (I mean the swine, though the priests have scarcely any stronger marks of intelligence in their countenances) are fed from the funds of the temple, and literally roll in fat. Whether they die a natural death, or are made to contribute to the support of the priests, I do not know, but the preservation of life is a part of the Buddhist religion. I attended the service, which is performed daily by the priests without any worshipers. About twenty officiated, and the service, which consisted of chanting, intoning, ringing of bells, striking a tom-tom, and various bowings and genuflections, with marchings up and down the temple, was very like that which may be witnessed in any Roman Catholic church. The chanting was well done, and had a pleasing effect upon the ear. I have before remarked upon the similarity between the Buddhist temples and ceremonies and those of the Romanists, and every where it was the same.

There is nothing picturesque in the ordinary dress of the Chinese. Like the Japanese, they wear the everlasting dull blue cotton, all excepting the really wealthy, and, unlike the blue of the sky, which it is *very* unlike, it becomes any thing but pleasing to the eye after one has looked upon some millions wearing it. The Chinese, too, are the reverse of neat in their personal habits, and one soon comes to associate this with the blue cotton clothing which is seen wherever clothing is used at all. Consequently we came to doubt whether the grand display of gorgeous attire of which we had read was not all in the imaginations of the writers, but we had an opportunity while in Canton to confirm all that we had read and heard.

Some of our friends informed us two or three days in advance of a grand procession which was to take place in honor of one of the gods, an uncouth image which was to be taken from the temple and paraded through the streets, and a friend very kindly made arrangements for us to view it from the balcony of a large tea-merchant's hong. The street itself, like the others through which the procession was to pass, was about eight feet wide—not a very grand theatre for such a display. But they must needs use such avenues as they have, and there are none much wider. We went early, in time to see the operations connected with the assorting, mixing, and flowering of the teas, which last consists of mingling with the leaves of the tea various flowers, the chief of which is the jessamine, to give it fragrance. Soon after we arrived the requisite number of cups was placed before us, the choicest tea of the establishment placed in each cup, the hot water poured on, and a second cup or saucer placed over the first to preserve the flavor, the universal mode of making tea in China. To one who is accustomed to having milk and sugar added, this decoction is very insipid; but the hospitality must be accepted, and it was renewed, on this as on other occasions, as often as the proprietor, who could not speak or understand a word of English, imagined we were thirsty.

We waited more than an hour for the procession to arrive, and, in the mean time, were the objects of as much curiosity as the procession itself. During the two hours that it was moving, we (especially, if not wholly, the lady that was with me) fairly divided the honors of the day with the Dragon god. The Chinese, like the Japanese, never become tired of looking at foreign ladies (in the case of American ladies I do not wonder), and while we looked at the pageant that was passing before us, men, women, and children stared into the balcony, as if such a sight as an American lady had never been seen in Canton. How many of them bestowed upon us the usual compliment, *Fan-kwai* (foreign devils), I could not tell.

After we had waited long, the sound of tom-toms, and cymbals, and gongs, and triangles, and then of Chinese flutes and various rude instruments, was heard, and one of the most gorgeous processions that I ever beheld passed before us. There was more or less sameness between different parts, but there was a great variety, especially in the costumes of the persons composing it, and in the richly-embroidered canopies which were carried along in large numbers. I made some notes of the component parts of the procession, and will copy only a specimen. Of course I am unable to picture the scene as it moved on like a panorama, or like the endless turning of a kaleidoscope in which the gayest colors and richest combinations appear.

First came a band of police-officers (as in New York) to drive away the crowd who had assembled in the narrow street to see the sight; then men carrying immense Chinese lanterns, ornamented in every conceivable manner with rich colors; next a company of small boys elegantly dressed in silks of various colors, with caps embroidered in gold, and set off with the feathers of the golden pheasant three feet in length; music consisting of a sort of flageolet, with cymbals and gongs; coolies bearing vermilion and gilded tablets with Chinese inscriptions (which I did not attempt to copy); more boys on foot, elegantly dressed as before; silk banners in various colors borne aloft; a boy on horseback, his own dress of the richest description, and the housings of his horse richly embroidered (boys thus dressed and decorated in every imaginable way were distributed singly through the procession, until in its different parts there were more than a hundred, in a city where horses are scarcely ever seen); a rich canopy of silk embroidered all over with birds of gay plumage (and such canopies came along every minute in the long procession); elegant sedan chairs, cases elaborately carved and ornamented, carried by the coolies, and containing gifts to the god; boy bands of music, and boys on horseback dressed in fancy costumes, representing sages of the empire and emperors, some with long flowing beards and some with bows and arrows; a large white crane pouncing down with joss-sticks in its mouth as an offering; fruits and confectionery in endless variety for the god to eat; glass cases containing jewelry and precious stones, including the Chinese jade-stones, loaned undoubtedly for the show; companies of men dressed in the most costly silks, crimson, salmon, orange, green, blue, etc., the colors of the dresses and the different parts blended and contrasted with exquisite taste; large, lofty embroidered silk canopies *passim*, and so of the Chinese lanterns and Chinese music; boys richly dressed and painted, carried on platforms, and girls carried in a similar manner, resting on rods of iron concealed, and apparently suspended in air, as if caught up in the act of dancing or performing some gymnastic feat. Toward the close of the procession came the public executioner, with the heavy sword which takes off the head at a blow.

This does not begin to complete the catalogue, but, as far as it goes, it is a faithful transcript of notes made on the spot. It was a perfect marvel to see such a pageant got up by the dull-looking Chinese, and to observe what a variety of scenes the turns of the kaleidoscope would bring up as the pageant moved on.

I saw, in the course of my walks, two large wedding processions. One I encountered in a narrow street, and was squeezed into a corner during the time of its passing, but it was a curious sight, and well worth a squeeze to see it. The parties did not seem to be present, and the procession was composed mainly of the presents made, or supposed to be made, to the bride, which were on their way to her home. They consisted of all sorts of articles that would be likely to enter into the outfit, the housekeeping, and living of a newly-married couple. There were tables, chairs, trunks, boxes, blankets, etc.; even fowls in coops, and vegetables in baskets. I heard it suggested, as the long procession was passing by, that the Chinese are not behind the more civilized nations in the art of swelling the display of presents on such occasions, and that a large portion of the articles that I saw moving in such grand ceremonial, like those which we sometimes see so ostentatiously displayed on tables in the Western world, were hired for the occasion, and might be seen the next day gracing other nuptials.

Another procession of a similar character I met at one of the ferries between Honam and Canton, and, as the boats are small, it was a long time in passing over. The boats were plying back and forth for nearly an hour, at the end of which time, having finished my call and returned, I observed it just leaving the river. This procession was even gayer and more varied than the one I had met in the heart of the city, and was designed, like all others, to attract attention by its gorgeous character. Nor was it a failure in this respect. Great numbers of persons were standing around discussing the value and beauty of the articles, and, I presume, making their comments upon the parties and families interested, who obtained their satisfaction in being talked about by the street-goers. Whether they found a place in the gazette I am not able to say, as I did not read the Chinese papers next day.

I came once, in the city of Shanghai, upon a long funeral procession which was preceded by a powerful band of music—powerful in amount of noise and not of music. The mourners, real or professional, in white, were carried in sedan chairs, and at different intervals in the course of the procession companies of men in long white garments filled up the train and kept up a constant wailing, making the scene mournful even in the midst of the crowd which always fills the streets of a Chinese city. Not the most grotesque ceremonies, nor the most matter-of-business circumstances, can divest death of its solemnity or bereavement of its touching character. The imagination will always supply enough that is melancholy.

A much simpler funeral I saw outside the walls of the same city. It consisted of two common coolies who were bearing to the grave, slung upon a pole, the coffins of two children apparently five or six years of age. They were not attended by a single relative or friend, but were to be buried like dogs. Children in China are not considered worth a funeral, or even mourning, unless they have arrived at the age of eight or ten years.

## XI.

#### CHINESE MANNERS AND CUSTOMS.

One of the most curious but not the most agreeable parts of a traveler's experience in going round the world is to be found in the great diversity of manners and customs in regard to eating and drinking. One can accommodate himself readily to many new circumstances in which he finds himself on stepping into a new country, but he can not always make his taste agree with the tastes of the people among whom he is thrown. Happily, in this age of the world he finds some of the staples of life much the same the world over, so that he is not obliged practically to put the most fastidious of the senses to the strong test which it had to endure, when traveling, as one of the fine arts, was more in its infancy; but he can still indulge in observation and speculation to his heart's content.

The Chinese from time immemorial, at least from the days when we studied the pictorial geography, have been celebrated for the range of their animal diet, and for some of the luxuries of life which are peculiar to the celestial kingdom. To begin with the first course, soup. All the world knows that in China they have a delicacy which has not reached other parts, in birds'-nest soup. One of my first inquiries, as I got into the streets of Canton, was after this commodity, or the nests from which it is made, and I was taken into a fine shop, fitted up in a costly manner, where it was the only article sold.

Birds'-nests are a great luxury in China, being within the reach of the wealthy alone. They are sold at prices graduated according to the quality of the article, none of any value bringing a less price than their weight in silver, and some bringing almost their weight in gold. Nests are sold as high as $30 or $40 a pound. The nests are simply a mass of pure gelatine, secreted in some way by a species of swallow (*Hirundo esculenta*), and deposited against a wall, just as the swallows in our country stick a nest of mud against a beam. Some naturalists maintain that the gelatine is formed from a sort of sea-foam which the swallow gathers, and which is exuded from the mouth of the bird. It resembles the gelatine known by the name of isinglass, and the purer sort is almost transparent. There is nothing repulsive in its appearance, and its origin is just as honorable and commendatory as that from which our jellies are made at home—I am disposed to think more so. The nests come chiefly from the island of Java, where they are obtained with great labor, and often at much peril, from deep caves along the coast. Some of these caves on the southern coast of the island are approached only by a perpendicular descent of great depth, by means of ladders, the raging of the sea below preventing all approach from the water. When collected they are assorted into different grades, those which have not been occupied by the birds bringing the highest price, and the other grades prices according to cleanliness and quality. From one to two million dollars' worth are imported every year into Canton. I put a fine specimen of the nest into my trunk for importation into America.

The Chinese do not have as great a variety of animal food as the Western nations, but they make use of some which most nations reject. I find a great diversity in the testimony of travelers and residents in regard to the use of "rats, cats, and puppies," some of the latter (I mean the residents) stoutly affirming that such animals are not eaten at all, or, if so, only in cases of extremity, where nothing else in the shape of food can be obtained. But I have seen all these exposed for sale in the markets of Canton in the very heart of the city.

There are dog markets where nothing else is sold, and where day after day I have seen dogs dressed and ready cooked. There are several such markets in the city. Rats also, alive and dead, fresh and dried, are regularly and constantly sold, and I have seen them in all these stages of preparation as I have been passing. One plump fellow I saw suspended by his tail from a market-hook waiting for a purchaser, but all the while struggling to escape, while the dried specimens hanging around him mocked his agony, and awaited their destiny with more composure. There is no more reason for denying that such animals are regularly sold in the markets of Canton for food than that beef and mutton are sold in the markets of New York. And yet it is nevertheless true that the mass of the people do not use them. Their use is confined to those who are unable to obtain flesh meat that is more expensive.

Another staple in the line of animal food is pork. Chinese pigs are celebrated the world over for their excellent quality, and, as well as Shanghai chickens, have long been imported into America. They are raised with great care —as carefully, if not more so, than the children. They are often kept in little cages in the shops and houses, where they receive every attention, and are fed with the choicest food instead of living on what is thrown away. And a very quiet and well-behaved race they are. They are carried about the streets in baskets just large enough for them to be slipped into with their legs folded, and in this state are laid away at the markets and other places, but I do not remember ever to have heard in China a single note of that dulcet music which is their peculiar forte in other parts. Perhaps it is out of gratitude that they remain so quiet, for I have been told that, until the government interfered and required that they should be carried in baskets, they were slung by the heels across a pole, a mode of conveyance which would very naturally develop their musical powers.

The fruits of China are generally poor and destitute of flavor. We had some fine grapes from the extreme north, but the only fruit in the south that was in season and really palatable was the Amoy pumelo, corresponding to the West India shaddock.

The cultivation of small feet is not altogether peculiar to the higher classes, nor to those who are exempt from labor. It is regarded as a mark of distinction, but only as conformity to fashion distinguishes its votaries. In every city great numbers of women, perhaps a quarter or more of the female population, may be seen toddling about the streets on their pegs, looking very much as if their feet had been cut off and they were walking on the stumps. It is difficult to balance themselves in walking, and they frequently resort to a third peg in the shape of a cane to keep themselves straight. The custom of closely bandaging the feet from infancy is not so injurious as might be supposed, but it greatly interferes with locomotion.

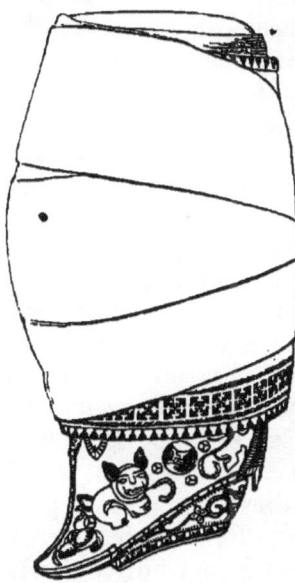

CHINESE SMALL FOOT.

Every one who visits China or reads about it is naturally curious to learn something about the great staple of the country, which has become the common beverage of the world. The tea plant is a shrub which, left to itself, would grow to the height of twenty feet and more, but as cultivated for the production of tea it is cut down and kept down to four or five feet in height. It is raised chiefly in the central regions. The leaves are gathered several times during the season, the earliest, tender leaves being accounted the best. The first crop is usually gathered in the third year from planting, and at the end of about seven years the plants are renewed or cut down to the ground, new shoots springing up from the roots. Plants treated in this way will live for twenty-five or thirty years and produce good crops.

The difference between *black* and *green* teas is not a difference of nature, but of manufacture; both may be produced from the same identical shrub, according to the treatment of the leaves. In preparing *green* tea the leaves are dried, or roasted as the process is called in China, by artificial heat, in pans, almost immediately after being gathered. After about five minutes roasting they become moist and soft, when they are placed on the rolling table and rolled with the hands. They are then restored to the pans, which are kept in motion for about an hour, at the end of which time they are well dried. The color at first is a dull green, but it becomes *fixed* or brighter after a short time. It is afterward sifted and *fired*, or heated, before being packed for market. The high color of green tea is often imparted to it by drugs, which are not the most wholesome for a beverage. For *black* tea, the leaves, on being picked, are spread out in the open air for some time, then tossed about until they become soft, when they are roasted in pans for a few minutes, and then rolled, after which they are exposed to the air for several hours, and finally dried slowly over the fire until they acquire the color which is permanent. The process of drying produces a chemical change in the juices of the plant, and the difference in the process of greater or less exposure to the atmospheric air in the curing accounts for the difference in the color and flavor of the two kinds of tea.

In preparing it for market, fragrant flowers are distributed through the tea as it is placed in the chest, to add to its flavor. The jessamine is most commonly used on account of its fragrance. Tea is unquestionably often adulterated, and, perhaps, most frequently by the mixing of spent leaves with those that are fresh. In the vicinity of Shanghai I saw old leaves revamped in this way in large quantities. When we remember the immense quantity consumed in the empire, and that the mode of preparing the beverage is not by thorough steeping, but simply by pouring hot water upon a small quantity of leaves in each cup, leaving much of the strength still in the leaves, it does not appear strange that even the Chinese should resort to this mode of adulteration. We are sometimes shocked at the thought that barbarous nations should adulterate any thing designed for market, when adulteration is one of the most common, if not most refined arts of civilized life.

Who does not remember how he was puzzled, when a child, with the idea that the Chinese, living on the opposite side of the globe, must of necessity be standing on their heads; and, although the matter was fully explained on the principle of universal gravitation toward the centre of the earth, the puzzle never seemed to get entirely out of the youthful head. Children of larger growth, on coming to China, find a hundred puzzles where before they had only one. The Chinese seem to be standing on their heads in almost every respect; they reverse the general orders of society in more ways than I can attempt to enumerate. In China the mariner's compass does not point to the north, but to the south; in other words, the index is placed upon the opposite end of the needle, a fact which must be kept in mind by those who follow the compass, as it might make some difference in laying their course, whether they go north or south, east or west. So in regard to the different points of the compass, they reverse the occidental order, and call northwest westnorth, southeast eastsouth, etc.

When they meet a person whom they wish to salute, instead of taking him by the hand and giving it a hearty shake, the ordinary salutation with us, they shake their own hands, putting them together and moving them up and down. In most civilized countries it is considered a mark of respect, and even of ordinary politeness, to take off the hat, unless it be for one with whom we are on the most familiar terms. But the Chinese, on the contrary, regard it as showing undue familiarity to uncover the head, and although they may remove their shoes on coming into your presence, they never think of removing the hat, or cap, or whatever they may be wearing. The general head-gear of the men is a sort of skull-cap. If a Chinaman wishes to do you special honor, instead of placing you at his right hand, you will have a seat or a standing-place on his left. When invited to a feast or other entertainment, the men and women, although invited together, do not eat together, but occupy separate rooms, a custom which is only partially imitated in strictly English society, where ladies are expected to retire early by themselves, in order to give the gentlemen an opportunity to smoke and drink to their hearts' content.

I am sorry to say that the female sex is not regarded with much respect until it wears the honors of maternity. Girls in China are of very little account. While at Canton I visited, by invitation, the house of a wealthy and highly educated man, one of the Howqua family. I found him in his library, surrounded with books and works of art, some of which he had executed himself. His house was an extensive palace, and every thing about it, as well as his manners and conversation, indicated high culture and refined taste. His little boy coming into the room, I asked the father how many children he had, and his reply was "One, and two daughters;" as if the daughters were not deserving of the name of children. The lady who accompanied me, and who soon afterward was admitted to the wife's apartments, laughingly attempted to impress upon his mind the superiority of the feminine portion of his household, including the two daughters. He took it all in evident good humor, but it was more than doubtful whether any impression was made upon his mind in that direction.

The style of dress in China is not only different, as a whole, from what we are accustomed to, but there are some strange transmutations which strike the attention of a traveler. The men very commonly wear a sort of petticoat — a loose, close garment reaching to the feet, while the women, on the other hand, wear trowsers or pantaloons, literally and not metaphorically. I may say that the latter wear the pantaloons metaphorically as well as literally, for, contrary to the general ideas in regard to the position and influence of woman in these Oriental countries, there is no part of the world where family authority resides more in the woman. The wife may not have the same high position outside of the family, but maternal authority in China is well nigh supreme, and grand-maternal authority is sometimes still greater. A mother does not lose her right to command her son when he marries or becomes the head of a numerous household of his own, but continues to hold the sceptre over succeeding generations.

The dress-makers and milliners in China are men instead of women, and the various trades and occupations are singularly mixed up. Having occasion to order an Eastern hat, or topee as it is called, as a protection against the sun, the rays of which often prove fatal, even in the cool season, I sent my measure through a friend. A day or two after, word was brought to my room that the tailor was at the door waiting to see me. On sending for him, I found it was the tailor who had made my hat, and who came to see whether it was a fit. In the streets of a Chinese city, almost every man you meet has a fan either in his hand or tucked in his dress, back of his neck; while, on the other hand, the women indulge freely in a habit which in our country is supposed to belong to the other sex—that of smoking. The men wear their hair as long as it will grow, longer than any modern reformers that I have ever seen in America, while the women carefully put theirs up.

In China, when a man gets angry with another and wishes to be revenged upon him, instead of killing the object of his hatred he kills himself. The principle on which he does it is the supposition that the man whom he hates will be answerable for his murder, and will be more heavily punished by evil spirits in this world and in the world to come than if his life had been taken. It is certainly, for society, a safer mode of administering vengeance than that which prevails in civilized countries, where the pistol and bowie-knife are made to do their work upon unsuspecting victims. The Canton policemen have quite as original a mode of performing their services. Instead of looking for marauders, they go about the streets at night sounding a loud rattle or tom-tom, which may be heard at least a mile, and which seems intended to warn all misdoers that an officer of justice is at hand, and that they must accomplish what they have to do and get out of the way before he arrives.

The language of China is another of its contradictions. The spoken language is never written, and the written language is never spoken, so that one may be familiar with Chinese books, and not understand any thing of the conversation of the people; or he may be proficient in the colloquial tongue, and not understand a word of what he reads. In reading a book, the Chinese begin at the end (that is, at our end) and read backward; they read from top to bottom instead of across the page, the lines running downward, and numbering from right to left. The running title of the book or page is at the side instead of the top of the page, and the contents of the chapter at the end instead of the beginning. The notes, which with us are at the bottom or in the side margin, in Chinese books are at the top of the page.

The Chinese have a custom quite peculiar to themselves of ordering their coffins and having them sent home long before they have any thought of dying. They take peculiar pride in selecting the best materials, having them made good and strong, and, when they can afford it, in the most expensive style, and then they take great pleasure in showing them to their friends, keeping them where they may be seen by all who call. For the same reason, perhaps a motive of pride, they preserve the bodies of their friends in the house sometimes for weeks and months after death, making a display of the costly receptacle.

I might greatly extend this catalogue of contrarieties by speaking of the manner in which their schools are conducted; of the old men flying kites, and the boys looking on; of wearing white instead of black for mourning; of all classes whitening their shoes with chalk instead of blacking them; of mounting the offside of the horse when they ride, etc. But this is enough.

China and the Chinese are a great mystery to the world at large, and scarcely less of a mystery to the dwellers in China than to those who never set foot within the Flowery Land. The people of the country are a study, but a study in which little actual progress is made. I have heard those who have been here ten years or more confess that they knew as little of Chinese character, and were almost as unable to comprehend the national traits, as when they first came to this country. The Chinese are a very stolid, incommunicative, undemonstrative race, so that a foreigner may be associated with them, or may have them in his house as servants, and constantly in his presence for years, and know no more about them at the end of this period than the first day he saw them.

I have found one key which, if it does not unlock the mysteries of the Chinese mind, explains the uniform and stereotype character which the nation has maintained for centuries, and which it seems determined to maintain for centuries to come. A Chinaman is a Chinaman in every part of the empire and the world over. He is nothing else, and can be made nothing else, and he has been the same for long ages. One explanation of this is to be found in the fact that the educated and ruling class of the country are all cast in one mould. The ideas of the nation were formed more than two thousand years ago; and the only system of education which has existed since that time has, *per force*, not only compelled the people to adopt these ideas, but has ground them into their very natures, and made them a part of the national character, as much so as the peculiar features of the countenances of the people.

All who have read any thing about China must have met with frequent references to the "Competitive Examinations," which are the great stimulus to education. The Chinese are eminently a literary people, a large portion of them being able to read and write, while the highly educated class is very numerous. But this is not the result of any such system of general instruction as prevails in American or European countries. The schools do not comprise the mass of the children, nor are they of a high class. The education of the people is in a great measure voluntary, and, such as it is, is secured by its being the only road to position in society and to political preferment. The "Competitive Examination" is the ordeal through which all must pass successfully in order to secure any high standing, and this examination is a sort of mould in which the Chinese mind is cast, and from which it comes out uniform in shape and character. It is conducted on this wise:

The empire is divided into provinces and districts, for each of which there is a separate examination — the district, the provincial, and the imperial. No one is required to go through an examination, but it is open to all, with the exception of a few classes, such as the children of executioners, jailers, prostitutes, etc. Before any one can be a candidate for the lowest, the district examination, he must have passed through a satisfactory examination before a magistrate, and must present satisfactory testimonials as to his parentage, character, etc. At the appointed time, the candidates, who usually number many thousands, assemble at the capital city of the district, and have assigned to them subjects for essays and a poem, which they are required to produce without assistance and within twenty-four hours. The most extensive arrangements are made for the accommodation of this vast number of persons, and also to prevent their obtaining any external aid. The essays are carefully examined by government officials, and so rigid is the ordeal that usually not more than one in a hundred passes the test. The successful competitors receive the degree of B.A.—not Bachelor of Arts, but "Beautiful Ability." And the point peculiarly noteworthy is, that all the themes are taken from the writings of the Chinese sages. The essays are not only expected to be a reflection of their teachings, but it is impossible that it should be otherwise, inasmuch as the previous training of the candidate has been confined almost exclusively to their writings. Only those who receive the first degree in the district examination are allowed to compete for the second in the provincial.

The provincial examination occurs once in three years at the capital of the province, where a large hall, as it is called, is devoted exclusively to this purpose. The one at Canton (the capital of the province of Quang Tung) which I visited is 1330 feet long, 583 feet wide, and contains cells, arranged in long rows like stalls for horses, for 8653 candidates. The whole inclosure is surrounded by a high wall, and each row of cells is inclosed, and under the supervision of an officer, whose duty it is to prevent all communication between the candidates or with the outer world. Here they are shut up, after having been carefully searched, to prevent their taking in upon their persons any thing that might assist them in the preparation of their essays. Themes, taken as before from the "Classics," or "Four Books," are then given to them on several successive days; the essays and poems, which must be produced within a given time, are carefully copied in red ink to prevent recognition by the examiners of the source from which they come, and they are then subjected to the rigid criticism of literary men appointed by the imperial government. On the close of the examination, the names of the successful competitors are posted upon the outer wall, and are heralded throughout the province. They bear about the same proportion to the whole as before — one to a hundred. They receive the second degree, A.M. — not Masters of Arts, but "Advanced Men"— and become candidates for the third and highest examination, which is held triennially at Peking, and which is equally rigid with the preceding.

Those who pass and receive the last degree become eligible to public offices, and enter into the most honored and ruling class in the empire. Only two or three hundred out of the thousands who have passed the lower succeed in the imperial examination; but in this, as in the lower, they have the privilege of trying again, and thus many present themselves triennially, term after term. In this way fifty or a hundred times as many as are successful in obtaining the prize, receive the training and become educated members of the communities to which they belong.

There is no prize presented to the mind of a Chinese youth which is such a stimulus to unbending effort as the third degree. It comprises all that his ambition could desire—social position, office, honor, wealth. The successful candidate, on his return to his home from the capital, is feasted and fêted, and frequently a pagoda or some other building is erected in his honor, and as a memorial of the honor which he reflects upon his native city.

I have referred to this subject only as giving something of an insight into Chinese character, and as showing why it is that the Chinese remain so much the same, while other nations are undergoing change. They are educated in a system of ideas which have been handed down through twenty centuries; the hoary-headed antiquity of these ideas makes them venerable in their eyes, and it is not strange that they wish future generations to travel in the same path which they and their fathers have trod so long. The teachings of the Chinese sages, Confucius, Mencius, and others, are the fountain of their ideas. Few natives live up to their own standards, and it is not strange that the Chinese practically depart from the wise instruction of those sages; but this is the mould into which the educated minds are all poured, and it appears to account for many of their national characteristics.

## XII.

### RELIGIONS OF CHINA.

The prevailing forms of religion in China are Confucianism, Buddhism, and Tauism. The former, which is the faith of the educated and influential classes, is more a system of philosophy and of morals than a religion. It is founded on the teachings of the great Chinese sage who flourished about five centuries before the Christian era, whose reputed writings contain a vast amount of practical wisdom and of pure morality. The Chinese owe much to Confucius, and they would be a much better people if they followed his precepts more closely. Buddhism is an importation from India, where it had its rise, and from which it passed over Eastern Asia and to the adjacent islands. It is now declining, and the temples devoted to its worship are in many places going into decay. Tauism lays claim rather to the vulgar and uneducated classes. It is a mystic sort of religion, deals in incantations and astrology, and, like spiritualism, pretends to intercourse with the departed dead as well as with acknowledged evil spirits. The priests are generally ignorant men, and, through mystic art and by playing upon the superstition of the people, maintain their ascendency over them.

There is no more striking or more universal trait of Chinese character than its intense superstition. The religious element appears to be wanting; they are simply superstitious, and no nation is more so. The spirits of the air, the earth, and the sea are a constant terror to them, and their acts of worship are designed to ward off such influences rather than to pay homage to any exalted being. They use all sorts of charms to keep off from their persons, and houses and farms the world of evil spirits which in their belief are going hither and thither. Ancestral worship is universal. No matter in what part of the world they live, the Chinese wish to be brought home when they die, and buried with the generations that preceded them; and while they live they pay great respect, a reverence amounting to worship, to their departed ancestors, making pilgrimages to their graves, adorning their tombs, erecting tablets to their memory in costly ancestral halls, burning incense, joss-sticks, and candles, and presenting offerings. They reverence their dead grandfathers more than their gods.

One of the most common offerings that the Chinese make in their worship is exceedingly characteristic—a sort of counterfeit money, pasteboard dollars covered with tin-foil, resembling silver dollars, and marked accordingly. This is sometimes offered to a large amount, counting it at its nominal value, and a Chinaman will not only pride himself on making an offering to his god or his ancestor of several thousand dollars, which cost him only a trifle, but he will fairly chuckle over the thought that his stupid god or his dead ancestor, not knowing the difference between the counterfeit and the genuine, will give him credit for the full amount in good money.

They have numberless inferior gods—the God of the Earth, the God of the Sea, the God of Wealth, the God of Letters, the God of Thunder, the God of War, the Kitchen God, etc., etc., which are represented by grotesque images or pictures. The thieves and the gamblers each have their god. They make their appeals to the gods by the use of the lot, every temple being provided with a box of sticks or straws for the purpose. This superstitious disposition to rely upon the lot is carried into all the affairs of life. The Chinese are all gamblers, gambling every where and for every thing. Even the little boys, as I have often seen, in going up to a fruit-stand, almost invariably cast the die to determine whether they shall have double or nothing for their money.

The efforts to propagate Christianity in China have not

CASTING LOTS BEFORE A GOD.

met with as much success as in some other countries, but they are far from being a failure, and there are manifest reasons which, while they account for the want of enlarged success thus far, do not in the least degree discourage those who have undertaken the work. Nowhere have Christian missions had greater obstacles to overcome. The opening of the free ports did not open China to free intercourse with the rest of the world. The traditional seclusion of its inhabitants, and their hostility to foreigners and to all foreign notions, exist to this day in all their force. The mass of the people regard all other nations as outside barbarians, and it is the interest of the educated class to keep alive this hatred. They salute missionaries, as well as others, in the streets with the title of foreign devils, not knowing or not appreciating the motives with which they come to teach a new religion.

Foreign intercourse thus far has been carried on by force. The ports were opened, not by the free consent of the Chinese, but by the guns of foreign powers. The Chinese wished to live by themselves, neither interfering with others nor interfered with; but for purposes of gain, and by force of arms, foreign nations compelled them to admit the commerce and the merchants of the world. This of itself was enough to prejudice the nation against missionaries who come from the same lands with the ships of war that battered down their forts and their cities. It is not strange that Christian teachers should find it hard even to gain the ears of those who have been thus treated. And, furthermore, this force was employed to open China to commerce for the express purpose of compelling the authorities to admit one of the greatest curses ever thrust upon any people.

The Opium War and the present opium traffic are a dark blot upon the history of the British government. No one can visit the cities of China and witness the debasing and destructive effects of opium on the multitudes of miserable victims which it is daily depriving of mental and physical vigor and consigning to the grave; no one can read the piteous words in which the Chinese commissioners have besought the British representatives not to force this destructive drug upon the nation; no one can recall the heartless manner in which such appeals were answered with threats, and then with broadsides from vessels of war, until the way was made open for the wholesale introduction of opium into all parts of the empire, and wonder, after such proceedings on the part of a Christian government, that the Chinese do not seem well disposed to accept the Christian religion. It is not strange that they should put the two together, and regard them with the same hostility. When Sir Rutherford Alcock, the British embassador, was taking his leave of the government at Pekin to return to England on a furlough, Prince Kung said to him, "Now that you are about to return to your own country, we wish you to take with you your opium and your missionaries." Could any thing be more natural? And yet there are those who impute the slow progress of Christian missions in China not to the obstacles which have been placed in their way, but to the cause of missions itself.

PRINCE KUNG.

The Rev. J. R. Wolfe, a Church of England missionary of long experience in China, writes:

"There is not a particle of truth, as far as my experience goes, in the statement that the Chinese people are opposed to the propagation of Christianity, or dislike the missionaries simply because they are such. There is, however, one thing which the Chinese people dislike, and which has tended more than any thing else to produce hatred for foreigners, and cause misery and ruin to multitudes of the Chinese people themselves, and that one thing is the act of the British government in compelling the Chinese people at the point of the bayonet to buy the opium, when they most virtuously and patriotically protested against it. I have invariably found in my journeys through the country that this act of the British government is remembered with deep and lasting hatred by all classes of the people, and is handed down from father to son as one cause why the English should be held in everlasting hatred and contempt."

While I was at Canton, one of the missionaries with whom I was crossing the river in a ferry-boat fell into conversation with two or three intelligent Chinese, and the first reply of the person he addressed was, "You are bringing opium into the country to destroy us, and we do not want to have any thing to do with your religion."

In no other country has the personal example of irreligious men from Christian lands done more to prejudice the people against Christianity. Too many of those who go to foreign parts lay aside even the restraints of morality by which they are bound at home, and set before the heathen an example of license in living which becomes a libel upon the religion of their native lands. The people of those countries can not make the distinction which is made at home between those who profess to be governed by the principles of Christianity and those who do not; all are called Christians, and the name and cause of true religion must bear the burden of those immoralities. I could detail scenes which I have witnessed on these distant shores that were shocking to my own feelings as they would be to any Christian mind, and yet they were all laid to the account of Christianity.

The present attitude of the foreign merchants in China toward the Chinese is another hinderance to the success of efforts made to promote their conversion to Christianity. The spirit of the Opium War is still at work. Foreign merchants, with few exceptions, go to China without a thought of doing the Chinese any good, simply to make money. The opportunities for making large fortunes have gone by. The Chinese are getting a measure of the foreign trade into their own hands. Trade with the interior is still restricted. These and other causes have awakened the hostility of foreigners toward the Chinese, and now it is difficult to say where the greater degree of hostility lies, with the Chinese or the foreign traders. While I was in China, the desire for another war was prevalent among the foreign residents; I might say it was almost universal, and the motive was to break down the restrictions upon trade, and give foreigners greater opportunities for making money. After all the injuries the Chinese have sustained in the past, and with the feelings cherished toward them at the present time, I do not at all wonder that they are ready to spew every foreigner, missionary as well as merchant, out of the land. I do not mean to intimate that Christian missionaries share in this anti-Chinese feeling; they do not; but the Chinese do not comprehend the different motives which actuate the two classes.

The difficulty of acquiring the language so as to become familiar with it has been a great obstacle. A single fact will give some idea of this. Through the instrumentality of the American Presbyterian Mission, metal types have come into use in printing Chinese. The Mission Press at Shanghai is the most extensive printing establishment in the empire. On entering it, I was confronted with a series of amphitheatres, in the interior of each of which stood a compositor, and I saw at a glance the immensity of the work which every one who learns to read, or write, or print the language has to encounter. Each of these amphitheatres was what printers call a case, containing, not twenty-six letters, as in English printing offices, but more than six thousand different characters or types, and, with the combinations, more than thirteen thousand. The Dictionary of Dr. Morrison contained forty thousand separate characters, which must become familiar to the eye, and various inflections must be given to similar words to express the ideas associated, or one may fail to express what he means. In no language are ludicrous errors more apt to be made by giving a wrong accent or inflection, and thus entirely changing the sense.

But, notwithstanding all these difficulties, a great work has been already accomplished. Few even of those who are familiar with the current work of missions in China have any adequate idea of what has actually been done. Protestant missionaries are almost the only persons who have ever mastered the language. Not one merchant in a hundred, scarcely one in a thousand, makes even the attempt to acquire it either for reading or speaking. All the Chinese Dictionaries for English students have been made by missionaries. The only writers who have prepared books in Chinese designed to instruct and elevate the people have been missionaries. I have before me a catalogue of nearly a hundred works in Chinese on various sciences, history, geography, medicine, law, etc., all of which have been prepared by Protestant missionaries. They have done more than any and all other men to promote a knowledge of Chinese literature. They have established and maintained in Chinese cities hospitals which have been a great blessing to the people, and which are doing much to prepare the way for the reception of the Gospel of Christ. At Canton a hospital was established in 1835 by Dr. Peter Parker, then a missionary, which has been a house of mercy to hundreds of thousands. During the year that I was at Canton there had been 26,457 patients, many of whom required skillful surgical treatment. During my stay in that city several surgical operations of the most delicate and difficult nature were performed. The hospital is now in charge of a skillful physician and surgeon, Dr. Kerr, of the American Presbyterian Board.

Nor have the labors of the missionaries been without important spiritual results. In 1850 all who had professed themselves Christians did not number four hundred. Now there are about six thousand communicants in the various mission churches. The Presbytery of Ningpo has seven churches and about five hundred communicants. At Foo Chow there are about one thousand communicants. At Amoy, a station which was first occupied by Rev. David Abeel, the devoted missionary whose fervid and eloquent appeals in behalf of the cause of missions will never be forgotten by any who heard them in his native land, there were, when I was in China, nearly thirteen hundred communicants, with thirty-two stations and twenty-eight chapels, chiefly in the country round about. These are only some of the fruits which have been gathered.

In no part of the world is the medical branch of the missionary work of more importance than in China. There are many parts of the empire where a missionary, in going out to preach the Gospel, or to distribute books or tracts, would be driven away by a mob, if he did not fare worse; indeed, this is true of almost the whole interior of the country, but there is not a single spot, city or country, town or village, where a medical missionary may not at any time set himself down, and, within an hour, make himself perfectly at home with the people—administering to the sick and suffering, and, at the same time, preaching the Gospel with entire freedom. It is simply marvelous, when we remember the hostility of the Chinese to foreigners, that physicians have such ready access to the people, although there is a reason for it. The Chinese have no thoroughly educated physicians. Their aversion to handling the dead is so great that they have no students of anatomy. The only really educated physician of whom I heard was educated in America. At the same time, they seem to have implicit faith in the medical skill of foreign physicians, and in their presence lay aside their national hatred.

Dr. Kerr gave me an account of a visit he once made, in company with another missionary, a preacher of the Gospel, to an interior town which had been the scene of violent demonstrations against the *Fan-kwai* (the foreign devils). As soon as he found a place to sit down, and announced the object of his visit, he was surrounded by an eager crowd, and all day long he ministered to the sick, who came to him by hundreds, while his companion preached without any molestation. But for his being a physician, they would have been mobbed, if not torn to pieces. When they went to their boat at night they had a perfect ovation; the streets were lined with people who were attracted by the benevolent character of their visit.

The first Sabbath that I spent at Canton I visited in the morning the chapels and schools of the London Wesleyan Missionary Society, and heard a sermon delivered with great earnestness and solemnity by a native preacher. The whole service was in Chinese. The hymns which were sung were "Rock of Ages," and "Grace, 'tis a charming sound." The congregation gave close attention, and the whole scene was impressive. At the close of the preaching I went into the schools and examined the young children in some of the general facts of the Old and New Testament histories, and I am sure that no children of the same age in America could give more ready or intelligent answers to the inquiries which were made. From there I went to the Treasury-street Chapel, under the charge of Rev. Mr. Preston, of the American Presbyterian Board, a neat and attractive building, situated in the very heart of the old city, and on one of its great thoroughfares. The front is always open, and passers-by drop in to hear the Word spoken, some staying through the service, but most moving on after listening for a while. Some came in with heavy burdens on their heads, and set them down while they listened. One lad came bringing two cages of birds, which he placed on the floor. He soon became evidently interested in what he heard. This service is kept up every day, and thousands thus hear the message. There are several such places open in the city in connection with the different missions, and, although the speakers are sometimes interrupted with questions and objections, they are never molested.

The foreign merchants, who are absorbed in their commercial enterprises, as a general thing, take little interest in the missionary work, or in the elevation of the Chinese. But one honorable exception I desire to name (there are others), that of the house of Oliphant & Co. Not only at home, but in China, have they made large gifts to promote the cause, and they have more than once placed their vessels at the disposal of the missionaries. In 1835 they gave to Mr. Medhurst and a companion in his work the use of a vessel for a missionary voyage of some months among the ports of China, and the following year they sent out from America another vessel to be employed in the same service. Their example is one which might better be followed than that of men who seek only to make gain out of this heathen people, and do nothing to elevate them, or to make them acquainted with the Gospel from heaven.

## XIII.

### MACAO, SINGAPORE, AND PENANG.

THE sunniest, brightest spot that I saw on the whole coast of China is Macao. For this reason I do not regret reserving a visit to it as the last before leaving for other Oriental lands. It is but a few hours' sail, in a pleasant American river steamer, from Hong Kong.

On our way down the bay the captain entertained us with stories of his encounters with Chinese pirates, which still infest these rivers and bays. I had seen some specimens—desperate-looking fellows—in the criminal court at Canton, where they were undergoing torture, a Chinese mode of examination; the judges informing us that they had been on the rack several hours, and were still unwilling to confess their crimes. As we were running down the bay to Macao, the captain informed us that the waters were still swarming with these desperadoes, who were watching every opportunity for seizing vessels, from a steamer down to a row-boat, and that they would not hesitate to put to death all on board who stood in the way of their rapine. One way in which they accomplish their purpose is for a large number to take passage on a steamer on which there are usually very few European passengers, and to seize the vessel. They have a strong temptation to do this in the fact that these steamers often carry treasure back and forth. We had then on board a large amount of specie; but the captain mildly assured us we had nothing to fear from the crowd of Chinese on deck below, as he had an armed man at each companion-way, who would instantly give the alarm if any attempt to seize the little steamer should be made. All this was very assuring; but I found his stories far more than confirmed in the records of Hong Kong, which I afterward examined. They contained, for every year, so many accounts of piracies in the vicinity, that it seemed to be the commonest of crimes. Some were committed in the very neighborhood of Hong Kong, and many on the river between that place and Canton.

One of the regular passenger steamers between Hong Kong and Canton, not long before, was the scene of a desperate encounter with these river pirates, who had come on board with the intention of taking the vessel and murdering all its officers. They seized their opportunity, shot the pilot and several of the officers, but the captain, with the aid of a lady, who handed out to him through a window one musket after another, kept them at bay until he had assistance, and the ruffians were overpowered or killed. There are no people that would plan an enterprise more remorselessly than the Chinese, or carry it out in colder blood. Indeed, from all that I have learned of Chinese character, they appear to me more destitute of that element of our nature that we call conscience than any other people I have ever known.

While we were listening to the captain's piratical yarns the city of Macao hove in sight. It stretches along a beautiful bay and up the hill-sides, and, with its cream-colored stone buildings, looks very much like an Italian town on Lake Como or Maggiore. Its whole appearance, as you approach it, is picturesque. Macao, in reality, is not a Chinese town. It was first occupied by the Portuguese in 1557, and is said to have been allowed them as a residence and a trading-place on account of their efforts in destroying the pirates which infested the coast. During the last century, while the trade of the East India Company with Canton was at its height, it enjoyed a high degree of prosperity, and became the resort and the home of foreigners from all nations. It has more than once proved a refuge for foreign merchants when they have been driven out of the ports of China, and it was for a long time the resort of Christian missionaries when they could not be admitted into the empire itself. It received a fatal blow when, by the treaty of 1842, the ports of China were thrown open, and Hong Kong became a British colony. It is now almost entirely deserted by foreigners for purposes of trade, though still resorted to, especially by invalids, on account of the salubrity of its climate. Its inhabitants are almost exclusively Chinese and mixed-breed, descendants of the Portuguese.

MACAO.

Macao was never actually ceded to the Portuguese. They continued very reluctantly to pay the imperial government an annual rental of 500 taels until 1846, when an order was given by the Queen of Portugal that the Chinese Custom-house on the island should be closed, and the semblance of Chinese authority obliterated. The execution of this order by the Portuguese governor Amiral awakened intense hostility on the part of the Chinese population of the island, which was no doubt fostered by the officials of the empire. The governor, soon after, in opening a new street, removed several tombs—a desecration which, in their eyes, afforded good cause for visiting their vengeance upon him. As he was one day riding on the public drive near the Barrier, attended by an aid-de-camp, several Chinamen rushed upon him, dragged him from his horse, and severed his head and his hand from his body (the other hand having been lost in battle). The whole thing was done so instantaneously that, although in open day, no one could detect the ruffians. The head and hand were sent as trophies to Canton, whence they were afterward obtained by negotiation. This transaction led to the assertion by the Portuguese of exclusive jurisdiction over the island, but the claim has never been acknowledged by the Chinese. The island has become the chief seat of the coolie or Chinese slave-trade, great numbers being shipped from this port.

The European aspect of the town, utterly unlike the low, dull, gloomy Chinese cities, makes it very pleasing to the eye after visiting the latter. There are a number of fine buildings, some of them beautifully situated on hills embraced within the city limits, and affording charming views of the town, the harbor, and the adjacent waters. Some of the old Portuguese churches are elaborate specimens of architecture. The façade and ruins of St. Paul's, which was destroyed by fire many years ago, are very picturesque. The Church of Our Lady of Sorrow, a quaint old building, occupies the crest of a hill, which affords one of the finest views of the town and its surroundings. A large wooden cross, twenty-five or thirty feet in height, stands in front of the church, and overlooks the bay. A curious legend is related as its history. A devout (or undevout) sailing-master, some time in the last century, in a violent storm at sea, when he had little hope of again seeing land, made a vow that, if his vessel should be preserved, he would erect a cross out of the mainmast in

COOLIE BARRACOONS AT MACAO.

front of this church, and he fulfilled his vow. The church is called the "Sailors' Church," and a gentleman who has long resided at Macao assured me that it is a common custom with the sailors to bring various parts of the rigging of their ships up the steep hill to this church to have them blessed.

A beautiful though lonely spot is known as Camoens's Garden, where the great poet, the author of the Lusiad, walked, and mused, and wrote. The grotto which bears his name, and a monument to his memory, is a curious formation of rocks in the midst of extensive grounds, that are laid out with great taste, and shaded with large Oriental trees. It is just such a spot as a poet would select for the indulgence of his fancy, and it has probably lost none of its beauty by the lapse of time. Camoens was born in 1524. He came to the East in 1553, and for a satire upon the Viceroy of Goa was banished to Macao. Just at the entrance to the beautiful grounds of which I have spoken stands the English Chapel, and immediately behind it is the Protestant Cemetery, composed of a series of terraces, the whole very carefully and neatly kept. It is just such a quiet and beautiful spot as any one might choose to lie down in and sleep till the final waking. It is consecrated, not for, but by the graves of Morrison, the first and one of the noblest of the band of missionaries to the Chinese, and several members of his family. Other missionaries were also buried here.

The last evening of our stay in Macao, Captain Endicott (a name well known in New York), who had resided here more than thirty years, and of whose death I have heard with sorrow since leaving China, drove us out to the Barrier, making the entire circuit of the island, a charming drive of several miles, much of it along the sea-shore. On our way we passed the temple in which the treaty with China was concluded and signed by the United States Commissioner, the Hon. Caleb Cushing, and the Chinese Commissioner Keying, the former not being allowed to enter China proper. The Chinese, like the Japanese, have no special reverence for their temples, and often use them for secular purposes.

We returned to Hong Kong from Macao, and made our preparations for another voyage upon the restless, treacherous China Sea, the worst of all seas on which I have had occasion to sail. Before embarking for Calcutta we were assured that at this season of the year, the last of November, we should have a delightful passage to Singapore, with only enough of the northeast monsoon to keep the air from stagnating, and the sea from becoming like molten glass. But I have learned to put little faith in predictions of the weather, even by sailors, having been obliged so often to interpret prophecies by contraries. I now wait for the weather to come before building upon it any substantial castles. We found the predictions in regard to this voyage as much at fault as ever. But, before writing out my log, let me introduce the reader to our ship, with its passengers and crew.

There is no regular line of mail steamers between Hong Kong and Calcutta direct. The English Peninsular and Oriental mail steamer (always called in the East "the P. and O. Line") leaves Hong Kong once a month, touches at Singapore, and then runs across to Point de Galle, the southern cape of the island of Ceylon, where the passengers for Calcutta are transferred to another steamer, which touches at Madras on its way up to the Hoogly. The French steamers of the *Messageries Imperiales* also touch at Singapore and Ceylon, but do not go to Calcutta.

There are large, fine steamers, engaged principally in the opium trade, which take passengers back and forth, and, as there is no opium going to India, the voyage in that direction is made very comfortably. They touch at Singapore and Penang. In one of these, the Hindostan, Captain de Smidt, we took passage. Going on board, we stowed ourselves and our luggage away, and then began to look around for our fellow-passengers, who, with the crew, formed such a curious commingling of races, that I took the trouble to ask the captain for his part of the catalogue, which I found to be as follows: The captain was a Belgian by parentage, born at the Cape of Good Hope, a British subject, and had spent all his life upon the sea, a true cosmopolitan. He was, by the way, a noble specimen of the sailor, well educated and well read, very affable and communicative. The first officer was a Scotchman, the others Scotch and English; the quartermasters were Portuguese, the gunner half Malay and half Portuguese, the carpenter a Chinese, the firemen Chittagong Indians, who stand the heat better than any others; the crew, a savage-looking set of fellows, were Malays, Bengalese, Hindoos, Persians, Arabians, Bombay, Muscat, and Zanzibar men — one or two of them real African negroes.

Among the passengers we numbered eight Americans,

who took possession of one side of the deck, which, in anticipation of hot weather, was to be our home day and night for nearly a fortnight. On the opposite side of the deck were several wealthy Jews, the ladies in a blaze of diamonds as they came on deck; three Parsees, two of whom, a gentleman and his wife, were our fellow-passengers on crossing the Pacific Ocean. Two Armenians subsequently came on board. The deck-passengers were Chinese, Bengalese, Hindoos, Mohammedans, and I do not know what all. We did not want for variety; but, strange to say, notwithstanding the numerous nationalities, and the fact that the most of our passengers were residents of Oriental countries, the only language that was ordinarily spoken was English. This enabled us all—Jews and Gentiles, Parsees, Hindoos, Mohammedans, and Armenians—to become well acquainted, and we had a very pleasant time during the voyage. Nor was religious conversation debarred. Oriental and Western politeness allowed us to speak freely of each other's views without any offense being given. It would be rare to find so many religions represented where such freedom of intercourse and of conversation was enjoyed.

We had but fairly got out of the harbor and from under the shelter of the headlands when we caught the monsoon, blowing fresh and strong. It upset all our calculations in more senses than one, but the sweet assurance was given us that the wind would go down as we got farther south. On the contrary, the farther south we ran the more heavily the wind blew. There was one consolation—it was a fair wind, but as it increased, the huge waves came chasing us from behind, threatening all the while to overwhelm us. Not being able to move about much of the time, we sat or lay on deck watching the great seas as they towered above the stern, coming on with all their force, as if determined the next time to pounce upon us and wash us all from the deck: but our ship never failed to obey the law of gravitation which gives the highest place to the lighter body, and just at the critical moment she would lift her stern gracefully and allow the swell to pass underneath. This she continued to do for five days, the monsoon increasing all the while, and tossing us up and down most inconveniently.

In the evening of the fifth day out, when we were within about two degrees of the equator, dark clouds were seen gathering in the west, which soon overspread the sky and the sea, the blackness of which was relieved only by fierce flashes of lightning. Presently the rain came down in a tropical deluge; and while the elements were all in wild commotion, the engine suddenly stopped, the ship swung round into the trough of the sea as helpless as a log, and then commenced that awful rolling of the vessel which is far more terrible than driving before or even facing a storm. The heat was too great for us to go below, and we preferred to remain on deck, sheltered only by an awning, and take the chances of the storm; but as the ship rolled heavily from one side to the other, as if about to roll completely over, we were thrown about or compelled to cling fast to whatever was within reach. Some of the passengers were overcome with terror, expecting by the next lurch of the ship to be pitched into the sea. One poor Jewess, who came on board with a fortune on her person in the shape of diamonds and emeralds, shrieked aloud and called upon God to save her. It was to all of us more or less a scene of terror, aggravated by the absolute blackness of darkness that surrounded us. As soon as the ship began to recover herself, a voice by my side commenced singing,

> "Tossed upon life's raging billows,
>   Sweet it is, O Lord, to know
> Thou didst press a sailor's pillow,
>   And canst feel a sailor's woe.
> Never slumbering, never sleeping,
>   Though the night be dark and drear;
> Thou, the faithful, watch art keeping;
>   'All, all's well,' thy constant cheer."

The moment that the engine stopped I comprehended the cause. I had learned from the captain that we were drawing near a rocky part of the China Sea, in which were several islands, and in the thick darkness and descending torrents of rain it was impossible to see the course; we might at any moment strike a rock or run ashore; it was safer to let the ship drift than to drive her with the engine. The storm of rain became so severe that we were at length compelled to go below, but all night long the ship was starting and stopping, and when the morning came, instead of being to the west of Bintang Island, as we should have been, we had drifted with the currents thirty miles to the east. The morning light was very pleasant to the eyes, and so was the sight of Singapore, with its beautiful groves of palm, and its substantial buildings stretching along the shore for one or two miles.

We did not at all regret to say farewell to the China Seas. Three times had we tried them, and found them always turbulent, although we had taken them at the best season of the year. Often, while tossing on the waves between Hong Kong and Singapore, was I reminded of a voyage made over the same sea by a beloved friend, Walter M. Lowrie, who subsequently perished by the hands of pirates near Shanghai. He came to China in 1842. On the 18th of June of that year he left Macao for Singapore in a sailing vessel, and, after being driven hither and thither by tempests for two months, the ship put in to Manilla. On the 18th of September he sailed again for Singapore, but on the 25th of the same month the ship struck a hidden rock far out at sea, and was wrecked. The crew and passengers took to the boats, and after spending five days under a burning sun without shelter, and with little hope of seeing land, they at length reached the island of Luban. There he found a vessel bound for Hong Kong, in which he returned almost to the point from which he started, having been gone just four months on a fruitless voyage. Five years afterward, as he was on his way from Shanghai to Ningpo in a native boat, he was attacked by pirates and thrown into the sea. While struggling in the water, he cast the Bible, which he had kept in his hand, into the boat, and then sank. This precious relic was saved and restored to his friends, but his body still sleeps in the sea. He was one of the noblest of that band who have devoted their lives to the service of Christ and his Church in the evangelization of China.

A few miles northeast of Singapore we crossed the 180th meridian west or east of New York, being then precisely on the opposite side of the globe to our home. Neither did we fall from the deck of the ship, nor did the ship fall from the sea, nor did the sea fall off from the land, but all things continued to gravitate as at home. We were just twelve hours in time from the friends whom we had left behind; it was midnight with us, but high noon with them. This might have been the proper time to drop a day in our reckoning; and right glad should we have been to drop four or five days, if we could have avoided the tossings of the sea. This part of the voyage over, we sailed at length on a bright, beautiful morning into the harbor of Singapore.

It was a delightful sensation, after five days and nights of incessant tossing, to feel once more at rest, and still more delightful were our sensations when we stepped ashore and found ourselves in an earthly paradise, the most enchanting spot that I have looked upon in any latitude or in any clime. As I wandered among the groves of spice, and palm, and every form of tropical and Oriental vegetation, I caught myself continually repeating the words of the old Mogul inscription, "If there be a paradise on earth, it is this, it is this!"

Singapore is situated on an island of the same name, just at the extremity of the Malacca peninsula. It is an English colony, having been ceded to Great Britain in 1824. Some one has explained the name as meaning "the place of lions," rather an extraordinary name for a place where lions never were known. The island once abounded in tigers, which are still occasionally met with. In former times, it is said, they carried off and ate one man a day on an average. A resident of more than thirty years, who had made the languages of the East a study, informed me that the word Singapore means a place to touch at, a very appropriate name. It is, in reality, the touching-place for all steamers which pass eastward or westward, from whatever quarter they come. Constant communication is kept up with the rest of the world, and scarcely a day passes without a visit from one or more of the grand fleet of steamers which are driving sails from the Eastern waters as they have driven them from the Atlantic. Singapore is not an undesirable place for residence, being on the great highroad of the nations east and west. But its chief attractions consist in its delightful climate and its rare productions. Situated only one degree north of the equator, it enjoys perpetual summer, and the atmosphere being moist from the vicinity of the sea, and the frequent showers with which it is visited at all seasons, the heat is never oppressive, the thermometer seldom rising above 90°. I have before me the meteorological record of an entire year, in which the greatest heat was 88° and the lowest 73°. In general attractiveness it is very similar to the island of Ceylon, just across the Indian Ocean, with this exception, that while in Ceylon, according to Bishop Heber, "only man is vile," in Singapore the horses are equally vile. On going ashore, we were met by the first crowd of hackmen that we had seen since leaving the Western continent, and they seemed, from their exorbitant demands, to be in correspondence with the fraternity in New York; for when we came to settle accounts, they always had some plea on which the original demand was increased. The horses, too, were mere rats, scarcely able to draw an empty carriage. More than once, in ascending a slight hill, I was obliged to alight and assist them up, or leave the carriage and its other occupants in the interior of the island. But the island itself surpassed, in the variety and richness of its vegetable growth, all that I had conceived of the natural grandeur of the tropics.

Before reaching the harbor, we saw from the steamer, first with the glass and then with the naked eye, large plantations of banana, cocoanut, and other varieties of the palm, stretching along the coast for miles. The cocoanut grows here with great luxuriance, the fruit of enormous size, and the leaves attaining the length of twelve or fifteen feet. It is cultivated for the sake of the oil, which is used for illuminating purposes. The bananas, although considered very fine, are not so large nor so highly flavored than those from the West Indies. I hesitate not to record the general remark, that the fruits of the East Indies, with very few exceptions, are much less rich in flavor than those of the West. It is in spices of all kinds that the East has the superiority, and of these we had a fine specimen at Singapore.

At the invitation of the proprietor, we took a morning walk into a grove of nutmegs occupying several acres. The tree grows to the height of about twenty-five or thirty feet, resembles a pear-tree in its general appearance, and bears a fruit about the size and shape of an ordinary Seckle pear. The grove was in full bearing. Every morning a man walks through, carefully examining each tree to see if the fruit has opened, the cracking of the outer shell being an indication that the nutmeg is fully ripe. This opening of the shell reveals an inner case of the brightest vermilion, the ordinary mace of commerce; and when this is removed the nutmeg is found inclosed in a third shell, much harder than the outer one. I gathered several specimens, preserving some of them in their original tri-fold envelopes.

Mr. P. Yoakim, a wealthy Armenian merchant, who was our fellow-passenger from Singapore to Calcutta, and to whom I was indebted for much information in regard to his beautiful island home, has an extensive spice plantation a short drive from the town. It will abundantly repay any one who touches at Singapore, and has the time to make the excursion, and the gentlemanly proprietor will give him a hearty welcome. This plantation has on it

12,000 cocoanut-trees, 1500 nutmeg-trees, with cinnamon, clove, and all kinds of spices. The clove grows in large clusters upon the extremities of the branches of a large tree, and was in season when we were at Singapore. Mr. Yoakim has an orchid house of great extent.

The Rev. Mr. Keasbury, who has spent more than thirty years as a missionary at Singapore, and who, although not connected with any society, is still prosecuting his work vigorously — preaching, teaching, and superintending a printing establishment that is sending out among the various classes of natives, and into other regions along the Malacca coast and among the islands, a knowledge of the Gospel, has reclaimed from the jungle, about two miles out of town, a small plantation, which yields all the fruits and spices of the tropics, with a profusion of shade, made more delightful by its fragrance. Among the trees and shrubs that I saw in his grounds were the following: pineapple, cocoanut, bread-fruit, orange, mango, jack-fruit, mangostine, durian, custard-apple, coffee, chocolate, nutmeg, clove, cassia, etc., together with a large variety of shade and ornamental trees, among which was the banyan.

The drive to Mr. Keasbury's was one of the most beautiful imaginable, the road being lined with bungalows and plantations laid out with exquisite taste, and adorned with all the luxuriance of tropical vegetation. One of the most conspicuous trees upon the island was the fan-palm; not the palm from which fans are made, but a large tree having the symmetry and shape of a fan, as flat as if it had been placed in a press, although the circle of the leaves alone is at least twenty feet in diameter. The tree resembles the tail of a peacock when fully spread. This singular tree is also called "the traveler's fountain," on account of the large amount of water secreted by it, which flows out when the tree is punctured, affording to the traveler an abundant supply. There is at Singapore a botanical garden or park, over the entrance to which is an inscription, "Open only to subscribers and strangers." It is well laid out and well kept, with a large variety of trees and plants from different climes. Houqua's Garden, some miles from the town, is in the stiff Chinese style, distorting instead of cultivating nature—a process which neither in itself nor in its results has any attractions for my eye. One can not go amiss at Singapore in looking for the beautiful. The whole island is covered with what seems a spontaneous growth of all that is graceful and attractive in vegetation, and animal life is not wanting to enliven the scene. The jungle and forest abound in birds of the richest plumage, tribes of monkeys chatter among the branches of the trees, and occasionally a tiger makes his appearance when hard pressed for something to eat.

The second morning of our stay we spent in company with Rev. Mr. Grant, a missionary representing the Plymouth Brethren, and Major Malan, of the British army, stationed here (a grandson of the departed patriarch of Geneva, Dr. Cæsar Malan), in visiting the Gospel-house, the school for young girls established by Miss Cooke, now in England, which is supported chiefly by the work of the pupils. The embroidery is sold at a public annual fair, and is quite equal to that found at the Oriental bazars.

Singapore was once a very important missionary station, not so much in its relation to the permanent population of the place as on account of its affording an opportunity to exert an influence upon China and other neighboring countries. It was ποὺ στῶ, a standing-place on which to operate while the Celestial Empire was closed against foreigners. For a long period there has been a large Chinese population on the island, so large as really to afford a broad field for the missionary to work. If I am not mistaken, there were at one time as many as thirty missionaries here; but just as soon as the Chinese Empire was thrown open, the force moved on, and now the station is almost abandoned. Mr. Keasbury and Mr. Grant are the only missionaries whom I met. There are in the town of Singapore four Protestant churches, two of them Chinese; four Roman Catholic, of which two are also Chinese; one Armenian; one Jewish synagogue; three Mohammedan mosques; one Hindoo temple; one Chinese Buddhist temple, and some minor places of worship.

For its size, Singapore has the most conglomerate population of any city in the world, almost every nation being represented. The variety in costume and general appearance strikes the stranger at once. It was the more noticeable to us, coming from Japan and China, where the ordinary dress of the people is perfectly uniform, a dull blue cotton. The wharf, as we were leaving, was one of the gayest scenes that we have met with. A large crowd, in all the colors of the rainbow, occupied the bund. There were Jews and Jewesses elegantly dressed and glittering with jewels; Armenians, the ladies fine-looking and splendidly dressed; Mohammedans with large red turbans; Bengalese; Malays in all sorts of bright colors, and many of them in plain dark color, that in which they were born; then there were English, and French, and other Europeans in their own national costumes. Besides the people, there was a grand display of gay-colored birds for sale—parrots in green, crimson, scarlet, yellow, white, etc. While we were waiting for the steamer to be off, boys, who seem to belong to some amphibious tribe, amused the passengers by diving from boats for pieces of money thrown into the water, invariably catching them before they reached the bottom, which was six or eight fathoms below. In the midst of this variegated scene the order was given, and we were once more upon the sea.

We entered the Straits of Malacca, and had a quiet and pleasant voyage to Penang, which we reached early on the morning of the second day. As it was Saturday, the Jews and Jewesses on board had a long discussion in regard to the propriety of going ashore to spend the day, as it was their Sabbath. Some of them were really conscientious, but others were disposed to treat the question in a very Rabbinical way. One Jew maintained that they might go ashore, but not go out in carriages, as that would be contrary to the command, "*Seven* days shalt thou labor," etc., this being the form in which he repeated it, and according to which he had probably been most accustomed to observe the day. Another thought it right to ride on an elephant on the Sabbath, but not in a carriage. The result of the discussion was that some went on shore and spent the day as they chose, while others, more conscientious, remained on board and played cards for money.

Having a note of introduction to the Rev. Mr. Macdonald, an Independent missionary at Penang, I went ashore to present it. Calling at the bungalow of the chief commissioner of police to make some inquiry, we were very courteously received. He immediately ordered his carriage and sent an officer to take us to the residence of the missionary, where we spent the morning in very pleasant intercourse with those whom we had met as strangers. It was truly delightful to enjoy their Christian society on this other side of the world, and as pleasant to them, they assured us, to have a call from travelers who felt an interest in them and in their work for the Master's sake. Mr. Macdonald is the only missionary now at Penang, and his labors are distributed among the various races which compose the population of the town, among which, very strangely, the Chinese appear to be the most numerous. They occupy a separate portion of the city, forming a distinct community. The Celestials, indeed, are scattered through all the cities east of India. Even Calcutta has a large Chinese population. They are possessed of great enterprise, and, the population of China being so dense, the motive to emigration is strong. A few years since a fearful riot occurred among the Chinese at Penang, growing out of some of their clannish ideas. The whole community became involved in it, and it was not quelled until nearly a thousand lives were lost.

As our steamer was to lie all day at Penang, Mr. Macdonald proposed a drive through the town and into the country, a proposition which we were nothing loth to accept. The city itself is even more beautiful, at least some portions of it, than Singapore, and the country has the same luxuriant, tropical appearance, abounding in cocoanut groves, the cocoanut and betelnut being among the chief productions. During our drive we called upon a wealthy Mohammedan, Mahomet Noordin, the head of the Klings, who owns a large part of the native city of Penang. It was just after noon, and as we drove up to the doorway the servant said his master was asleep, and "no man was so brave as to disturb him between the hours of twelve and three." We insisted on his announcing our arrival, but he was resolute until I produced my card, and Mr. Macdonald, writing his own name on it, told him to take it to his master.

We waited a few moments, expecting him to return without having presented it, but some one had been brave enough to present the card, and we were shown into the private rooms of the chief, where he received us not only with cordiality, but with Oriental flattery. He expressed great delight at seeing us, and when we apologized for having disturbed his slumbers, he said "it made him very much happy to have a visit from us, but that if the lieutenant governor had called at that hour he would not have received him." He then led us into his public reception-room and ordered cheroots and wine, of which, being a Mohammedan, he could not partake, but he had it placed before us, each glass on an elegantly-chased silver salver. Mr. Macdonald at first declined to take wine, saying, "I am very much like the Mohammedans in one respect—I take very little wine." Mahomet Noordin immediately retorted with a hearty laugh at his own wit, "And I am very much like the Christians—I drink plenty of brandy and water." He talked very intelligently about America and of different Europeans whom he had met at Penang. He asked how long we were expecting to stay, and said if I would come to Penang and live he would give me a bungalow, with every thing that could make us comfortable, and that if I would stay for only a week he would have a house made ready for us, and that his horses and carriages should be at my command, all of which generous offers I was obliged to decline.

The old gentleman (for he was quite advanced in years) took us around his extensive house, pointed out one large building after another which he had gradually added to his home, and then pointing to one small house in the centre, in which he had first received us, a low and comparatively mean-looking building, said, "That was my father's house." Although he had added house to house, he still retained the paternal roof for his own home.

A mountain lying back of the city affords a magnificent view of the town, the country around it, and of the sea; but it requires the greater part of a day to make the ascent, and we had not time for the excursion. Besides, a heavy rain came on, in the midst of which we were obliged to make our way back to the steamer in an open boat, the boatmen embracing the occasion to demand an exorbitant fare. Soon after we had reached the steamer the wind increased, and, as the tide was running with great velocity, it was with immense difficulty that some of the passengers reached the steamer and got on board.

These tropical regions are as prolific of animal life as of vegetable. The most venomous snakes are quite at home in all these beautiful places, and they do not disdain an inviting bungalow for a residence. As we were driving through the city of Penang a house was pointed out to me in which the proprietor found, on coming home one day, two boa constrictors occupying his parlor and waiting to give him a warm embrace; but he declined the compliment, and chose to have them put out of the way.

We resumed our sail through the Straits of Malacca. On the third day out from Penang we passed a chain of islands which crop out occasionally from the sea, evidently a continuation into the ocean of the mountains of Burmah. This chain runs down to the island of Sumatra, and separates the Andaman Sea and the Gulf of Martaban from the Bay of Bengal, which we presently entered. The Andaman Islands are a penal settlement, to which the mutineers from India were sent to the number of several thousands. Some portions of the islands are said to be inhabited by cannibals, into whose hands and jaws some of the mutineers fell in making an attempt at escape.

The Bay of Bengal was like a mirror, and scarcely was the dying swell from a wave to be seen. The air was delightfully warm, and in the calmness which settled down over the sea great numbers of flying fish, tempted from their native element to try their wings in a lighter atmosphere, skimmed along the surface in flocks. Immense sea-turtles also came to the surface to sun themselves, and were not roused from their slumbers until we were just upon them. These waters are inhabited by snakes which sometimes reach a large size, very inconveniently making their way into cabin windows, or on deck when a stray rope hangs over the side by which they can work their way on board. We saw them, but happily had no visit from them on board. Some of our passengers took the precaution to close their ports, lest they should find in their cabins these unwelcome visitors.

While sailing up this sea we were often tantalized like the travelers in the desert, only they are deceived by what appears to be water, while we had the promise of land which never came in sight. I had never before seen a marine mirage, but for days the state of the atmosphere was such that we seemed to be approaching shores which loomed up in the distance. As we sailed on and on, the shores were ever as far off as at first, and ever as near, and finally they would fade away into air.

As we were drawing near the mouth of the Hoogly we began to meet the East Indiamen, homeward bound. Their occupation will soon be gone, now that steam is monopolizing not only the passenger, but the carrying trade of the ocean, especially if the Suez Canal should prove a success; but with all the speed and the modern appliances for luxury on the steamers of the present day, I do not doubt that there was more of comfort in some of the large East India ships which made the voyage around the Cape. The great drawback to comfort was the length of the voyage, but even this enabled those who had weak stomachs to become accustomed to the sea, and as "hanging is nothing when one gets used to it," so it is of the ceaseless rolling of the sea.

---

## XIV.

### CALCUTTA.

CALCUTTA is about a hundred miles from the mouth of the Hoogly, one of the outlets of the Ganges. The greater part of the distance up from the sea the banks of the river are a wild jungle, through which are scattered, sometimes in groves, the cocoanut and other palms, the whole vegetation having a strictly Oriental aspect. The banks of the stream are as flat as those of the Lower Mississippi. Near the mouth of the Hoogly stands a monument, sad as a memorial, and strikingly suggestive of adventures which are still to be met with in all parts of India. It marks the spot where a young lady once disappeared in the grasp of a tiger. A vessel from home was detained by the tide, and a number of passengers concluded to go ashore and while away the time by a stroll among the palms. One of the party strayed a little from the rest, when a scream was heard; they ran to her assistance, but only in time to see her carried off by one of the tigers that still infest the jungles, even in the vicinity of the towns.

As we approached the city of palaces, the signs of cultivation, and at length of Eastern wealth, became more frequent. For several miles the river on either hand was

ENTRANCE TO THE HOOGLY.

lined with rich plantations and costly residences. The palms, acacias, and other tropical trees were as fresh and vigorous as if it were not the third day of winter. About two miles below Calcutta, among many of the choice trees of the tropics, stands one of the finest specimens of the banyan tree in all India. I do not know the number of its trunks, but one of these trees is described as having three hundred and fifty large branches that have shot down and become rooted, forming three hundred and fifty large trees, and more than three thousand smaller ones, making from one tree, still joined together by its branches, an immense grove.

On the opposite shore is the palace of the ex-King of Oude, who was dethroned by the East India Company and brought to Calcutta as a sort of prisoner of state. He was allowed to retain a large portion of his wealth, and still has a princely, if not a royal revenue. His buildings are very beautiful, extending a long distance upon the river's bank. Among them was a temple, the dome of which was burnished gold, dazzling the eyes in the bright sunlight. We were detained several hours opposite his grounds waiting for orders from the Custom-house, and had abundance of time to study all the beauties of the place. Nothing in the ample grounds of the dethroned monarch attracted my attention like a small but beautiful kiosk which stood directly upon the river's bank. It was about twelve or fifteen feet square, with a dome-shaped roof; its sides were open, but grated with iron bars, and within was a royal Bengal tiger pacing up and down in all his majesty. I do not know whether the royal owner of the grounds designed this as a satire upon the power which had dethroned him and taken possession of his territory, but if so, it was, indeed, a biting satire.

The order from the Custom-house came at length, and we steamed up to the anchorage directly opposite Fort William, which stands upon a vast open plain, known as the Maidan, quite to the south of the city. As we approached the ghaut, or landing-place, we found gathered on the shore one of the most curious crowds that we ever beheld. All nations and all costumes appeared to be represented, the crimson garments of the Bengalese and Hindoo women predominating, while turbaned, and gowned, and trowsered men and women of all complexions and styles of dress filled up the picture. Awaiting us was a large fleet of native boats, manned by the most voracious cormorants that we have met with in any part of the world. Their shoutings and fightings, one with another, to secure the landing of our persons and our baggage (we were not fifty yards from the shore), would have silenced the builders of the towers of Babel. It became necessary for us to shout and fight as vigorously as they, in order to prevent our baggage from being carried off into a score of separate boats; but at length we were landed.

Then came another tug of war. Not one of the boatmen would carry the baggage up the bank to the gharries or carriages, about fifty feet distant, and the same process of fighting and shouting was renewed, the army of the Philistines in the mean while having increased as we reached the shore. I steadfastly refused, in the most vehement Orientalisms I could command, to pay one of them a single copper pie until I saw every thing on the gharries, by which time the number of clamorous creditors had still farther multiplied, and each one demanded enough for all, whether he had touched our baggage or not. Never before or since have I found it so hard to pay an honest debt, only because it was impossible to select from a crowd of rapacious Hindoos, who all looked as much alike as if they were the same man, those to whom the debt was actually due. At length, seeing that all was ready, I selected the one who was most violent in his demonstrations, handed him what I thought was right, motioned to the rest to get their dues from him, and, leaving him to be torn in pieces by the crowd, sprang into the gharry and was off for the hotel. I never learned whether the man survived the combined charge, but I could do no better. The longer I parleyed in English, the larger and more imperious the crowd of Hindoos became, and there was neither native nor English police to whom I could appeal.

Arrived at Spence's Hotel, we were provided with rooms after stipulating to give them up for the Duke of Edinburg and suite, who had engaged them for the following week. They were immense quarters, Oriental in style and accommodations. We were abundantly supplied with servants — four, and sometimes five, who seemed gifted with omnipresence, were always at hand to wait on two of us. With their dusky forms clothed from head to foot in white; moving about without shoes, noiselessly, and without uttering a word, they were like so many lost spirits, or like

Hindoos in grave-clothes. When waiting on us at our table they wore white muslin hats, with immense brims covered with the same material, and, excepting that they were clothed in white instead of drab, we should have fancied ourselves served by the spirits of some of the followers of George Fox or William Penn. As the shades of night came on, and we grew anxious to try the effect of sleeping on shore, we found it next to impossible to relieve ourselves of their presence. We signified to them, as well as we could, that their duties for the day were over, and that we were about to retire. We motioned them out of our quarters, and fancied that we had seen the last of them for the night, but scarcely had we turned around when the same dark ghosts in white stood before us. They had stolen, without a sound, through another door into the room, and were waiting for our orders, which were that they should disappear, and at length they did.

We were enjoying our first sleep on land, after many days and nights of tossing on the China Sea and the Bay of Bengal, when, just after midnight, we were roused by the most hideous screams that ever assailed our ears. The cries were not altogether human; they were inhuman, infernal. It seemed as if a legion of demons had broken loose from their confinement, with a commission to drive sleep from the pillows of Calcutta. As often as we attempted to quiet ourselves to rest, the same shrieks would startle us from our incipient dreams, until we gave up in despair, if not in terror. We could not form a conception of the nature of the beings from which they proceeded. In the morning we learned that it was the nightly serenade of jackals, which have the run of the streets after midnight, and which, if not protected by law, are perfectly safe from all harm, on account of the valuable service they render as public scavengers. They are quite harmless themselves, excepting their cries, which rob all new comers of sleep. They are never seen by day, skulking away into sewers and dark recesses, where they lie until they are summoned to make their round of the city. Nor was it in Calcutta alone that we heard them, but in every city in India that we visited during the winter, with the single exception of Bombay. Their cries, especially when a whole pack join together, approximate so near to the human, that I have heard it interpreted thus: A large pack of jackals start upon their nightly round in search of their appropriate food. Suddenly one in advance of the rest breaks out into a shrill, hideous scream, "Here's a dead Hindoo." The whole pack immediately scream, "Where? where? where?" A score of the ghouls answer with a short, shrill bark, "Here! here! here!" and then the whole crowd of jackals send up, in the otherwise still night, a howl over their discovery that may be heard for miles. This was the serenade that awakened us, and scarcely a night that we were in the country did they fail to send a thrill of horror through our souls.

The jackals are the night-scavengers of Calcutta. Those of the day are the crows, the kites, and the adjutants. The crows, as in all parts of India that I have visited, swarm throughout the city by myriads, keeping up an incessant "caw, caw, caw." They spend the night quietly on the trees, not much less than a thousand sometimes selecting a single tree, and taking an hour of fighting and shouting in concert before they become fairly settled for the night. Even after they have become quiet, and you imagine that at last their noise is over for the day, some dispute arises among them, and the whole thousand start up from the tree in violent altercation, and again go through the same course of fighting before they are settled again. Nor are they satisfied with the refuse of the city for a living; they come boldly into the open windows and lay their beaks upon any food that is within reach. The first morning that we were in Calcutta our breakfast had been set in the anteroom, but before we could lay claim to it the crows had entered, and, supposing it was intended for them, had made way with a good share of it. Once they took it before our very eyes, without so much as saying "By your leave." The kites, a species of large hawk, are not so numerous, but they are numbered by thousands, or tens of thousands, and are continually sailing over the city or along the streets, excepting when they see some tempting provisions, in which case they do not hesitate to swoop down and bear it off, even from the midst of a crowd of pedestrians or carriages. They have the freedom of the city in common with the crows. The adjutant, an immense stork, standing, in his stockings, as high as a man, belongs to the same army, and enjoys the same freedom, but he is a gentleman, carrying himself with as much dignity in his daily walks as if he were a major general instead of a mere adjutant, and never intruding where he does not belong. Much of the time he stands on one leg, with his neck drawn down into his body and his immense visor closed, in a meditative mood, and so perfectly motionless that you might easily mistake him for a bronze statue. The snakes form a part of his rations. The residents of Calcutta seem as unconscious of the existence of the crows, the kites, and the adjutants, and even of the jackals, as if such specimens in natural history were never heard of within a thousand miles of the city.

Calcutta may be called the European capital of Asia. It has been the seat of British empire for more than a century, and the centre of British influence for the whole East. Its commercial supremacy is probably well-nigh ended since steam and the opening of the Suez Canal have changed the route of commerce between Europe and the East. Bombay is now the port of India, as Calcutta is thrown more than ever off the great highway to China. But no other city will ever have such a combination of Oriental and Occidental grandeur as the "City of Palaces," the name it bears in the East. The name is not unmerited, although we do not find either the architectural beauty of the West, or the lavish expenditure of the old dynasties of the East. It was founded by the East India Company near the close of the seventeenth century, on the site of a small village called Kali-kutta (the village of the Goddess Kali), from which the present name of the city is derived. A temple of the goddess, south of the city, is still frequented by multitudes of devotees at the period of the annual worship. The official name of the city, from which public documents, I believe, are dated even to the present day, although executed at the Government House a mile distant, is Fort William. The fort was erected in the reign of William III. of England, and named from this sovereign. It is an extensive fortress, standing in the midst of the Maidan, a vast open plain extending more than two miles up and down the Hoogly, south of the city. The northern portion of the Maidan, known as the Esplanade, is occupied by the government buildings, which front upon a well-kept park known as the Eden Gardens. The viceroy's palace occupies the most conspicuous site, and, although possessing no great architectural beauty, is an imposing pile.

The portion of the Maidan bordering on the river for a mile below the Government House is the great fashionable drive of Calcutta, answering to the Prater of Vienna, or Rotton Row in Hyde Park. Every evening, just before sunset, when the heat of the day has passed, all Calcutta turns out for an hour's drive up and down the strand. The sight is one of the gayest to be seen in the suburbs of any city, and one of the most peculiar. Nowhere in the East is there any thing to equal it, and nowhere in the West any thing like it. Europeans with gay equipages, from the viceroy's scarlet and gold, with his Sepoy outriders, down to the unpretending gharry, move on in a steady line, three or four abreast, until night comes on. Notwithstanding the occupants of the carriages are chiefly Europeans, the scene is decidedly Oriental. Coachmen and footmen, some of them splendid specimens of the various tribes of India, are all in Eastern costume, the colors and style of which are as varied as the races of Hindostan. The wealthy Baboos have their place in the grand procession, and when we were in Calcutta there was a grand gathering of Rajahs and native princes from all parts of India, who had come down to meet the Duke of Edinburg and take part in the durbar at Government House. One who would study Oriental life should not fail to be on the strand at Calcutta an hour before sunset.

The residences of the merchants, and those connected with the civil and military service, are east of the Maidan, the whole of this part of Calcutta being known as Chowringee. The dwellings, many of which may in truth be called palaces, though not architecturally beautiful, are isolated, standing in the midst of squares, and surrounded by a profusion of the ornamental trees and shrubs of India. The suburbs of the city toward the south, in the direction of the palace and grounds of the ex-King of Oude, stretch out into the region of the palms, acacias, mango, bamboo, and peepul trees, which grow with great luxuriance of foliage. In tropical countries leaves often take the place of branches. The stately palm, the glory of the tropics, is as destitute of limbs as the mast of a ship, but a single leaf is fifteen or twenty feet in length, and each tree is crowned with a drooping mass. Such a tree has no need of branches. In the palm-clad suburbs of Calcutta stands the country house of Warren Hastings, where that brilliant though erring statesman, the governor general of India, maintained a splendid hospitality. The place is now among the historic scenes of the East; but one can not recall the events connected with his rule and conquests, even in the midst of the prosperity of India, without a long-drawn sigh.

There are few public buildings of much note. The Government House, built by the Marquis of Wellesley, and the new government offices on the Esplanade, are the most imposing. The post-office is a large and fine building, erected in part on the site of one more memorable in history than any other within the limits of the city or in this part of India. It is the "Black Hole of Calcutta." In the year 1756 Fort William was taken by Surajah Dowlah, Nabob of Bengal, a feeble garrison being left to defend it after the governor and others had escaped to the ships. The prisoners, 146 in number, were thrust into a room only eighteen feet square, with two small, obstructed windows, where, in the intense heat of a Calcutta night, on the 18th of June, they were shut up without water or any means of relief. With heat, and thirst, and suffocation, many of them became maddened, and the horrors of that night never can be depicted. Bribes, and prayers, and the raging of despair were all ineffectual to move the hearts of the guard. In vain the prisoners, in the agonies of thirst and of suffocation, entreated to have the nabob informed of their condition; they were told that he was asleep, and could not be disturbed. In the morning twenty-three ghastly forms had just life enough left to crawl from the room when it was opened; the rest, 123, were piled upon the floor, putrid corpses. No scene connected with Calcutta is more indelibly graven on the memory of the world than this; but all traces of it are obliterated from the spot by the erection of new and stately buildings.

The new Cathedral, the seat of the bishopric which has been held by such apostolic names as those of Heber and Wilson, is a fine building, it may be called elegant, finished as it is with such admirable taste and in such beauty. It is already becoming filled with monumental marbles, among which the statue of Bishop Heber is the most striking. There are several fine churches, English and Scotch. The college buildings of the Free Church, and the Scotch Kirk, are worthy of note for their extent, if not for their beauty. The Bishop's College, on the right bank of the Hoogly, two miles below the city, makes more pretension to taste and elegance.

The native and the European quarters of the town are distinct, the former having very narrow streets and more or less of squalor in its whole extent, but the portion occupied by foreigners (Europeans have no native-born descendants of pure blood in India) is laid out upon a broad scale, and built up with appropriate magnificence.

The city is supplied with water from immense tanks, reservoirs of one or two hundred feet square sunk into the ground, but left entirely open. The natives walk down into them, bathe their bodies and wash their clothes, and then fill their jars or goatskins with the water for drinking and other domestic use. This is a specimen of native cleanliness.*

The streets are watered by a truly Oriental method. Each waterman has, instead of a cart, a goatskin taken off entire, and forming an immense bottle, left open at the neck. This is suspended by a strap over the shoulders of the coolie, who seizes the neck with one hand, and, as he walks along, deftly throws the water hither and thither. Large numbers of these coolies are kept constantly employed spirting the streets, which are as well watered by this method as by our own.

Of the institutions of Calcutta, one of the first that claim-

---

* The following, from an India paper, is a specimen of Hindoo metaphysics, and also of the stress that is laid upon ceremonial uncleanness above actual filth.

"At the last meeting of the Sanatana-Dharma Rakshami Sabha, the president, Rajah Kali Krishna Deo Bahadoor, read an opinion on the water supplied to the Calcutta residents from the municipal water-works. He says that the water, being destitute of the sanctity of the Ganges, can not be used for religious purposes, but can be employed for drinking or domestic use without prejudice to caste. Rice, milk, turmeric, and other things become pure by boiling, and can be used by virtue of the authority that says that edible articles become purified by purchase. The water-rate may be considered in the light of value paid, and the water become drinkable. Besides, it is written in the *Satatapa vachana* that articles prepared in a cow-shed by a shopman or by a machine, though not purified, are not considered unclean; also that fluid, as in a running stream, is considered pure. The *Shruti* says that health is most important, and that religion comes next; and as water is called *jivana*, or life-giver, and as good, pure water preserves health, the fluid can be used without detriment to caste. The great bulk of water is also a test of purity in the same way, as a number of persons in a boat does not affect purity. The president farther states that he visited the water-works in company with several respectable Hindoos, and examined the machinery, and found that India-rubber, and not leather, as was supposed, is used in certain parts of the machine; cocoanut oil is used to lubricate the works, and that no forbidden substance is used in connection with the pumps. He concludes by submitting to the other members of the Sabha his opinion that the water is wholesome, and that it would be unwise to remain in doubt and sustain loss by not using the same."

ed a visit was Dr. Duff's College, as the great Free Church of Scotland Institution is called. Although it is many years since Dr. Duff was compelled to leave India by the failure of his health, his indomitable energy and ardent spirit having worn out his comparatively feeble frame in that trying climate, his name still adheres to the college which he founded and brought to a high state of prosperity. He came to India in 1830, and began his educational work with a class of five scholars, which, in a few days, increased to more than a hundred. It soon became necessary to have permanent accommodations for those who were coming in such numbers to receive instruction in Western science, which is quite as different from Oriental science as the fact that the earth revolves around the sun is in advance of the idea that the sun revolves around the earth, or that the earth stands on a tortoise. A site for a college was selected on Cornwallis Square, one of the pleasantest quarters of the city, extensive buildings were erected, a corps of teachers was supplied by the Church at home, and as many as eight hundred scholars were going through a course of instruction.

When the institution had reached this advanced stage, the disruption took place in the Church of Scotland, and the Free Church was organized. The result was that the missionaries, to a man, decided to go with the Free Church. They followed the example of the Free Church ministers at home, who gave up churches and manses, and began their work anew. They abandoned the mission property, and every thing connected with the college, to lay another foundation. It was but a few years before the new college numbered nearly fourteen hundred pupils, while the old, which had, in the mean time, been supplied with fresh men from the Kirk of Scotland, had nearly as many. The number has fallen off considerably within the last few years, owing perhaps to the founding of other schools by the government and by private munificence. These institutions are open to students of all religions, and the mass-of them are Hindoos or Mohammedans. Only in rare instances have they renounced the faith of their fathers, while fewer still have become real Christians.

It is not the desire to become acquainted with Christian truth, much less to become Christians, that induces so many youth to crowd these foreign seminaries of learning. They are anxious to become qualified to fill the various lucrative posts which, in connection with the civil service, and the commerce and business of the country, are open to the natives. This is the great stimulus to study, and a successful course and an honorable graduation in the missionary, as well as in the government colleges, is usually a passport to a good situation. But this army of educated men may yet be brought into the Church of Christ, in that great religious revolution that is to pass over India, the promise of which we have in the Word of God, and the signs of which are to be seen all over the land.

The Bishop's College, occupying a fine Gothic building, beautifully situated on the botanic garden or park, on the banks of the Hoogly, two or three miles below the city, has a more limited class of students. It was founded by Bishop Middleton in 1820 for the purpose of training up, under the discipline of the Church of England, a corps of preachers and teachers, to be employed by that Church in disseminating the truths of the Gospel in India. The number of students is small, but the arrangements for their education in the languages of the East, and in general literature and science, are very extensive.

Besides the institutions I have named, there are several others of a high order. Among these are Doveton College, founded, I believe, by a man whose name it bears; the Martinière, founded by General Martin, who amassed a large fortune in the East, and who established a college at Lucknow; the Sanscrit College; the Hundu College; the Mohammedan, etc. There is also a medical college, with a large corps of able professors, at the head of which is Dr. Joseph Fayrer, a distinguished surgeon of the British army, who was at Lucknow during the memorable siege, and in whose arms the commanding officer, Sir Henry Lawrence, breathed his last. A large hospital, which I visited in company with Mr. Duff, an eminent merchant of Bombay, and son of the Rev. Dr. Duff, is under the charge of this faculty. Dr. Fayrer has been engaged, by a series of experiments upon animals, in endeavoring to discover an antidote to the venom of the snakes that abound in India, by which thousands of lives are lost annually, but thus far without success.

The Asiatic Society, located at Calcutta, was originated and established by that eminent scholar and Christian, Sir William Jones, who went out to India in 1783. Having been appointed to the bench of the Supreme Court of Bengal, he devoted himself with intense ardor to the study of the languages of the East as the means of fitting himself for usefulness in India. He is said to have acquired in the course of his life twenty-eight different languages, and to have become familiar with the literature of each. It was he who gave the noble testimony to the Bible, all the more weighty because coming from one whose professional pursuits were not theological, and who was also so well qualified by his eminent learning to bear such testimony: "I have carefully and regularly perused the Scriptures, and am of opinion that this volume, independent of its divine origin, contains more sublimity, purer morality, more important history, and finer strains of eloquence than can be collected from all other books, in whatever language they may be written." The Asiatic Society, which he founded, and of which Warren Hastings was the first president, was formed for the purpose of preserving the history and the memorials of India and the East generally. It has now an immense collection of volumes, and manuscripts, and specimens in natural history, and relics of all sorts. The large building in which they have been kept was long since overflowing, so that it was found necessary to store the additions elsewhere. An extensive range of buildings on the

Chowringee Road was approaching completion when I left Calcutta, and when it is opened it will be one of the most interesting museums in the world. I máde the acquaintance of the scholarly superintendent, who expressed an earnest desire to establish some system of exchanges with similar institutions in this Western world.

Excepting in what is known as the Zenana Mission, the Americans are not represented among the institutions of Calcutta; but that work is one of great importance, and in India is absolutely essential as the complement of Christian missions. It is not altogether new, but in its specific form was undertaken only ten years since by the "Woman's Union Missionary Society of America for Heathen Lands," whose head-quarters in India are at Calcutta, under the superintendence of Miss Hook, a lady of rare culture and refinement, and of great energy of character. Their field of operation is the zenanas, the homes of the women of India. Of course I was not able personally to observe the prosecution of this work, but I became familiar with its character and prospects, and was happy to learn that it is full of promise. The ladies of the mission, who go out daily among the zenanas, are cordially received, and many of the wealthy natives express an earnest desire that their wives may be instructed.

There is no spot in India more sacred in the eyes of the Christian world than Serampore, beautifully situated on a bend of the Hoogly, about fifteen miles from the city of Calcutta. Every one who is at all familiar with the history of missions in the East knows how intimately this place is associated with the names of the earliest and some of the best men that have gone out to preach the Gospel in Asiatic countries. In the beginning of the present century it was the cave in which the prophets were hid when they were forbidden to preach in British India. Being a Danish possession, it was not under the control of the East India Company, and here Carey and Ward set themselves down to study the languages of the East. Here they planted their printing-presses, and from this spot they sent forth millions of pages of Christian truth into all parts of Asia and the Islands of the Sea. Here, too, the apostle Judson, several years later, found a temporary refuge when he was forbidden to land at Calcutta, as if he and his companions from America had conspired against the peace of the country.

The history of Carey and his labors is known the world over. He was born in a small interior town in England. His parents, being poor, apprenticed him at the age of fourteen to a shoemaker, whose trade he seems never to have mastered; for, in after years, when dining at the governor general's in India, as he overheard some supercilious Englishmen speak of him as a shoemaker, he turned and corrected him, saying he was only a cobbler. (On his deathbed he was ministered to by the wife of the Governor General of India, and the Bishop of Calcutta came to ask his dying blessing.) While learning his trade in England, he indulged his thirst for knowledge by a course of reading, and at length turned his attention to languages, and enlarged his field of study, until he became a well-read Biblical scholar, and at length was licensed to preach the Gospel in the Baptist connection. In reading the accounts of Cook's voyages around the world he was deeply moved in heart toward the heathen, and stirred up his brethren with his own zeal until they resolved on a mission to the pagan world, and Carey himself was sent. On arriving in India he was obliged to conceal himself from the knowledge of the East India Company, whose policy was altogether opposed to efforts for the conversion of the natives. For many years he labored in great seclusion, supporting himself by working on an indigo plantation. In the year 1800 he was joined by Marshman and Ward, from England, when they established themselves under Danish protection at Serampore. They seemed almost to be endued with the gift of tongues, so successfully did they devote themselves to the acquisition of languages and to the translation of the Word of God into the numerous tongues of the East. They established presses on which the Word of God was printed in languages spoken by at least half the pagan world. They laid the foundation for a college of a high order, and erected for it a building which even now is regarded as one of the finest structures of its kind in India. They procured a choice and extensive library, which is still a rich repository of learning and a monument to their own enlarged ideas and acquisitions.

A great part of the expense of these enterprises they bore themselves. It is wonderful that a few poor missionaries could do such a work; but they were earnest men of genius, and they lived not unto themselves. Dr. Carey received for thirty years more than a thousand rupees a month (equal to $6000 a year) for his services as professor in the College of Fort William, at Calcutta, and translator to the East India Company; Mr. Ward received as much more from the printing-office, and Mr. and Mrs. Marshman about the same from teaching; and yet, while they were receiving these princely sums, they ate at a common table, and drew from the common fund only twelve rupees each, or four dollars a month. The remainder was devoted, by a mutual contract, to the purposes of the mission, and was employed in spreading the Gospel. The cost of the Chinese version alone, which they prepared and printed, was 20,000 pounds sterling, or $100,000. The words of the agreement which they signed when they entered on their work were, "Let us give ourselves up unreservedly to this glorious cause. Let us never think that our time, our gifts, our strength, our families, or even the clothes we wear, are our own. Let us sanctify them all to God and his cause." Now that life's labor is over, these devoted men sleep together on the spot consecrated by their many years of toil in the service of the Master.

Here, too, Henry Martyn, of blessed memory, lived for a time and studied, fitting himself for his short but important life-service in India and Persia. Nor is this spot without special interest for Americans. When the first band of missionaries from our own country to the East reached India, this was the only spot in all the land in which they could find a resting-place even for a day.

All these associations were so many powerful attractions, and I gladly accepted an invitation from Dr. George Smith, the accomplished and learned editor of the *Friend of India*, to visit him at his home at Serampore. I found him awaiting me at the station, and we drove first to the cemetery, known as the Westminster Abbey of India, where Carey, and Marshman, and Ward were buried. Carey wrote his own epitaph, which is inscribed on a plain cenotaph:

WILLIAM CAREY:<br>
BORN 17TH OF AUGUST, 1761,<br>
DIED 9TH OF JUNE, 1834.<br>
"A wretched, poor, and helpless worm,<br>
On Thy kind arms I fall."

I visited the college where those prophets taught; I stood in the pulpit where Carey preached, and saw the room in which Marshman died. Dr. Smith pointed out to me the site of the pagoda in which Henry Martyn devoted himself with such assiduity and success to the study of the languages in which he afterward preached the Gospel. The college building is still in excellent repair, and the library was most tempting in its choice collection of books, among which I would fain have lingered. But, as elsewhere, I suffered from the bane of travelers, want of time, and I could not linger in any of the many interesting scenes in which I found myself.

We drove out to the grounds of a wealthy Baboo to witness a Hindoo festival that had been in progress two or three days, and which was then at its height. It was in honor of some one of the multitude of gods which the Hindoos reverence, but in the form of an entertainment for the people, who had come together in great numbers in holiday attire. In various places by the roadside and in booths, or under canopies, were groups of statuary formed from the plastic mud of the Ganges, which is superior to the finest statuary clay. Some of the groups were in caricature, but others were perfectly life-like, evincing real genius in the extemporaneous artists. In a large inclosure, separated from the crowd of natives, a sort of musical drama was in progress, the music and the words appearing improvised, but falling on the ear with pleasing effect. Every thing was conducted with strict decorum, and the whole scene, as I witnessed it for a few moments while the shades of evening were falling—its perfect novelty, its strictly and strangely Oriental features, and its surroundings of bamboos, and palm-trees, and other tropical vegetation—formed a picture which can not easily be forgotten. Crossing the Hoogly to Barrackpore, and passing through the grove of an immense banyan-tree, I reached the station of the East-side Railway, and was shortly in Calcutta again.

## XV.

### GOVERNMENT OF INDIA; EUROPEANS, ETC.

The Hindoos claim for their country and nation an antiquity which ought to satisfy the most enthusiastic advocates of the long geologic periods. They make it out that things have been going on somewhat after the present order for indefinite ages—four or five thousand millions of years; that in the early days of their race people used to live a hundred thousand years; that they were the matter of thirty-five or forty feet in height, etc.; but the records of those ancient times are not very authentic. Nothing satisfactory is known either of the country or the people before Alexander the Great crossed the mountain barrier on the north and extended his arms onward toward the peninsula. This was a little more than three hundred years before the Christian era. From that time to the present we have records more or less authentic, first of the Hindoo rule of about thirteen centuries, and then of the Mohammedan, including the reign of the Mogul emperors, exceeding in splendor all that the world has seen out of Hindostan, and reaching down to the complete occupation of the country by British power.

It was the wealth of the Mogul dynasty which first led European cupidity to turn its eyes toward the East. The discovery of the passage to India around the Cape of Good Hope, six years after the discovery of America by Columbus, opened up the whole of India to the commerce of Europe. In the year 1600 a commercial company was chartered in England under the name of the East India Company, which continued to increase in power, and to extend the objects and limits of its sway, until it had taken possession of all India; and at length was compelled to turn it over completely to the crown of Britain. The East India Company, which had been a mine of wealth and an engine of almost unlimited power to its corporators, was abolished by act of Parliament in 1858, the year after the great mutiny, having been gradually shorn of its privileges and power by the same authority in successive renewals of its charter. Its immense wealth and power may be inferred from the fact that its gross revenue for the year 1850 was £135,000,000, or nearly $675,000,000. Its expenditures were at a corresponding rate.

The Empire of India, which includes a number of provinces or presidencies such as Bengal, Bombay, Madras, etc., and extends over a territory of a million and a half square miles, with a population of two hundred millions of people, is now administered by a viceroy, or governor general, who has under him, in the several provinces, governors, lieutenant governors, and commissioners, some of the native princes retaining a semi-independent position in their own territories. All the great native rulers were dethroned and their territory appropriated in the conquests made by British arms.

For two centuries and a half India was ruled for the benefit of the East India Company. This was a commercial enterprise, undertaken for the sole purpose of making gain; it did not pretend to establish itself for the purpose of doing good to the inhabitants of India; trade, and gold, and diamonds were the objects sought, while the welfare of two hundred millions of people was among the last things considered. Even the claims of religion, humanity, and justice were too often treated as if they had no binding force in that longitude. Not the splendors of successive conquests of territory from native kings and princes, nor the brilliant administration of such men as Warren Hastings, can blind the world to the wrongs and crimes which marked the progress of British empire in the East. It is in many respects a dark record, unworthy of a Christian or a noble people. But that is all changed since the East India Company was abolished, or, if not *all*, the purpose and the general administration of the government is changed. India is now ruled, not for the sake of extorting money from an unwilling, subjugated race, but for the good of the people of India.

It is with great pleasure that I bear testimony to the high character of the men who have the administration of affairs in that empire, as well as to the promising aspect of the country in its material, educational, social, and religious interests, as being full of promise. I doubt if any country has more conscientious and intelligent public officers controlling its destinies. There are reforms yet to be consummated. The extreme caution of the rulers prevents them from taking the bold stand assumed by the home government in favor of Christianity and against some of the enormities of idolatry and heathenism; many evils growing out of the peculiarities of the people, the variety of races, the inveterate nature of hoary prejudices, yet remain to be removed or remedied; but, judging from the promise of the present, India bids fair to become again a mighty empire in the East, and to outshine in real glory the splendor of the old Moguls.

The viceroyalty of India is the highest office under the British crown, and, considering the extent of its sway, and the population over which it is exercised, is the most important delegated office in the world. The power is not as absolute as was that of the governor general in the palmy days of the East India Company. Being directly responsible to the home government, the viceroy is under statutory checks; general legislative power also is in the hands of councils, provincial and general, so that a uniform and complete system of government, and one which might be called constitutional, extends over the whole of India. The outward dignity of government is maintained by a liberal provision for its support. The viceroy has a salary of £25,000 (five times that of the President of the United States), with as much or more for incidental expenses; an extensive palace and complete establishment at Calcutta, with provision for a country residence and a summer capital on the Himalaya Mountains, to which the governor general and the supreme council remove during the hot season.

The salaries of officials in India are generally large, and the immense army of office-holders employed in all the departments of government, the revenues for their payment being drawn from the country itself, makes this possession one of incalculable value and importance to Great Britain. It is the source from which a large representation of the higher and middle classes obtain their support. The younger sons of the aristocracy who can not be maintained in affluence, and a large force of others who are able to obtain appointments, are sent to India to fill the offices in the various branches of the military or civil service. There is a charm about Oriental life which makes it attractive. The pay is liberal. Some officials receive enormous salaries, with the promise of pensions after the term of service has expired; and at the end of seven years, as a rule, officers high and low have a furlough of a year on half pay, with the expenses of a journey homeward paid.

This rule, in the form of a custom, extends even to clerks in banks and other private corporations. It is not strange, therefore, that India is regarded at home as a sort of El Dorado.

I have spoken of the great change which has come over the administration of affairs in India since it became more directly dependent upon the British crown. The change is noticeable every where, but in no respect more than in the extent and thoroughness of the educational work carried on by the government. I was aware that a system of public instruction had been organized, and that institutions of learning had been established at various points, but I was not prepared to find that these institutions were of such a high order; that so many of the youth of India, Hindoo and Mohammedan, were enjoying and profiting by these advantages, or that such liberal provision was made by the government for their support and for general education. Within the last ten years the progress of the work has been rapid. The appropriations for this object by the government for the year previous to my arrival in the country amounted to nearly nine millions of rupees, or more than $4,000,000. This was distributed over the whole of the empire, so that every school conforming to the requisitions of government received its share.

A University is established in each of the three presidencies of Bengal, Bombay, and Madras. These are examining bodies only, but colleges and schools of various grades are established in all the different provinces. In Calcutta alone there are eleven colleges of a high order, including the institutions of the Kirk and Free Church of Scotland, the students of which, on completing their course of study, appear before the University on examination for their degrees. In Lower Bengal there are five colleges, and in the northwest provinces and the Punjaub, seven. There are, besides, similar institutions in Bombay and Madras. These colleges are all thoroughly equipped with professorships filled by scholars who have had a university

P

education at home, some of them men eminent for their attainments, and have all the appliances for a complete education in the arts, sciences, and languages. In the year above referred to there were, in the colleges and schools taught, aided, or inspected by the state, 662,537 scholars. These were, with very few exceptions, natives.

Too much attention and too large a proportion of the appropriations have been devoted to the higher institutions, without suitable provision for the education of the masses. One reason for this is, that it has been the policy of the government to educate native youth for its own service in the various departments of civil life, and for this purpose mainly the colleges were originally founded; but, now that so large a number have enjoyed these advantages, it would accord with the general policy of the government to elevate the people by diffusing the blessings of a sound education. Such a course, I believe, is to be pursued. A general system of schools for the country, approaching our own public-school system, has been under consideration, and will probably soon be adopted.

The standard objection against the government schools and colleges of India is that they are not Christian in their character; that the course of instruction has tended rather to favor than to oppose idolatry. There is too much ground for the objection; but, after becoming more familiar with the character of the people, and with the peculiar circumstances of the government, I could better appreciate the difficulties of establishing a system which should be avowedly hostile to the religious convictions of the people. It is not considered as the province of our own government to teach religion in its public schools, and there are difficulties in India in the way of teaching Christianity through governmental institutions of which we know nothing. Since being in India I look with more hope than before to the results of the work of education which is carried on by the government. It must aid in the overthrow of idolatry, and of other forms of false religion which have so long prevailed in the land. Many, it is true, become infidels on becoming convinced of the absurdity of the science which has formed a part of their own religious systems, but this may be only a transition state, not unnatural as the effect of correct scientific instruction without the pervading and prevailing influence of Christian conviction. This conviction must come from a higher source than mere human instruction.

The general attitude of the government toward the systems of idolatry has undergone an entire change. The time was, and not many years ago, when the East India Company derived a large revenue from the temples and places of pilgrimage for devotees; when English soldiers were compelled to bow down and do reverence before the false gods for the sake of securing the favor or avoiding the hostility of the natives. A long indictment was recorded against the former rulers of the land, and they were convicted not only of wickedness, but of folly, when, in the great mutiny of 1857, the very men whose favor they had courted became their deadliest enemies; and when, from the beginning to the end of the rebellion, not a single Christian convert in the land was known to lift his hand or give any information against the English. The authorities have learned wisdom and righteousness by this terrible experience.*

---

* Meadows Taylor, in his History of India, speaking of the administration of Lord Auckland, says:

"All connection between the English government of India and Hindoo temples and their idolatrous ceremonies was abolished under imperative orders from the Court of Directors and the Board of Control. All revenues derivable from these sources were abandoned, and the temples and their endowments placed under the management of their own priests. It will hardly now be credited how much honor had used to be accorded to idols and their worship before this most necessary exactment of April 20, 1840. Up to this time troops had been paraded at festivals, salutes fired, and offerings by the Company presented to idol deities, and the European functionary of the district was obliged, often most unwillingly, to take a part in heathen ceremonies originally conceded to conciliate the people, but which had grown by usage into a portion of the ceremonies themselves. It is still stranger to record that it was not till the lapse of years that a final disseverance from and abandonment of pilgrim taxes was effected."

The European population of India, of whom the natives of the British Isles form by far the largest part, is about 160,000. They are chiefly engaged in the public service, military and civil, although in the principal cities there is a large mercantile population. There are very few Europeans in India who were born there, and scarcely one whose parents were natives of the country. From a remote period the children of English or Scotch parents have been sent home, not merely to be educated away from the evil associations of the land, but to be raised in a more healthful climate. Children of foreign parents are more exposed to the injurious influences of the climate than those who come to India in adult years. It was mentioned to me also as a singular fact, that women born in India of European parents seldom become mothers, a proof of the deleterious effect of the climate upon the constitution; consequently one rarely sees children in the families of the foreign residents, or much more rarely than in other countries. They have either not been born, or they have been sent home. The trial which missionaries have been called so often to endure in sending their children from the home circle and from parental care is one which is shared by a large part of the foreign residents, who are engaged either in the public service or in mercantile business.

There is another class, the children of European fathers and native mothers, called Eurasians, East-Indians, Half-castes, etc., numbering about 80,000. Being a sort of connecting link between the two races, they are commonly acquainted with the foreign and the native languages; many of them have had special advantages of education, and many of them occupy positions of usefulness, as clerks or agents of the government. They are easily distinguished by their European features from the natives, and, being almost as dark as the natives, are never confounded with Europeans. They are not reputed to possess the same mental or physical vigor, or to have as much enterprise of character as foreigners.

During the hot season all business requiring active exertion is crowded as much as possible into the early morning, especially if it makes exposure to the sun necessary. The army-drill is over by eight or nine o'clock, traveling is done by night, and during the middle of the day the struggle for existence is most wisely managed by ceasing the struggle altogether, and giving one's self up to perfect quiet. The slightest exercise instantly produces violent perspiration, and the same effect follows the suspension of the *punka*. The *punka* is a broad fan suspended overhead, and usually stretching across the room; in the dining-room reaching the length of the table. It is moved by coolies in an ante-room, who, by means of a cord attached to the *punka*, draw it back and forth. Every private house, every place of business, and every assembly-room is supplied with this indispensable requisite. The churches have immense *punkas* suspended over the heads of the congregations, which wave back and forth majestically during the entire service. The first time that I was called upon to address a congregation through such a medium, I found it far less suggestive of ideas and suitable emotions than if I had been speaking to the people face to face. But even the heat of a church would be unendurable without the *punkas*. They are quite as essential at night in the homes during the hot season. No sleeping can be done without them. Nor are they such a severe tax upon the coolies as might be supposed. The coolies are paid for the service; it is their only support; they luxuriate in the heat as do the natives of Africa, and they have their time for rest. Few natives of any country in the East die of hard work.

Europeans in India live much more freely in respect to eating and drinking than is generally supposed to be consistent with such a climate, but it may be that the waste of the human system demands a generous supply to repair it. I have never been in any land where free indulgence within the bounds of temperance was more generally the rule. Foreign residents rise early all the year round, and take a cup of tea, with toast, or some light food, immediately on rising. This is called *chota hazril,* or the little breakfast. About nine or ten o'clock comes the real breakfast, usually an elaborate meal of fish, eggs, and some preparation of rice, with meats. At one o'clock *tiffin,* a still more hearty meal, is taken, and at seven or eight o'clock dinner, which is the meal of the day, and which is much after the pattern of an English or American dinner. This generous style of living seems to agree with the people; for, instead of the yellow or dark-skinned, shrunken, liver-diseased race that I expected to see, I found the gentlemen robust and rosy-faced, to my great astonishment, and the ladies equally well favored. (I speak of health, not of beauty, for in this respect the ladies always and every where bear the palm.) They assured us that we found them at their best, in the midst of the cool season, when they were luxuriating in a genial temperature; but, from the general aspect of the foreign residents, I felt convinced that India had been greatly belied, or that foreigners had learned how to adapt themselves to its climate better than in years past.

The subdivision of labor is carried in India to its very utmost limit. Every servant has his own sphere, and it would be about as difficult to move him from it as to turn one of the planets from its orbit. It almost reaches the point that one servant who takes up an article must have another to lay it down for him. This necessitates the employment of a large number to do the work of a household. Fortunately, the rate of wages is very low, or it would require a fortune to live at all. A family, however small, living in any style, must have a *kansuma,* a butler or steward; *kitmutgar,* a head table-servant, besides a table-servant for every member of the family; *bobagee,* or cook; *meeta,* man-sweeper; *metrane,* female sweeper; *musalche,* to clean knives and wash dishes; *surdar,* head bearer, with eight common bearers if he keeps a palanquin, to pull punka, etc.; *durwan,* gate-keeper; *dobey,* washerman; *bheestie,* to bring water; *abdar,* to cool the water; *chuprasse,* a confidential messenger; *coolies*, to carry marketing and other burdens; *chokedar*, watchman; if he keeps a carriage he must have a *gharry-walla*, or coachman, with a *syce*, or groom, for each horse, who runs with the horse; and so on, almost without end. Some of the servants must be Mohammedans, for the Hindoos will not touch certain dishes, and the Mohammedans, on the other hand, have their antipathies in household service which must be consulted.

Among the chief objections to a residence in India is the extreme heat during the greater part of the year. Frost seldom occurs south of the Nerbudda, and even in the far north the winter season is known as such only by the cool nights. This season is very short, and from March to June the heat increases with great intensity. Hot scorching winds prevail, the earth becomes parched, and vegetation withers. Nor is the degree of heat graduated by the latitude, excepting that it is more intense in the extreme north than in the central or southern parts. The great plain of Hindostan suffers most. I was informed by a gentleman who has resided near the Himalaya Mountains, on the plain, for thirty years, that he had often seen the thermometer for weeks standing at midday in the shade at 110, 120, and 130, and at night it seldom falls, during the hot season, below 90 or 100. This would be almost insupportable but for the punkas, which are kept moving night and day. The mountains and the high table-lands afford a refuge, like "the shadow of a great rock in a weary land," to those who are able to remove. In June, when the heat is at its greatest, the clouds pile up, and the southeast monsoon bursts upon the land, attended with terrific storms of thunder and lightning, and torrents of rain. Every thing becomes saturated or swollen with moisture, as it was parched and warped with heat before. This rainy season is not of long continuance, and under the influence of the succeeding heat the land bursts forth into vegetation, which advances, under occasional rains, with wonderful rapidity and beauty. The southeastern coast is not reached by the monsoons until late in the year.

The quantity of water that falls in the rainy season varies greatly in different localities, according to distance from the coast and the mountains, the sea and the low marshy lands supplying moisture which the mountains condense. Sometimes a short distance makes a vast difference in the rainfall. At Bombay the average fall in the year is about 75 inches; on the Ghauts, south of Bombay, it is 254 inches; while a little farther inland, at Poonah, over the mountains, it is only 23 inches. According to the same authority, the fall of rain on the Khasia hills is 600 inches, fifty feet. This immense fall of water is attributed to the passing of the air from the sea over 200 miles of swampy country, by which it becomes surcharged with moisture, that precipitates itself when it strikes the mountains, and falls in torrents as long as the monsoon prevails in that direction. Only twenty miles farther inland the amount is 200 inches. I met in India a veteran army officer who had spent twenty years in Assam, the eastern part of India. He gave me an extract from the meteorological record that he had kept in that country for many years which contained some remarkable statistics. In one year, 1862, there fell at Chorra-poongee 725 inches of rain, a little more than sixty feet, probably the heaviest rainfall ever noted at any place on the earth.

The sand-storms of India are even more remarkable than the rain. They are violent whirlwinds, occurring occasionally in the dry season, gathering up the dust and carrying it over the country in such volumes as actually to make midday as dark as midnight.*

\* Lady Baker, in her Letters from India, gives the following description of one of these sand-storms:

"Scarcely had the servants fastened firmly to the ground the large curtain which formed our tent door, and which was generally festooned back with green wreaths of mango-leaves, when the tent shook and swayed backward and forward, and in a few moments every thing was covered more than an inch deep with the finest dust, which had filtered through the numerous folds of the canvas. It was impossible to read or work; the candles only gave a little gleam of light through the thick atmosphere, and all we touched was gritty. For four long hours our imprisonment lasted, and it was not until sunset that the servants pronounced it safe to release us. As soon as the

A SAND-STORM.

One of the greatest luxuries in India is American ice, which at the principal ports is received in large quantities, and is freely used. It comes from Boston, and is no inconsiderable item in the trade with Bombay and Calcutta. A

tent-flaps were lifted up, we all burst out laughing at each other—such objects you never saw! No one had an eyebrow or an eyelash to be seen; the bronzed and red complexions which outdoor life had produced were all hidden under a thick coating of dust, and we needed only a few streaks of paint to have looked like Clown in the pantomime, for our faces were quite as white as his. We could see the dense cloud moving on to the southwest, but all was beautifully clear behind it; only a slight haze between us and it showed that the atmosphere was not quite free from dust a little beyond us. I looked at the horses: they were all as white as if they had been powdered with flour; and the water-carriers were busy filling the large goatskins which serve them as water-jugs, to give every live thing which had been outside a good drink, and to wash the dust out of their eyes and ears. The camels had buried their noses in the sand, and did not appear to have suffered at all."

cargo of ice will waste from one third to one half in the passage to India by the way of the Cape of Good Hope, but even with this waste it is a profitable shipment. The raw material costs little; a cargo is very speedily packed in a vessel, and when it reaches its destination in the East it is sold at an immense advance. The price of ice at Bombay and Calcutta varies from two and a half to five cents a pound, according to the supply, and even at these rates it is accounted as indispensable to living as in American cities, and the luxury is inconceivably greater. Owing to the extreme heat it can not be sent far into the country, but in former times it was sent to the wealthy nabobs and English residents on the heads of relays of coolies, fifty or sixty miles in the course of a night, and it is now sent much farther by rail. It is also manufactured artificially in the interior at no greater expense than its importation. At Allahabad there is a large establishment where the manufacture has been successfully and profitably carried on. If it be a blessing in America, where the thermometer sometimes reaches 95 as the extreme heat of the day, what a boon must it be in the north of India, where for days and nights together the thermometer does not fall as low as 100, and where it often reaches in the day 120 and 130 degrees! But the most of the people in the interior of India never saw ice, and comparatively few know any thing of its use. It is a miracle in their ideas.

## XVI.

### PUBLIC WORKS; PRODUCTIONS.

The material development of India has gone forward with great rapidity within the last quarter of a century, more especially since it came directly under the control of the home government. One of the first enterprises undertaken was the construction of public roads. As the military and civil power of the English became more extended, it was found necessary to have better modes of transportation, and the old East India Company undertook the construction of carriage-roads over the country. The work was vigorously prosecuted, and at great expense. The Grand Trunk Road extends from Calcutta to Peshawur, on the borders of Afghanistan, a distance of 1400 miles. These roads are no insignificant works. They are laid out by the best engineering skill, and executed in the most substantial manner. For more than a thousand miles from Calcutta northwest no grading was required, excepting on very short distances, but farther north the work was heavy. From Lahore to Peshawur, a distance of a little more than 250 miles, the road passes over 103 large bridges and 459 smaller ones, through six mountainous chains, and over immense embankments on the marshy borders of rivers. Its estimated cost was more than one million sterling. There are branch roads over the Sewalic range of the Himalayas, in Bengal and the Punjaub, some of which are admirable specimens of engineering and grading, the surface being as smooth as the roads of England or of France. The soil itself furnishes the material for their construction. Through a great part of the plains of India, small nodules of limestone, called *kunker*, are found in large quantities a foot or two below the surface. It looks, when taken from the ground, as if it might have been broken up for making a Macadam road. When packed with the soil and watered, it forms a concrete, making a hard road-bed as smooth as it is durable. There are several thousand miles of these Macadam roads, frequently shaded with trees on either side to protect travelers from the rays of the sun.

A work of still greater importance to India has been the opening of extensive canals, designed not so much for transportation as for irrigation. The rains are very unequally distributed over the country; they are not altogether equal in amount from year to year in the same locality, and the seasons are so uniformly divided into rainy and dry that the soil and the crops frequently suffer, and the people in consequence, for the want of natural irrigation. Under the old Mogul emperors extensive canals were dug for the purpose of watering the plains, but the East India Company had been long established before any systematic attempt was made to supply the deficiency. In the mean time great scarcity of rain, and floods in other seasons, had brought on destructive famines, which more than decimated the population in large districts. The distress and loss of life were fearful. This suffering stimulated the government, though but too tardily, to provide against such calamities by an extensive system of irrigation. The Ganges Canal, the chief work of this nature, reaching from Hurdwar, near the sources of the river, to Cawnpore, where it re-enters, 810 miles in length including its main branches, was an immense undertaking, but it has been an immense benefit to the country. The main canal is 150 feet wide, is the channel of a rapid stream, and in its course crosses the Solani River by what is said to be the most magnificent aqueduct in the world. This structure alone cost a million and a half of dollars. The Bari Doab Canal, between the Sutlej and the Ravi, nearly 500 miles in extent, cost the government more than seven millions of dollars. The Ganges Canal alone irrigates a million and a half of acres, and is not only a great public benefit, but a source of large profit to the government.

The telegraph was early introduced into India, connecting the principal cities north and south, east and west. During the mutiny it proved of incalculable importance. Wooden poles being less durable in that climate than in our own and many other countries, the wires to a large extent are erected on stone or brick pillars. There are now 14,000 miles of telegraph wires in India, all under the control of government, and subject to a uniform tariff, without regard to distance. A message of ten words may be sent from one end of the empire to the other for one rupee, about fifty cents in our money. Within the last few years the telegraph service has brought a small profit to the government. The postal service is a source of revenue, although the postage is cheaper than in any other country, being a half anna (or one cent and a half) for any distance in the empire.

The greatest change of a material nature that has taken place in India has been through its railways. In no other part of the world has this improvement wrought such a revolution in travel, or made such a general innovation upon established customs. In Oriental countries time is a commodity that has no appreciable value. In making a journey, as in any and all the business of life, it has been a matter of no account to the natives whether weeks or hours were consumed; it was all the same to them. Even after Western ideas had taken root, speed was a plant of very slow growth. An American missionary informed me that when he first went to India he was three months in making the journey from Calcutta to Allahabad, a distance of 630 miles, which is now made regularly in about twenty-four hours. I met another gentleman in the north of India who said that, when he came to the country, less than twenty years ago, he was five months in making the passage from Calcutta to Dehra. When the railroad was opened from Delhi to Umballah in 1869, making a continuous line from Calcutta about the same distance as to Dehra, and not far from it, a special train made the entire distance, 1154 miles, in forty-one hours—not a slight reduction from five months. In old times, the common mode of travel up country was by the River Ganges, in boats which were pulled and poled against the current at the rate of a very few, if any, miles a day. Sometimes the progress was rapidly backward with the current. If great haste was required, the palanquin was resorted to; and in India coolies are not the most rapid travelers in the world.

The introduction of railways was at first strongly opposed by the natives and by some Europeans, but under the encouragement and substantial aid of the East India government the work was undertaken. Very few persons out of India appear to have any idea of the extent to which this branch of internal improvements has been carried. The first train of cars in India was set in motion in 1852, not twenty years ago, and now there are more than 5000 miles of railway in operation. The East Indian Railway extends already nearly 1500 miles from Calcutta to the northwest, near the borders of Afghanistan. The Great Indian Peninsular Railway, from Bombay to the northeast, with its branches, is of almost equal extent, and, besides these, there are several important roads. The East Indian had a very practicable route laid out for it up the Valley of the Ganges. That part of India is a vast plain, resembling our Western prairies, or even more level and extensive. For more than a thousand miles there is scarcely a single embankment or cut of any extent. Indeed, from Calcutta to the Himalaya Mountains one rarely meets the slightest elevation. This made the construction of that road very easy; but in the west is some heavy work. For a hundred miles out of Bombay the Great Indian Peninsular Railway runs over and through a range of mountains by a succession of ghauts, over immense embankments and viaducts of masonry, and is carried, within a short distance, through twenty tunnels cut in the solid rock. These works have been executed at immense expense. An idea of the solidity of the railways of India may be gathered from the fact that, notwithstanding so much of the country is an open plain, making their construction, excepting through occasional ghauts, comparatively easy, the average cost of the 4000 miles completed at the opening of the year 1869 was $85,000 per mile. There are now more than 5000 miles in operation. They were built by private companies, the government guaranteeing five per cent. interest upon the capital invested, without which they could not have been undertaken. The amount of interest thus advanced by the government up to January 1st, 1869, was about

$125,000,000, of which more than half had been repaid from the revenues of the roads. Throughout the entire peninsula the rails were laid with a uniform gauge of five feet six inches. The narrow gauge, I learn, has since been adopted. The weight of the rails varies from sixty to eighty-four pounds the yard.

The route by rail from Calcutta to Bombay *via* Allahabad, a distance of 1470 miles, was completed in March, 1870, a month too late for me to avail myself of its facilities for a part of the distance; but the event was considered one of great importance by travelers to and from the north and east of India. Formerly passengers from England to Calcutta and the cities up the valley of the Ganges had sailed direct to Calcutta by the Cape or through the Red Sea; but now they land at Bombay, where they take the rail to Allahabad, 845 miles, and thence to Calcutta, 625 miles, or to the north of India. The time between Bombay and Calcutta, according to the Indian Bradshaw, was sixty-nine hours. It may be shortened ere this.

Contrary to general expectation, the railways have been immensely popular among the natives. They are a traveling people, having been accustomed from ancient times to make long pilgrimages, and, as soon as they became familiar with the sight of the cars, they began to crowd them in great numbers. The system of caste was at first an objection, inasmuch as a high-caste Brahmin was wont to consider himself polluted if even the shadow of a low-caste man fell upon him, and much more if he touched him. The companies were strongly importuned to establish caste cars, in conformity with the social regulations of the country; but the government wisely forbade it, and the advantages of this rapid mode of travel were found to be so great that these stern prejudices were overcome; and now, all who are not willing to pay for the exclusive use of a car are packed together promiscuously. Mohammedans and Hindoos, Brahmins and Pariahs, may be seen sitting cheek by jowl as composedly as if they had all been made of one flesh. The railroads of India are thus having an important influence in breaking down the power of caste.

The cars in India are after the European pattern, divided into compartments, but not equal in comfort to those of the same classes in England, and altogether inferior to those of our own country. The report of the Commission sent to the United States by the East India government to examine our railroads, to which I have already referred, was altogether favorable to our system of construction and management of cars, and especially of the Pullman cars. Immediately upon the publication of the report, an order was given for the remodeling of the carriages and the construction of others having the accommodations of the Pullman cars. An application was also made, through the British minister at Washington and our own Secretary of State, for a competent American engineer to aid in remodeling their whole railway system. Not in our own country have I heard more enthusiastic praises than I heard all over India of the grandeur and success of the great enterprise which laid an iron band across our wide continent, and built upon it those rolling palaces which pass from ocean to ocean with the fleetness of the wind and almost with the ease of a balloon.

In making mention of some of the productions of the country, the one to be named of first importance as a source of revenue is the great curse of China. Opium had been raised in India long before it came under British rule, but in 1773 the East India Company, becoming aware of its great pecuniary value, assumed the monopoly. It has ever since been raised under the direction and for the benefit of government. The amount exported, nearly all to China, in the financial year of 1869–70, was in value $58,466,650. The rulers of India and its merchants talk about the opium market, and the profits of the sale, as they do in London of consols, and as we do of our government securities, just as if it were not an unmitigated curse to the Chinese, who were compelled at the cannon's mouth to take it when they steadfastly refused. The government auction sale at Calcutta is a scene of more excitement than I ever witnessed at the Paris Bourse or among the brokers of New York. I came one day, in the business quarter of the city, upon a crowd of thousands of Mohammedans, Hindoos, Parsees, and other natives, not to speak of Europeans, who were wild with excitement. For a moment I imagined that a riot had broken out; but I soon learned that it was the monthly opium sale, in which more persons are interested than in the sale of stocks in our markets.

Opium is produced almost exclusively in Bengal, in a district lying along the Ganges, about 600 miles long and 200 broad. It is the dried juice of the capsules of the common white poppy, extracted before the seed is fully ripe. The poppy-fields, when in full bloom, resemble green lakes studded with white water-lilies, the tract of country in which they grow being perfectly level. The following account is given of the raising of the poppy and the manufacture of the drug:

"The seed is sown in the beginning of November; it flowers in the end of January, or a little later, and in three or four weeks the capsules or poppy-heads are about the size of hens' eggs, and are ready for operating upon. The collectors each take a little instrument called a *nushtur*, made of three or four small blades of iron notched like a saw; with this they wound each full-grown poppy-head as they make their way through the plants in the field. This is done early in the morning, before the heat of the sun is felt. During the day the milky juice of the plant oozes out, and early on the following morning it is collected by scraping it off, and transferred to an earthen vessel which the collector carries. When this is full it is carried home and transferred to a shallow brass dish, and left for a time tilted on its side, so that any watery fluid may drain out. This watery fluid is very detrimental to the opium unless removed. It now requires daily attendance, to be turned frequently, so that the air may dry it equally, until it acquires a tolerable consistency, which takes three or four weeks. It is then packed in small earthen jars and taken to the go-downs, or factories, where the contents of each jar is turned out, and carefully weighed, tested, valued, and credited to the cultivator. The opium is then thrown into vast vats, and the mass, being kneaded, is again taken out and made into balls or cakes. This is done in long rooms, the workmen sitting in rows, carefully watched by the overseers to insure the work being properly performed. The balls are wrapped in layers of poppy petals and taken to a drying-room, placed in tiers on latticed racks, and continually turned and examined, to keep them from insects and from other injury. After being fully dried they are packed in chests for the market."

The drug is supposed to cost the government, laid down in Calcutta, 400 rupees ($200) per chest. On arrival at the government go-downs in Calcutta, it is sold by public auction, in lots of five chests, to the highest bidder. On the fall of the hammer the buyer has always the option of there and then securing as many succeeding lots as he wishes at the same rate as the lot he has just bought. The purchaser of any parcels has to pay, on the fall of the hammer, bargain-money at the rate of 50 to 100 rupees per chest, and the balance of purchase-money within a fortnight. It is not compulsory, however, to take immediate delivery of the opium, as the government allows it to remain, free of warehouse charge, for an indefinite period. These auctions take place once every month, a price of 400 rupees per chest being placed on the drug. All it realizes over and above this price goes toward increasing the revenue, and is a profit to the government. No private individuals are allowed to store opium in their go-downs; all so found is looked upon as smuggled, and confiscated. When a buyer wishes to export his purchases, they are shipped for him by the government agent. For this production and traffic the government alone is responsible.

Another of the important and somewhat peculiar productions of India takes its name from the country, indigo. It is the product of a plant of the order *Leguminosæ*, and genus *Indigofera*, of which there are between one and two hundred species. The species cultivated in India, *Tinctoria*, grows to the height of three or four feet. The dye was known to the ancients, being taken to Greece and Rome from India, from which it was called *Indicum*, and hence indigo. The coloring principle is contained in the stems and leaves, which yield a colorless fluid, that is changed into the beautiful dye by fermentation. The seed is sown in drills; the plants are tender, and require great care; in about two months they begin to flower, producing a pale red flower, when they are cut and laid in mass in great stone cisterns, covered with water, and kept down by heavy weights. In the course of twelve or fourteen hours fermentation commences, the whole mass appears to be boiling, and bubbles of air of a purple hue begin to rise. When this process is complete the liquid is drawn off into another vat, and violently agitated until the coloring matter begins to precipitate itself, when it is left to settle. The water is again drawn off, and the indigo dried and prepared for commerce. The production for the financial year 1869-70 amounted in value to $15,890,225. More is produced in India than in all other countries together.

The good housewives, who are well acquainted with the mode of testing indigo by putting a lump into water to ascertain whether it is good or bad, but who do not precisely know whether the good will sink or swim, and *vice versa*, may be informed that the best quality will float on water. The poorer qualities, having much earthy matter, sink. The finest indigo, in a dry state, will scarcely make a mark on white paper.

## XVII.

#### THE NATIVES OF INDIA; CASTE, ETC.

BEFORE reaching India, I met with a very intelligent gentleman who had spent many years in that country. In the course of conversation I made some remark in regard to native society, to which he immediately replied, with an exclamation, " Native society ! Why, there is no such thing. The women (referring, of course, to the more wealthy classes) never see any one, and the men spend their time between eating and sleeping."

This is a strong way of putting the matter; but, with exceptional cases, it is the truth. There is no social life among the native population of India. The woman is no society to her husband, the only man whom, as a rule, she ever meets; the man is no society to his wife: he regards her as belonging to an inferior order of beings, created only to minister to his pleasure and comfort as a servant; there is nothing like social intercourse between brothers and sisters; and outside of the family, society, in our understanding of the term, has no existence. Life is a dreary waste, judging it by the standards which prevail in all countries with which we are most familiar.

It is not for the want of people that there is no society in India. Within the compass of 1900 miles in one direction and 1500 in another (taking the diamond-shaped country in its greatest length and breadth) there are two hundred millions of people thrown together. The most numerous of these are the Hindoos, who compose three fourths of the population, or about 150,000,000. Then come the Mohammedans, who number about 25,000,000. The remaining eighth is made up of the aboriginal tribes, whose immediate descendants still number several millions, the Parsees, the Buddhists, the Jews, and the Christians. There is also the same sprinkling of other nations which is to be found in almost every part of the world where an exclusive system has not prevailed.

The Hindoos are not the original possessors of the soil. When they came into the land, some thousands of years ago, they found it already occupied by a people who had strayed over there not long after the dispersion. These tribes, after some twenty-five or thirty centuries, may still be found a distinct people in Orissa and other parts of India; but they are so small a part of the population that the Hindoo may be regarded as the native race; and not merely because the most numerous, but because it has for so long a period given character to the country. Though not always the reigning element among the people of India, the Hindoo has been the pervading element; his religion, the Brahminical, has been the catholic religion; and the great feature of Hindooism, caste, has stamped itself upon the country as its prevailing type, a social system of greater power than any other that has appeared in our world, save only the divine system of Christianity, which is destined to triumph over all.

The Mohammedans, who, many centuries before the introduction of European commerce and power, established themselves by successive conquests, and at length became the ruling class, retain their religious characteristics, though adapting themselves in many of the habits of life to the country of which they took possession. They introduced a splendor of architecture and a gorgeous style of life, which culminated in the magnificence that marked the Mogul dynasty, the monuments of which have not passed away with the destruction of their power in the East.

It is one of the marvels of Oriental life that these different races, having religions not only different, but diametrically opposed, have lived together with so little outbreaking hostility. The Hindoos are the grossest idolaters that have ever existed. Their forms of idol-worship and service have reached the lowest degradation, and yet the Mohammedans, whose religion is essentially a protest against idolatry, have lived with them for long centuries, and each have maintained their own religion intact. The Mohammedan power came into India with its chief weapon of conversion, the sword, in hand, and for a time it was plied not without effect. Some succeeding emperors exhibited the spirit of proselytism, but, as a general thing, Mohammedans and Hindoos have lived together with remarkable tolerance of each other's antagonistic faiths.

The Sikhs, who were once a powerful community in the north of India—powerful with their swords, and even now physically the finest race in all the land—were the product of an attempt to combine the two religions. After this new religion had been well established, it ended in attacking both Hindooism and Mohammedanism; but, though it developed a hardy, warlike community, who are still distinguished as soldiers, it has never had any great influence upon the religious thought or faith of the country.

Of the Parsees, the followers of Zoroaster, and descendants of the ancient Fire-worshipers of Persia, who are confined chiefly to the city and vicinity of Bombay, I shall speak in another place.

This brief enumeration of some of the constituent elements of the population of India will give little idea of that curious piece of mosaic upon which one looks when he lands in that interesting country. In Eastern Asia, in China or Japan, for instance, every thing is of one type. The Japanese or Chinaman that you meet on entering his country is the Japanese or Chinaman that you meet everywhere. His face is the same. His form is the same. His dress is the same. But every thing is different in India. The mixed crowd that we saw on the banks of the Hoogly as we reached Calcutta, with their varied costumes of diverse colors, was only a picture of the great multitude that one sees in traveling through the country. The very aspect of the people is a study of which one never grows weary, it is so diversified. The many languages that he hears will remind him of the confusion of tongues at an earlier period of the race. The occupations of the people, so different from those to which he has been accustomed, will be to him an endless source of entertainment, if not of instruction. If he goes into their bazars and market-places, his curiosity will be still more excited. Their habits and customs, as far as he is allowed to observe them, will keep awake all his powers of observation.

The costumes of the Hindoos are the same that were worn long centuries before the Christian era. That of the men usually consists of two pieces of wide cotton cloth, one of which is wrapped around the waist and falls to the calf of the leg, the other thrown loosely over the shoulder. A shawl or turban of some kind upon the head completes the dress. The women have a single piece of cloth, silk or cotton, plain or colored, eight or ten yards long, which is first partly tied around the waist, forming a garment that reaches to the feet; the rest is then passed around the body and over the head, falling down the back. A tight bodice is frequently worn underneath. The dress, especially that of the women, has a graceful appearance, and, as the colors are often bright, a company together presents a striking appearance. Until after the Mohammedan conquest no clothes that were cut or sewn were worn, and by some they are still regarded as unlawful. But loose trowsers are now frequently worn, even by Hindoos. The wealthier classes among the natives, both Mohammedan and Hindoo, indulge freely in dress, wearing the richest brocades and finest muslins, trimmed with gold and silver lace. They are all and equally fond of jewels and other ornaments, the women having no limit to their decoration except the extent of their means. The most valuable gems are usually set uncut, some of them having been handed down in their rough state through many generations. The natives of India have an almost instinctive appreciation of pure and valuable gems, which are estimated, not according to their outward aspect, but their intrinsic worth. The common people exhibit their fondness for jewelry by a profusion of ornaments. They have rings in their ears and rings in their noses, necklaces, armlets, and anklets without number, winding off with rings on their toes. The rings worn in the nose are usually put through the side of the nostril, and sometimes are several inches in diameter—extremely inconvenient, to say the least. The different races and religions may all be distinguished by their dress, even though it be of the same general style. The Hindoos, for instance, fasten the tunic, or vest, upon the right side; the Mohammedans on the left.

The condition of woman among the natives of India, as in all the East, has been very defectively represented. She is nowhere elevated to her true position as the equal companion of man; she is excluded from the ordinary social intercourse of life; her apartments are usually in striking contrast with those of her assuming lords, barren of furniture, and cheerless in appearance; her person is decked with costly apparel and more costly jewels, but only as a doll is ornamented to gratify the pride of the possessor; among the poorer classes she is often made a mere beast of burden; by none is she deemed worthy of education; and yet, with all this, I was surprised, after all I had heard, to find that she exerts so great an influence, and that so many women, breaking through all the disadvantages and obstacles which surround them in Oriental life—not by stepping out of the narrow sphere assigned them, but by mere force of intellect and character—make their power felt. The truth is, that since the foundation of human society, woman has been a power in the world the world over. In India, as in China, the mother, ignorant as she is, has the moulding of the rising race, and not a few hold the sceptre in the household even over those who claim to be of a higher order by virtue of their sex.

In the records of all the ages there are evidences of the great influence of woman among the Hindoos, and still more among the Mohammedans. The most beautiful, costly, and magnificent monument ever erected to a mortal stands to-day in the heart of Hindostan. It was built by one of the Mogul emperors as the tomb and memorial of his wife. While she lived she held his heart and his throne in her hands, and when she died he poured out his wealth upon her grave. A still more remarkable woman was the wife of the Emperor Jehangeer, of whom the historian writes, " Her influence over the emperor must have been as great as the most ambitious of her sex could desire. He took no step without consulting her, and on every affair in which she took an interest her will was law. Previous to his marriage the emperor had been intemperate, capricious, and cruel. Through her influence his habits and conduct were greatly improved, if not entirely reformed. The ceremonies, manners, and usages of the court were remodeled by her; its splendor was increased by her arrangements, while its expenses were diminished by her management." These are exceptional cases; but the influence of woman in the East, notwithstanding her general degradation and her disadvantages, is far greater than we are often told. Nor are the women of the higher classes so unhappy as is generally supposed. Their wants are fewer than those of women in more enlightened countries, and such as they feel are usually well supplied. Not being educated, they are generally content, if not happy in their lot.

There is still a large amount of wealth among the natives, although so many kings and princes have lost their territories and their revenues by the encroachments of the latest conquerors of the country. Some of them live lavishly, after the style of former sovereigns. I saw recently a statement in one of the India papers that the Maharajah of Travancore ("May his weight never be less," exclaimed the editor), in anticipation of his investiture with the dignity, was weighed in scales against gold, and the gold distributed among the Brahmins. The gold was coined into pieces varying from 9.28 grains to 78.65 grains. The whole expense of the ceremony, including the feeding of some ten thousand Brahmins, was acknowledged to be 160,000 rupees, which, with other ceremonies that must be performed before the Maharajah's elevation, would amount to more than $150,000.

The subject of food is one of paramount importance with all classes of the natives, not merely as to how it shall be obtained, but still more as to what shall be eaten. The Brahmins eat no animal food of any kind, having a religious abhorrence of the destruction of life. Some of them have the water they drink carefully strained lest it should contain a gnat. Even eggs are forbidden, as possessing the germ of animal life. All Hindoos of every caste abstain from beef. Mohammedans, of course, eschew pork. Brahmins and others of high caste abstain from all intoxicating drinks, using only water or pure milk. In Bengal the people live largely upon rice, but in the north of India wheat, and barley, and other cereals are the staples. Very little animal food is used by any of the natives.

The most striking characteristic of Hindoo society, if society it may be called—that which constitutes its very frame-work, as much as do the bones and tendons of the human system, the like to which is found among no other people, from the civilized to the savage—is caste. Most nations and tribes have their distinctions, some of them hereditary and strongly marked, but nowhere else is there such a system of caste as that which is found in India. It is very difficult to describe it so that it may be comprehended by those who have not seen its workings, although its rules are well defined and more unchangeable than the laws of the Medes and Persians.

The term *caste* is of modern origin, derived from the Portuguese in the thirteenth century, but the thing itself is as old as the Aryan invasion, centuries before the Christian era. The Aryans, from whatever quarter of Asia they came, brought with them a well-defined, social, and civil polity, which at once took root in a congenial soil, and has continued to flourish until the present time. Its roots run deeper and are more firmly fixed than those of any other social system in existence. Caste, which is not without its advantages in such a state of society as that which has prevailed in India, is, nevertheless, the mighty barrier which opposes all progress and elevation, and the great obstacle in the way of the Gospel of Christ.

According to the *Laws of Menu*, a work supposed to have been written about nine hundred years before Christ, Hindoo society is divided into four grand classes: 1. The *Brahmins*, who are said to have emanated from the mouth or head of Brahma, the Creator, and who are the chief of all created beings, the head of society, the teachers and priests for all others. A Brahmin is to be treated with the most profound respect even by kings; his life and person are protected by the severest laws in this world, and by the most tremendous denunciations for the world to come. They are supposed to have the power of blessing and cursing all others. 2. The second class, the *Kshatryas*, who sprang from the shoulders and arms of Brahma, are the *military* class, and have something of a sacred character; they are the executive class. The Brahmins draw up and interpret the laws, but the *Kshatryas* administer them, so that these two classes are in a measure dependent upon each other. 3. The third class, the *Vaishyas*, sprang from the thighs or loins of Brahma, and are the *mercantile* class, the men of business. It is their province to carry on trade, cultivate the soil, keep cattle, and to acquire and practice all useful knowledge. 4. The fourth class, the *Sudras*, sprang from the feet of Brahma. They are the *servile* class; they are to serve the three higher classes, especially the Brahmins, and never to aspire to the dignity or privileges of the others; they are neither to acquire property, nor to acquire knowledge by reading, but to remain in an abject condition all their days and through all generations.

These may be called the ideal laws of caste as found in the ancient books, but the two middle classes have now no very distinct existence. The Brahmins are the only high caste, the other three having been subdivided until there are eighteen principal and more than a hundred minor classes, every trade, and profession, and employment forming a separate caste, from which no one can rise to a higher, or even descend to a lower. A man, by breaking the rules of his particular order, as by eating or drinking with a person of a lower caste, becomes an *outcast*, and will be equally spurned by those above and below him. The distinction is hereditary, and does not depend upon any acquired position. No outward social rank confers the privilege. The poorest Brahmin in India would consider himself defiled for all time, and would be so considered by all others, if he were to eat with the Emperor of the Russias. The Governor General of India could not find a man of the lowest caste who would be willing to partake of his hospitality. Brahmins are often found in comparatively humble positions in life, but the loftiest Hindoos who do not belong to their caste must pay them reverence. At Calcutta I saw a high-caste Hindoo who was employed by a wealthy merchant as a porter, but the rich Hindoo could never pass the high-caste man who was waiting at his door without making a humiliating sign of obeisance and of real subjection.

The rules of caste are broken not by crime. A man may commit murder, adultery, theft, or perjury, and even be convicted of such crimes, without losing caste; but if he violates any of the ceremonial laws, especially if he should eat with a European, or even with a Mohammedan of India, or with any one not belonging to his class, he would be degraded, and only by the most humiliating process of atonement, and by paying an enormous sum, could he be restored, if at all. A Brahmin was once forced by a European to eat meat. Although his offense was involuntary, he could not be restored after three years' penance, even by the offer of forty thousand dollars ransom. He subsequently regained his former position by the payment of a hundred thousand. While I was in India a high-caste Hindoo was present at an entertainment, partly social and partly official, given by Europeans, and partook of some article of food in their society. He was afterward compelled to pay a heavy fine, and to eat the excrements of beasts, and humble himself before an idol with costly presents, before he could be recognized by those of his own caste. It is not merely the pride of a clan, or the rule of a sect; there is an inborn, ingrained feeling in a Hindoo which makes the laws of his caste seem inexorable and essential. He is bound by an invisible but mighty chain, which it is next to impossible for him to break. If he violates the rules of caste he is driven from home, and friends, and society, an object of contempt and execration, and any friend who should give him shelter or countenance would become an outcast. Neither parents, nor wife, nor children would be allowed to hold intercourse with him.

This is the penalty that every Hindoo incurs who becomes a Christian, and caste thus proves one of the most serious obstacles to the progress of the Christian religion. Even the lowest Sudra becomes an outcast if he enters into fellowship with Christians; and partaking of the holy communion is an act which would effectually cut him off from all future intercourse with his own people. It is a severe test, but just such a test as was indicated by the promise of the Savior: "Every one that hath forsaken houses, or brethren, or sisters, or father, or mother, or wife, or children, or lands, for my name's sake, shall receive an hundred fold, and shall inherit everlasting life." The Roman Catholics, on coming to India in the sixteenth century, finding the power of caste so strong, conformed to it, employing low-caste priests to minister to those of low caste, the Jesuit fathers carrying the sacraments to the sick and dying only in secret and by night. But it was justly said of them that they became Hindoos instead of making the Hindoos Christians. Swartz and other German missionaries made some concessions to caste, but all English and American Protestant missionaries have consistently and persistently refused to give it any place in the Christian Church.

*Pariahs*, a numerous class, are lower than the *Sudras;* they are literally outcasts; but even they have their distinctions and their rules, to which they rigidly adhere, although they occupy the lowest depths in the social scale.

The system of *caste* is becoming undermined by education and by the influence of Christianity. Intercourse with intelligent Europeans is slowly operating upon the public mind to weaken its power. The introduction of railways, as I have already mentioned, by compelling men of all castes to sit together, often crowded into a compact mass, has done much to overcome the senseless notion that one man is spiritually defiled by touching another, or by any simple act of social intercourse. The destruction of the system does not seem so hopeless or so remote as it once did.

## XVIII.

### CALCUTTA TO BENARES.

I HAVE interjected some information in regard to the government and people of India in order that I may be more free to continue the narrative of the journey as far north as the Himalaya Mountains, and thence to Bombay.

Down to the last hour of our stay in Calcutta, which had been protracted many days, our visit was full of interest. We had entered it perfect strangers, but among the Scotch and English residents, as well as among the American representatives, we had found warm friends, whose acquaintance we would gladly have cultivated longer, but our plans of travel through India made it necessary to improve the cool season. In that far-off land there is a warmth of hospitality that is all the more welcome so far from home, and we recall with great delight the pleasant social scenes in which it was our privilege to mingle. Nationality was quite forgotten until we were invited specially to meet a party of American friends, when thoughts of the Stars and Stripes, and talk of cities and scenes over which they wave, and of mutual friends whose home was beyond all the seas, quickened the pulsations of our hearts. The United States have some noble representatives in Calcutta, of whom I would speak did not the rules of hospitality forbid.

We regretted being obliged to leave just at the time we did, as we should miss the grand durbar to be held in honor of Prince Alfred, who was to arrive within a day or two. We had seen the displays at Shanghai and Hong Kong; but his coming to Calcutta, the capital of England's richest possession, was the occasion of one of the most brilliant scenes witnessed in India since the days of the old Mogul emperors. The ruling dignitaries from all parts of the empire were summoned to the capital, and with them were invited the native princes and rajahs of high degree, who came prepared to join in the demonstrations with all the show of Eastern pomp and circumstance. Trains of elephants had been sent from the north, and the procession was to be one of true Oriental magnificence. The scene at the Government House, when all the princes appeared in full costume and dignity, was dazzling beyond description.

It was a beautiful moonlight night when we were driven to the banks of the Hoogly, to cross over to the cars of the East India Railway that were to take us twelve hundred miles to the north. The shadows had fallen over the streets of the City of Palaces; the noisy tumult of the day, in which thousands of Orientals and Europeans had joined, making the thoroughfares a scene of gay confusion, was over; in almost profound stillness we passed up the Chowringee Road, by the Government House, through the main streets, past the site of the Black Hole, now occupied by stately buildings, and reached the bank of the river. The tide was out, and we were obliged to commit ourselves to the arms of the coolies, who carried us through the deep mud of the river to the small boat in which our luggage was awaiting us. We were not subjected to the trick which the boatmen played upon some other travelers. The price of ferriage had been agreed upon beforehand, but in the middle of the stream the ingenious Hindoo boatmen demanded more pay, and gave their passengers the choice of complying with the demand or leaving the boat. The latter alternative was not altogether convenient in the circumstances, and they were compelled to hand over the extra pay.

Howrah, the terminus of the East India Railway, is directly opposite Calcutta. It is a place of no importance in itself, but the railway station and the works of the road, with its extensive business, have built up a small town on the borders of the jungle. Here, in a dimly-lighted dépôt, and still more dimly-lighted cars, we arranged ourselves for a journey of twenty-four hours, our first experience of railway traveling since leaving the shores of America.

Although the day had been exceedingly warm, and the sun's rays oppressive, if not dangerous, before morning we wrapped ourselves, in the sleeping-car, with all the clothing we could find, including traveling-shawls and blankets. During the winter months, over a great part of India, the nights become extremely cold, so that the warmest covering is agreeable. Not until the next morning, and after we had noticed that the outside of our car attracted special attention at each stopping-place, did we discover that it bore the following placard: "Whole carriage, two compartments to Benares reserved: party of American ladies and gentlemen." For its exclusive use (though not on the principle of caste) we were indebted to the kindness of a friend at Calcutta and the politeness of the railroad officials at Howrah.

Our railway guide-book was to us something of a curiosity from the novelty of the names of the towns that we passed: Pannaghur, Raneegunge, Seeterampore, Ahmoodpore, Maharajpore, Sahibgunge, Bhangulpore, and many other *pores*, not including Putty-muddy-fudge-pore, of which I have read. The suffix *pore* is as common in India as *town* or *ton* in our own country, and the signification is much the same.

There is little in the scenery going north from Calcutta that is attractive. At one or two points the country breaks out into some demonstrations of grandeur, but the vast plain of the Ganges is almost wholly without variety. It is generally in a state of cultivation—not high cultivation, for the whole country has the appearance of exhaustion from its effort to sustain so many millions for thousands of years. Occasionally we passed through rich rice-fields, and the crops were green as in summer-time, but nowhere did we see the signs of good, thrifty tillage. One reason doubtless is that the people are not landholders, and are not stimulated to keep the land up to the maximum of its producing capacity. It was a novelty in agriculture to see camels yoked to the plow like oxen, and elephants working in the field with the sagacity of farmers. They are frequently employed in the East to perform work which requires a discriminating eye and good judgment, and this, too, without an overseer. They are trained to lift and pile lumber with their trunks, which they do with as much exactness as if they used a plumb-line.

A striking peculiarity of the great plain of India, and indeed of the whole of Asia, from the east to the west, as far as I have seen it, is the destitution of forests. With all the beauty of verdure and foliage which marks Japan, I did not see, within the thousand miles of the empire that I traversed, a single forest of any extent. The whole coast of China, along which I sailed more than a thousand miles, and the interior, as far as I penetrated it, had only sparsely scattered trees. Farther inland there are heavily-timbered districts, but I saw none. There is not the sign of a forest from Calcutta to the mountains, although a large part of the country is in jungle. Even the Himalaya

R

Mountains that I subsequently crossed, and the second range that I ascended, were only sprinkled with trees, in comparison with the grand old dense forests of magnificent growth which form one of the sublime features of American scenery. And to anticipate still farther; Syria, including the mountains of Lebanon, is almost destitute of trees. All that remain of the cedars of Lebanon can be counted in a few moments. The plain of India, which led me into this digression, has scattered groves of palm, and acacia, and guava, and mango, and many other Oriental trees, but they are all planted for shade or fruit. Centuries ago the forests were cut down to supply the necessities of an immense population, but the soil does not appear to have the reproductive power that is a marked feature of our own.

The night had gathered around us before we reached Mogul-Serai, where we were transferred to another short road, by which we reached the bank of the Ganges opposite Benares. Crossing by a bridge of boats, we entered by moonlight that ancient and magnificent city—in the eyes of a Hindoo, the holiest spot on the face of the globe.

India has three capitals, although two of them are more historic than real; Calcutta, the actual capital, the seat of the British viceroyalty; Delhi, the Mohammedan capital, the seat of the old Mogul dynasty; and Benares, the ancient Hindoo capital, still regarded by Brahminists as the centre of the world. It is the Mecca of the Hindoos, the point to which their most sacred thoughts turn, and where, of all places, they think it blessed to die. Indeed, it is an article of Hindoo faith that the vilest sinner, if he dies within a circle of ten miles around Benares, is sure of passing at once into everlasting bliss. Thousands are brought to the shores of the Ganges at this spot, that they may drink and bathe in its waters, and die within the charmed circle, with their eyes resting on the sacred river. As soon as the breath has departed, their bodies are burned upon its banks, and the ashes thrown to mingle with its waters.

Water taken from the ghauts is carried by pilgrims over the whole land, and every where regarded as holy water.

The city, one of great antiquity, has passed through many and great mutations. Hindooism, and Buddhism, and Mohammedanism have here successively reigned, the former all the while clinging to the soil as its own sacred inheritance. One ancient city, about five miles from the present site, has passed away, almost from memory, leaving scarcely a trace behind. I spent a morning among its sparse but massive ruins, accompanied by the Rev. Mr. Sherring, the learned antiquarian and historian of Benares, and the Rev. Mr. Hutton, both of the London Missionary Society, to whom I was indebted for most of the pleasure and interest of my sojourn.

The modern city, if I may apply such a term to one that has stood unchanged for centuries, is the most magnificent in its architecture, and the most strictly Oriental in aspect of all the cities of India. There are grander structures at Agra and Delhi, and there is more of show at Lucknow, but nowhere else does the traveler find himself dreaming over so constantly the fancies which filled his imagination when, as a boy, he read the tales of the East, or when, in riper years, he lingered over the pages of its history. Perhaps I should make some qualification in speaking of the grandeur of this or of any Oriental city. In no other part of the world does distance lend so much enchantment to the view as in the East. Domes and minarets, and palaces with lofty, fretted porches, and palm-trees, and Oriental skies, form a picture that is truly enchanting; but when one attempts to thread the narrow winding alleys that are called streets, and is jostled at every step by men, and women, and donkeys, and camels, and sacred bulls, to say nothing of an occasional elephant, whose huge dimensions appear to require more than all the space between the walls, he loses sight of the magnificence, and is absorbed with the realities of the place.

But, even with these qualifications, the views of Benares

which linger in my memory are the grandest recollections of all the cities of the East. As seen from the lofty minaret of the Mosque of Aurungzebe, the domes of a thousand temples, the minarets of three hundred mosques, and palaces without number, which princes have built, that they may live and die in sight of the holy river, make up a magnificent picture. The city is skirted with palms and acacias, and the deified peepul, all which add to the beauty of the scene.

But, to see its real grandeur, one must look upon it from the Ganges. Benares is situated on a bluff, rising precipitously from the river. Its most massive structures have their foundations laid in the river itself, and rise up a hundred feet by terraces or ghauts, broad stone stairways, so that the palaces, and mosques, and temples overhang the river. The style of architecture is gorgeous, and the whole scene so enchanting that, as one floats down the stream, he seems to be gazing upon a city built in fairy land. Even now, as I look back upon it, and attempt to trace with my pen the impressions that were made upon my mind, I seem to be dreaming.

The city stretches two or three miles along the Ganges; but its chief magnificence is crowded into a single mile above the bridge of boats. The English town known as Secrole stands entirely by itself, and is laid out with broad streets finely shaded, and a grand esplanade for military evolutions. In driving toward the river for the purpose of making the passage down the Ganges in an open dinghy to obtain this view, we came at length to the city proper, from which, by the narrowness of the streets, carriages are excluded as effectually as by impenetrable walls. Ordering the carriage to make a circuitous route in order to meet us below, we took to our feet, and soon came to the *Doorgha Khond*, a temple dedicated to the goddess Doorgha, but actually devoted to monkeys. Hundreds and thousands of these caricatures of humanity, made more impudent by being petted, if not worshiped by the Brahmins, who are their humble servants, filled the temple and the adjoining courts, and swarmed into the streets and neighboring grounds, and grinned at us from every house-top, and garden-wall, and tree. They have the perfect freedom of this part of the town.

Taking a boat, we slowly descended the river, admiring the splendid panorama of Oriental architecture as it seemed to move past us. First comes the *Man Mandil*, the observatory of Jai Singh, a grand structure, which still has, on its broad stone roof, charts of the heavens drawn by Indian astronomers in the days of the Mogul emperors. Large instruments that were in use centuries ago are in its galleries. Here is the ghaut leading to the Golden Temple of Shiva, the reigning divinity of the city, where, on the following day, we saw the worshipers, some of them of high degree, bringing their offerings in successive groups, to be laid on the altar and washed with the water of the sacred stream. Hindoo temples cluster thick around, and sacred places, holy wells, and shrines, all visited by devotees, reminded us of Paul's visit to Athens, where "his spirit was stirred within him when he saw the city wholly given to idolatry." The idols of Benares number more than half a million.

Then comes a succession of ghauts, broad terraces and flights of steps of hewn stone which line the river's bank, and overhanging balconies, from which the princely proprietors look out upon the river which seems to them so near to Paradise. Here we reach the great Mosque of Aurungzebe, the Mohammedan pride of the city, whose foundation walls rise up from the water's edge, the building towering up in massive beauty, and the minarets piercing the air still higher. Great numbers of Hindoos, men and women, have come down the long flights of steps to bathe in the Ganges, and all along we see them performing their ablutions with religious solemnities, hoping thus to wash away their sins. Others are worshiping the river itself, bowing often and repeating their prayers, absorbed in their devotions, and apparently unconscious of the pres-

THE GRAND MOSQUE.

ence of others. Every now and then we come to a landing-place devoted to the burning of the Hindoo dead. We pass pile after pile made ready for the cremation. From some the smoke and flames are ascending to perfume the city, making this quarter of the town almost unendurable excepting to a Hindoo.

Leaving the river, we climbed one of the ghauts by a flight of more than a hundred steps, and re-entered the city, threading our way through the narrow streets. Presently we encountered one of the Brahminy bulls, a race of animals held sacred as the gods, and, knowing the fanati-

BURNING THE DEAD.

cism of the Brahmins, who adore them, and the imperious nature of the bulls themselves, we gave him a wide berth. These animals, from time immemorial, have enjoyed the freedom of the city, no one being allowed to molest them in any wise, or even to interfere with their predatory habits. If they choose to enter a china-shop, no one must say nay, and if a grocer's stock happens to strike their fancy, the proprietor would not dare to interfere with their claims.

They are, consequently, always in good condition, living on the fat of the land. A few years since they had multiplied to such an extent, and had become so imperious in their exactions, that the English local authorities determined, if possible, to rid the city of the nuisance, or at least to thin them out. But how to do this without exciting the horror of every Hindoo, and, perhaps, raising a rebellion, was the problem. To kill the Brahminy bulls would be a thousand times worse than to behead so many princes. At length the problem was solved; it was decided to turn them out to graze in the jungle, where the tigers, who have no Brahminical scruples, made short work with them, and the city was relieved.

We had ordered our carriage to meet us at the bazar, near the residence of the Rajah Sir Deo Narain Singh, a distinguished native prince. During the terrible mutiny of 1857 he had remained faithful to the British government, and had rendered important service, for which he was made a Knight Commander of the Star of India. The queen had made personal acknowledgment of his services by sending an elaborate piece of silver plate bearing an appropriate inscription. The gentleman who accompanied us, a resident of Benares, being on terms of familiar acquaintance with the rajah, proposed a call, and, nothing loth, we complied.

Passing through an outer court-yard, in which several elephants were in waiting, we entered a large flower-garden, rather stiffly arranged, but admirably kept, and, ascending a flight of steps, were met by the rajah's eldest son, who has since succeeded to the title and honors of the father. Giving us a cordial welcome, and inviting us to the reception-room, he ordered refreshments and entertained us with conversation in English, expressing great regret that his father was absent on his estates in the country. He gave an order to one of the servants, who presently returned with two glittering silver garlands called *malas*, and the young rajah, throwing them over our necks, said, "This is the way we express hospitality in our country." We retained them and wore them away. Another servant brought perfumery for our handkerchiefs, and, as we were leaving, we were presented with bouquets of flowers from the garden.

The next morning, as we were at breakfast, word was brought that the rajah's servants were entering the compound with baskets on their heads, and they appeared with presents from the young prince. There were all sorts of vegetables, a box of Cabool grapes, raisins, nuts, a large circular cake of rock candy, etc., etc. About two o'clock he called upon us in a carriage, with his attendants. Being a high-caste Hindoo, we were unable to show him the usual rites of hospitality, but we entertained him according to the best of our ability, and gave him a hearty invitation to visit our country, where we might reciprocate his attentions.

As he was leaving, he informed us that one of his elephants should be at our service if we would like to make an excursion into the country. Soon the elephant, with mahout and another attendant, appeared. He was a noble specimen of his species, and, somewhat peculiar, mottled or spotted on his breast. Obedient to command, he came down upon his belly, and even then we required a ladder to mount to the howdah, the tower upon his back. This was our first experience in elephant riding, and, although the excursion was one of great pleasure, the motion was just about as agreeable as that of a boat in a short chopping sea, or, to draw a comparison from the land, it was very much like making an excursion upon the back of a small mountain.

I find that in the East the elephant, while he has full credit for his sagacity, does not bear the high reputation for fidelity which is current in the West. Even the best of the race, and those which have been long domesticated, are liable to freaks which have the appearance of insanity, in which they sometimes attack their most tried friends.

The year before, an old schoolmate of my own, who has been many years in Siam as a missionary physician, and whom I expected to visit on my way, Dr. S. R. House, having occasion to go out several days' journey from Bankok to perform a surgical operation, took the usual mode of conveyance for a long journey, with suitable attendants. One morning, having spent the night in his tent, as he was preparing to start, he passed by his elephant, which, for some unaccountable reason, struck him down with his trunk and tore him fearfully with his tusks. He was obliged to perform for himself the office of a surgeon, sewing up his own wounds, and it was several days before he could be moved from the scene of his injury. This treachery on the part of elephants may be owing to the fact that they are usually taken wild and subdued by severe discipline, and probably are not thoroughly tamed. They may lay up the remembrance of their subjugation and injuries, and watch for an opportunity to avenge themselves.

But to return to the rajah. I was pained, on reaching home, to receive the intelligence of the death of the noble Hindoo, the father, through the following tribute to his worth which appeared in the *Friend of India:*

"The death of Rajah Sir Deo Narain Singh, K. C. S. I., which occurred at Benares suddenly on Sunday evening, August 28th, is a great loss, not only to the city, but to India generally. During many years he occupied a foremost place among the natives in all matters connected with the prosperity of the country. He was a man of very liberal views. His mind was noble and benevolent, and he had no sympathy whatever with those mere party questions which injure one class of the people by benefiting another. Of good natural intelligence, frank and courteous, enthusiastic and enterprising, his opinions on all matters that came before him were those of a thoughtful, fearless, and honest man. Sincerity—valuable every where, and especially so in India—was his distinguishing characteristic. He has been cut off in the prime of life and in the maturity of his powers. On several occasions of difficulty and danger he rendered invaluable assistance to the government, and, indeed, he was ever a stanch and loyal friend. In the year 1857 he was the chief native adviser of the English officials in Benares, and it is not too much to affirm that the safety of the city and neighborhood during those perilous times was, to a large extent, secured by his devotion and counsel. For the important services he then rendered, the government conferred upon him the title of rajah. He was one of the first native members of the Legislative Council of India. The part which he took in the debates of the council, during his term of office, proved him to be a man of independent thought, of clear judgment, and of earnest sound convictions. No man in Benares was for a moment to be compared with him in zeal for public welfare. His house was open to all comers who visited him for consultation and advice. For eight years he presided over the Benares Institute, and was the life and soul of that society. His death gave a sudden shock to the city, and both Europeans and natives alike felt that they had lost their truest and most faithful friend."

I subsequently received a copy of the *Friend of India* containing an account of the investiture of the son with the titles and dignities of the father, "in recognition of the faithful and eminent services of the late rajah." He is now the Rajah Sumbhoo Narain Singh. May he long wear his honors as worthily as his father!

The last morning that we spent in Benares we devoted to visiting some of the Hindoo temples, in which the city abounds. They are erected in honor of all sorts of gods; many of them by private munificence, in fulfillment of vows or under some religious impulse. Some of the temples of Benares are costly, and have a show of splendor about them, especially the Golden Temple; but it is more in show than reality. Even the Golden Temple, which is the pride of the Hindoos of Benares, and which more than all others is resorted to by pilgrims from afar, is not attractive either in its external or its internal appearance. The pointed dome, which is characteristic of this style of buildings, is not without beauty of outline, but there is usually nothing in the surroundings of these temples to make them pleasing, and they are far from being neatly kept.

A HINDOO TEMPLE.

In almost all respects they are in striking contrast with the magnificent mosques of the Mohammedans in the same cities, and there is a good reason for the contrast. When the Mohammedans subdued and took possession of India, they destroyed the monuments of the ancient religion, using the material for building their mosques, and at the same time prohibiting the erection of temples, excepting of very limited dimensions. Throughout the North of India, therefore, the Hindoos scarcely have any thing that can be called temples; they are all diminutive structures—mere shrines. Out of the hundreds or thousands that I saw, I think there was not one that would measure more than twenty-five feet in its greatest diameter. It is different in Southern India, where some of the most extensive structures in the world are to be found.

The ordinary services at the temple are not elaborate. The worshipers present offerings of flowers, fruits, jewels, money, etc., which become the perquisite of the priests. The life of a Hindoo is one of ceaseless devotion to his religion, and the visit to the temple may be only the last act in a long service or pilgrimage, or the initial step to some such enterprise, and consumes but little time. There are, indeed, occasions of grand ceremonial when the gods are taken out for an airing, but the shrines themselves afford no room for any gathering of the people. The assemblages take place at some consecrated spot, like the banks of the sacred rivers. As we approached the Golden Temple, we found it occupied by a small party of distinguished pilgrims from the up-country; and when they had retired it was flooded with the water of the Ganges, which had been poured upon their offerings to sanctify them. The temple, within and without, was in a very filthy condition.

Benares has a distinction in Asiatic history as the spot where the founders of Buddhism commenced the propagation of that religion. At one period it was firmly established in various parts of India, but at length was driven out to seek its home in more Eastern countries, where it is still exerting its sway over hundreds of millions. The ruins of Sarnath, an extensive Buddhist establishment near Benares, and the monasteries cut into the rocky mountains in the west of India, which I subsequently visited from Bombay, bespeak the firm hold which it once had upon the people among whom it originated.

The gold brocades of Benares are among the most costly and elegant fabrics of the world, rich and exquisite beyond description, and as costly as they are beautiful. As the merchants took them out of the safes and displayed them to us, we could almost imagine that the Mogul dynasty, in

RUINS NEAR BENARES.

all its gorgeous splendor, was to be re-established; we could not imagine how otherwise there could be a demand for such fabrics. Some of them were held at 900 rupees, or $450, the square yard.

## XIX.

### BENARES TO ALLAHABAD.

The night is the time for travel in India at all seasons of the year. As there was little that was attractive in the scenery through which we were to pass, we left Benares at the same hour of the evening at which we had entered it. We crossed the Ganges in the beautiful moonlight, which spread a wondrously weird sheen over the massive monuments to the false prophet, upon its thousand diminutive Hindoo temples and shrines, and along its magnificent ghauts. . Were we in the mystical land of the Arabian Nights, or in the dream-land of Hindoo mythology, or in the midst of the splendor of the old Mogul dynasty? We could scarcely say until we had crossed the Ganges, and entered the dépôt to take our seats in the railway cars. This was a modern reality.

At Chunar we passed a fortress celebrated alike in Mohammedan history and Hindoo mythology, near which, upon a lofty eminence, the Supreme Being is supposed to be seated personally, though invisibly, a portion of every day, and the remainder of the day at the sacred city of Benares.

Near Mirzapore, a few miles farther north, is the temple of the Goddess Kali, which in former times was the resort of the Thugs, the discovery of whose existence as a complete and extensive organization not many years since struck terror into the hearts of all the residents of India. To this temple they came to worship, and to present their offerings to their tutelary divinity before entering on any murderous expedition—a fearful instance of the power of a false system of religion to blind its devotees to the nature of crime. The goddess is represented in Bengal with a hideous black face and mouth streaming with blood, a very fury in appearance. Thuggism, if not a religious organization, was the next thing to it. The fraternity, while living by murder and robbery, were scrupulous in all their religious observances. They were even more pious in their way than the banditti of Italy, who would not for all the world eat meat on Friday, while they would not hesitate to cut off the ears of a refractory traveler, after robbing him, on any day in the week. The Thugs never undertook a criminal expedition until they had propitiated their Goddess Kali, with whom they afterward divided the spoil; and, being intensely superstitious, they were easily deterred from the commission of a crime, not by any enormity which it involved, but by the slightest evil omen. If one of their number happened to sneeze as they were starting upon an expedition, or if they met a woman with an empty pitcher, or heard an ass bray, the expedition was abandoned. They were not ordinary robbers. Their depredations were made only upon travelers, natives as well as foreigners, and murder was always the first step in the robbery. This is the explanation of the secrecy that they maintained so long. The pirate's maxim, "Dead men tell no tales," was one of their fundamental principles. They invariably put their victims to death, usually by strangling with a cord, and then buried them out of sight. Each gang had its *jemadar*, or leader; its *guru*, or teacher; its *sothas*, or entrappers; its *bhuttotes*, or stranglers; and its *lughaees*, or grave-diggers. These would usually meet at some town, often as pretended strangers to one another, select their victims, fall into company with them, and travel for days before seizing the opportunity for their meditated crime.

The discovery of this extensive organization was made in the year 1829. Individuals, and even gangs, had been detected from time to time, and, on being convicted of murder, had been executed, but it had never been known that all over India a secret association existed, with officers, and regulations, and pass-words, which had been devoted to this species of crime. One evening in the year named above, as Major Sleeman, the Deputy Commissioner of the English for the Saugor District, was seated at the door of his tent, a native came up to him in great haste, threw himself at his feet, and begged to make a communication of great importance, but to his ear alone. Mrs. Sleeman, who was present, retired, and the man then confessed that he was the leader of a gang of Thugs, who were near, and that the grove in which Major Sleeman's tent was pitched was filled with the graves of those who had been murdered from time to time. A search was made, and his words proved to be true. The gang was apprehended, information was obtained from one and another source until the proof of the existence of the organization in nearly every province and district of India was obtained. A knowledge of their proceedings, their regulations, their secret signs, and of the fearful extent of their crimes, was obtained and laid before government. The most thorough measures for their suppression were adopted, and carried out, it is now believed, with perfect success. Every known Thug throughout India was apprehended, and although the number was so great that condign punishment could not be meted out to all, the organization was broken up. The least guilty were formed into a sort of penal colony at Jubbulpore, where they were kept employed at various trades, secluded from intercourse with their former companions and with the community generally. It is hoped that, in the course of time, the traditions of this iniquity will so die out as to preclude the possibility of its revival. No statistics of the number of its victims during the ages in which it has had an organized existence could possibly be obtained, but the number must have been very great.

The following case, which I find in the records of Colonel Sleeman, will give an idea of the course which these murderers pursued, and of the remorseless perseverance with which they followed up their victims. It is drawn from the confessions of a Thug who had been apprehended and convicted of the crime.

S

"A stout Mogul officer, of noble bearing and singularly handsome countenance, on his way from the Punjaub to Oude, crossed the Ganges at Gurmuktesur Ghaut, near Meerut, to pass through Meradabad and Bareilly. He was mounted on a fine Turkee horse, and attended by his *kitmutgar* and groom. Soon after crossing the river he fell in with a small party of well-dressed and modest-looking men going the same road. They accosted him in a respectful manner, and attempted to enter into conversation with him. He had heard of Thugs, and told them to be off. They smiled at his idle suspicions, and tried to remove them, but all in vain; the Mogul was determined; they saw his nostrils swelling with indignation, took their leave, and followed slowly.

"The next morning he overtook the same number of men, but of a different appearance, all Mussulmans. They accosted him in the same respectful manner, talked of the dangers of the road, and the necessity of their keeping together and taking the advantage of the protection of any mounted gentleman that happened to be going the same way. The Mogul officer said not a word in reply, resolved to have no companions on the road. They persisted; his nostrils began again to swell, and, putting his hand to his sword, he bid them all be off, or he would have their heads from their shoulders. He had a bow and quiver full of arrows over his shoulder, a brace of loaded pistols in his waist-belt, and a sword by his side, and was altogether a very formidable-looking cavalier.

"In the evening another party that lodged in the same *serai* became very intimate with the butler and groom. They were going the same road, and, as the Mogul overtook them in the morning, they made their bows respectfully, and began to enter into conversation with their two friends, the groom and the butler, who were coming up behind. The Mogul's nostrils began again to swell, and he bid the strangers be off. The groom and butler interceded; for their master was a grave, sedate man, and they wanted companions. All would not do, and the strangers fell in the rear.

"The next day, when they had got to the middle of an extensive and uninhabited plain, the Mogul in advance, and his two servants a few hundred yards behind, he came up to a party of six poor Mussulmans sitting weeping by the side of a dead companion. They were soldiers from Lahore on their way to Lucknow, worn down by fatigue in their anxiety to see their wives and children once more after a long and painful service. Their companion, the hope and prop of his family, had sunk under the fatigue, and they had made a grave for him; but they were poor unlettered men, and unable to repeat the funeral service from the holy Koran; would his highness but perform this last office for them, he would, no doubt, find his reward in this world and in the next. The Mogul dismounted. The body had been placed in its proper position, with the head toward Mecca. A carpet was spread; the Mogul took off his bow and quiver, then his pistols and sword, and placed them on the ground near the body; called for water, and washed his feet, hands, and face, that he might not pronounce the holy words in an unclean state. He then knelt down and began to repeat the funeral service in a clear, loud voice. Two of the poor soldiers knelt by him, one on each side, in silence. The other four went off a few paces to beg that the butler and groom would not come so near as to interrupt the good Samaritan at his devotions. All being ready, one of the four, in a low undertone, gave the *shirnee* (the signal), the handkerchiefs were thrown over their necks, and in a few minutes all three, the Mogul and his servants, were dead, and lying in the grave in the usual manner—the head of one at the feet of one below him.

"All the parties they had met on the road belonged to a gang of Jumaldehee Thugs, of the kingdom of Oude. In despair of being able to win the Mogul's confidence in the usual way, and determined to have the money and jewels which they knew he carried with him, they had adopted this plan of disarming him—dug the grave by the side of the road in the open plain, and made a handsome young Mussulman of the party the dead soldier. The Mogul, being a very stout man, died almost without a struggle, and his servants made no resistance."

It was past midnight, but a night almost as bright as the day, when we rolled over the magnificent bridge that spans the Jumna at Allahabad, just above the union of its waters with those of the Ganges. The bridge is one of the most costly railway structures in or out of India. It is built of iron imported from England. The foundations of the high stone piers on which it rests were laid in the ooze of the river, which, in laying the foundations, seemed to be almost without bottom. The rise of water in the rainy season, which sometimes reaches forty feet, made it necessary to have elevated piers; and the bridge, which is three quarters of a mile in length, makes a fine appearance in the ordinary stages of the river.

We were delighted, on reaching the station at so late an hour of the night, to find the Rev. Mr. Walsh awaiting us. I had known him when a boy, but long ago he turned his steps eastward to preach the Gospel in the land of the Hindoos and the Mohammedans. Since the death of another friend and classmate, the Rev. Dr. Owen, Mr. Walsh has been the father of the American Mission at Allahabad. Taking us in his gharry, we drove mile after mile through the broad streets of this capital, until it seemed that the streets had no end; and when under these quiet Eastern skies, in the beauty of the night and in our pleasant converse, we almost wished they were endless. At length we reached the bungalow of the American Mission, and found a resting-place in an American home.

Allahabad (which means *the City of God*), a name given to it by the Mohammedan conquerors of India, is one of the sacred places of the Hindoos. It has been a point of much importance in all the changes which have occurred among the rulers of Hindostan, and has been fortified from time to time under different dynasties. The present fortress, a mile and a half in circuit, situated at the junction of the Ganges and Jumna Rivers, was built by Akbar, one of the Mogul emperors, three hundred years ago, on the site of an ancient Hindoo fortification. It has been remodeled and strengthened by the English, and has been of incalculable value to them. During the mutiny of 1857 it proved the salvation of many of the English residents at Allahabad; and contributed greatly to the final recovery of British power in India. It has acquired much importance within a few years by the removal of the capital from Agra to this place. A new city, with broad avenues and spacious squares, has been laid out, and large public buildings, including some of the finest barracks in India, have been in course of erection. Many beautiful bungalows have been built, and are surrounded by extensive grounds; and although, like our own Washington, Allahabad, for the present, "is a city of magnificent distances" rather than an imposing capital, it bids fair to become one of the finest towns in the peninsula. In the mutiny, every foreign residence was destroyed, with every public building, excepting the Masonic Hall, which the natives did not dare to attack on account of the spirits that were supposed to guard it. This building was pointed out to me in a remote part of the town, a lonely monument of the terrible scenes which it survived.

Allahabad has long been one of the most important mission stations of the American Presbyterian Church. It was selected not only on account of its large population, but as a centre of influence for the whole north of India, and in one respect it has a peculiar importance. It is the chief place of pilgrimage, and through the multitudes that gather here every year an influence may be sent out into every part of the land. Situated at the confluence of the two most sacred rivers of Hindostan—the Ganges and the Jumna—the spot is regarded by all Hindoos as one of the holiest places in the world. They come to it from all parts and at all times of the year to bathe where the two rivers meet, and thus to wash away their sins. There is an annual mela or gathering at this place in the month of January, when hundreds of thousands come together; and every twelfth year, owing to some propitious conjunction of the stars, there is a special gathering, when the number of the pilgrims is sometimes counted even by millions.

I first reached Allahabad in December, on my way to the north; but, after visiting the Himalaya Mountains, I returned to be present at the opening of the great mela on the 12th of January. It is held on a vast plain—a tongue of land lying between the two rivers, which in the rainy season is completely overflowed. When the pilgrims assemble they pitch their tents upon the plain, and for the space of a month it is the most populous city in India. I learned afterward, from one of the missionaries, that two millions were present at one time, and I could easily comprehend it from what I had seen.

I took my stand, one day, in a thoroughfare leading to the grounds, to see the people pouring in by crowds, many of whom came from hundreds of miles up and down the country. I had seen them far up to the north, the week before, coming down in large companies. They continued to arrive at all hours of day and night for days and even for weeks, like a continuous procession. Some of the wealthier people came on elephants, others on camels, many of them, especially the aged and feeble, in carts drawn by bullocks or cows, but most of them on foot, with the dust and dirt of their long pilgrimage upon them. In the vast crowd were thousands of *faquirs* or devotees, who were almost naked and covered with dirt, their hair matted with filth, more disgusting in their appearance than swine, and accounting themselves all the more holy because of the excessive filth in which they had chosen to live. Bathing in muddy streams and living in abominable filth seem to be the two prominent articles in the creed of the Hindoos, at least of those who pretend to eminent holiness—the very reverse of the Christian maxim that "cleanliness is a part of godliness." More abominable or more horrid specimens of human nature than these *faquirs* can scarcely be conceived; and the more painful part of it was, that the poor ignorant people had been taught to regard these filthy, depraved brutes in human shape as pre-eminently holy. Some of the devotees had made their pilgrimage all the way upon their hands and knees, others by dragging themselves along the ground, and one man, perhaps more, by measuring his length like an inch worm, lying down, making a mark at his head, and then lying down with his toes at the mark, and so making his slow progress toward the consecrated spot. One man whom I saw at the mela had held his right hand above his head eleven years, and was, of course, accounted an eminent saint.

The Brahmins keep up these festivals for the sake of making money out of the pilgrims. Each one is required to pay his tax as he comes to bathe, and so a large revenue comes to the coffers of the Brahmins of the district. The *faquirs*, too, extort money from the people on the ground of their sanctity, but a more transparent set of knaves I never looked upon. They showed it in their countenances; but long practice and established custom had given them an ascendency and power over the people. One of the first acts of a pilgrim (the *faquirs* excepted) is to have his head shaven by regularly appointed barbers, under the assurance that for every hair he loses he secures to himself a million of years in Paradise; a favor for which he is compelled to make a return in money according to his means. By this operation the pockets of the pilgrims are as well fleeced as their heads. Then comes the bathing; and a sorrowful sight are those tens of thousands of poor, sin-burdened heathen, going down into the water and devoutly washing themselves, in the vain hope of washing away their guilt. All classes and all ages go down into the water; even the women of the higher class being exempt, for the time, from the law of custom which compels them to live in seclusion. I longed for the gift of speaking, not only to their ears, but to their hearts, of that fountain for sin and for uncleanness which has been opened by a dying Saviour, and which is free and near to all, without any painful pilgrimage. But this is done by faithful missionaries, who have their tents pitched at various points among the crowd, and who improve this occasion for imparting religious instruction, and not without success.

After the pilgrims have been shaven, and have bathed and performed other religious services, they devote themselves to social intercourse, to traffic, and often to all manner of wickedness, so that the mela becomes a mixed scene, the religious part bearing but a slight proportion to the whole. I believe that the whole system of idolatry in India is now sustained more by the avarice of

Brahmins, who become wealthy from their perquisites and by the incidental gains connected with it, than by the religious feelings of the people. Priestcraft has a mighty power in keeping up rites which, if left to the choice even of ignorant people, would speedily come to an end. At the great mela at Allahabad I heard many confess that Christianity was better than their religion, but they are bound by education, and custom, and caste. It is not a slight evidence, though only one of many, that the religion of Christ has taken hold of the people of India, to see preaching-tents established by the Hindoos, with readers and preachers, who endeavor to counteract the preaching of the Gospel by drawing away and holding the attention of the people. I had seen the same thing in China. In the city of Canton the Chinese have built a beautiful chapel, in all respects like the Christian, where they have regular preaching. Amid the melancholy scenes connected with this great aggregation of heathenism at Allahabad, there is much that gives promise of a bright day at hand, when the gross darkness that has so long covered the people will be dispelled.

The only witness against the British government for its complicity with the idolatry of the Hindoos that I saw remaining in India was at Allahabad. In the fort there is a passage leading to extensive subterranean vaults, which from time immemorial have been regarded with great veneration by the natives. They pretend that the passage leads to Benares, nearly a hundred miles distant, and that a third sacred river once coursed through it. The multitudes who come on pilgrimage to Allahabad all enter this vault, pay their devotions, and make some offering, on which they pour the water of the Ganges and the Jumna to consecrate the gift. There are numerous shrines, all, I believe, of the *Lingam*, the obscene object of Hindoo worship, which are constantly covered with flowers and kept wet with the holy water. Formerly the pilgrims who entered were required to pay a tax of one rupee each to the government, which became an immense revenue. The tax has been abolished, but I saw these obscene pagan shrines still standing, and the devotees in crowds presenting their offerings and paying their worship before them with the British flag flying over their heads on the fort. It is a reproach and a shame to a Christian government, and the more so because connected with a fortress which belongs exclusively to the government.

## XX.

#### THE MUTINY; CAWNPORE AND LUCKNOW.

AFTER I had been several weeks in India, the question was asked me, by one who naturally enough wished to know how I had been impressed with the country and its people, "What, of all that you have seen, has struck you most forcibly?" I replied, "The fact that no two persons seem to entertain the same ideas with regard to any subject."

I was never in a country where there is such a diversity of sentiment in regard to questions of public policy, the right mode of dealing with social problems, or even in regard to many matters of fact. Scarcely any thing appears to be settled in the general opinion of the people—the Europeans, I mean. The very names of places and things are without any established rules. Every writer has his own orthography, and every speaker his own pronunciation of native words. The languages of the country have never yet found their equivalents in the English tongue. I was told that there are sixty-four different ways of spelling the name of *Lodiana*, a town in the north of India, and that each one has good authority for it. I have seen the name of the beautiful valley of the *Dehra Doon*, that I visited among the Himalaya Mountains, written *Dehrah, Deirah, Deira, Deyra, Deyrah, Dera*, and so on *ad libitum*.

But in no respect was I more struck with the diversity

of sentiment among intelligent and well-informed persons than in regard to the cause of the terrible mutiny of 1857, which came so near extinguishing the power of the English in the East. I not only felt a strong desire, in going over the ground where its fearful scenes were enacted, to learn more than I had known before of the causes which led to it, the impelling motives which fired the natives, but I imagined that I should be able to obtain such knowledge by personal intercourse with the residents, many of whom had been there during its progress and suppression. But almost every intelligent man in India seemed to have his own theory in regard to the matter, and very few, on comparing notes, would be found to agree. It certainly speaks well for the independence of thought in that land, but it shows also that this awful episode in the history of the British occupation of India is still involved in much mystery. And this is just about the truth in regard to the matter. I doubt if any rebellion of equal extent and importance ever before occurred which could not be traced more directly and more clearly to its origin.

The nearest approximation that I made to a definite opinion of my own, after careful investigation of all the sources of information, and all the opinions current, is, that the mutiny was a sort of blind movement on the part alike of Mohammedans and Hindoos (though more the former than the latter) to cast off the foreign yoke which had been placed on their necks by a series of usurpations, too often attended with the very crimes of which the natives themselves had been guilty in past ages. One monarch after another had been dethroned by the agents of the East India Company, and his territory added to the Company's possessions, or made tributary. It had become clear that the same power, unless absolutely destroyed, must cover the whole land, and the opportunity was seized, when the English military force was reduced to its lowest limits, to rise and attempt to annihilate the foreign element. In the spring of 1857 there were only about twenty thousand

British troops in all India. The army was composed almost altogether of native troops. There was not a European regiment at Calcutta, nor at Benares, nor at Delhi, nor at many other important points. There must have been conference or conspiracy for some time previous, for the mutinous spirit manifested itself almost simultaneously from one end of Hindostan to the other. The train had been laid, and the explosion passed with frightful rapidity from one city and district to another.

The occasion for such a rising, too, was opportune in more respects than one. A prophecy had long been in circulation among the natives that on the hundredth anniversary of the battle of Plassey, which secured the supremacy of the English in India, their power would be destroyed. That battle took place June 23, 1757, and the eventful day was drawing nigh. The success of such a revolt seemed the more assured by the defenseless state of the English in the country at the time. The introduction of greased cartridges was another coinciding element. This has been regarded by some as the actual cause of the mutiny, but it was simply a coincidence, and was made use of as an incitement to revolt. Artfully was it seized upon, and successfully was it employed. To make use of the new cartridges according to regulation, the soldiers must bite off the end before inserting them in the musket. The report was circulated through the whole army that they had been greased with a composition of tallow and lard—the former an abomination to the Hindoo, and the latter to the Mohammedan. The Hindoo would as soon draw a razor across his throat as put a particle of the fat of the cow to his lips, and a Mohammedan would perish before he would have any thing to do with the fat of the swine. The report was circulated that by this means the English intended to compel both classes to abjure their religion, and it was effectively used as one of the instruments by which the troops, Hindoos and Mohammedans, were stirred up to revolt.

It is a very remarkable fact that no satisfactory evidence

has ever been found that the rebellion had any real head or leader, or that it was designed to re-establish any one of the old dynasties, or to found a new one. Conspiracy there must have been, but there were no arch-conspirators, and there was no well-executed plan of action. Some have implicated the effete family of the old King of Delhi; some have regarded the ex-King of Oude, a sort of state prisoner at Calcutta, as being its moving spirit; some have given the same position to the monster Nana Sahib; but I do not think there is any proof that any one of these, or others who have been named, played any such ambitious part in the terrible drama. The mutiny was more Mohammedan than Hindoo in its origin and in progress; but this, perhaps, was owing to the fact that the Mohammedans had been so long the ruling race.

Equally mysterious with its origin were the means used in preparing for a concerted movement throughout India. At the commencement of the year 1857 it was noticed that a peculiar kind of small cakes of unleavened bread, called *chupatties*, were distributed through the whole country. A messenger appeared at a village with these cakes, he sought out the head man of the place and gave him six, with the charge that he was to send six more to the next village, and so they passed from one end of the land to the other, and exerted a talismanic power which has never been explained. Just about the same time lotus flowers were sent to the native soldiers at the various cantonments, and they, too, passed from hand to hand with the same effect. Strange to say, the peculiar significance of these tokens has never transpired, so profoundly have the secrets of the mutiny been preserved. The history of the world will scarcely furnish a parallel to the anomalies and mysteries connected with this whole matter.

The first serious signs of disaffection appeared at Dundum, near Calcutta, in January, 1857. The Sepoys objected to the greased cartridges, but they professed to be satisfied when they were excused from using them. The same disaffection showed itself, and from the same ostensible cause, soon after at Barrackpore, opposite Serampore, on the Hoogly, where incendiary fires also occurred. A general order for the whole army was then issued allowing the soldiers to tear off the end of the cartridge instead of biting it, but it had no good effect. All this time the English authorities slept, as it were, in profound security, ignorant of the storm that was so soon to burst upon them. Other and more serious disturbances took place, but without awakening apprehension. It was not until April that the country was roused. Scenes of insubordination and violence occurred at Meerut, far to the north, extended to Delhi, and spread with fearful rapidity until the whole army was in revolt. Forts and towns were seized by the rebels, the English officers and residents slaughtered without mercy, or subjected to the most horrible outrages that fiends could inflict. The magazine in the great fort at Delhi, which contained a vast amount of stores of all kinds, guns, and ammunition, was defended by a small force of English against a horde of rebels until the unequal contest could no longer be maintained, when, instead of surrendering to the enemy, the feeble garrison applied the torch to the train, and thousands of the assailants perished with the besieged in the explosion. Straggling Europeans escaped destruction at Delhi and other places to wander for months in the jungle, some to be preserved almost by miracle from all horrible forms of death. Incidents of this character occurred which are too harrowing to be repeated.

At Allahabad, a native regiment stationed in the town suddenly revolted; shot down the superior officers and bayoneted the younger; attacked the residents, men, women, and children, cutting them in pieces while alive; children were tossed on the bayonets of the native soldiers before the eyes of their mothers, and atrocities committed which the pen can not record. The remnant of English who escaped took refuge in the fort, which was besieged by the Sepoys. A train of powder was laid, and the besieged were prepared to blow themselves up and perish in the explosion, as at Delhi, the moment the fort should be taken. But English troops arrived from below, and they were preserved. All through the mutiny the fort was a rallying-point for the English.

From Delhi, and from other cities where the English families were congregated, women and children made their escape from the general massacre—sometimes in small companies, but generally alone—and wandered for days exposed to the intense heat of the summer sun, when they could scarcely exist in the shade, and at night lay down in the jungle without shelter, and at last perished from hunger, fatigue, terror, the stroke of the sun, or the wild beasts. At Agra, the foreign population, with few exceptions, succeeded in reaching the fort, where they had time to shut themselves in before the bursting of the storm; and here they endured a voluntary but fearful imprisonment more than four months, not knowing any thing of the fate of their friends or what might be going on in other parts of India. I met at Delhi a lady who passed through this long siege, enduring the agony of suspense in the fear that all the rest of India was in the hands of the Sepoys.

But the chief horrors of the mutiny centred at Cawnpore, and were perpetrated under the orders of the monster Nana Sahib. This station was occupied by Sir Hugh Wheeler with a small body of English troops, who had under their protection several hundred women and children belonging to the families resident in the city and the neighborhood. Having no fortress, they hastily intrenched themselves by throwing up earth-works on the open plain. The space they occupied was about two hundred yards square, and included a few small buildings. There were nine hundred persons in all within this narrow space. A murderous fire was opened upon them by the Sepoys, which, with famine, the burning sun of June, the close confinement, and other causes, told fearfully upon their numbers from day to day. Many died, and some went raving mad.

At length the enemy began to pour upon them red-hot shot, which fired the buildings, the sick perishing in the flames. The soldiers would have cut their way through the multitude of Sepoy soldiers, even at the risk of all perishing in the attempt, but for the hundreds of women and children who were under their protection.

While in this extremity, they received an offer from the rebel leader, Nana Sahib, that if they would abandon the intrenchments and the treasure which they had been guarding, the survivors should be furnished with boats and an escort to take them down the Ganges to Allahabad. It was not until Nana Sahib had signed the contract and confirmed his promise with a solemn oath that the offer was accepted. Conveyances were provided for taking the wounded, the sick, and the feeble to the river, about a mile distant. They were in the act of embarking, when, by the order of Nana Sahib, a battery opened upon them and numbers were slain. A few boat-loads hastily rowed across the river, but they were seized by the Sepoys, the men all sabred, and the women and children carried back to the camp of the monster who had thus violated his pledge. For weeks they were incarcerated in a building at Cawnpore, where they were subjected to the brutality of the Sepoy troops. A rumor having reached the rebels that a military force was on the march from Allahabad to rescue the captives, an order was given that they should be slain—not an unwelcome order to those who were suffering a thousand deaths. At sunset on the 15th of July, volleys of musketry were fired into the doors and windows of the building, after which the bayonet and the sword did their work, until all were supposed to be dead, and the building was closed for the night. The next morning it was found that a number were still alive, who, upon being brought out, either threw themselves or were thrown into a large well in the compound, with the dead of the night before. Thus perished all who had survived the slaughter of the ghaut, nearly two hundred in all. The whole number of victims at Cawnpore was about one thousand. The army, under Havelock, entered Cawnpore the day after the massacre, driving out the rebels before them; and when they reached the building which was the scene of the massacre, found it strewed with the relics of the departed ones—remnants of clothing, ladies' and children's shoes, locks of hair, and other mementoes—and the floor covered deep with their blood. The brave soldiers were almost maddened by the sight.

On the plain at Cawnpore is one of the most beautiful parks in the East, laid out in exquisite taste, and planted with trees, and shrubbery, and ever-blooming flowers. In the midst of this park rise the marble walls of a sacred inclosure, in the centre of which, over the fatal well, stands a marble statue—an angel having in his arms the palm-leaves, emblematical of martyrdom and victory. This park was laid out and planted after the mutiny, and called the Memorial Garden; but it seemed designed as much to mitigate with its beauty, as to preserve by its monuments, the memories of the spot. The pedestal, on which stands the angel, bears the following inscription:

"SACRED TO THE PERPETUAL MEMORY OF A GREAT COMPANY OF CHRISTIAN PEOPLE—CHIEFLY WOMEN AND CHILDREN—WHO, NEAR THIS SPOT, WERE CRUELLY MASSACRED BY THE FOLLOWERS OF THE REBEL NANA DHOONDOPUNT OF BITHOOR, AND CAST, THE DYING WITH THE DEAD, INTO THE WELL BELOW, ON THE 15TH DAY OF JULY, 1857."

While General Wheeler and his command, with his precious charge, were still in their frail intrenchment, the mutiny broke out at Futteghur, higher up the Ganges. This has long been one of the chief stations of the American Presbyterian missions to India. All the Mission buildings, including a valuable printing-office, were destroyed. The foreign residents were put to the sword, the English officers and civilians being the first to suffer. The survivors, including four American missionary families, attempted to escape in boats, hoping to reach Allahabad. The Americans were Rev. Messrs. Freeman, Campbell, Johnson, and

McMullen, with their wives, and two children of Mr. Campbell. Mr. Freeman had been my classmate and intimate friend at Princeton Seminary.

The large party, one hundred and thirty in all, floated down the Ganges, all the while in terror of the natives. Twice they were fired on by the Sepoys, and a lady, nurse, and child were killed. Once, as they landed at evening to cook some food on the shore, they were surprised by a zemindar, who made them his prisoners; but they were released on the payment of a large ransom. On the fourth day the boats ran aground near an island a few miles above Cawnpore. The whole party went ashore and concealed themselves in the long grass, where they remained in constant apprehension of discovery, and with little hope of escape. In this hiding-place they assembled for prayer and preparation for death, the missionaries leading them to the throne of God's mercy to seek grace for the hour of greater trial that awaited them, and exhorting every one to steadfast trust in Him who would bring salvation even in death. The record of those solemn scenes was derived from four native Christians, who were the only survivors. Near the close of the fourth day they were discovered by a body of Sepoys, who came upon the island, made them prisoners, and, deaf to all appeals for mercy and offers of ransom, took them across the river on the way to Cawnpore. Though exhausted with long fasting and anxiety, they were tied together with ropes, and men, women, and children compelled to take up the line of march on foot. Night overtaking them, it was spent on the plain in the open air, the Sepoys keeping guard over them to prevent their escape. Early the next morning they were taken into Cawnpore to Nana Sahib, who ordered them to be drawn up in line on the parade-ground, where they were indiscriminately shot down. Those who survived the volley of musketry were dispatched with the sabre. When they were first seized by the Sepoys, the missionaries dismissed the four native Christians, advising them to seek their own safety, but in no circumstances to deny their Lord and Master. One of them, a man who had been a servant to the Maharajah Dhuleep Singh, disguised himself, followed the captive party, and was a witness to the last fearful scene in which their lives were offered up. From him the knowledge of their fate was obtained.

The remarkable fact that from the breaking out of the mutiny to its close not a single Christian convert took any part in the fearful outbreak, is the most emphatic condemnation of the blind and fatal policy of the East India Company in discouraging the propagation of Christianity among its dependent population in India, and especially in the army. The chaplains of the army, Christian ministers, were strictly forbidden to interfere in any manner with the religion of the native troops. This tenderness was repaid by the revolt of those who had been dealt with in such mistaken policy. The whole conduct of the native troops during the rebellion was strikingly characteristic of Oriental and Indian character. The most of them joined in the mutiny at the very commencement, many of them exhibiting the ferocity of wild beasts. Some hesitated for months, and at length joined the mutineers. Some regiments remained loyal to the English during the rebellion, resisting all inducements to engage in the revolt, even when it promised to be successful, and at the very last mutinied when it was evident that it must be suppressed. Some, though comparatively few, remained faithful to the end. So made up of contradictions and mysteries is the native character.

What became of the monster Nana Sahib is one of the mysteries of the rebellion. Whether he perished in the suppression of the mutiny, or escaped to die in exile, no one knows to this day.

It was evening when we reached Cawnpore. By twilight we drove across the parade-ground where so many brave and tender hearts had ceased to beat. It was late before we were all arranged for the night at Noor Mahomed's hotel in a distant part of the town; but the moon came out to look upon the scene once so fearful, now so placid, and I could not resist the impulse, even at that weird hour, to visit the places so full of interest to all who have read the story of the Sepoy rebellion. I wandered down to the Ganges, to the *Suttee Chowra Ghaut,* where General Wheeler's force was treacherously slain. It was a lonely spot, and the stillness of the grave reigned over it, broken only by the ripple of the flowing river, the cry of the night-birds, and an occasional howl of a jackal. In that quiet hour, with the personal and the historic recollections which came thronging upon the heart, the interest of all India seemed to centre in Cawnpore.

The next morning, after spending an hour in the Memorial Garden, we took leave of Cawnpore and went on to Lucknow, the scene of the memorable siege.

Lucknow is about forty miles to the northeast of Cawnpore, with which, and with the East Indian Railway, it is connected by a branch road. The Cawnpore Station is on the opposite side of the Ganges, which we crossed by one of the usual bridges of boats, which are much better adapted to these swift-flowing and rapidly-rising streams than one might suppose. As we crossed the bridge early in the morning, I looked up the stream for the island on which one of the large companies that had been massacred by the orders of Nana Sahib had been seized on their flight down the river from Futteghur, after lying concealed for three days in the grass. The same river on which they had floated still flowed on in its course; the same landmarks were scattered along its shores, but the fearful scenes which they had witnessed were among the things of the past.

It was near noon when the domes and minarets of Lucknow rose into view, and grand was the sight. Few of the cities of India could compare in outward splendor with the capital of Oude as it was before the mutiny, or even as it now stands. It lays claim to great antiquity, dating far back in the shadowy periods of Hindoo history; but

The King of Oude, whose possessions were the last to be seized by the East India Company, reigned here in great splendor. He had just completed the Kaiser Bagh — the extensive palace which forms the most striking feature in the view of the city, having expended in its construction and embellishment eighty lacs of rupees (about four millions of dollars) — when the British authorities informed him that they required his extensive and rich dominions, and that he must lay down his sceptre and his crown. Lord Dalhousie, who was then governor general, proposed to settle on him a large pension; but the king, very naturally, was reluctant to resign his authority and his revenues, and steadfastly refused to put his hand to any deed of conveyance. When compelled to retire, he sent his queen to England to plead his cause before another queen, Victoria; but before she returned the mutiny of 1857 broke out, and his fate was sealed. He now resides, a sort of prisoner, on his own purchased estate, two or three miles below Calcutta, on the Hoogly. By many this seizure of the territory of Oude and the sale of the personal property of the king is regarded as the immediate cause of the rebellion.

There is more of show in the city of Lucknow than of solid grandeur, such as we see at Benares, or of the exquisite taste and almost inconceivable costliness that we find at Agra and the old Mogul capital at Delhi; but with its domes, and minarets, and imposing structures, it is a realization of all one's dreams of Eastern magnificence. The palace, gorgeous in its style of architecture, and colored to resemble a vast structure of gold, with its lofty dome of real gold, looms up before the eye; the *Hoseinabad Imaumbara*, built by Ali Shah, and elaborately ornamented; the *Jumma Musjid*, the Grand Mosque; the magnificent marble tombs of former kings, more beautiful than the palaces; the *Great Imaumbara*, the architects of which were commanded to produce a building which should be unlike any others ever built (in which they succeeded), and which should surpass them all in beauty and magnificence (in which they failed); the *Dilkhoosha* palace, where the heroic soldier, Sir Henry Havelock, breathed his last; the *Martinière*, from the dome of which the mountains of Cabool are seen, though a hundred miles distant—these, and many other striking buildings, set like gems in the midst of Oriental foliage, give a grandeur to the views of the city which can not be transferred to the written page. A drive through Lucknow and its suburbs is one of rare beauty and of indescribable interest.

Notwithstanding all this Eastern splendor, I felt wonderfully like entering a familiar city when entering Lucknow. Years before I had become familiar with its appearance and localities in reading the history of the memorable siege, in which the garrison of British soldiers, protecting hundreds of women and children, were surrounded by 50,000 Sepoys, and subjected to a murderous fire day and night, without any communication with the outer world for 113 days. I had followed the noble Havelock and his brave troops in their long march under the burning sun of India, and as they cut their way through the multitudinous Sepoys into the Residency, only to find that their force was still too feeble to compel the enemy to raise the siege. I had read with the same intense interest the story of the final relief of the besieged, by Sir Colin Campbell, with his Highland brigade; of their going forth by night, leaving the city in the hands of the rebels; and of its final capture the following year by the most heroic fighting recorded in the annals of war. All these scenes were so familiar that I did not feel like being in a strange city.

After finding quarters at the Imperial Hotel (it bore about the same relation to a genuine republican hotel that a marble tomb, with its one lonely couch, does to a cheerful home), our first visit was to the Residency, the scene of the siege. It was the former residence or palace of the British commissioner, and occupied a slight elevation, an area of a few acres, within the city. At the breaking out of the mutiny, the *Muchee Bhowan* fort, being found untenable, was blown up, and the garrison retired to the Residency, where they threw up earth-works, and endured the long siege.

By the kindness of Dr. Fayrer, of Calcutta, former surgeon at the Residency, I had been furnished with diagrams and notes made during the siege, which greatly aided me in reviewing its memorable history. The original garrison, as it left the fort, numbered about 1700 men, of whom nearly half were native troops. At the relief there were left, including sick and wounded, only 350 Europeans and 133 natives. Several hundred women and children spent the five months of the siege chiefly in the cellars of the buildings, where they awaited their rescue in anxious and protracted suspense.

It was a mystery I could not solve, excepting in the reflection that the Almighty had thrown a shield over this company of imperiled souls, that for so many months they not only could endure the privations, and suspense, and anxiety, and heat, in such quarters, but still more that they could survive the storm of iron hail which day and night was poured upon them by tens of thousands of infuriated native troops. Their numbers were greatly reduced by death, but the preservation and final escape of any seemed the next thing to a miracle. At any hour within the many months of the siege, the enemy, by mere force of numbers, might have carried the whole place by storm, and put the entire garrison, with the women and children, to the sword. But they had no leader of sufficient courage, and the hand of God held back the mutineers.

With melancholy interest I went into the *Dilkhoosha* Palace, where General Havelock, after escaping uninjured the perils of war, sank under an attack of dysentery, and died while the British forces were making their successful escape from the city. I visited also the summer palace of the king, *Alum Bagh*, two or three miles out of town, to which the body of Havelock was carried, and where a force was left to hold the place until the recapture of the city the following year. The tomb of the hero stands in the centre of the garden, and bears a long and very inappropriate inscription.

The inscription on the stone that marks the grave of Sir Henry Lawrence, in the cemetery of the Residency, seemed equally infelicitous: "Here lies Henry Lawrence, who tried to do his duty. May God have mercy on his soul." The explanation should be made that these were words which this excellent man uttered as he was sinking into the arms of death. Like Havelock, he was a man of decided Christian character. After being struck by the fatal shell, as he was lying in the open veranda of Dr. Fayrer's house, to which he was carried, and while exposed to the constant fire of the enemy, he asked to have the holy communion administered to him, many of the officers joining in the service. He expressed his firm trust in the atonement of Christ for the pardon of his sins, and his hope of heaven through the merits of the Savior. He spoke in words of deepest tenderness, and with bitter tears, of his absent wife and daughter, whom he should not see again on earth. He then earnestly entreated all around him to prepare for the realities of another world, reminding them of the vanity of all earthly distinctions, and, referring to his own honors, asked, "What is it all worth now?" and died.

It is an ungracious task to spoil a romantic story, but the thrilling incident connected with the siege of Lucknow, read the world over with such intense interest — the hearing of the pibroch of the Highlanders under Sir Colin Campbell by a Highland girl long before any sound or tidings of the approaching army reached any other ear, related as an instance of the Highland second-sight or hearing—was a pure fiction.

Two or three weeks after I was at Lucknow, and while I was still in the country, I received by post a copy of a newspaper in Persian, printed at Lucknow, which contained the following notice of our visit at that place. I have the original now before me, but I give a translation made by a Hindoo friend who had not yet attained to a very accurate use of the English language:

"VOYAGE ROUND THE WORLD.

"Dr. Prime, with few of his friends, left New York in August, 1869, and, after visiting few places in America, came to Pacific; from thence on a steamer to Japan and China, and, after seeing some famous cities, he left for Calcutta, and reached in December. From there he came up country to Lucknow *via* Allahabad. He has now left for Agra and Delhi, and afterwards he intends to visit Egypt, Constantinople, and Turkey, and then direct to his native land. We think that this will take about fourteen months.

"What a nice thing is this, that people can journey throughout the world with great ease and comfort. And from this we find a strong proof that the earth is round."

## XXI.

### AGRA AND THE TAJ.

From Lucknow we returned to Cawnpore, and took the cars of the East India Railway for Agra. At Toondla Junction, where we were to make a change, we had the only rain that fell while we were in India, and this was out of season. We reached Toondla after midnight, and, while waiting for the train, the heavens grew black, and shot forth shafts and sheets of lightning, accompanied with heavy thunder. It rained heavily until morning.

On reaching Agra we made our way to Beaumont's East Indian Hotel, pleasantly located in the midst of a charming compound outside of the native town, and we flattered ourselves that we had reached a delightful retreat, in which we could spend a few days luxuriously in this old capital of the Timours. But, alas!—We had a bungalow all to ourselves, but the bungalow was nearly all that we had. Our sleeping-rooms were without furniture excepting a bedstead and mattress. We found that we were expected to furnish the bedding ourselves. In India Europeans have been in the habit of traveling with tents, taking with them all the comforts and necessaries of life.

When I first reached Calcutta I wrote to an old friend in the extreme north, informing him of my arrival, and asking him to secure accommodations for our party at a hotel or government bungalow in the city in which he was residing. I received in reply a hearty welcome to the country, with the assurance that, as there was no hotel in the place, he would arrange for the accommodation of the entire party at private houses *provided* we brought our own beds and bedding with us. When we reached Agra we had not laid in a supply of linen, and inquisition was at once made at the principal hotel in the city, but, after the most diligent search, only four sheets could be mustered for seven persons, not all mated. Of course, no one could have more than a single sheet, and not every one could have even that.

We found it almost as difficult to make a living at the table, the commissariat being as poorly supplied as the wardrobe. The servants were all natives who had never found it convenient to cultivate the English language, and we had no time to cultivate the Hindustani, Persian, Mahratta, or any of the numerous dialects of the region, so that we fared ill while we were guests at the East Indian hotel.

After a vain attempt to gather up the fragments of the sleep which we had lost on the rail and at the stations during the night, we sallied forth to visit the renowned fort and palace of the emperors. Agra, or, as it was once called, Akbarabad, first rose to importance in the beginning of the sixteenth century, and from 1526 to 1658 it was the capital of the house of Timour. Here, for more than a century, the Moguls lavished their wealth on costly buildings to be occupied while they lived, and erected still more costly structures in which to repose after they were dead.

The fortress, which is a mile and a half in circumference, and which contains the palace, was built by the Emperor Akbar. It stands upon the banks of the Jumna, the massive walls on the river side being sixty feet in height, and commanding a magnificent view of the river and country. When it was built it was a fortress of immense strength, but the mode of warfare has changed in modern times; it would not now be regarded as impregnable. It served, however, as a shelter to the European families during the four or five months of the mutiny in which they were shut up and shut out from all communication with the rest of the world, but kept secure from the hordes of mutineers that swarmed around them. Nearly six thousand refugees from the city and the neighboring country were thus protected.

As a specimen of the manner in which the old emperors were accustomed to fortify their palaces, it may be mentioned that when Agra was taken by the British in 1803, among the spoils found within the fort was a cannon of twenty-three inches bore, the metal eleven and a half inches thick at the muzzle, fourteen feet and two inches in length, and weighing ninety-six thousand pounds. It carried a ball of cast-iron weighing fifteen hundred pounds. This stupendous piece of ordnance was blown into fragments by the orders of a British officer, who perhaps had some fear that he might live long enough to feel the weight of one of its balls.

The entrance to the fortress is strongly protected by towers and passages elaborately constructed, such a gateway as none but a powerful assault could force. We drove through it into the grand court, and alighting, entered the Diwan-i-maum, the ancient judgment-hall in which the Mogul emperors dispensed justice after the manner of the times. Strange as well as splendid scenes had passed within those walls, when an empire rich beyond all precedent yielded its immense revenues to fill the coffers and swell the state of those despotic monarchs.

The palace stands in the same inclosure, one portion of its walls, with its stone balconies, overhanging, at a dizzy height, the walls of the fort itself. It was built by Shah

Jehan, grandson of Akbar, and, like every thing in architecture that he undertook, was executed at immense expense and in exquisite taste. This emperor celebrated his accession to the throne by a festival which, according to Khafi Khan, cost more than fifteen millions of rupees (a sum equal to $7,500,000); and although he expended hundreds of millions on costly structures and their adornment, and hundreds of millions more upon his army, he had in his treasury, when he died, more than $100,000,000 of coined money, besides a vast accumulation of the precious metals in bullion, jewels, and precious stones.

The palace was laid out upon a scale of great magnificence, designed alike for the entertainment as well as the luxurious living of its inmates. One of the court-yards was arranged in mosaic for a game resembling chess, in which the men, living persons, made the moves according to the order of the emperor and his guests, who were seated in the fretted marble balconies above. The bath, a suite of marble rooms, was set with thousands of convex mirrors, which multiplied the artificial lights by myriads, making it a scene of splendor indescribable.

The *Motee Musjid*, or Pearl Mosque, standing near the Judgment Hall, is an exquisite specimen of architecture and of the sculptor's art, of the finest marble, the interior carved in flowers and vines, chaste and simple, but surpassingly beautiful. It is not alone the Pearl Mosque; it is the pearl of mosques, unequaled in purity and beauty by any similar structure.

But all that we had seen in the forts of Akbar and the palace of Shah Jehan was eclipsed by another structure, the most sublime and beautiful that now stands upon the face of the earth. This, I believe, is the unqualified testimony of every one who has seen the Taj.

About a mile to the south of the fort at Agra, upon the right bank of the River Jumna, lies a beautiful park, about a quarter of a mile square, planted with the choicest trees, and shrubs, and flowers of the East. More than eighty fountains, scattered along the avenues of this park, throw their jets into the air, which sparkles with the falling drops as with a shower of diamonds. It is surrounded by a high wall, and guarded by a magnificent gateway, a building fifty or sixty feet in height, which, with any other surroundings, would be studied and admired for its architectural grandeur, and the beauty of its carving and mosaic ornamentation. No one would imagine it to be simply the portal to greater beauty and grandeur, but such it is.

We enter beneath this majestic arch, and find ourselves within the park. A broad avenue, skirted with lofty cypresses, acacias, and other Oriental trees, and tanks of aquatic plants and *jets d'eau*, reveals, at its extremity, an object which at once rivets the eye, and steals over the heart like a strain of delicious music, or like the melody of sublime poetry. It is the Taj, the peerless Taj, the mausoleum erected by the Emperor Shah Jehan as the tomb of his favorite begum, Noor Mahal, in which they now sleep side by side. She died before him in giving birth to a child, and it is stated that, as she felt her life ebbing away, she sent for the emperor, and told him she had only two requests to make: first, that he would not take another wife and have children to contend with hers for his favor and dominions; and, second, that he would build for her the tomb he had promised, to perpetuate her memory. The emperor summoned the medical counselors of the city to do every thing that was in their power to save her life, but all in vain.

Shah Jehan, who was devotedly attached to her, at once set about complying with her last request. The tomb was commenced immediately, and, according to Tavernier, who saw its first and last stones laid, it was twenty-two years in building, with twenty thousand men constantly occupied upon it. It cost, in actual expense, in addition to the forced labor of the men, more than three hundred lacs of rupees, or about fifteen millions of dollars. Such a building, including the cost of materials, could scarcely be erected by paid labor at the present time, even in India, for $50,000,000.

As this building is acknowledged by every traveler to be unrivaled, and the sight of it declared by many to be worth a journey round the world, I will give a more minute description of its situation and its prominent features.

At the extremity of the beautiful park or Oriental garden of which I have spoken, on the river side rises a terrace of red sandstone twenty feet in height, and a thousand feet broad. The walls of the terrace on all sides are of hewn stone, and its surface is paved with the same material. At the extreme left of this terrace stands a magnificent mosque, an appendage to the main structure, the Taj. It is the place of prayer for the faithful, who come to visit the tomb of the favorite of the Mogul emperor. This building alone must have been very costly, but as it would destroy the symmetry of the grand mausoleum by occupying one side of the central building, the emperor had another mosque, a perfect counterpart, erected on the opposite extremity of the terrace, a thousand feet distant, of no use excepting as a *jowab*, or answer to the first. The one is held as a sacred place; the other, in the eyes of a Mohammedan, has nothing sacred about it; it is simply the complement of the first.

On the lofty terrace of sandstone rises another terrace of pure white marble, its walls of cut stone laid as regularly as the courses of a marble building. This terrace is three hundred feet square. At each of its four corners there stands a circular marble minaret, about twenty-five feet in diameter, diminishing in size until at the height of a hundred and fifty feet it is crowned with an open cupola, commanding a magnificent view of the Taj with its surroundings, of the River Jumna, the city and fort of Agra, and of the adjacent country. I ascended to the top of one of these minarets, and had photographed upon my memory a view which I am sure no time can dim.

In the centre of this marble terrace, equidistant from

the four lofty and graceful minarets, stands the building which for more than two centuries has been the admiration of every eye that in all that period of time has rested on it. It is an octagon, or it might perhaps be more correctly described as a square with each of the four corners slightly cut off, and is crowned with a high swelling dome, having the gracefulness of outline which seems to have been an inspiration in the Mohammedan and Oriental styles of architecture. The building is one hundred and fifty feet in diameter; the crescent upon the summit of the dome nearly two hundred feet above the pavement. The structure is built from foundation to topstone of the purest marble, so perfect in its preservation and so unspotted in its whiteness that it looks as if it might have been erected only yesterday. Standing upon its marble pedestal, it vies in purity with the clouds that are floating by. A cupola of the same material rests upon the roof on each side of the dome. The exterior of the building is carved in graceful designs, the front elaborately wrought, but in such perfect taste as to fill the eye like a picture in colors. No description will convey to the mind any idea of the effect of the engraving on the arched doorway. It is elaborate, but not florid, giving to the solid marble almost the lightness of a cloud. Indeed, the whole building, as you look upon it, seems to float in the air like an autumn cloud.

Let us enter—but breathe softly and tread gently as you step within. It is the sleeping chamber of Noor Mahal, the cherished wife of the Mogul emperor, Shah Jehan, and here, beneath this magnificent dome, they lie side by side, each in a couch of almost transparent marble, set with precious stones, and wrought exquisitely in tracery of vine and flowers. Nowhere else has human dust been laid away to slumber in such superb repose—so beautiful, so silent, so sacred, so sublime. In such perfect, exquisite taste is every thing within as well as without, that it is more like a creation than the work of man. The whole interior, which is lighted only from the lofty doorway, is open from wall to wall, and from the pavement, to the summit of the dome, with the exception of a high marble screen standing about twenty or thirty feet from the outer wall, and extending entirely around the building. This is cut in open tracery, so as to resemble a curtain of lace rather than a screen of solid marble. One who has seen the veiled statue of a master artist can appreciate the deception, if deception it can be called where none was intended.

The sarcophagi containing the remains of the empress and of her faithful lover, the Mogul emperor, lie in the crypt below, which is reached by a marble stairway. That of the former has inscribed upon it, in the graceful Arabic characters, "MOONTAJ-I-MAHAL, RANOO BEGUM" (Ranoo Begum, the Ornament of the Palace), with the date of her death, 1631. The other has inwrought the name of the emperor, with the date of his death, 1666. To this day they are covered with fresh flowers, strewed by faithful hands, in recognition of the fidelity which reared the structure.

Upon the main floor, directly over these marble slabs, and under the canopy of the open dome, stand the cenotaphs, designed simply as the representatives of those below, but carved in tracery and set with gems in no ostentatious or gaudy style, but so beautifully and tastefully that one lingers around them as he stands before some masterpiece of art, never satisfied with looking. Upon the cenotaph of the queen, amid wreaths of flowers, worked in gemmed mosaic, are passages from the Koran, in Arabic, one of which reads, "Defend us from the tribe of unbelievers." This inscription was made by the Emperor Shah Jehan, who seemed to think no words too sacred to be recorded upon the tomb of one whom he loved so devotedly; but his own son, Aurungzebe, who placed the marble in memory of his father, in accordance with Mohammedan custom regarded the words of the Koran as too holy to be engraved—the difference between conjugal and filial love. In the same devotion to his wife, Shah Jehan caused the

Koran to be inscribed upon the interior of the Taj, in mosaic of precious stones, jasper, lapis lazuli, heliotrope, chalcedony, carnelian, etc. The whole of the Koran is said to be thus inwrought, and yet it has the appearance of a light and graceful vine running over the walls. With the sentences of the Koran, thus traced upon the marble in such costly material, are interspersed fruits, and flowers, and running vines, all of precious stones inlaid, designed to represent one of the bowers of Paradise in which the emperor had laid the light of his life to sleep her last sleep.

While we were standing beneath that lofty dome, the silence of the tomb reigning even over its exquisite beauty and grandeur, voices at my side commenced singing:

"In the hour of pain and anguish,
In the hour when death draws near,
Suffer not our hearts to languish,
Suffer not our souls to fear.
And when mortal life is ended,
Bid us in thine arms to rest,
'Till, by angel bands attended,
We awake among the blest."

The singing ceased, but far up in that snow-white vault, as if among the fleecy clouds of heaven, an angel band caught up the strain, not as an ordinary echo of reflected sound, but as if prolonging the notes. It continued as long as the original song, and at length gradually died away, only as the song of angels would cease to be heard when they enter the portals of heaven. This echo is as marvelous and as celebrated as the Taj itself, and I know not in what building or in what part of the world another like it can be heard.

All this description may seem to the reader simply extravagant, but not if the reader has ever looked upon the building described. Every one who has seen it will simply say that words are powerless to express the ideas which its sublimity and beauty inspire. I could only compare the emotions which it excited to those awakened by listening to exquisite music, and the building to some sublime poem, whose words transport the soul out of itself. The very first glimpse of the structure, as I entered the gateway a quarter of a mile distant, and looked down the long avenue of acacias and cypress, was overpowering, and I felt at every step as I drew nearer that I must withdraw my gaze or be overcome. Often, as I stood within the Taj, its silent grandeur was equally overpowering. Moonlight is said to add greatly to the effect of the whole scene, giving to the building the appearance of a cloud-castle built in air.

According to the records, Shah Jehan had planned another structure precisely similar to this for his own tomb, on the opposite side of the Jumna, to be connected with it by a bridge, but he wisely concluded to sleep by the side of his beloved begum.

As we left the Taj and lingered in the park, we found it vocal with the song of birds. Richly-colored paroquets made their homes along the cornices of the surrounding buildings and upon the gateway, and, by a singular though somewhat sentimental coincidence, the only turtle-doves that I saw or heard in India were two mates that sighed their melancholy notes upon the evening air as a requiem over Shah Jehan and his beloved Noor Mahal.

On Christmas morning we rode out several miles from Agra to Secundra, a station of the English Church Missionary Society known as "the Christian Village." We heard, long before reaching it, the sound of the church-going bell, a strange sound in a heathen land. This missionary station, which comprises a considerable community, has been organized on the principle of separating the native Christians from their ordinary associates in order to protect them from the evil influences by which they are surrounded among their own people, and also to give to the natives at large an illustration of the influence of the Gospel of Christ upon a community, important ends to be accomplished, but only at the expense of losing the leavening and aggressive power of religion working through the relations

U

of society. It has too much of the community principle about it to commend it to general adoption. But in this case a great and beneficent work has been done, and this Christian community has become a light in the land. Before we reached the place the congregation had assembled at the neat English church, whither we at once directed our steps, and where an interesting and impressive sight greeted our eyes and moved our hearts. The building, which was well filled, had no benches, the whole congregation, according to Oriental custom, being seated upon the floor, each one clothed in pure white, the women and girls with their long muslin garments drawn over their heads as veils. All devoutly engaged in the service, joining in the responses, and in prayer bowing their foreheads to the pavement. The services were conducted in the Hindustani tongue, and were unintelligible to us, but before us was a congregation of people who had been called out of the grossest idolatry, now devoutly engaged in celebrating the birth of the Saviour of the world, joining with Christians of all lands in the song of the heavenly host, " Glory to God in the highest, and on earth peace, good will toward men." As I looked upon them in their devotions, the vision of the Apostle John in the Isle of Patmos came up before me, and I seemed to hear the inquiry, " What are these which are arrayed in white robes, and whence came they ?" and then the response, " These are they which came out of great tribulation, and have washed their robes and made them white in the blood of the Lamb." This was one of numerous scenes witnessed in India, which show that the Gospel of Christ, through the power of the divine Spirit, is making its conquests and giving promise of a day when it shall completely triumph over idolatry and superstition.

The tomb of Akbar, one of the Mogul emperors, stands near Secundra, in the midst of a quadrangular court a quarter of a mile square. A heavy wall surrounds the square, making the inclosure a fortress. The mausoleum in which lie the remains of the great emperor is three hundred feet square, and vies in magnificence, though not in beauty, with the Taj, rising to the height of a hundred feet in five terraces, with cloisters, galleries, domes, and cupolas elaborately wrought. The roof of the highest elevation is flat, one hundred feet square. In the centre stands a cenotaph of pure marble, elaborately carved with the *Now Nubbey Nam*, the ninety-nine names of God, from the Koran. It is covered with a cupola, not for the protection of the cenotaph, but to guard the names of God from the storm. The roof is surrounded by a lattice of carved marble, and at each corner is a beautiful marble cupola, light and graceful. The sarcophagus which contains the dust of the emperor, on the ground floor, is reached by a descending passage similar to that of the great pyramid of Egypt. The whole structure is almost as massive as the pyramids.

Akbar was the most powerful sovereign of his day, and a man of independent if not enlightened views. He opened the places of honor and responsibility to all races and all religions, and by his liberal and tolerant policy secured to a greater extent than most Oriental monarchs the affections of his people. His sons having all died in infancy, he made a pilgrimage to the shrine of a celebrated saint at Ajmere to sue for an heir. He went with his whole family on foot a distance of three hundred and fifty miles, at the rate of four miles a day. Walls of cloth were put up on each side of the road, and carpets spread for the royal pilgrims the entire distance. On reaching the shrine, he was referred to another saint still living at Secree, where he was promised an heir that should live to a good old age. The empress afterward gave birth to a son, who became the renowned Jehangeer. Akbar then took up his residence at Futtehpore Secree, about twenty miles from Agra, where he founded a summer capital, covering the hills with magnificent buildings, the very ruins of which are among the most impressive testimonies to the grandeur of the Mogul court. When he died, the treasures that he had heaped together—coin, jewels, plate, brocades, etc.—were estimated at seven hundred millions of rupees (about $350,000,000). His crown, studded with jewels, was valued at twenty millions of rupees. One of the historians of India thus describes the splendor of his reign:

"The greatest displays of Akbar's grandeur were at the vernal equinox and on his birthday. They lasted for several days, during which there was a general fair, and many processions and other pompous shows. The emperor's usual place was in a rich tent, in the midst of awnings to keep off the sun. At least two acres were thus spread with silk and gold, carpets and hangings, as rich as velvet embroidered with gold, pearls, and precious stones could make them. The nobility had similar pavilions, where they received visits from each other, and sometimes from the emperor. Dresses, jewels, horses, and elephants were bestowed upon the nobles. The emperor was weighed in golden scales against gold, silver, perfumes, and other substances in succession, which were distributed among the spectators. Almonds and other fruits of gold and silver were scattered by the emperor's own hand, and eagerly caught by the courtiers. On the great day of each festival the emperor was seated on his throne in a noble palace, surrounded by his nobles, wearing high heron-plumes, and sparkling with diamonds like the firmament. Many hundred elephants passed before him in companies, all most richly adorned, and the leading elephant of each company with gold plates on his head and breast set with rubies and emeralds. Trains of caparisoned horses followed, and after them rhinoceroses, lions, tigers, panthers, hunting leopards, hounds, and hawks, the whole concluding with an innumerable host of cavalry glittering with cloth of gold."

Intending to leave for Delhi in the afternoon, we shortened our stay at the tomb of Akbar, and hastened back toward Agra. But, alas for human calculations in Oriental lands! our horses were factors or tractors in the calculation which we had not taken fully into the account. One of the miserable beasts gave out, and, after walking about two miles, we impressed an *ekka*, one of the rough carts of the country, and so reached our hotel. Here a new misfortune awaited us, revealing visions of the Black Hole of Calcutta, or some vile prison, not at all agreeable to our fancy in that land of the Moguls and the Hindoos.

Having hastily arranged our baggage, our bills duly paid (with the usual necessary abatements), our luggage all upon the gharries, we stepped in and gave the order to start, on which I settled back into my seat in the vain expectation that it would be obeyed. Again I looked out and repeated the order, using the strongest Hindustani words that I could command, but it was of no avail. Stepping out to see what was the matter, I was confronted by a native policeman, whose orders had been more forcible than my own, and I at length learned that the whole party were under arrest for stealing one of the four sheets that we had been able to muster on the day of our arrival. Of course we were very indignant, but police officers the world over seem to have a common understanding not to regard indignant looks and high words as conclusive proof of innocence, and our warm expressions were received with great coldness. I had once, in a strange city in my own country, been arrested for passing counterfeit money, but then I was near enough to my own friends to communicate with them, and establish my innocence. Now we were ten thousand miles away from those who would certify to our previous good character in regard to thieving, and the circumstantial evidence was decidedly against us. When our party of seven arrived at the hotel, there were four sheets distributed among us as the extent of the accommodations of the first hotel in Agra. As we were about to depart, only three sheets could be found, and what supposition was more reasonable, what proof could be more positive than this, that we had stolen the fourth, and that it had been secreted somewhere in our baggage. Of course it was not to be thought of for a moment that one of the dozen Hindoo servants, or one of the traveling merchants or mendicants who had been coming and going through the bungalow all the day long, had taken it. We were the culprits beyond all question, and must submit to an examination. Cooling down in a measure, we ordered the trunks to be taken from the gharries, and full search to be made;

but, when we consented to have it done, they did not wish to do it, like the Frenchman who, in a financial panic, made haste to draw out all his deposits from the bank, but when he found the teller ready to hand it over, he declined to take the money; he wanted it only in case the bank was not willing to pay. The next order of the police was to have the ladies' satchels searched. By this time matters grew somewhat serious, and we made inquisition for the host, Mr. Beaumont, who had not appeared on the scene, whether privy to it or not. To him we could talk in round English, and we improved the opportunity. He became our bail, notwithstanding we gave him the assurance that after such treatment we certainly should not stop at his hotel the next time we came to India. The whole affair was undoubtedly a ruse on the part of the servants, who had secreted the sheet, thinking they could extort money from us, in payment for the loss, by calling in the police to arrest us. After the affair was all over, there came an apprehension on our part that, as the sheets had been folded in the morning in anticipation of our departure, one of them might possibly have been packed unnoticed with our baggage. We reached the cars in season, and at midnight, by moonlight, crossed the lofty iron bridge over the Jumna at Delhi, and entered the renowned capital of the Mogul emperors, more than a thousand miles from Calcutta. We made deliberate inquisition, but not a trace of the missing sheet which had occasioned our arrest at Agra was found, and we had the proud satisfaction of feeling that we had not only escaped the prisons of Agra, but were 'guiltless of the felony.

## XXII.

### DELHI.

The vicinity of Delhi is a field in which the antiquarian may revel in endless delight. Within a circle of less than twenty miles, one dynasty after another has established its capital and ruled in splendor, and then passed away, leaving the field to the conqueror, who, instead of occupying the same site, has founded a new city, and left the old to crumble into ruins. In this way numerous cities have been scattered over the plain, the monuments of some remaining to this day, while the very history of others has been lost. One monument, the loftiest single column in the world, stands about ten miles from Delhi, in the midst of magnificent ruins, of which there is no satisfactory account in the records of India. Old Delhi, as it is called, the last forsaken site, is in greater perfection; the walls remain, and much of the city is yet standing, but its halls are deserted; vagabonds and beasts of prey share its hospitality alike. But if the region is a field for the antiquarian, the present city, for a long period the capital of the Mogul empire, is the home of fancy and the field for romance.

Delhi was founded by Shah Jehan about two centuries and a half ago. When his golden sun arose he determined to mark the day by erecting a monumental city. Leaving Agra, which had been built chiefly by his grandfather, the renowned Akbar, although greatly beautified by himself, he came to Delhi and laid the foundations of the gorgeous capital. It is inclosed by a wall of granite five and a half miles in circuit, and is entered by twelve strongly fortified gates—the Calcutta, the Cashmere, the Lahore, etc. One of these, the scene of an heroic and successful assault by the English during the mutiny of 1857, like the fort and the city itself, has a modern tragic history of the deepest interest. One principal street, the Chandnee Chowk, 120 feet wide, divides the town, and is daily the scene of more strictly Asiatic display than any other street in India. It is alike the Boulevard and the Broadway of Delhi. On either side are shops and warehouses of the wealthy merchants; the centre is a broad terrace or promenade, shaded with acacias and other ornamental trees. During the day the Chandnee Chowk is a busy mart of trade, but toward evening the loaded trains of camels and other beasts of burden disappear, the hum of business dies away, and a scene of Oriental leisure and display ensues. The promenade is thronged with persons in all the varied costumes of the interior of Asia, while richly-caparisoned Arabian horses, elephants with gayly-dressed riders, and not a few English carriages belonging to natives, pass up and down the broad street. Other parts of the city are equally curious in their way. The grain markets are one of the sights. Camels and buffaloes, with their heavy freights, come and go like ships entering and leaving port, and a noisy multitude, scarcely less bewildering and far more entertaining than the crowd of a Western produce exchange, almost fascinate a stranger. The people of the city at all hours of the day, but still more toward evening, may be seen at home on the flat roofs of their houses, apparently unnoticed by and unnoticing their nearest neighbors. One feels, in treading the streets of Delhi, that he has reached the heart of Asia, and every thing is so intimately associated with the old Mogul dynasty that its ancient scenes of barbaric splendor are continually rising up before him.

The fortress, built by Shah Jehan for a palace, extends nearly a mile along the river, and is protected on all sides by a strong wall forty feet in height, flanked with bastions and turrets. The main gateway, the Lahore, is a tower of great strength. Entering through the archway, which once was richly ornamented with flowers in mosaic and with inscriptions from the Koran, and passing into the grand court, we came to the *Diwan-a-im*, the hall where the emperor gave free audience to all who had any petition or cause to present. It is an immense canopy, supported by pillars of stone, with an elevated throne on one side, the wall inlaid with mosaics of precious stones representing flowers and fruits, birds and beasts. The *Diwan-i-khas*, or hall of private audience, is smaller, but it is a gem of beauty. It is an open marble pavilion, resting on massive pillars and Moresque arches, the marble highly polished, and having almost the transparency of alabaster. The marble balustrade is exquisitely carved in elaborate perforated work. At each corner of the roof stands a marble kiosk with a gilded dome; the ceiling was once composed of gold and silver filigree work, for which the goldsmiths of Delhi are celebrated to the present day. One side of the *Diwan-i-khas* opens on the court by which we entered, and commands a view of the whole interior of the fortress; another looks out upon the palace gardens, which are still kept in great beauty; a third affords a charming view of the River Jumna, while the fourth, which is closed, rests upon the walls of the royal zenana. On the side that is closed once stood the famous "Peacock Throne," the admiration, if not the envy, of the world in the days when the Mogul dynasty was at the zenith of its splendor. It is thus described:

"The throne was six feet long and four feet broad, composed of solid gold inlaid with precious gems. It was surmounted by a gold canopy, supported on twelve pillars of the same material. Around the canopy hung a fringe of pearls; on each side of the throne stood two *chattahs*, or umbrellas, symbols of royalty, formed of crimson velvet richly embroidered with gold thread and pearls, and with handles of solid gold, eight feet long, studded with diamonds. The back of the throne was a representation of the expanded tail of a peacock, the natural colors of which were imitated by sapphires, rubies, emeralds, and other brilliant gems. Its value was estimated by Tavernier, a French jeweler, who saw it in its perfection, at six millions of pounds sterling, or thirty millions of dollars."

This famous Peacock Throne was taken away by the Persian conqueror, Nadir Shah, who not only stripped the palace, but signalized his conquest and the subjugation of the Mogul capital by ordering the slaughter of a hundred thousand of its helpless inhabitants, men, women, and children. He sat with the conquered emperor in the *Diwan-i-khas*, sipping his coffee, while the dead were piled in the streets. As we trod this marble hall, once the scene of imperial splendor, memory and fancy bringing up the contrasts of grandeur and cruelty, glory and humiliation which had here been witnessed, and as we thought of the many changes which had come over the face of things since Shah Jehan sat upon his throne of brilliants, we could only look in sadness upon the delusive inscription which the emperor had engraved in the beautiful Arabic characters upon the marble walls: " If there be a paradise on the face of the earth, it is this—it is this—it is this."

Only a portion of the adjoining seraglio remains, but the *Hummaums*, or royal baths, rooms of the purest white marble, with inlaid borders, marble floors and tanks, and a fountain in the centre of each room, have a richness and exquisite beauty that is almost inconceivable in connection with such simplicity of material. The *Motee Musjid*, or Pearl Mosque, a miniature of the Pearl Mosque at Agra, is a pearl itself, built exclusively of white marble, and giving one an idea of purity such as no other material suggests.

The *Jumma Musjid*, accounted the grandest mosque in the East, stands upon an eminence in another part of the city. Its paved court, 450 feet square, having in the centre a large marble reservoir of water, is skirted on three sides by a colonnade of red sandstone, with a marble pavilion at each corner. The building is very imposing, and, with the lofty minarets, forms one of the most striking objects in the city, whether seen from a distance or near at hand. The view from its summit, taking in the city and fort, the river and a vast extent of the surrounding country, is sublime. Long did I linger upon it to study the strange map which lay before me, and to ponder over the history of strange events which had been written on it by the hand of time through more than a score of centuries.

We devoted one day to the *Kootub-Minar*, eleven miles from Delhi, and to the intervening monuments and ruins which are thickly scattered over the plain in all directions. The Kootub-Minar is a fluted column 240 feet in height, more than 100 feet in circumference at the base, and gradually diminishing to forty feet at the summit. It is divided into five stories by projecting balconies, which surround the tower and add greatly to its beauty. There are many curious but evidently designed coincidences in its construction. The lowest and upper stories make precisely half the height; the lower story is just twice the diameter, and the whole column is five diameters in height. For what purpose the column was erected is a problem which the antiquarians of India have not solved, but their solution is not at all essential to the admiration of a structure which is pronounced the finest of its kind. There it stands, in the midst of the ruins of an almost forgotten city, towering up toward the heavens in solitary grandeur. One is fascinated as he follows up its beautifully fluted sides until the lines mingle at the summit, and as he gazes its proportions swell and rise, and his thoughts become lost in the clouds. I have a sort of passion for climbing heights, and could not resist the impulse to travel up the spiral staircase to the top (there were only three hundred and seventy-five steps), to look out from this elevation upon the ruined cities and magnificent mausoleums, and upon the city of Delhi in the distance. The view was many times worth the climb.

At the foot of the *Minar* are the carved fragments of the *Musjid-i-Kootub-ul-Islam*, which was erected as the grand mosque of old Delhi. It was constructed by the Mohammedan conqueror from the spoils of twenty-seven Hindoo temples at the close of the twelfth century. Some of the arches and pillars are exquisitely sculptured. Among them stands an enigma in the shape of an iron pillar five feet in circumference and fifty feet in length, cast in a single shaft. It stands erect, the base by actual investigation having been found nearly thirty feet below the surface of the ground. It has stood there more than a thousand years, but when, by whom, or for what purpose it was erected is unknown. It furnishes solid testimony, to the weight of fifteen or twenty tons, that heavy castings are not among the modern achievements of art.

In all parts of the world there is only a step between the sublime and the ridiculous, and no one must expect to find it widened in Oriental lands. It is rarely that we make the attempt to look through magnificent structures and imposing ruins into the regions of the past, without being called back to the present by some plaintive cry for charity, or a repulsive demand for backsheesh from the pretended lords of these crumbling heaps of stone. On this occasion, after we had descended from the Minar, we were summoned to witness a feat which every traveler must witness, and for which every one must pay. We were taken to an immense well, eighty-five feet in depth and about fifty in diameter. A half dozen nearly naked natives stood upon the wall around the edge, waiting for the nod that seals a contract to pay them for the exploit. We nodded, and at once they sprang with outstretched arms and legs, kept in this position until within about twenty-five feet of the bottom, when they suddenly straightened themselves, plunging feet foremost into the water, and soon reappeared, swimming on its surface. They speedily reached the top by an underground passage and demanded their pay, and would not have been satisfied if we had given them ten times the usual amount. But it is their only means of support, and they have followed plunging into the same well from their childhood, and their fathers before them for many generations, and perhaps for centuries.

I shall not attempt to describe the wilderness of ruined

cities, of magnificent tombs and mosques that lie between Delhi and the Kootub-Minar; nor the ruins of the grand Astronomical Observatory of Jay Singh, the scientific Rajah of Jeypore, who erected the complete observatory at Benares. It is on the same grand scale on which these wealthy nabobs and emperors wrought all their works. The dimensions of the gnomon of the equatorial dial as it now stands give an idea of its extent, the hypothenuse being 118 feet, and the perpendicular 56 feet.

The English government has done much since the mutiny for the improvement of Delhi. The Queen's Gardens, in the midst of the town, are laid out with great taste, and carefully cultivated. A collection of living animals and birds, and other specimens in natural history, adds to the attractions of the park. A large ornamental building for public and scientific uses has been erected on the Chandnee Chowk, called the Institute. In its large municipal hall we had the pleasure of meeting several of the native princes. For these improvements the Mogul capital is under many obligations to the Rev. James Smith, an English Baptist missionary, who has also held a commission under the government for promoting the scientific advancement of the native population. A costly memorial church has been erected to commemorate those who fell in the terrible mutiny, which burst upon this city with terrific force at its very beginning. The revolt commenced at Meerut, forty miles distant, and after the massacre of Europeans, men, women, and children, at that place, the Sepoys set out in a body for Delhi, where the native troops joined them, and commenced the slaughter of their officers. The magazine, which contained an enormous supply of guns, powder, and warlike stores, was in charge of Lieutenant Willoughby. Seeing the state of affairs, he closed and barricaded the gates, and then, laying a train of gunpowder, prepared to blow up the arsenal should resistance prove unavailing. Nine Europeans kept thousands of Sepoys at bay until at length they were exhausted and likely to be overpowered, when the match was applied, and more than a thousand mutineers were blown into the air. All the Europeans in the city who had not made their escape on the appearance of the Sepoys were massacred. The English families were tied in rows, and shot and sabred without mercy. The assassinations were accompanied by horrid atrocities. Others, who escaped—tender women and helpless children—wandered for days under the burning sun, lying down at nights in the jungle. Delhi fell completely into the hands of the mutineers, but its recapture was one of the most heroic achievements of the recovery of British power in India.

While at Delhi I had occasion to send homeward letters of some importance, and not being disposed to trust them to the uncertainties of the native servants at the hotel, I determined to deposit them with my own hands in the post. It afforded a new occasion for admiration of an institution the marvels of which seem to be forgotten in the newer and greater marvel of the telegraph. I never cease to wonder at the thought that one can go into almost any remote corner of the earth, and write his thoughts on a slip of paper, and drop it into a little box, even in the dead of night, when every one else is asleep, and that with all the speed of steam the identical slip of paper will travel over land and sea, and search out the friend to whom it is addressed, no matter in what other corner of the earth he may dwell, and deliver the certified message. With the telegraph different and even remote countries are actually bound together, and although thousands of miles intervene, you may, by means of a wire, hold by the button the one to whom you are speaking. The wire is an absolute link. But the postal service depends upon detached messengers, who must traverse sea and land, and seldom do they fail to execute their commission. I do not know that I have ever failed to receive a letter out of the numbers that have been addressed to me in all foreign parts, or that any one that I have sent has failed to reach its destination. Some of the former have been great travelers. Several that were addressed to me from home while I was in India, through the sagacity of New York clerks were sent by the way of China, and arrived in the north of India after I had left the country; but they traveled on, hoping to reach me at Cairo, where they made another halt and search, and then came on to Constantinople, where they overtook me precisely five months after they had started upon their travels.

Inquiring at the hotel at Delhi the way to the post-office, I was told it was a short distance beyond the fort. I traveled onward and onward until I almost despaired of reaching the place. At length, after various inquiries of natives of all Oriental regions, made chiefly by holding up my letters, I was directed to a back alley, which I found led to an old temple, or mosque, or something of the sort, and this was the Delhi post-office. A Eurasian who spoke English was in charge, and seemed to be the only living being within the premises. At the window I asked for stamps, and was directed to a sleepy Mohammedan who was lying on the pavement outside, and who was any thing but a promising looking dealer in government securities. When I made known what I wanted, he drew from the folds of his loose garment a muslin bag, from which he produced the requisite amount of stamps, as suspicious in appearance as the dealer himself, but I paid for them, and, affixing them to the letters, again presented them at the window. The Eurasian advised me to cancel them myself, adding that if I did not some one in the office might remove them from the letters and sell them again. Their appearance indicated that they had gone through this operation several times already. It was a new idea to me, that of canceling my own stamps before mailing my letters, but I complied, and then dropped them into the box, having little faith in their ever seeing America. I learned afterward that they were all received in due time, and in good condition, and I have now more faith than ever in international posts. This is rather a long story about what some may think a small matter, but those who have been 10,000 miles or more from home do not esteem it a small matter that by international arrangement they may hold direct and free communication with those they have left behind, and the motto which I have elsewhere recorded as found graven over the arch of the post-office at Hong Kong will recur as among the expressive sentiments of inspired wisdom : "As cold waters to a thirsty soul, so is good news from a far country."

## XXIII.

#### AMONG THE HIMALAYAS.

At Delhi we were more than a thousand miles from Calcutta, but we had not yet reached the northern limit of our journeying in Hindostan. We were bound for the Himalayas, and in some doubt whether to return by the route we had taken, or to go up to the Indus, make our way to the sea by that river, and so down to Bombay. The weather having become sufficiently cool to travel with comfort by day, we took the cars at 11 o'clock. In the afternoon we passed Meerut, an important military station, and memorable as the scene of the first outbreak of the mutiny.

Just at evening we reached Saharunpur, where we left the rail to make an excursion of a few days among the Himalaya Mountains. This town is pleasantly situated on the great plain of India. It was one of the earliest stations of the American Presbyterian Mission, and is occupied by the Rev. Mr. Calderwood, who met us at the cars, and who, with his family, made our short sojourn one of great pleasure. An interesting incident connected with our visit was the close of the examination of the mission school, and I regarded it as a peculiar pleasure to be invited to distribute the prizes to a large number of native youth, two of whom bore the familiar names of Alexander McLeod and James T. Wylie.

Saharunpur is a military station, and is the location of the government stud. The horses of the country are miserable specimens of their race, and it became a matter of necessity to the military service to establish on a large scale a dépôt where they could be reared from better stock and for hardy service. The stalls were not full, but we found nearly two thousand horses occupying quarters almost fit for the officers of an army, and altogether superior to the cantonments which soldiers often consider very desirable. The horses, when old enough for service, are found to have cost the government from one to two thousand rupees each, and those of Arabian blood from two to five thousand rupees. Some of the Arabians were splendid animals. We soon had an opportunity to contrast them with the natives of the country bred in the usual way.

Having made arrangements to cross the Sewalic range of the Himalayas from this point, we left Saharunpur in the morning in what the natives called an *omnibuckus*, but it bore in plain English on one of the panels the following notice: "Omnibus No. 1, Gunquaram, Head office Meerut, LicensedatSeharunpur, 10 June 1869, tocarry 5 passengers, with 62 lbs luggage, Drawnbytwohorses." The two horses were comparatively decent animals, and we congratulated ourselves that if we had not found real Arabian steeds, we had at least fallen upon tolerable specimens of the Indian race. But we learned to our sorrow that they were intended only for show, designed to entrap unwary travelers by making a good appearance on leaving town, on the principle upon which strictly honest fruit-dealers inevitably place the finest specimens at the top of the basket. The road, on starting, was as level as a railway track, well metaled, and shaded on either side with bamboo, cassia, and other trees. With our gallant steeds we were promising ourselves a triumphant passage over the mountains, but just as we were

X

in the full tide of expectation, only three or four miles out of town, we suddenly hauled up at a post-station, and two miserable rats were put into the carriage. The word of command was given, and the whip duly applied, but the more the persuasive arguments were used, the more they would not start, excepting backward. One of them insisted again and again on putting his heels into the front of the omnibuckus, and the other persisted in attempting to stand erect on his hind heels. And these were a fair type of the horses that we took in at every station on the way, excepting that some of them were even worse.

The East India Company built one of its finest roads over this pass, in order to reach the Dehra Valley and ascend the mountains to the summer resorts of Mussoorie and Landour. It is as skillfully engineered and as substantially built as the roads over the passes of the Alps, and decidedly smoother. The summit is pierced by a tunnel reducing the extreme elevation. Long before reaching the summit, and when we were approaching the more difficult and dangerous parts of the pass, the horses were detached, and sixteen coolies took the carriage in charge, and drew us over and down the descent on the other side, a distance of eight or ten miles. We were accustomed to being carried by coolies in sedan chairs in Japan and China as well as in India, but not to using them as horses, and, had there been any other way of crossing the mountains, we should have demurred; but there was no other (I had the offer of elephants on the return), and then these coolies have no other means of making a living. It is the business which they and their fathers have followed. They would lose caste, and lose all means of a livelihood if they should attempt any thing else, so that to employ them was a mercy and not a degradation. Besides, we remembered that when some distinguished dancer or singer visits the metropolis of our own country, or any of the gay capitals of Europe, it is not uncommon for young gentlemen of the highest breeding to aspire to the level of beasts of burden, and, taking the horses from the carriage of the danseuse or cantatrice, to harness themselves like donkeys and drag her to her hotel. With these precedents in mind, we quieted our scruples in regard to being drawn by coolies over the Himalaya Mountains.

In going through the pass we came upon a splendid, full-grown leopard that had just been caught in a trap, and were in the region of wild beasts of all kinds. A gentleman whom we met had seen, not long before, a huge wild elephant cross the highway on which we were traveling, and, in ascending the second range of the mountains the following day, we frequently saw around us the fresh tracks of leopards in the snow. India, considering the density of its population, is marvelously infested with wild beasts, and not merely in the mountainous regions, but in the jungles of the plain. The government has made great efforts to exterminate them, but without any apparent impression upon their numbers. One reason for this want of success is that the natives regard the wild beasts—man-eating tigers in particular—as divinities, whose wrath it is more safe to appease than to arouse, and accordingly they will not hunt or kill them even when exposed to their ravages.*

Tiger-hunting is still a favorite sport in many parts of India, and it is not uncommon for an ordinary party to bag half a dozen tigers in a single excursion. At Calcutta I met an American gentleman who had shot five the summer previous.

Since leaving India, I have received from Dr. Fayrer, of

---

* "In the Chanda district, one of these man-eaters killed, in a short time, 127 persons, and stopped all traffic for many weeks on the road. Another slew 150 people in three years, causing the abandonment of the villages, and throwing 250 square miles out of cultivation. During six years, in Bengal proper, 13,401 deaths were reported by wild beasts, of which 4218 were ascribed to tigers, 4287 to wolves, 1407 to leopards, and 105 to bears; the rest to other animals. The British government, on the other hand, paid in the same time $32,500 in rewards to secure the destruction of 18,196 wild animals. As much as $500 has been offered for the head of a man-eating tiger."—*Indian Mail.*

Calcutta, who accompanied the Duke of Edinburg (Prince Alfred of England) on his tour in the north of India, the following account of a tiger-hunt with elephants in the vicinity of Lucknow:

"*February* 23*d.* The camp is situated just on the river bank, and the exact spot is known as Kullean Ghaut. The narrow stream divides the British territory from that of Nepaul, the tract of country on the opposite side having been given over to the Nepalese since the mutiny. It contains the finest forest land in India. The gift was probably more valuable than it was at the time supposed to be. The royal standard of Britain is hoisted on one side, while that of the prime minister, the virtual ruler of Nepaul, is on the other. The Mohan abounds with alligators and gurrials. On the 22d one of Sir Jung's men was carried off and eaten by an alligator when bathing in the river.

"Fourteen years ago this used to be a splendid hunting-ground. It is said to be so still, notwithstanding the encroachments of civilization and cultivation. A tiger has already been heard of, and after breakfast he is to be sought for. Sir Jung Bahadoor is to cross the river to meet H. R. H. in British territory after breakfast, and will accompany him throughout the day. The weather is getting warm, fleecy clouds obscure the sun, but diffuse rather than intercept its rays. Sir Jung's camp resounds with barbaric music.

"After breakfast the Nepalese minister crossed the river on a bridge thrown over for the occasion, and rode up to H. R. H.'s camp. He was preceded by his body-guard and a band of music. H. R. H. and suite received Sir Jung, with Colonel Lawrence, the political agent, Colonel Thomson, the commissioner of Seetapore, Captain Young, settlement officer, and eight of his principal sirdars, nearly all colonels, who were presented to the duke. The maharajah, who is a slight, active, and wiry-looking man of about fifty-three, with fair Mongolian features, was dressed in a military uniform, and was decorated with the Grand Cross of the Bath. His head-dress was made of the most costly jewels, said to be worth about £15,000. The visit lasted only a few minutes, and shortly after H. R. H. got into the howdah, and, crossing the river, was joined by the Maharajah Sir Jung Bahadoor in a plain blue cotton shooting-dress, with a broad sola hat, and the Maharajah Sir Digbija Singh, G. C. S. I., of Bulrampore, in a dress very like it, only colored green. The combined party, with a line of above four hundred elephants—one hundred and thirty belonging to H. R. H.'s camp—proceeded in the direction of an extensive grass and tree jungle, where the tiger had been marked down, and where, during the last few days, he had killed several buffaloes. On the way some small game was shot, but on approaching the vicinity of the tiger's abode all firing ceased, and arrangements were made by Sir Jung for surrounding the brute. After beating in a long line through a belt of sâl forest, skirting the long grass, the line was gradually formed into a circle, and the elephants were brought so close as to touch each other. It certainly was a magnificent sight, and one seldom witnessed. They were all thoroughly trained and stanch, as the result proved when the tiger tried in vain to break the line, or rather circle. The inclosure being complete, H. R. H. on the same howdah, a large square one, with Sir Jung Bahadoor, went into the circle, and the tiger soon revealed himself, although the grass was as high as the howdah, with occasional vacant places. He was fired at by the duke alone, as all the rest of the party were requested not to fire unless the tiger got on any elephant's head. H. R. H. wounded him severely, and he made several charges round the line, but the elephants stood firm, and he could not get out, though he tried hard to break through. He fell at about the third shot from the duke's rifle, and then the whole circle closed in on him. He was soon padded, and proved to be a fine male tiger ten feet one inch in length, and very heavy.

"It was a most exciting scene; the wildness of the place, the magnificent line of elephants, and the steadiness with which they and their mahouts carried out the orders of the maharajah, were remarkable, and all were much pleased, none more so than H. R. H., with the sport; though perhaps, in a strictly sporting sense, the tiger may be considered to have been rather hardly used. The Nepalese elephants are well trained, and are so frequently employed by Sir Jung in tiger-shooting and elephant-hunting that they can not be surpassed. They are worked in line by the bugle calls, and are taught to go at a pace that no other elephants can equal. The maharajah is a great sportsman, and spends a considerable part of each year in the Terai. After padding the tiger the party moved on the line, and general shooting commenced. The party returned to camp in the evening, after an excellent day's sport on the banks of the Mohan with a bag of about twenty deer, one tiger, and a quantity of partridges, hares, pea, and jungle fowl. In returning to camp just before dark an accident occurred, which was attended with very serious consequences to a mahout, and in which two persons in the howdah had a very narrow escape. An old but very famous elephant made a false step, and, being weak, fell over against a tree and crushed the howdah. The native gentlemen jumped out, while the mahout, an old man who, at the time, was not on the elephant's neck, but was trying to drag the howdah over to one side, as it had become crooked, was crushed between the howdah and the tree, and sustained a very serious injury to the left hand. The wound was temporarily dressed, and he was taken into camp, where it was found necessary to amputate part of the hand. But for this unfortunate accident the day had been a most successful one. The weather was fine, a moderate breeze tempered the heat, and the wild scenery of the forests, the grassy plains on the banks of the river, which are themselves very picturesque, with the ever-varying interest of the working of the magnificent line of elephants, made up a scene that has seldom been equaled.

"*February 24th.* Before leaving camp this morning a camel-man of the maharajah's was brought in with a rather severe wound in the left thigh, just above the knee. He was wading across the Mohan, which there was not up to his hips, when he was suddenly seized by a large gurrial, and dragged down. Some Sepoys who were close at hand rushed to the rescue, and one of them so severely wounded the great lizard that it let go and tried to make its escape; he followed, thrusting his bayonet into it, and having fired all his (six) cartridges, he clubbed his musket and belabored it until the stock was broken. The brute by this time was so far *hors de combat* that it turned over as though dead, and was dragged on shore, and brought into camp with the man it had bitten. Fortunately the grip had not been very firm, and a portion of integument only, about five inches in circumference, had been torn away, leaving a painful and tedious, though not a dangerous wound. The gurrial was an enormous brute over sixteen feet in length. He was opened, and his stomach found quite empty, with the exception of about twenty or thirty pebbles, from the size of peas or marbles to a hen's eggs. These are useful for purposes of digestion, and are probably always found in the stomachs of these Saurians. This incident quite settles the question as to whether the gurrial does take other food than fish, although, from the conformation of his jaws, he is not able to seize so large a morsel, or inflict so great a wound as the alligator."

But the wild elephants, tigers, leopards, wolves, etc., formidable and destructive as they are, may be regarded as rather ornamental than otherwise in comparison with the lesser vermin which swarm over the whole country during the rainy and hot seasons. Of these the most dreaded and the most deadly are the snakes, from the hooded cobra, which sometimes attains the length of ten feet, down to the innumerable venomous snakes no larger than a riding-whip. It is stated on good authority that in the year 1869 there were 11,416 deaths from the bites of snakes in the single province of Bengal. From actual statistics, it has been estimated that in all India there are from 20,000 to 40,000 deaths from the same cause every year. The snakes live and multiply not only in the jungle and open country, but in the villages and cities. They come into the grounds and houses of all classes; they make their homes in the thatch and drop down from the rafters; they creep into the beds; they lie around among the kitchen utensils, and even ensconce themselves in the parlors. I heard many thrilling narratives of adventures with these unwelcome visitors. The smaller vermin are still more ubiquitous, and a still greater annoyance. Scorpions and centipedes are abundant, and every where dreaded. The white ants move in armies, and are terribly destructive. Scarcely any thing in the shape of furniture or clothing escapes their ravages, and their tastes are decidedly literary. They will go through an entire library in an incredibly short space of time, leaving nothing to be perused by those who come after them. If a book is carelessly left within their reach, the form of it may be found, but the entire contents has been devoured.

The day was all spent and the night had overtaken us before we had completed the descent of the mountain. For hours we rode on in the darkness, until late in the evening of the last day of the year 1869 we alighted at the home of the Rev. Mr. Woodside, in the charming valley of the Dehra Doon. This valley is one of the gardens of India, a vale of Cashmere transferred a little to the south. Sheltered on all sides by the Himalayas, which stretch themselves four and five miles into the skies, it has all the year round a genial climate (if the intense heat of the summers can be called genial), the trees of all climes, the plants of the tropics, and the fruits of the north growing side by side. The bamboo flourishes with great luxuriance, and the palm rears its stately crown. Extensive tea plantations occupy the plain.

It was a joy which no words can express to meet in this lonely but lovely valley, in the very heart of Asia, American families at home, and to have these homes opened to us with as much cordiality as if we had been their nearest kindred. The days that we spent there were all red-letter days, and when at length we were compelled to say farewell, it seemed more like taking a new departure from home than going homeward.

## XXIV.

### ON THE HIMALAYAS.

It was well into the new year before we could say goodnight or think of rest, but we were to be up and on the wing before the morning light. In anticipation of our arrival at Dehra, Mr. Woodside and Mr. Herron, of the American Mission, had arranged an excursion to the sanitary cities of Mussoorie and Landour, perched upon the very top of the second range of the Himalayas, between seven and eight thousand feet high. They are crowded during the heat of summer, being a delightfully cool resort from the plains below, and, indeed, from all parts of Hindostan, but in the winter, when we made the ascent, they were deserted. Simlah, to which the governor general moves his court in the summer, is a hundred miles farther north.

We rose long before the sun to greet the opening year. A drive of five or six miles across the valley, through a charming country, brought us to Rajpore, where the arrangements for ascending the mountain were to be made. One of our number, too feeble to endure the day's ride, was taken up in a *jhanpan*, a sort of sedan chair, the rest making the ascent on horseback. The cities are in full sight from the plain below, and show themselves at different points during the ascent, but we were long in reaching them. Slowly we toiled upward, encouraged by an occasional glimpse of the summit, and often repaid for our toil by the views of the Dehra valley, until at length we reached a point where the Sewalic range that we had crossed the day before sank so low that we could look over upon the great plain beyond. The road passed deep precipices, over one of which the wife of an English officer, the year before, had gone down several hundred feet and was instantly killed. Troops of monkeys, looking old and wise enough to be the ancestors of Darwin, sat grinning at us from the trees. Wild peacocks, with plumage as gay as the domestic bird, are abundant on the mountain, where they are shot as game. We had dined on them two or three days before. At length we reached Mussoorie, and, passing through it, were soon at Landour, which is on the very crest of the mountain. I could not but marvel at the boldness of the man who first conceived the idea of building a town upon this lofty ridge. There is not half an acre of level ground any where to be found. It is a simple line of peaks, with here and there a spot on which an eagle might build his nest. It may be a hundred feet down to the next eyrie, but every rock on which a house could be fastened has been seized upon, until towns of considerable extent have grown up. It is a place of great attractiveness to those who are suffering from the scorching heat of the plain, but all the while that I was on the mountain I was haunted with the thought that if I were to spend the night in any one of these numerous homes, I might, simply by stepping

A GORGE IN THE HIMALAYAS.

out of bed, plunge thousands of feet down the mountain sides. The elevation is nearly three times that of the Catskill Mountain House, and it appears as if one might almost step into the Dehra Doon.

I can scarcely attempt to describe the magnificent views afforded at this elevation. On one side lies the Dehra Doon, one of the fairest valleys in all the East, smiling in its verdure and foliage, although it was now midwinter. Farther on is the Sewalic range of the Himalayas, and still farther, in full view, the great plain of India, fifteen hundred miles in extent. On the opposite side, toward the northeast, peak after peak of the snowy range, stretching out into Thibet and Cashmere, lifts its snowy head into the clouds. One of these, separated by a narrow valley from the point on which we stood, measures 22,330 feet. Another, in the distance, is 25,700 feet high; and still another, Mount Everest, reckoned the loftiest point on the surface of the globe, is 29,000 feet by barometrical measurement. Several of these peaks have been ascended by adventurers and scientific parties, but we did not attempt to go so far into the clouds, among the everlasting snows. We were very hospitably entertained at Landour by Dr. Kellett, the British surgeon, who had made preparation to receive us, and we left with him a pressing invitation to return our call on the next New-Year's day in New York.

Retracing our way down the mountain sides, we were overtaken by the darkness of night, and passed the last hour or two in no little apprehension of the precipices which invited us below. But we reached our home at Dehra in safety, having met with no misadventure in this delightful and ever-memorable excursion to the top of the globe.

The following day, which was the day of rest, we spent in this peaceful valley, greatly enjoying communion with the happy circle of Americans whose hearts are drawn closely together in this far-away part of the earth, and who became very near to us before we parted with them. In the morning I heard a sound which transported me homeward. As it fell upon my ear, the tone was so familiar that I exclaimed, "That is one of Meneely's bells;" and so it proved. It had crossed the ocean, and crossed the plains of India, and crossed the Himalaya Mountains before us, and there, in the heart of Asia, it was calling a congregation of native Christians to the house of God. We worshiped with the natives in their own tongue a part of the day, and in the evening, at an English service, I spoke some words of Christian encouragement to the Americans and others to whom our tongue is familiar, and so we spent the sacred day at the farthest point from home I had ever reached; and yet we were not away from home—we were still among friends. In one respect I almost envied the mission families their lot, for I know not a missionary station in any part of the world more charmingly located. It is one of the fairest spots in our memories of the lands of the East.

Rising very early on Monday morning, I rode out with Mr. Woodside to the government tea plantations, and gathered the leaf for myself, though not for use. The tea of India we decidedly preferred, while we were in the country, to any that we drank in China or Japan, perhaps because it was made in more civilized style. We came upon a company of Thibetians, one of whom was praying in the early morning with a machine, a small wheel turned upon a handle—a very convenient way of saying one's prayers, and quite as efficacious, no doubt, as using the form of words where the heart is not found. The tongue may become a praying machine as truly as the wheel of this traveler of Thibet.

Many urgent and tempting inducements were presented to us, by the English as well as the American residents, to prolong our stay in the beautiful valley, and gladly would we have yielded could time have tarried with us. In anticipation of our arrival, various plans for improving the sojourn had been laid. I found that arrangements had been made for a public lecture on the Pacific Railroad, which

A PRAYING MACHINE.

had awakened almost as much interest in that remote region as in the United States. They had read and heard so much about this enterprise, and of the comfort and charm of travel by the Pullman palace cars, that they wished to have it all confirmed or dispelled by one who had actually traversed the road. Many of the English residents were intending to take this route homeward. But, having laid my own plans for a long time to come, I was compelled to decline the invitation. Had we yielded to all the tempting propositions to lengthen our stay in many places, to see more that was to be seen and to enjoy more that was to be enjoyed, especially in the society of the friends whom we met, we should still be tarrying or wandering far away among Oriental scenes, and perhaps should never reach home at all.

The English commissioner sent us a polite offer of elephants to take our party over the mountains, but we had already tried this mode of conveyance to our satisfaction. We returned to Saharunpur as we came, being taken by coolies over the most difficult part of the route. Mr. Woodside and Mr. Herron accompanied us several miles on the way, and at the ascent of the mountain we bade them farewell.

Several months before leaving America, in arranging my programme for the year of travel, I decided to spend the first week of January, 1870, in this part of India. My object in doing so was to pass the week with the American Mission families and the native churches in the religious services of the period, now known the world over as "the Week of Prayer." Lodiana, from which the general mission takes its name, is the place from which, in 1858, an invitation was sent out to Christians every where to spend the first week in each year in united prayer to God for the conversion of all nations to Christ. That concert is now observed throughout Christendom, and has become a bond of union and of interest among all who look for the renovation of the world through the Gospel of salvation. I commenced the week at Dehra Doon, then came to Saharunpur, where I joined with the native Christians and the mission family in similar services. I spoke to the natives through an interpreter, and, bidding them and our friends of the mission farewell, went on in the evening of Tuesday to Amballa, fifty miles farther north. Here I was welcomed by an old friend, Rev. John H. Morrison, D.D., who has spent between thirty and forty years in India, and, after joining in the same interesting services at this place, went on with him seventy miles to Lodiana, where we met with several missionaries and the native Christians in the chapel in which, twelve years before, the resolution was adopted and sent out into all the world to devote the week to this holy purpose. In that distant land, and amid the many sacred associations, it was a week of peculiar interest.

I had now reached the extreme northern limit of my travels, having abandoned the plan of going to Bombay by the River Indus and the Indian Ocean on account of the low stage of water. Thus far my journeyings had been accomplished in exact accordance with my original programme, and I was not willing to trust to the uncertainties of navigation through a river of shifting bars and shallow waters, when I could lay my course by the hour according to a previously arranged time-table.

Before leaving Lodiana I went into the native town to witness the manufacture of the Cashmere shawls, one of the principal branches of industry. I called also upon two Cabool princes, who were living in exile upon a small pension from the British government. They were sons of Shah Shujah, one of the last native possessors of the renowned Koh-i-noor diamond, which now belongs to the British crown. The early history of this gem is as romantic and as tragic as that of an Eastern princess. It has cost many a prince his eyes, and many a one his life. It was found in the mines of Golconda, in Southern India, and first belonged to the viceroy of the province, a native of Persia, who afterward presented it to Shah Jehan, the Mogul emperor who built the Taj for Noor Mahal. After lying in the imperial treasury near a century, it was carried off by Nadir Shah, the king of Persia, who invaded India in 1738. It passed through several royal hands. Some of its possessors had their eyes put out, and others were assassinated in the strife to gain possession of the treasure. One of these princes, after he had lost his sight, had it taken from him on the plea that such a gem could be of no value to one who had no eyes with which to see its beauty. The father of the princes whom I met at Lodiana, while sharing the hospitalities of the Maharajah Runjeet Singh, the Lion of Lahore, was put to the torture and compelled to give it up to his host. The diamond remained in Runjeet Singh's family until the Punjaub was conquered by the British, when it was seized and presented by the captors to Queen Victoria.

Dark has been the history of this brilliant, reckoned second among the most valuable gems of the world. When found it weighed 900 carats. It was reduced by cutting, first to 279 carats, then to 186, in which state it was shown in the Great Exhibition of 1851. It has since been recut, and now weighs 123 carats, being valued at about $600,000.

## XXV.

#### LODIANA TO BOMBAY.

On the 6th of January we turned our faces southward and homeward, taking the Delhi and the East Indian Railways to Allahabad, where we paused again for a few days. As we passed through Cawnpore, the native and foreign communities were agitated by the recent occurrence of a *suttee*, the burning of a widow on the funeral pile of a husband. In studying the state of society in India, I found that there is more to commend this practice to Hindoo widows than is generally supposed. They are not driven by the mere law of custom to immolate themselves when thus bereaved. It is not affection for the husband which leads them to cast their own bodies into the flames which consume the dead. It is the future of the widow, her degraded, hopeless, helpless condition, that makes her choose death rather than life. The suttee was abolished by law in 1829, and now rarely occurs. All who take part in it are regarded as aiding and abetting murder, and are treated accordingly.

Our last evening at Allahabad was spent with a pleasant party of English and American residents, our host being a veteran English officer who had spent forty years in the military service in India. He was apparently unaffected by the climate, which had sent tens of thousands home to England, and many thousands to their long home. The evening passed delightfully, and soon after midnight we took the cars bound for Jubbulpore. By morning we had left the great plain, and were among the hills. There was little that was interesting in the face of the country; no picturesque scenery; no high cultivation. By noon we reached Jubbulpore, where the only break in steam communication around the world occurred, a space of 167 miles to Nagpore. The gap was filled a month or two later by the completion of the rail through from Allahabad to Bombay, connecting Calcutta with the latter place by rail.

Jubbulpore is the station to which the Thugs were consigned when the murderous clan was suppressed. They are organized in a sort of penal colony, under the superintendence of British officers. Some of the more desperate and dangerous characters are in irons, and all are kept at hard labor. Even the children of the Thugs are under surveillance, and not allowed to go out into the country, lest the seeds of this infernal band should again be spread over the land, and its horrid crimes be repeated. Here we were to make arrangements for the only formidable journey that we encountered during all our travels, and it was a journey which we have occasion to remember until the journey of life is over. We were not shut up to Hobson's choice in regard to the mode of conveyance, a variety of vehicles and of motive power being presented to our selection. There was the palanquin, the ancient carriage of India, a long black box in which one person can lie down but can not sit up, and which becomes exceedingly tiresome after traveling fifty or a hundred miles. It is carried by coolies, four at a time, and if the journey is designed to be speedy, relays are required every few miles. They travel night and day, though in the warm seasons it is customary to journey only by night, and seek repose and shade during the day. Then there were the bullock-carts, drawn by oxen, which are sometimes very fleet, but which, in a long journey, make slow progress. As time is of little account in Oriental countries, the bullock-carts are a favorite mode of conveyance. The distance between Jubbulpore and Nagpore is made by these carts in four or five days, which was enough to condemn them in our eyes. The conveyance that we selected, chiefly on account of speed, was the *dak-gharry*, the government post-carriage, which resembles the palanquin, although larger, is set on wheels, and drawn by animals that are dignified by the name of horses, three abreast. It has this advantage over the palanquin: it can be arranged so as to enable one to sit up, but in general it is furnished with a flat bottom, on which a mattress is spread. The passengers (each gharry will accommodate two, and no more) lie down with their feet toward the horses, and are driven night and day almost at railroad speed, and without any regard to bruised muscles or broken bones.

The entire distance, 167 miles, we were assured would be made in twenty-four hours, and, as time was something more than money, we made choice of the dak-gharry, not wholly unaware of the severe pommeling to which we must be subjected, though not altogether aware of the severe trial of physical strength and endurance that we must pass through. Accordingly, I engaged two gharries at the government post-office, one for myself and wife, and another for the young lieutenant, paying one hundred rupees, or fifty dollars, for each, a large price considering the wear and tear of flesh, for which no allowance was made. The rest of the party engaged gharries of a private company which run their vehicles over the same route.

It was late in the afternoon when we were fairly launched. Going out from Jubbulpore for several miles we met large numbers of natives, some of them gayly dressed, returning from a Hindoo festival which they had been celebrating on the hills. Four miles from the town we descended into the valley of the Nerbudda, where the scenery became more attractive. The "Marble Rocks," situated on the river some miles below the ghaut at which we crossed, are celebrated in the annals of this part of India for the bold and striking views of which they form a part, and are a place of great resort.

During the whole journey the horses were changed every five miles, and every time that fresh ones were put in it appeared as if they had just been caught wild, and were then for the first time put into harness and introduced to the gharry. The first move was for all three to attempt to jump over each other at the same moment of time, an exploit the absurdity and impossibility of which they had not learned by years of experiment. The next move was for half a dozen natives to seize hold of the wheels, and two or three to take the horses by the head, while all together set up a hideous shout that frightened the miserable beasts out of their senses, and away they went as on the wings of the wind, under the lash and shout of the driver the whole five miles of each post, seldom going at a less rate than ten, and often, I believe, twelve miles an hour. We were driven with such reckless speed over the plains and down the hills that at every new stage we committed ourselves anew to the care of Providence, confident that, without special protection, we must be dashed into our original elements before the next five miles were up. But we came through alive.

A great part of the distance, especially that which we passed in the night, is a jungle, which, like every available spot in India, is still kept for raising tigers. At one of the stations we learned that two soldiers, who were on duty at the place, had been carried off not long before by tigers, and eaten. We concluded that there were two tigers at least in that part that were not hungry; but, as night was coming on, I took from my traveling-bag, that had been my pillow, an excellent revolver, that I had not loaded since leaving home, and, carefully inserting five metallic cartridges, lay down to sleep in the gharry, fully prepared, as I supposed, for savage beasts and for still more savage men, of which there are such in India even since the Thugs have been suppressed. The next morning I found, on examination, that in the dim twilight, and in my inexperience with fire-arms, more especially with metallic cartridges, I had inserted the latter with the powder toward the muzzle and the ball toward the stock, so that, if we had been attacked during the night by one of the rovers of the jungle, I should have shot myself, and not the tiger.

About two o'clock at night I became delightfully conscious that we were making no headway in our journey. The sensation was so peculiar and refreshing I did not move to inquire into the cause even after we had been lying still for half an hour or more. Presently I heard a gentle tap at the sliding-door of the gharry, and the *coachwan* calling "*sahib! sahib!*" (gentleman, or sir) in those persuasive tones which in the East usually mean *backshish*. Supposing we were merely changing drivers, and that he was rousing me to obtain a fee, which he had no business to do at that unseemly time of the night, I made no answer. The *coachwan* retired, but it was not long before I heard the same gentle call—"*sahib! sahib!*" I rose, and found that the tire of one of the wheels of the other gharry had broken, and I was summoned to a council of war by the natives to determine what was best to be done in the emergency. We were happily in a small native village, and not in a jungle; but we might almost as well have been in the wilderness, so far as repairing damages was concerned. We found a miserable little smithy, but our only light was obtained from a string in a cup of oil, which scarcely made the dusky natives visible, and afforded little aid in mending the broken wheel. They had already removed the tire, and were preparing to weld it and put it on again—a very nice operation for an experienced wheelwright, and an impossibility in the circumstances. I remonstrated very fluently in good English against their undertaking so difficult an operation, assuring them that they could not accomplish it if they took a week for it, all of which they understood as perfectly as if it had been Hebrew. After three hours spent in ineffectual attempts to repair the break, they abandoned it as a hopeless undertaking, substituted a mail-cart for the other gharry, and we resumed the journey.

At frequent stages on the road the government has erected bungalows, where travelers can rest during the day, or spend the night, provided they carry their own beds and bedding. They are supplied with a few articles of furniture, the chief of which is a bedstead, and with the necessary means of preparing a meal, but they are not intended as hotels. About nine o'clock in the morning we reached the *dak* bungalow at Seonee, midway between the two ends of the journey, and paused for the first and only time on the route, excepting during the delay connected with the accident to the gharry. At this place one of the wheels of my own gharry gave ominous signs of failure, and the remainder of the journey we made with increased speed, and with increasing apprehensions of a wreck. But, through the merciful care of Providence, we reached the end of our ride in safety—more dead than alive, it is true, but with the vital spark ready to be resuscitated, as it was by a refreshing dinner and a good night's rest at Nagloo's Residency Hotel, in the pleasant town of Nagpore.

This was a journey that I would not undertake again for a large part of India; but, now that it is over and safely accomplished, we look back upon it with mingled feelings of pleasure and pain, in which the former predominate—pleasure in the thought that it is safely over, and that we enjoyed one of the last opportunities that could be afforded to any foreigners of sympathizing with the multitudes who, through all the past ages, have been pounded almost into gelatine by traveling in the dak-gharry over the hills of Western India. It is a luxury which can never again be enjoyed on any of the long routes. Travelers will hereafter pass from Calcutta to Bombay, by the way of Allahabad, without leaving the cars. The *dak-gharry* is among the joys departed never to return.

We were still 500 miles from Bombay, but we had the rail before us all the way. Our route lay through the Mahratta country, famous in the wars of the past centuries, and even in the conquest of the country by the British. All day long, every few miles we came upon the old forts standing in the midst of the plains, some of them having walls of great height. The time was when in this whole region no one was safe unless shut in by the walls of a strong fortress. One conqueror after another has swept over it with his armies, and even rival petty chieftains have made prey of the people and their substance. It is now devoted to the arts of peace.

The country through which we were passing is the great cotton region of India, a large portion of the land having been appropriated to its cultivation since the rebellion in our own country compelled the English manufacturers to look for a supply from some other source than the United States. India is the oldest cotton-growing and cotton-manufacturing country in the world. It produced cotton thousands of years ago, and from the earliest accounts cotton fabrics have formed the clothing of the inhabitants. Nothing equal to the finer qualities and the long staple of our Southern States has been produced, but it affords a large supply of the shorter staple. The production was immensely stimulated by the war in America cutting off the supply. The value of the crop of 1859-60 exported from India was £5,637,624. In 1864-5 it had risen to £37,573,637. After this there was a great falling off in its value, though not in quantity, the exports of the crop for 1869-70 amounting to £19,079,138.

. We were at Egutpoora, nearly 100 miles from Bombay, early in the morning. From this point onward the road passes through mountain scenery bold and striking, a perfect contrast to the most of India over which we had traveled. Within a few miles we passed through a long succession of tunnels, scarcely emerging from one before we plunged into another. This portion of the railway was immensely expensive, but it was among the first projected in the grand system of railways for opening up and fortifying the country. It connects the port of Bombay not only with the Deccan, but with the whole of northern and eastern India. Arriving at Bombay at eleven in the morning, we found pleasant quarters at the Byculla Hotel, in the suburbs of the city.

## XXVI.

### BOMBAY.

BOMBAY is situated at the extremity of an island of the same name. It was taken by the Portuguese after the capture of Goa, in the early part of the sixteenth century, and ceded in 1661 to Charles II., of England, as part of the dowry of his bride, the Infanta Catharine. King Charles gave it to the East India Company a few years later, and in 1865 it was made the seat of the chief presidency. On the opening of communication with England by the Red Sea route it received a new impetus, and its importance, if not its supremacy as the commercial capital of India, has been secured by the opening of railroad communication with all parts of the country. Its population and commerce have rapidly increased until it has become the successful rival of Calcutta. It is now a delicate matter to express an opinion in India as to which is the chief city, but it will be the fault of the people of Bombay alone if they do not take the lead. Admirably located, both in regard to its internal and foreign trade, at the western gateway of India, it is in direct communication with the richest parts of the country, and at the nearest point of communication with the whole western world.

Calcutta, on the other hand, is at the far side of India, near the head of the Bay of Bengal, and 100 miles from the mouth of a river which can be entered by large vessels only at certain stages of the tide. Bombay has a fine open harbor—a little too open, it is true, during the prevalence of the southwest monsoons, but it may be farther protected without great expense, and the navies of the world might here ride at anchor. As one of the results of the American war, which opened a market for the cotton of India, and other causes, the city became inflated in 1865 with the promises of a golden harvest, and launched out into extravagant speculations, as if the business of the world was to be concentrated at this point. But the bubble burst almost as soon as it was blown, and a disastrous collapse occurred. Waste lands, that had commanded enormous prices, were suffered to lie waste, and those which were bought at fabulous rates while still under water were never reclaimed from the sea. The people of Bombay became sadder, but wiser, from this experience, and now the city is on a career of assured prosperity. All my observations convinced me that it is destined to be the great city of India, if not of the whole Eastern world.

In its general aspect Bombay is the most lively city of the Indies. Its population of nearly a million is very multifarious. Nearly all the tribes of Hindostan are represented, Hindoos, Mussulmans, Parsees, Indo-Britons, Indo-Portuguese, Europeans of various nations, Americans, and natives of Western Asia. The costumes of the people are varied and gay beyond description. The streets are thronged by a busy multitude on foot, on horseback, and in carriages, many of the latter gaudily trimmed and drawn by bullocks.

The city is not so remarkable for its public buildings or its public institutions as Calcutta, and for the reason that the latter has been the real capital of the country, the seat of the East India Company, where its wealth was concentrated, and in a great measure expended. But some por-

A BULLOCK CARRIAGE.

tions of the town, especially that known as the Fort, which is commensurate with the ancient bounds of the city, contain many fine buildings. The town-hall is a massive structure, with apartments not only for the public service, but for scientific and historical purposes. The rooms of the Royal Asiatic Society, with its library and museum, are full of interest to every intelligent stranger who desires to study the past as well as the present of India. The Elphinstone Circle, named from the Hon. Mountstuart Elphinstone, who succeeded to the Bombay presidency in 1819, is the Wall Street of Bombay, and the centre of its most important commercial operations. The government was erecting new and spacious buildings for public use, and the whole foreign portion of the town was putting on the promise of coming greatness.

The Parsees, numbering more than 100,000 of the population of Bombay, embody a great part of the wealth of the city, and are the most intelligent and enterprising of the natives of the country. No small part of the mercantile business of the East is in their hands, and leading houses have branches in Paris and London, as well as in Eastern Asia. Their dress is peculiar, partly European and partly Oriental. They have a sort of caste like the Hindoos, and are forbidden to marry excepting among their own people; nor do they usually eat what has been cooked by one of another religion. A well-educated Parsee gentleman and his wife were among my companions in crossing the Pacific Ocean. They mingled freely with the other passengers and ate at the same table with them. On returning to Bombay, he was called to account for violating the rules of his race, and his situation became so uncomfortable in consequence that he removed to London to take charge of a branch of the house with which he is connected. With all their intelligence, the Parsees are still greatly under the power of their ancient superstitions, and there are no more bigoted religionists among the tribes of Asia, not even among the Mohammedans. In their religion they are disciples of Zoroaster, who lived several centuries before Christ, and they are usually known as fire-worshipers, reverencing the sun, moon, and other heavenly bodies, and even fire itself, although the more intelligent do not admit that they pay actual worship to these objects. The distinction is very much the same with that of Romanists in regard to the worship of images; the intelligent and truly devout may use the image as an aid to the imagination, while the ignorant worship nothing but the image. In their temples fire is kept continually burning by priests, who maintain that it has never been extinguished. They feed it with fragrant spices, and treat it as if it were a god. The priests even cover the lower part of their faces with a mask when they approach the sacred fire, lest they should defile it with their breath. Their reverence for fire forbids them even to burn tobacco into smoke.

Nothing connected with the Parsees is more peculiar than their treatment of the dead. They have a large cemetery on Malabar Hill, near Bombay, the highest ground in the vicinity, selected on this account, that no one may look into it. The very approaches to the spot are guarded with the most jealous care by men who form a distinct class or caste, and who, from one generation to another, are not permitted to mingle with the rest of the people. The cemetery contains a building devoted to the preservation of the sacred fire, buildings for the priests and those who have charge of the dead, and five round stone towers called "Towers of Silence," each about sixty feet in diameter, and forty or fifty in height. These are the receptacles of the dead.

When a death occurs, the body is taken to the gate of the cemetery and delivered into the hands of the priests. No one is allowed to enter the walls with the dead. After a prescribed ceremonial, the body is taken to one of the towers and laid on a grate upon the top of one of these towers. A flock of hideous vultures is always waiting to devour the flesh, and the bones fall into the body of the tower below in an indiscriminate heap. It is the most revolting mode of disposing of the remains of departed friends of which I have any knowledge, but the Parsees adhere to it with a tenacity which borders on fanaticism.

Through the influence of the Parsee gentleman to whom I have alluded, we obtained an order from a high official in their community to visit the cemetery. Even with this order we had much difficulty in gaining admittance, and were constantly followed and closely watched by the attendants. We walked through the grounds, which were a picture of desolation, and saw the vultures seated upon the towers, anxiously awaiting their human prey; but the arcana of the place were carefully guarded. We had already seen more than often falls to the lot even of the Parsees themselves.

The Hindoo mode of disposing of the dead is far less repulsive. We had been dining one evening with a friend whose bungalow was on Malabar Hill, the most beautiful of the suburbs of Bombay. The drive was through groves of cocoanut palms, and the bungalow was embowered in a luxuriant growth of vines and trees, making the place one like fairy-land. It was late when we returned to town. Across the bay, on the Bombay side, a row of brilliant lights stretched along the shore. In the deep stillness of midnight and the strangeness of the whole scene, they had a mysterious look, and, on inquiry, I learned that they were the funeral piles on which the Hindoos were burning their dead, a more appropriate use of fire than to worship it, and a more becoming mode of treating the remains of the departed, ashes to ashes, than the horrid funeral rites of the Parsees.

We devoted one day while at Bombay to a visit to Elephanta, a lonely island lying six or eight miles across the bay, which we reached by a sail-boat placed at our disposal by Mr. Kittredge, of the American house of Stearns, Hobart & Co. We were accompanied by Mr. and Mrs. Harding, and Mr. and Mrs. Ballantyne, of the American Mission, Mr. Chauntrell, an English barrister, and Dr. Bhau Daji, a Hindoo gentleman, to whom I was indebted not only for many polite attentions, but for much scientific information, as well as for many hours of pleasant intercourse. He has a high standing as a man of science, and is in correspondence with men of learning in this country and in Great Britain. The caves of Elephanta are deserted Buddhist temples, immense caverns cut into the solid rock. Colossal Buddhist figures still remain in comparative preservation. Their history is not known with any degree of certainty, but they are supposed to have been made in the sixth century.

Another day was spent, at the invitation of Dr. Bhau Daji, in a visit to more extensive excavations in the mountains of Kenhari, twenty miles from Bombay. We left in a carriage before daylight, and drove twelve or fourteen miles to the mountains, where horses and palanquins were awaiting us. I chose one of the latter, and, bestowing myself in the box, was soon sound asleep, and woke up in the wilderness as we were approaching the object of our visit. Like the caves of Elephanta, the excavations at Kenhari are involved in mystery, but they are supposed to have formed a Buddhist monastery. They are more than seventy in number—one room a cathedral, with pillars and aisles, all cut into the solid rock as square and smooth as the rooms of a house—are scattered along the mountain in galleries, and are not only deserted, but miles from human habitations. No fitter place for anchoretic life and meditation could be found if it were formerly as lonely as it is now.

One morning Dr. Bhau Daji invited us to his house, romantically situated in the midst of a grove of tall cocoanut palms, to witness the performances of a troop of Indian jugglers. We had seen a similar performance at Delhi, at the house of an English gentleman with whom we dined, but were in no wise impressed with their superiority to their own craft in other lands. Those at Bombay were more expert, but not one of them could equal Hermann, the prestidigitateur, in the variety and skill of his marvelous feats. From what I saw and all I heard, I am inclined to believe that the tricks of Indian jugglers, so celebrated the world over, appear more wonderful as rehearsed in the stories of travelers than when seen on their own ground. The great feat which I have often heard described as the marvel, if not the miracle of such performances in the East, the almost instantaneous growth of a mango-tree from the seed to fruit-bearing, in the dry earth, before your eyes, I saw twice in India, but I saw enough to make it clear that it was mere sleight-of-hand. There were other performances that were to me more wonderful than this, in which there was no attempt at deception.

While we were enjoying the delightful shade of the palms in the compound of our host, the servants ran as nimbly as monkeys up the tall cocoanut-trees, and threw down the fresh fruit for our entertainment. But neither the milk nor the meat is at all tempting in any stage. I prefer to leave the cocoanuts to be manufactured into oil, for which purpose they are raised all over the East.

Among the curious places in Bombay was the hospital for aged and infirm animals. It was open to all races save the human, from the elephant down to the smallest domestic animal. If any poor dog happens to break his leg, or meets with any disaster, or is overtaken by sickness, he will find provision here for his comfort and relief, if he can be relieved. A large square in the midst of the city, with suitable shelter, is devoted to this benevolent though rather sentimental object. The numerous invalids and unfortunates were any thing but a pleasing sight, and it appeared to me more of a work of mercy to end their misery than to prolong their days.

## XXVII.

### BOMBAY TO CAIRO.

WHATEVER may be the feelings of the reader, I leave this land of the Hindoo and the Mohammedan, of palms and palaces, with the deepest regret that time will not wait while I tarry longer among its strange scenes. Thus far it has been the most interesting country that we have reached, not alone nor chiefly for its Oriental and tropical scenery; nor for its venerable and varied history, running back through thousands of years, and down through changing dynasties, some of which have been maintained in splendor such as the world has not seen elsewhere; nor for the remarkably diversified character of its numerous races, which altogether make up one of the most curious pieces of mosaic that the population of the globe will furnish; nor for the monuments of the past, which exceed in beauty, if not in magnificence, all that the ages have left in other lands; but still more interesting in the changes that are now taking place in the condition of its people, and in the promises for the future which every where meet the eye and strike the ear.

Not the glory of the past, the age of "barbaric gold and pearls," but a greater glory is yet to rest on India. I have looked with the deepest satisfaction upon the signs of a coming higher civilization, and the evidences that the light that is to lighten all nations is dawning upon its two hundred millions. India is not now altogether a land of darkness. The mass of its people are still bowing down to its gods of wood and of stone, or following the false prophet, but from Cape Comorin to the Himalayas the Sun of righteousness is lighting the peaks here and there, and giving sure promise of the coming day when Christianity shall triumph over superstition and false religion.

I rejoice heartily that India is under British rule. Whatever may be the errors, or even the crimes of the past, in connection with the extension of British arms, and in the complicity of the governing powers with idolatry, now that they have been so fearfully expiated in the mutiny of 1857, and since the power has passed directly into the hands of the home government, a new destiny awaits the land and the people.

I had timed our arrival at Calcutta so as to spend in India the only two months of the year in which one can travel with comfort, December and January; and our departure, so as to avoid the stifling heat of the Red Sea, which becomes almost insupportable in summer. On the 24th of January we went on board the steamer Krishna, which was lying at anchor in the harbor. The waters of the bay were quiet, but outside we had a taste of the sea. As we passed the light-ship, a boat came off to the Krishna to put a passenger on board. It was already dark; the waves were running high; and as a sailor in the boat caught the rope that was thrown him, the boat receded with a returning swell, he was jerked into the angry sea and left struggling with the waves, the boat drifting far astern. Almost instantly the first officer of the Krishna jumped into the sea to rescue the man, and then there were two in great danger. They clung desperately to the rope, and twice were drawn to the ship and part way up its side, when a returning wave overwhelmed them, and they dropped again into the seething waters, the officer crying out "I'm done," and apparently giving up all hope. It was a frightful scene. In the darkness there seemed little prospect of saving either of them, and with anxious hearts we peered into the black waters, and could only pray that a merciful God might strengthen their arms and rescue them from what appeared an almost inevitable fate. The officer at length caught a buoy which was thrown overboard, the sailor clung to the rope, a boat was lowered, and, to the great joy of all, the men were both brought on board. It was all the work of a few minutes, but it seemed an age as I watched them in their struggle for life, and when they were safe I felt as if I had myself been rescued from a watery grave.

Once off the coast, the voyage through the Indian Ocean as far as Aden, 1660 miles, was without any striking incident. A strong northeast monsoon kept our ship steady, helped us on our course, and supplied us with plenty of fresh air, a great blessing in these Eastern seas. Our passengers were chiefly East India officers, in the military and civil service, with their families, and as we gradually became acquainted, the time passed pleasantly away. On the morning of the sixth day the shores of Arabia were in sight, and toward evening we descried the heights of Aden, ninety miles to the east of the entrance of the Red Sea. It is a mass of rock, connected with the main land by a low, sandy neck, and towering up to the height of 1776 feet. It was held by the Portuguese when they were stretching their arms and their commerce into the East. It was captured by the Turks in 1538, and held for three centuries; but in 1839, for an outrage committed upon a vessel sailing under English colors, the British government seized the place, strengthened its fortifications, and have kept a large garrison upon it ever since. It is called the Gibraltar of the East on account of its commanding position near the entrance to the Red Sea, and its great natural strength as a fortress. Owing to some peculiarity in its situation, it seldom rains at Aden, three or four years passing without a drop falling from the clouds, even when it rains on the main land near by. To supply this deficiency, the early occupants of the place, how long ago is not known, but it is conjectured as early as the sixth or seventh century, excavated immense tanks in the rocks, collecting the water when it fell, and preserving it for years. These ancient cisterns are still in use, and afford an abundant supply. Not long after we had touched at Aden there came a heavy rain, a flood, which not only filled the tanks, but swept away houses, and caused great destruction of property.

We took on board a small flock of Arabian sheep of the broad-tail species, the finest mutton in the East, and an important addition to our commissariat, and were again under way. Passing through the Straits of Bab-el-Mandeb (the Gate of Tears, or the Gate of Desolation, as it is variously interpreted), we entered the sea which, in all ages, has been a terror to navigators. This narrow strip of water covers a small space on the map, but it is more than 1200 miles in length, making a voyage of five or six days by steam, during which the shore is seldom seen on either side. Its navigation is difficult and perilous. The water is of great depth, but rocks and islands are scattered through it, and coral reefs abound, which seldom lift their heads above the waves to warn the sailor of his danger. The shores are almost entirely destitute of light-houses, and are occupied by not the most hospitable races of men, where inhabited at all. High winds prevail a great part of the year, making the navigation particularly undesirable for sailing vessels, which are now seldom seen.

Near the Straits, which are about twelve degrees north of the equator, we had another view of the constellation of the Southern Cross, which, in the clear skies of the Red Sea, was very brilliant in the early morning. The first evening we were off the town of Mocha, on the Arabian

Z

side, a name suggestive of good coffee, which lived in our memories, but formed no part of our experience on shipboard. The second day we were off the Zebayer Islands, called the Twelve Apostles, nearly opposite the landing-place of the British expedition against Abyssinia. We had on board one of the heroes of the war, who had served also with distinction in the suppression of the mutiny in India. He bore many marks of his heroism, having, as it was said, been cut to pieces and put together again. We afterward fell in with one of the original captives of King Theodore. He had his chains with him, and was bearing them home as a trophy. Farther on we passed Djiddah, the port of Mecca.

Two or three days before reaching Suez we encountered a fierce north wind, which never subsided until we were on shore. Every few minutes, on the last day or two of the voyage, a heavy sea would break over the bow of the ship, washing her decks from stem to cabin, which, with the cold blasts from the north, drove us all under shelter, and many to their berths. Nor were the high winds, and the coral reefs on which the British steamer Carnatic had struck and gone down a few weeks before, a large number of the passengers perishing, our only perils. In the midst of the gale and in the midst of the rocks our captain prepared himself to meet the danger by a drunken carousal, and became crazy with rum, one or two of his officers following his example. How we came safely through we never knew, excepting that we had the guidance and protecting care of the great Pilot who holds the winds in his fists and the waters in the hollow of his hand. This captain afterward fell overboard in the harbor of Bombay and was drowned.

It was not until the evening of the sixth day from our entering the Straits, and the twelfth from our leaving Bombay, that we dropped anchor at Suez—it may have been upon one of the chariot-wheels of Pharaoh. The sun had set before we reached the anchorage, which is five miles from the head of the gulf and from the town. As we could not go ashore until we had been inspected by the health officer, we fired heavy guns and threw up rockets, but there was no response, and we were compelled to spend another night upon the sea. But we were at rest, and the perils of the voyage were over.

Suez is not an insignificant town. It has a population of several thousands; its bazars are well supplied with goods for Oriental consumption, and there is more of an air of activity and business about it than one might expect in such a desert region. When the overland route to India was opened a few years since, Suez had a revival of the traffic it enjoyed before the discovery of the route to the Indies by the Cape of Good Hope; but the more re-

SUEZ.

cent opening of the Suez Canal may be another blow to its prosperity, by making all transhipment of passengers and goods needless.

Immediately on landing and getting comfortably established in the Suez Hotel, I took my Bible to read over the inspired account of the Exodus from Egypt, and went out to compare the account with the face of the country. It was the same land over which Moses led the children of Israel more than thirty-three centuries before. The same sands were still there, though the footprints of the departing host had been obliterated; the same sea rolled before us; the same mountains frowned from the southeast; the general aspect of the scene was unchanged. It was not difficult to obtain a perfectly satisfactory idea of the route by which the Israelites came thus far in following the cloudy pillar, although the precise point at which the miraculous crossing of the sea took place is still one of the problems of sacred geography. There is no doubt in regard to the route by which they came from Succoth to the sea. The path is clearly defined by the features of the country. A precipitous mountain range stretches from the shore diagonally to the northwest, leaving a sandy plain between it and the sea, from which they could not diverge. All this was so clear that, as I looked over the vast plain, I could almost imagine I saw the great host on their march, the pillar of cloud leading them on by day, and the great curtain hung up by the hand of God to protect them from their pursuers by night. But where was the point at which they heard the command of God to go forward, and were so marvelously delivered from their enemies?

Dr. Robinson is of the opinion that the crossing took place very near the site of the modern city of Suez; but his reasoning savors rather of rationalistic explanation than of a full acknowledgment of the grandeur of the miracle by which God effected this deliverance of his people. He explains away the miracle by referring it to natural and secondary causes, and in order to do so locates the crossing where the sea is now scarcely half a mile wide, and only deep enough to be navigable. It is true there are indications that the sand has encroached upon the sea, and that the latter was here more than a mile wide in former times; but even this scarcely makes the necessity of a stupendous miracle evident. From the point selected by Dr. Robinson they might have moved several miles farther south, or have passed up to the head of the sea farther north, as the shores in either direction are perfectly smooth. Every thing in the divine record shows that they were shut up to entering the bed of the sea at the very spot on which they stood when the Lord said unto Moses, "Wherefore criest thou unto me? Speak unto the children of Israel that they go forward; but lift thou up thy rod and stretch out thine hand over the sea and divide it, and the children of Israel shall go on dry ground in the midst of the sea."

From an examination of these localities, it appeared to me much more probable that they followed the sandy plain to the south, where the sea and the precipitous mountain range converge, and where it was impossible for them to move excepting in one direction. Pharaoh and his hosts were in their rear; they had fled until they could flee no farther; a mountain wall was on one side, and the deep sea upon the other: God divided the waters before them, and they passed through the midst of the sea.

At the point to which I refer the Red Sea must be five or six miles in width, and of great depth; but the whole account indicates that the crossing took place where the sea was wide. The Egyptians, pursuing the Israelites, "went in after them to the midst of the sea, even all Pharaoh's horses, his chariots, and his horsemen." It was in the midst of the sea that they proposed to turn back when they found that the Lord was fighting for the Israelites against the Egyptians. They turned and fled; but when the sea came back to its bed, of the vast army that had gone into it "there remained not so much as one of them." The simple narrative, the Song of Moses which he sang with the children of Israel to celebrate their deliverance, the allusions to it in other parts of the Holy Scriptures, show that it was a sublime miracle, not accomplished by a concurrence of ordinary means, and therefore that there was no occasion for selecting a place where it could be easily performed, but rather the contrary. The drying up of the waters was not effected alone by the strong east wind, for "the children of Israel went into the midst of the sea upon the dry ground, and the waters were a wall unto them on their right hand and on their left." In the Song of Moses it is said, "The floods stood upright as an heap, and the depths were congealed in the heart of the sea." This is not all poetic imagery.

While we were yet in the far East, on the way to Egypt, the ceremonial of the formal opening of the canal connecting once more the waters of the Mediterranean and the Red Seas took place, but the passenger lines were not yet established when we reached Suez. In connection with two or three English gentlemen, one of them a member of Parliament who had been sent out to investigate the expenses of the Abyssinian War, we chartered a small steamer at Suez to explore the canal, laid in a stock of provisions at the hotel, and left Suez about eight o'clock in the morning, expecting to be at Ismailia, fifty miles distant, by three in the afternoon. We steamed quietly along, stopping here and there to examine the work, climbing the high walls of sand thrown up on both sides to look out over the desert. We were well on our way toward the end of our inland voyage when an ominous gathering of steamers loomed up before us, very suggestive of one of those dead-locks predicted before the opening. We would fain have convinced ourselves that it was a mirage of the desert, but it was no unsubstantial apparition. We found, on coming to a halt, that the stoppage was produced by a float made fast in the middle of the canal for the purpose of blasting rock at the bottom, and that no craft could pass until the drilling was completed and the blast exploded, which would probably be near midnight—as it proved, and we did not arrive at Ismailia, which is on one of the lakes of the canal, until one or two o'clock in the morning.

NIGHT ON THE CANAL.

The Suez Canal was not a new idea to the man by whose energy and perseverance the seas have now become practically connected. It was projected by the ancient Egyptians, who must have had some sort of communication through the lakes across the isthmus. In 1798, Napoleon I., then commanding the French expedition to Egypt, proposed opening a ship canal through the same route. A commission appointed to make the survey reported that the Red Sea was thirty feet lower than the Mediterranean, which was considered a fatal objection to the enterprise; but the survey of the overland route to India in 1830 established the fact that the two seas are on the same level.

M. de Lesseps was then in Egypt, attached to the French consulate. He at once caught up the idea with enthusiasm, and by indomitable perseverance carried it out to its present success.

It was strange to find in old Egypt a city of palaces and parks not more than five years old; but such is Ismailia. It has sprung into existence by the touch of the Suez Canal, with as much rapidity and a hundred-fold more stability and beauty than the towns on the Pacific Railroad. From this point we struck out into the desert, and for hours traversed the sandy waste, the picture of dreary desolation. Once in a while we came upon some weary travelers or traffickers, who, with camels or donkeys, were dragging their way through the sands; but even this did not relieve the prospect, for we pitied the travelers who were making such slow progress, while we were driving onward by the force of steam over an iron pathway.

We were going down to the valley of the Nile by the same route which Abraham took when he went into Egypt to escape famine; by which the sons of Jacob went down to buy corn; and by which the grand funeral procession returned bearing the body of the patriarch to its resting-place in the cave of Machpelah (where, I have no doubt, it still slumbers undisturbed). At length we descried in the distance an oasis, a grove of palms, a beautiful sight always, but most beautiful when seen in the distance over a sandy waste, bearing the promise of green fields, upon which we presently came. They lie along the margin of the canal dug to carry the refreshing waters of the Nile over a wider extent of country.

We caught sight of Cairo just as the sun was going down beyond the Pyramids. Its golden light streamed over the domes and minarets, pouring itself in a flood upon the green fields and among the palms, and drawing a beautiful contrast between the buildings and the dark foliage in which they were set. The Citadel, with its Grand Mosque, towered above the rest of the city, having for its background the gray mountain, the mausoleum of long-buried generations. The broad valley of the Nile, dressed in living green, was spread out before us. For a while we forgot that we were travelers from a new world, and fell to dreaming of the Pharaohs and the patriarchs, until that intensely modern invention, the shrill whistle of the locomotive, restored us to consciousness, and summoned us to alight in the city of splendor, and dirt, and donkeys.

We had not seen the interior of our trunks since leaving India, and among the most pleasing anticipations of reaching Cairo was the general renovation that we were to undergo when we should again be admitted to the arcana of our luggage. But, on presenting our tickets, we were informed that the luggage had been left behind at Zagazig, half way to Ismailia. All we could do was to repair to Shepheard's Hotel and wait until it should arrive, if it came at all. I had no expectation of seeing it for at least two or three days, being confident that it had gone off to Alexandria and perhaps to London, with our English friends who had left us at Zagazig to take the steamer. But, greatly to my surprise, about ten o'clock in the evening the Egyptians came marching into our room with the lost baggage on their heads, and it was like getting home to get into our trunks once more.

They have strange chambermaids at Shepheard's. The one who waited on our room and attended to all the various duties of the calling, even to making of beds, was a courtly Frenchman, dressed as if for a dinner-party, and having the air of a refined and educated gentleman. It was really embarrassing to accept his services. One of the ladies, on arriving at the hotel, rang for the chambermaid. This gentleman presented himself. Supposing him to be the proprietor or chief clerk, she informed him that she had rung for the chambermaid. He very politely replied, in the best English he could command, "Madame, I am she."

## XXVIII.

#### CAIRO TO JERUSALEM.

My first expedition to Cairo, after recovering from the fatigues of our long voyage and subsequent journeyings by land, was to the Citadel; not so much to see the Citadel itself or the Grand Mosque, but for the panoramic view of the city and the valley of the Nile which it commands. This view alone would repay a traveler for coming to this far-off country, even if he should see nothing else. As you stand upon the parapet, the whole of Cairo, ancient and modern, lies at your feet. On the right are the tombs of the Caliphs and the Mamelukes. On the left is what remains of Old Cairo—called old by courtesy among the monuments of thirty or forty centuries. Beyond the city flows the Nile, encircling several beautiful islands. Farther on, across the emerald valley, the Pyramids and the Sphinx sit in silent majesty. A few miles up the Nile is the site of ancient Memphis, now nearly obliterated. The hills on either side of the broad valley, rising up as walls to say to the overflowing stream, "Thus far shalt thou come, but no farther," are inhabited by a silent multitude, unnumbered millions, unknown and undecayed, who await the coming of the resurrection morn just as they were laid in their tombs thousands of years ago. In the midst of this scene the old Nile flows on and overflows, as it has from the time of the Pharaohs and from the time of the flood, if not from all time. As he gazes one can not help but people the valley with the generations that have come and gone, and fill it up with the grand events that have transpired, until he becomes bewildered with their variety and with the succession.

Taking a carriage at the hotel, and crossing the Nile by the bridge of boats, we drove directly to the Pyramids, which are about ten miles west from the river. The carriage-road is an embankment of Nile mud from ten to fifteen feet high, making it available during the overflow and at all seasons of the year. It is shaded by large acacias, and the carriage-track is usually in excellent order. The viceroy has shown some sense in sparing a trifle from the vast sums which he is expending upon his numerous palaces for the construction and improvement of this road; and whether the natives bless him for it or not (it must greatly interfere with the donkey business), all foreigners who have occasion to visit the Pyramids will give him their benedictions. He might immortalize himself by effecting one reform—the abatement or abolition of the backshish nuisance. A horde of Arabs, nominally under the control of a sheikh, who is paid in advance for their services, stand ready to torment the money, if not the life, out of every new victim who falls into their hands. They give him no rest in making the ascent of the Pyramid, nor will they suffer him to enjoy, undisturbed, the magnificent prospect from the summit. And woe be to the luckless traveler who is persuaded to enter the chambers with money in his pocket, and without a large measure of courage and firmness.

There is no greater abatement to the pleasure of journeying in the East than this never satisfied demand of money. It meets the traveler at every turn, like the flies of the ancient plague, and comes up into his very bed-chamber, like the frogs, and there is no escaping it. Backshish is not asked as a matter of charity; every one who renders the slightest service, or who only makes an offer of service, or who even looks at you, whether you wish him to look or not, feels that he has established a claim to your purse, and dogs your steps with incessant appeals which it is impossible to thrust aside. The claim is made with such vehemence and pertinacity, that you are almost persuaded to

THE PYRAMIDS.

believe that in some way the miserable creatures who swarm around and follow you from place to place have become entitled to every thing you possess. If you could only purchase immunity by paying liberally there would be a satisfaction in doing it, but, like the flies in the fable, if you drive one swarm away, another at once takes its place.

I will not tax the reader with a description of the Pyramids, with which every one is familiar; nor of the Sphinx which sits a few hundred yards distant, looking out upon the valley of the Nile as it has looked for thousands of years, a strange monument to the strange ideas of the ancient Egyptians. After a stroll to the ruins of the old temples—long covered by the sand, but now excavated— we returned to Cairo over the same road, and through the same green valley which, at this season of the year, appears fresher and greener every time that the eye rests upon it. Nor shall I here record our excursions to Old

Cairo; or to the new palaces of the Khedive, on which he is expending millions of treasure, as if the wealth of the Indies were his; or to the island of Rhoda, where we were told the infant Moses was found in the ark of bulrushes—

A STREET IN CAIRO.

all these and other expeditions in the land of the Pharaohs must remain unrecorded for the present.

Bright and beautiful was the morning when we left Cairo—but what morning is not bright in the East, the lands of the sunrising? With the exception of one shower, of which I have made mention, we had not seen a drop fall from the clouds, and scarcely a cloudy day or hour, for many months. It is not pleasant always to live under a glowing sun, but smiling skies are usually welcome to a traveler.

Through the crowd of donkeys and donkey-boys, porters, and idlers, we made our way to and into the railway station, and into the cars bound for Alexandria, and were on our way toward the sea and toward other lands. Before leaving Cairo we heard that some home friends were coming up that day, and, meeting the train at the half-way station, I shouted their names while the cars were coming to a halt. There came back a response, and for a few brief moments we enjoyed one of those delightful interviews which can be had only thousands of miles away from home, after having been strangers in strange lands for many long months of travel. Our words of greeting and parting, our inquiries and replies, our items of information, which were confined to friends and matters of mutual interest, were brief and hurried, but into those few minutes we crowded an amount of pleasure that might be spread over many days of ordinary life. These stolen interviews in the wide desert—these snatches of home delight, as one flits by another in a strange land, are not to be measured by moments.

Our time in Alexandria we divided between the Catacombs, and Pompey's Pillar, and Cleopatra's Needle, and ancient and modern Alexandria. No one who has ever lived in the Republic of Letters can come to this spot and not be harassed with the remembrance of that wealth of learning which was here committed to the flames. What a treasure would the Alexandrian Library be at the present day! If one such repository had escaped the ravages of war, and of barbarism, and of time, what a flood of light would it shed upon the dark past! More than one million volumes are reputed to have been gathered in the Library and Museum, the most of which were burned during the wars of Julius Cæsar. The Library was subsequently restored and enlarged, but again the torch was applied by the Moslem conquerors. When importuned to save it, Omar coolly replied, "If these writings of the Greeks agree with the Book of God, they are useless, and need not be preserved; if they disagree, they are pernicious, and ought to be destroyed."

In what remains of ancient Alexandria there is nothing more interesting than the site of ancient Pharos, the first of those towers of light that now stud the shores of every sea, like guardian angels watching over the mariners. The light-house of Pharos is counted among the seven wonders of the world, and well does it deserve a place in the cataalogue. It was a massive building of pure marble, erected by the orders of Ptolemy Philadelphus, whose name was to be inscribed in the marble in front. The architect made himself infamous, but did not detract from the fame of his emperor, by a deceitful ruse. He engraved his own name in the marble, covering it with stucco, on which he placed the following inscription: "King Ptolemy to the Saviour Gods for the use of those who travel by sea." When, in the course of time, the stucco fell, it revealed another more durable inscription: "Sostratus of Cnidos, the son of Dexiphanes, to the Saviour Gods for all who travel by sea." There is a light-house now standing on the same site.

We were now bound as pilgrims for the Holy Land. Embarking at Alexandria on the French steamer, we were at Port Said, the Mediterranean entrance to the Suez Canal, early the next morning. Should the canal be a permanent success, this port will be an important station between the East and the West. Its formation was one of the most difficult parts of the great enterprise. The sea at this point being shallow, scarcely more than a mud flat, it was necessary to construct a harbor, and, at the same time, to excavate it to the proper depth. Two breakwaters were run out more than a mile into the sea, inclosing a harbor. As there was no stone for their construction, the great projector supplied the deficiency by making concrete blocks of sand and cement, which look like blocks of granite. A light-house, wharves, and other structures at Port Said have been built of the same material, and promise to endure the action alike of air and water for ages.

We left Port Said at 5 o'clock P.M. Late at night I was sitting on deck, enjoying the swell of the sea in the open air in preference to the confinement of the cabin, and by necessity became a listener to the conversation of two English gentlemen who sat near me. One said to the other, "What a host of Americans we have on board!" (The Americans comprised about two thirds of the passengers.) "Yes," replied his friend, "and it is the same wherever we go in the East. I should think they had room enough in their own country to wander in without coming over here in such crowds. Why! they can travel eight days and eight nights in one train of cars without stopping, but they do not seem contented even with that." And they voted that it was an unauthorized proceeding for American sovereigns to invade that part of the world in such numbers, evidently forgetting that they had stepped off from the little island of Great Britain without any better authority. It was gratifying to me to observe that they had become so familiar with the geography, or at least the extent of our country, which few have been able to comprehend.

Several years since I met, in a social circle in London, a very intelligent English lady, who, in the course of our conversation, feeling called upon to make some remark in regard to the country from which I came, said to me, "I see by the papers that you have had a fire in America," apparently regarding our continent as a small village compared with the immense extent of the British Isles. Having recently left New York, I felt bound to apologize for not having been at the fire, or, at least, for not knowing where it was, and replied that I did not know what one she referred to; that we often burned a large part of our cities over to build them up in better style. (It was a year in which there had been extensive fires in Milwaukie, St. Louis, and San Francisco, and other Western cities, some account of which had met her eye without making any particular impression.) To account for my ignorance, and to give her some idea of the extent of our country, I stated that not long before leaving New York I had taken a steamer in the interior of Pennsylvania and sailed a hundred miles down the Monongahela to Pittsburg, a thousand miles down the Ohio to the Mississippi, another thousand down the Mississippi to New Orleans, and that I was then a hundred and fifty miles from the mouth of the stream on which I had first embarked. This statement, although literally true, was such a tax upon her credulity that it suddenly stopped the conversation. She made no reply, evidently regarding me as another Baron Munchausen. But an English gentleman, who had traveled extensively in the United States, saw my unhappy position, and came to my relief. He said he had been on our Western rivers, and knew that what I said was true. A good understanding was restored, and all would have passed off well enough had not a young New Yorker present felt disposed to indulge in a bit of pleasantry and enlarge her ideas of American scenery. Noting her surprise, he said, "Madam, we have lakes in America so large that you might take up the whole of England and drop it into one of them, and it would not make a ripple on the shore." We were then all at sea again, and were both set down as incorrigible illustrations of our national fondness for large stories.

The United States of America are much better known to the world at large than they were but a few years since. Our late struggle for national life, affecting as it did, in one way and another, nearly every land, has made the nations better acquainted with our geography, our resources, and our strength, and never did the country or the nation stand higher in the estimation of the world than at the present time, if I may judge from the reception of Americans before and since the war. Fifteen or twenty years ago, as I can testify from personal experience, Americans, in traveling abroad, were constantly and often rudely placed upon the defensive when their nationality became known, and they are not in the habit of concealing it. It was not safe, even by the wayside or in a railcar, to address an Englishman on the most ordinary topic without an introduction, or unless he had first spoken; and when the subject of our country came up, it was the next thing to a declaration of war. I have many interviews of this character in memory.

Our late war, in all its history and its results, developing the indomitable energy of the people, their invincible attachment to the government under which they have attained to their present state of prosperity, and their independence of all foreign alliances, has greatly elevated the country in the eyes of the world. With no other people is this change more apparent than with the children of what we are wont to call the mother country. I take pleasure in bearing the most cordial testimony to the friendly bearing of Englishmen in all parts of the world, and to their friendly interest in our land. Time and again, as I have been passing through Eastern countries, where the interests of England are predominant, has the expression of such feeling been made, and with it the acknowledgment that while our war was in progress the sympathy of the more intelligent and influential classes of Great Britain, at home and abroad, was against us. They have as frankly confessed the cause; they thought we were becoming too powerful; they wished to see our strength divided, and for this reason they desired the success of the rebellion. But they now see their error, and heartily express the regret that they held the views and took the course they did. Such is the logic of success. May this international amity, which on both sides is now hearty, never again be interrupted!

It was evening when we left Port Said. When the morning came I rose early, and with no little anxiety looked out upon the sea. There is no harbor at Jaffa, and, as the anchorage is a mile from the shore, unless the sea is comparatively quiet, it is impossible to have any communication with the land. In rough weather the steamer does not stop, so that passengers are frequently carried by, and those on shore who have come down from Jerusalem to take the steamer are compelled to remain another week, and, perhaps, be doomed to a second disappointment from the same cause. Happily for us, it was calm, and we reached the shore without difficulty.

Jaffa is built upon a rocky hill directly on the sea, and the town rises so abruptly that it shows to good advantage. But if there be any beauty in its situation or appearance, the charm vanishes the moment one sets foot upon the shore and enters its dirty, winding streets, to be jostled by its miserable crowd of idle Arabs, camels, and donkeys. Our experience in getting ourselves and our baggage to the hotel in the American colony on the outskirts of the town, attended by nearly a score of porters who demanded backshish for all sorts of services, actual and imaginary, would make another amusing record, but there is not space for it. So many Americans were arriving that the people were indulging "great expectations," and nothing but princely gifts would satisfy them. I tendered the leader of the band that escorted us what was his due, but he indignantly rejected it, demanding five times as much, and, when I quietly put the money into my pocket, he and his whole crew lashed themselves into a towering passion in true Oriental style, and made all sorts of threatening demonstrations. Verily, it seemed as if the Philistines were upon us. In the course of an hour or two he expressed his willingness to accept what I offered, said he was satisfied, and added a "Thank you."

We tarried at this ancient harbor of Hiram and Solomon, and of Jonah's embarkation for Tarshish, only long enough to make arrangements for the journey to Jerusalem. A new road had been recently built, well graded, and affording a carriage-track twenty-five or thirty feet in width the whole distance; but the carriages were wanting, and we must needs take the saddle. The distance from Jaffa to Jerusalem is only thirty-six miles, but very few not inured to the saddle can accomplish it in a single day, while it is often done in eight or ten hours by those who have been hardened to the exercise, and sometimes in less.

It was afternoon on Saturday when we were prepared for a start. We had sent forward to engage rooms at the Russian convent at Ramleh, a few hours distant, where we were to spend the Sabbath—a far more quiet and desirable resting-place than the miserable city of Simon the Tanner. We rode out of Jaffa through the orange-groves that surround the city. The trees were still loaded with the golden fruit, and more magnificent specimens I have never seen. One gentleman whom I met cut a twig having on it six oranges which together weighed between seven and eight pounds, and another had two oranges that weighed five pounds.

Our course was over the beautiful plains of Sharon, then covered with wheat-fields in the early green, and decked with a profusion of wild flowers, and the ride was one of indescribable interest. We were traversing the plain which for thousands of years had been memorable in history and storied in song; the plain which had been trod by prophets and apostles; the plain which, time and again, in ancient and in latter days, had shook to the tramp of marching hosts. The classic sea was behind us; before us rose the hills of Judea; on our right, as far as the eye could reach toward Philistia, stretched the plains of Ajalon.

The gorgeous sun of Palestine had gone down in glory behind the sea before we reached our stopping-place, and, but for the gathering shadows, we would gladly have lingered longer on the plains to read upon them, and upon the skies of Judea, the long and sacred history of the past. We followed our dragoman through the winding streets of Ramleh, and were soon resting in our quarters on the house-top of the Russian convent. The lower and only story of the convent was appropriated to our horses and the pack-mules, while we ascended to the roof, a broad pavement, around which were rows of small rooms ready for our reception. Here we spent our first Sabbath in Palestine. The stillness of the wide plains surrounded us, scarcely broken by day or by night save by the muezzin's musical voice from the minaret adjoining, sounding forth the call to prayer. More than once were we roused from our slumbers by the solemn chant,

"Allah ekber! Allah ekber!
Eshedon en la Allah illa Allah!"

This is repeated seven times by day, and as often by night. The following is a translation of the usual form, varied only on Friday, the Mohammedan Sabbath:

"God is great! God is great!
I testify that there is no god but God.
I testify that Mohammed is the Prophet of God.
Come to peace! Come to happiness!
God is great! There is no god but God!"

On the Sabbath we gathered from their tents, and from the Latin convent, all the Americans whom we could find, and had our usual services on the house-top. It was literally a sacred day, and one to be consecrated in memory. We could enter into the feelings of the patriarch when, far away from home, he fell asleep by the wayside, and awoke to say, "Surely the Lord is in this place, and I knew it not. This is none other but the house of God, and this is the gate of heaven."

We rose at two o'clock on Monday morning to resume our journey beneath a brilliant sky. The stars were out in hosts—the same stars which shone upon the land of Canaan when Abraham first passed through it—the same stars which were shining when One, the brightest of all, was added to their number.  The moon was shedding its peaceful light upon the plains as we struck out again upon the track Zionward.  Soft as is the evening moonlight, and suggestive of sweet and sacred thoughts, the moonlight of the morning is softer and more sacred.  Entering, as we were, upon the Holy Land, and traversing the beautiful plains of Sharon up toward the Holy City, an awe of solemnity stole over us, and almost in silence we rode onward, hour after hour, until the east, toward which our faces were turned, became luminous with the advancing day.

And now the path became more rugged.  We were ascending the mountains which are round about Jerusalem, and which guard it like the walls of a citadel.  We paused but a short time to break our fast, and were again in the saddle pressing on to stand within the gates of Zion.  More than once, as we reached an eminence, expecting to see from it the city which was once "the joy of the whole earth," were we disappointed; it was still beyond.  At length our eyes beheld the sight.  As we reached the last height, the whole familiar scene, with all its hallowed memories, was before us.  We needed no one to point out the various localities.  It was a scene on which we had been looking from childhood.  We needed no one to say to us, That is the Holy City; there, to the right, is Mount Zion, the city of David; there, to the left, where rises the dome of the Mosque of Omar, is the site of the ancient temple; the height beyond, now looking so barren and desolate, is the Mount of Olives—the favorite resort of Him who came from heaven to sojourn upon earth, and the spot last pressed by his sacred feet ere he ascended to his native skies.  The memories of the sacred scenes which made the places so familiar even to our eyes came thronging upon our hearts, until we could scarcely collect our thoughts enough to imagine in what age of this old world we were approaching the Holy City, or whether it had any age other than that in which the most important events in its history transpired.

And this is Jerusalem! the mount where Abraham bound Isaac in the wilderness, and laid him on the altar! the city of David and Solomon! the spot which God selected for the display of his glory in the Holy of Holies! the place where he was long manifest in the flesh—where Jesus lived and taught! the city in which he was arrested and tried as a malefactor! This is the spot where he was stretched upon the cross, and where he cried "It is finished," and bowed his head and died!

Slowly and silently we wound our way down the hillside, past the Russian hospice, along the ancient wall to the Damascus Gate, passing through a strange crowd of frowning Mussulmans to the Mediterranean Hotel, and then we rested in Salem, the City of Peace. "Pray for the peace of Jerusalem: they shall prosper that love thee. Peace be within thy walls, and prosperity within thy palaces. For my brethren and my companions' sakes, I will now say, Peace be within thee."

## XXIX.

### THE HOLY CITY.

In the Hotel Mediterranean (it sounds almost profane to speak of a hotel in Jerusalem) we found more of comfort than one could expect, and, until another day had come, were not disposed to leave it to explore the city. But with the morning we went forth to trace the scenes which, eighteen hundred years ago, made this mountain so memorable in the history of our world and in the records of time. With little faith in the traditions that have mapped out the holy places in the sacred city, I determined to give myself up to the spirit of the scene, and, first of all, to follow, in imagination at least, the path the Saviour trod when he was led as a lamb to the slaughter. Accordingly, I told the guide to take us first to the house of Pilate. The one now bearing this name occupies the same general locality as that of the Roman governor, but there is nothing to establish the identity, and as little to assist one in recalling the scene of the judgment-hall. Following the *Via Dolorosa*, we come to the Chapel of the Flagellation,

VIA DOLOROSA.

and then to the Arch of the *Ecce Homo*, said to cover the spot were Jesus came forth wearing the crown of thorns and the purple robe, when Pilate exclaimed to the people, "Behold the man;" and then we followed, as near as we could, that strange procession which led the holy victim on toward Calvary. Here we are told the Saviour of the world sank under the burden of his cross, when Simon the Cyrenean was compelled to take it up and bear it after him; here we pass what are called the houses of Dives and Lazarus, and presently reach the spot where we are informed Veronica appeared with a napkin to wipe the sweat from the sacred brow, when the portrait of the Saviour was miraculously impressed upon it. The pretended relic is preserved as one of the chief treasures of the Basilica of St. Peter at Rome.

Making a slight ascent through a narrow street, we come at length to the open square in front of the Church of the Holy Sepulchre, a sort of bazar for the sale of relics, and a

CHURCH OF THE HOLY SEPULCHRE.

place of gathering for all sorts of pilgrims. The door of the church is closed. The time for the opening has come and passed, but the Turkish officials who have it in charge delay, and still longer delay, hoping that a party of strangers, not having the look of ordinary pilgrims, will tender backshish. At length we are admitted.

The Church of the Holy Sepulchre might more appropriately be called the Church of all the Holy Places. Tradition has so conveniently located many of them within a few yards of each other that they are all inclosed under one roof. Near the door is the "Stone of Unction," a marble slab, on which the body of our Lord is said to have been anointed for the burial. The dome of the building covers the Holy Sepulchre, which stands in the centre of the area—not a tomb "hewn out in the rock," according to the Scripture narrative, but a marble structure about six feet square, and the same in height, apparently built on the pavement. It is asserted that the surrounding rock has been removed, and that what remained was incased in marble, accounting for its present appearance. The whole structure is above the floor of the church, and bears no sign of attachment to the original rock. The coincidence of "stooping down" to enter or look within the sepulchre, as did Peter on the morning of the resurrection, is preserved by a low doorway through which we enter. About one third of the width of the interior is occupied by a marble slab representing the stone on which the body of Jesus was laid. It is fitted up as an altar, and on and above it are costly gifts, set thick with precious stones, presented by different sovereigns of Europe. A Greek priest was standing at the head when we first stepped within. He courteously gave us the names of the royal donors of the gifts recently made, and handed us from the altar some of the fragrant flowers that are daily placed there in profusion. The priests of the different sects in turn stand guard in the tomb, a necessary precaution with such a crowd of pilgrims and strangers. Free access to the holy places was allowed to all, nor was there any disorder or confusion in the crowd of visitors which thronged the church all day long.

A flight of steps leads to an upper chapel, which is said to cover the Hill of Calvary, and a round hole in the rock is pointed out as that in which stood the cross while the Redeemer hung upon it. A cleft in the rock, which is shown, is said to have been made when Jesus yielded up the ghost, "and the earth did quake and the rocks were rent." All the localities, even to the places where Mary, the mother of Jesus, stood while his body was prepared for the burial, and where Christ appeared to Mary Magdalene on the morning of the resurrection, are pointed out with the same precision.

Descending a long stone stairway, we were taken to the Chapel of St. Helena, and then to a still lower recess, appropriately called, in English, "the Chapel of the *Invention* of the Cross." I can have no faith in the miracle said to have attended the finding of the three crosses in perfect preservation three hundred years after the crucifixion. It is without satisfactory proof; the links in the chain of evidence are altogether too wide apart; and I can see no occasion for the miracle. Even the pretence has been used the world over to encourage a superstitious worship of the supposed relic instead of faith in the victim that hung upon the cross. I am equally incredulous in regard to the identity of most of the holy places. Without professing any accurate knowledge of the topography of Jerusalem, I have familiarized myself with the arguments of those who have endeavored to establish their verity, but it seems to me only fancy or superstition can be satisfied with the evidence.

On my first visit to the Latin Chapel connected with the Holy Sepulchre, the priests and monks had just commenced the vesper service preparatory to visiting the stations here grouped together. As I entered, a Capucin monk, whom I afterward found to be a jolly Irishman on a pilgrimage to the Holy City, handed me a Latin Breviary, and I joined the procession in the entire circuit, reading with them the description of the scenes connected with the death and burial of the Redeemer. The chants from the Latin Vulgate were well rendered, and would have been impressive even in other circumstances. At the close of the service, Father Antonio (he gave me his name as soon as it was concluded) conducted us through the chapels in possession of the Latins, showing us the relics which had been left in Jerusalem by the Knights of St. John, and treating us with great courtesy. I must confess I thought him rather profane in his bearing, for he spoke with a levity of the place which was far from being consonant with my feelings, even though I could not satisfy myself that I was, without doubt, upon the scene of the great events associated with the reputed holy places.

It is not a pleasant thought, even to those who have no superstitious reverence for any of the localities of the Holy City, that these places are in the keeping of the followers of the false prophet; and it is still more painful to contemplate the scenes of strife, amounting not unfrequently to bloodshed, that have occurred upon this sacred, if not holy ground. Nowhere else is the hostility between Latin and Greek Christians more intense or more ready to break out than on the very spot where, as they profess to believe, the Prince of Peace shed his blood for their redemption, and where his body was laid in the grave.

From the Holy Sepulchre we went to Mount Zion, the City of David, which is partially reclaimed from Mohammedan defilement, and from Oriental and Roman superstition, by the establishment of a Christian mission under Bishop Gobat, who has had much encouragement in seeking out the lost sheep of the house of Israel. Sad and miserable is the condition of the Jews in this city of their fathers, as it is in most parts of the world. Their quarter in Jerusalem, as in nearly every Oriental and European city, is the most wretched and filthy of all, and they seem here, as every where, to be suffering the curse which their fathers invoked upon themselves and their descendants when they cried, "His blood be on us and on our children." They still cling to the curse, even though they meet once a week to weep over the desolation of the Temple and the city. And even this is with most of them a mere formality. At the appointed hour I went out to the Wailing Place. More than a hundred Jews were assembled, but not more than one in ten appeared to enter into the spirit of the service. The rest were looking around upon the crowd as unconcerned, many of them more unconcerned, than the Gentiles who came merely to see the Jews. Even the Rabbi who read the penitential and mourning psalms, and those who joined him in weeping over the stones of the Temple, manifested no real grief.

"As the mountains are round about Jerusalem, so the Lord is round about his people from henceforth even forever." The city itself is set upon a hill, surrounded, excepting at one point, by deep valleys, while far above its highest elevation, to the north and to the south, to the east and to the west, rises the circle of mountains, hemming it in and guarding it on every side. In looking down upon Jerusalem thus peculiarly situated, I was often reminded of a precious jewel deeply set in gold to protect it against all injury and loss, and of the more wonderful setting of the human eye. Of the mountains that are round about Jerusalem, there is only one from which to view the city to advantage, the one most fraught with sacred memories. The second day after our arrival we crossed the brook Kedron and ascended the Mount of Olives, the nearest point of earth to heaven, if we may make such a comparison, because from this the Son of God ascended to the skies, leading the way for those who are to rise and live with him.

Before passing out of the walls we turned aside to visit the Mosque of Omar, on the site of the Temple of Solomon. The mosque itself, and the extensive grounds in the midst of which it stands, in years past were guarded with jealous care by the Mohammedans, and it was with great difficulty that Christians could gain admittance; but of late there has been little hinderance or objection. Arrangements having been made beforehand, we presented ourselves at the outer gate, and, provided with slippers for the more sacred parts of the inclosure, were conducted by a Mohammedan guide through the whole area, into the mosque and even beneath it, to the Cave of Rock, which we were allowed to examine thoroughly. This is one of the ancient places about which there can be no reasonable doubt. Here, within this square, once rose that magnificent building, the grandest and most glorious on which the sun ever shone; here it was that Jehovah came down and dwelt among men in the visible glory of the Shekinah, long before the Son of God dwelt on earth in the likeness of mortal man. Here the gorgeous Temple service was instituted and celebrated for centuries, until sacrifices and ceremonies were abolished by the offering up of the one great sacrifice, the Lamb of God. It was refreshing to meditate in the deep stillness of this sacred spot, where no idling intruders are permitted to enter, as in so many places, to destroy the sacredness of the scene.

Leaving the Mosque of Omar and the courts of the ancient temple, after visiting "the gate that is called Beautiful," we passed out of the city walls by St. Stephen's Gate, so named because the martyr Stephen was stoned just outside the gate. Descending the steep side of the mountain, we came to the bed of the Kedron, at the bottom of the Valley of Jehoshaphat. It was simply the *bed* for a stream, not a drop of water moistening its stones. In the rainy season a torrent sweeps through its entire length. Just as we commence the ascent of the Mount of Olives, we come upon what is called the Garden of Gethsemane, a square plot of ground, perhaps half an acre, surrounded by a high stone wall, and containing a few aged olive-trees, with plants and shrubs. The wall is confessedly modern, nor is there any conclusive evidence that the spot was the scene of the Saviour's agony and of his betrayal, while to my mind

THE BEAUTIFUL GATE.

the probabilities are all against it. There is nothing that marks it as a place for retirement. It was doubtless, then as now, on the frequented road from the city to the Mount of Olives, and a public place. The vague tradition connected with the spot is not enough to mark it as that to which Jesus retired for secret prayer, and in which he endured the mysterious agony when one of the heavenly host appeared to strengthen him, as his disciples, overcome with fatigue and sleep, left him to suffer alone. The inclosure belongs to the Latins, or Roman Catholics; but the Greeks, not to be outdone, have a garden near by which they assert is the real Gethsemane, thus bringing their rival claims into a sort of contempt.

And now we climb the Mount of Olives, in all probability by the very path so often trod by holy feet—the feet which last pressed the earth upon the summit of this mount.

JERUSALEM AND GETHSEMANE.

There is no other of all the sacred places in or near Jerusalem that may be visited with more confidence in its being the scene of events associated with the Saviour's life. I care not to know whether this precise rood of earth on which I am standing was the one on which Jesus stood when he spake the words of the Sermon on the Mount, or whether from this very spot he beheld the city and wept over it, saying, "If thou hadst known, even thou, at least in this thy day, the things which belong to thy peace," or whether on this precise spot he was talking with his disciples when "he was taken up and a cloud received him out of their sight." It is enough to know that the mountain on which I am standing was the scene of these great events, and that I am brought so closely into communication with the past, with the days of his flesh, and so near to that heavenly world in which I hope to see that form that was carried up in a cloud and hid from mortal sight. Indeed, it is a decided relief to my feelings, I might say an aid to my faith, it certainly with me is conducive to sacred recollections and pious emotion, that there is no one near to say that precisely here these words of Christ were spoken, or that this identical spot was last touched by his sacred feet. I can commune with the past far better without than with such meretricious helps. I found it very pleasant again and again to visit this holy mount, to linger around it, and from its summit to look down upon the Holy City, and backward into the past, and upward into the skies, as if through the opening made by the form of the ascending Redeemer.

The summit of Olivet being 300 feet above the Temple area, one looks directly down upon the city which is spread out before him like a map. Every building and every locality can be distinguished. Looking eastward, the Valley of the Jordan and the Dead Sea, although nearly twenty miles distant, and about 4000 feet lower, are seen so distinctly that one can hardly believe they are so far off. The surface of the Dead Sea is the lowest point on the face of the globe, being 1312 feet below the Mediterranean and the ocean, and to look into it from the Mount of Olives is like looking down into the depths of the earth itself.

I was greatly interested in tracing out the path that King David took when he fled from the treachery of Absalom. "And David went up by the ascent of Mount Olivet, and wept as he went up, and had his head covered, and he went barefoot; and all the people that was with him covered every man his head, and they went up, weeping as they went up." Nothing in the record of the reverses which kings have suffered could be more touching. The scene was constantly recurring to my mind as I went up the mountain from time to time, and I almost expected to meet Shimei as I passed over its summit. The Mohammedans were there with their curses, if he was not.

One day, as we came from the Mount of Olives, we followed the valley of the brook Kedron, past the tomb of Absalom, to the Pool of Siloam, a rapid fall of between 300 and 400 feet within a mile and a half; thence up the Valley of Hinnom, past the Jaffa Gate to the Damascus Gate, where we entered as on our first approach to the city. The same afternoon we rode out to Bethlehem, six miles due south from Jerusalem. After passing through the deep Valley of Hinnom, the road over the plain is the finest in the vicinity of the Holy City. We were in sight of several ancient villages mentioned in Scripture, that were lying off upon the neighboring hills. The Convent of Mar Elias, said to be erected on the spot where the prophet was ministered to by angels, and the tomb of Rachel, one of the few well-authenticated places in the Holy Land, were directly upon the road-side. And then we came to that spot, the grand illumination of the book of time, on which the Son of God appeared in the likeness of man. I looked out upon the hill-sides for the shepherds, and listened for the voice, "Behold, I bring you good tidings of great joy, which shall be to all people; for unto you is born this day, in the city of David, a Saviour, which is Christ the Lord," and the chorus of the heavenly host, "Glory to God in the highest, and on earth peace, good will toward men."

We entered the town of Bethlehem, where once the Lord of Glory entered our world in the lowly form of a little babe. We rode through the streets to the Church of the Nativity, and instead of meeting with the shepherds who said, "Let us now go even unto Bethlehem, and see this thing which is come to pass," or the wise men who came to pour out their treasures at the feet of the infant Jesus, we were surrounded by a swarm of imperious mendicants and traffickers in relics, who seemed determined to shut out all sacred thoughts of the place. The star that once "stood over where the young child was" had long since set, though shining brightly on so many other lands. May it soon arise again in all its glory on Bethlehem and all Judea!

Among the saddest of all the scenes connected with my pilgrimage to the Holy Land was a visit to Bethany, the one spot with which are associated many of the tenderest, sweetest memories of the life of our Lord, and more of our knowledge of his real humanity, his actual sympathy and friendship, than with all other places. Who has not, in reading the words, "Now Jesus loved Martha and her sister, and Lazarus," and of his resorting to Bethany to enjoy their society; and of the message the sisters sent him when Lazarus was sick, and his going to weep with them when Lazarus was dead; who, in reading all this in the Gospels, has not pictured to himself a rural village where he himself would love to stand, if not to dwell? But how changed is the present reality from the scene of his imaginings!

It is about two miles from Jerusalem. We left the city by St. Stephen's Gate, descending into the Valley of Jehoshaphat, passed Gethsemane, and took the path around the south side of the Mount of Olives, the very road by which, without doubt, the Saviour made his triumphal entry into Jerusalem, when "a very great multitude spread their garments in the way; others cut down branches from the trees and strewed them in the way; and the multitudes that went before and that followed cried, saying, Hosanna to the Son of David; blessed is he that cometh in the name of the Lord; hosanna in the highest." The scene, as it lay before us, was one of mere desolation. Utter sterility, without verdure or foliage save an occasional olive-tree, marked the whole way to Bethany. The path and the fields were heaps of stone, and the town of Mary and Martha, a miserable cluster of cheerless huts, with a more miserable crowd of children and grown people demanding charity, had not the first attractive feature. We looked into the reputed grave of Lazarus, and turned away in sadness at the desolation every where presented. And this is but a type of a great part of Palestine at the present day.

In these rapid sketches of travel over so large a part of the surface of the globe, it will be impossible to give even a continuous account of all our wanderings. I must omit the record of our excursion to the Valley of the Jordan and the Dead Sea, where we were attacked by the Bedouins in the dead of night, as we were encamped on the plains of Jericho. We escaped without injury or loss, but a party of our friends, who went down to Jericho soon after, fell among thieves, who stripped them of their raiment, robbed them of all they had, and threatened their lives.

The last day that we spent in Jerusalem was the day of rest. In the morning I attended the English service on Mount Zion, and heard an excellent sermon from the venerable Bishop Gobat. In the afternoon we had religious services of a social character at our hotel, attended by about twenty-five, chiefly Americans. Our landlord kindly prepared the dining-room for the services, and in this "large upper room, made ready," we joined in prayer and praise, and talked of the scenes which transpired in that Holy City nearly 2000 years ago — scenes in which the world has the same deep interest to-day as when they were transpiring on these holy mountains; which will never lose their interest while the world shall stand, and which will only have gathered fresh interest when the world shall pass away.

## XXX.

### TO DAMASCUS AND CONSTANTINOPLE.

The morning came on which we were to take our departure, and I can not say that I regretted to look for the last time upon the city, filled though it is with holy memories. I never had an intense desire to enter the earthly Canaan, although it had long been one of the unsettled purposes of my life to do so. Knowing its forlorn, desolate state, so different from what it must have been when Abraham dwelt at Mamre, or when David and Solomon reigned at Jerusalem, or when a greater than patriarchs and kings sojourned in the land; knowing how completely the traces of their footsteps had been obliterated, and the sacred scenes connected with their lives changed and desecrated, I could scarcely tell whether I desired most to gratify a common wish, or to cherish in my heart memories of the land derived from reading the Word of God. But, journeying homeward from more eastern climes, I could not pass by the land with which is linked all the most sacred history of the past, and with which are associated all the holiest anticipations of the future. I entered it; I traveled and tarried in it, and I turned away from it with a feeling of sadness, but with no regret.

I presume that every traveler experiences a measure of disappointment on entering Palestine, especially in visiting Jerusalem. He comes with all the sacred emotions that were excited in childhood, strengthened and deepened with his growth, now raised to their utmost by the very sight of the land. He does not expect to find it, as in days long ago, flowing with milk and honey, or to see Jerusalem as it was before the glory had departed; but few are prepared to see it so waste and desolate. While in Jerusalem, I found myself continually repeating the words of the lamenting prophet: "Is this the city that men call the perfection of beauty, the joy of the whole earth?" The frown of God is every where resting on the land; it may be read not only in the desolation of the Temple and of the Holy City, but in the dust of the earth and the stones of the field. The land lieth waste and mourneth, and no Christian traveler can fail to weep over it. It seems as if God had been sweeping it with the besom of destruction, obliterating the traces and attractions of its sacred scenes for the very purpose of preventing the idolatrous reverence for holy places which is even now carried to such an extent, and to impress upon the world the words of Jesus to the woman of Samaria: "Woman, believe me, the hour cometh when ye shall neither in this mountain, nor yet at Jerusalem, worship the Father. God is a Spirit, and they that worship him must worship him in spirit and in truth."

Early on Monday morning, our horses saddled and our baggage packed, we waited for the guard. From day to day, after our return from the Valley of the Jordan, we had accounts of fresh robberies and attacks upon travelers on the road to Jaffa. One poor Jew had been robbed and nearly murdered, and others had suffered in like manner. Through the American consul, Mr. Hay, I had made an application to the governor at Jerusalem for a guard, unless he would be responsible for our safe passage. He sent us word that we must have a military escort, which he proposed to send on his own account. After every thing was in readiness for the journey, we waited an hour, and began to grow impatient, when at length a *cavass* made his appearance with a message from the governor that we could go without the guard, and he would be responsible for any loss or damage that we might sustain. We could do nothing more, and accordingly we passed out the Damascus Gate, ascended the height, turned to take a last look of the city and of the mountains that are round about Jerusalem, and began the descent toward the Mediterranean. As the sun was setting we re-entered Ramleh, where we spent another night within sound of the muezzin's voice. With the break of day we rose to cross again the plains of Sharon, and early in the morning rode into Jaffa. The French steamer Tage was at anchor off the town; the sea was calm, relieving us of the apprehension that we might be compelled to lie over for many days (as were a party who came down the week before), and without any delay, and under the most pleasing promise of a smooth passage, we were taken on board.

About midnight we passed Mount Carmel, the scene of that sublime trial between the Prophet Elijah and the prophets of Baal, and early on the following morning were off Beyrout, the most homelike and the most beautiful city on the eastern shores of the Mediterranean. Indeed, it was a home to one who had been at my side in all my journeyings, for here, at the foot of old Lebanon,

"On that classical sea whose azure vies
With the green of its shores and the blue of its skies,"

she first looked out upon this little world which we had been surrounding, and now, for the first time since early childhood, she was returning to gaze once more upon these sublime mountains, and to look out from their heights upon this cerulean sea. I had no such memories to revive, but, from my first view of Beyrout, I wrote it down as just the place one might choose to be born in, if he should happen to have any choice in the matter. During the many days that we spent at this place, I was more and more charmed with its beauty, and never grew weary of looking out upon the blue sea and up the grand heights of Lebanon, or of watching the constantly shifting lights and shades. And when, as once, the brow of Lebanon grew dark and then angry with gathering clouds, and peals of thunder came rolling down its sides and echoing through its chasms, the scene became sublime.

No city in the East has been more changed within the

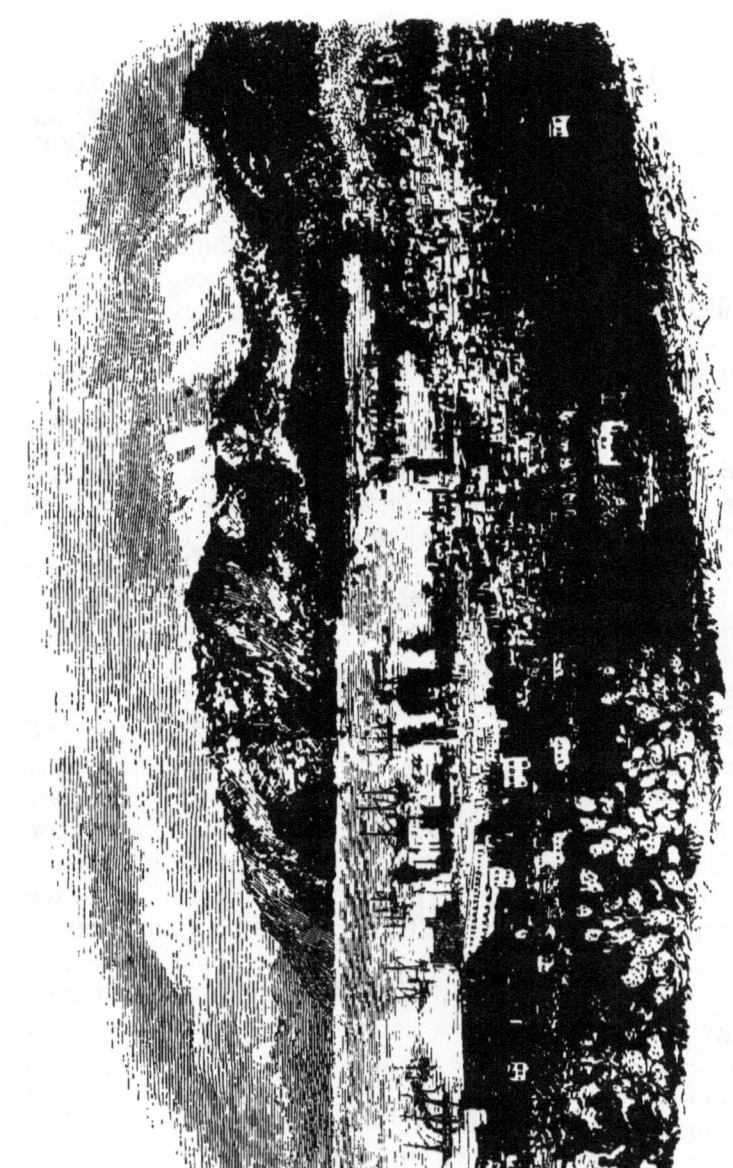

BEYROUT.

last half century than Beyrout. Fifty years ago it was a small town—a collection of mud and stone houses, surrounded by a wall, but having nothing imposing or attractive in its appearance. It is now a large, well-built city, a place of great and growing importance, having long ago burst through its mural inclosure. It has become also a moral centre for a large part of the East—the seat of extensive missionary operations, which extend over the mountains of Lebanon and far into the interior. When the first missionaries from America, Messrs. Goodell and Bird, with their wives, landed in 1823, they became first objects of curiosity, then of bitter hostility, and for a long time their lives were in danger. On the breaking out of the Greek Revolution they were obliged to leave the country for want of protection, but they were succeeded in after years by one of the noblest bands of Christian laborers that has occupied any part of the great field of the world, among whom were Dr. Eli Smith, the companion of Dr. Robinson in his biographical researches in the Holy Land; Dr. Thomson, author of "The Land and the Book;" Dr. Van Dyck, the eminent Arabic scholar; Dr. Calhoun, now of Abeih; Dr. Bliss, President of the Arabic College, and others—a galaxy of shining names.

Among the tribes inhabiting the mountains around Beyrout, the most peculiar and interesting are the Druses. They are a fine, noble-looking race, generally intelligent, and able to read and write. Their sacred rites are performed in strict seclusion, as secretly as the rites of Freemasonry. Among their articles of belief is the transmigration of souls, not into bodies of the lower animals, as some Oriental nations believe, but into those of other human beings. They hold that the number of the race, or at least of human souls, does not increase with the addition of new members to the human family; that when a man dies, his soul goes into the body of some infant who is born at the same time, and that the souls of all good Druses enter bodies born in China. On this belief is founded a tradition that there is in China an immense army of Druses, 25,000,000 strong, who are coming over to Syria, not only to liberate them from the Turkish yoke, but to put them in possession of this whole country, if not of the whole earth. In a visit which I made to one of the mountain villages, the Druses of the place learned that I had recently come from China, and I was waited on by one and another, among them a sheikh, who came to make a host of inquiries in regard to what I had seen of the country, which is to them, as it was not to me, a paradise. But the point to which I found they were desirous to come, and which they finally brought out, was whether I had seen any of this grand army of liberation. I assured them that, although I had been in different parts of the empire, I had not seen or heard of a single Druse in all China, and that I was quite sure I should have heard something about it if such an army existed there. My words sadly disappointed them, but it was evident they did not carry conviction to their minds. They fell back upon the firm belief that the army was yet to come from that distant country.

After the fearful massacre of 1860, in which many of the villages of Mount Lebanon were desolated, the French government sent into Syria an army of occupation, or protection to the Christians, which was withdrawn in a few years, but the army left behind it one monument for which thousands of travelers have blessed its memory. This is the splendid road across the mountains to Damascus. Such a road was a novelty in the East; the natives regarded it as a desecration of sacred soil, and an outrage upon the rights of donkeys and muleteers; but it has been a blessing to wayfarers, and has greatly facilitated traffic, not to say commerce, between these two cities.

The grandeur of the mountains of Lebanon exceeded all my anticipations. Not even after watching them from the sea, and then, day after day, from the city of Beyrout, was I prepared for such sublimity. They attain, indeed, no mean height, being 10,000 feet above the level of the Mediterranean; and, as if scorning to turn aside for any obstacle, this road mounts some of the loftiest ridges, and for miles runs along the brow of chasms two or three thousand feet deep. It was not at all in accordance with the ancient ideas of Oriental travel to be making the passage of these lofty mountains in a well-ordered French diligence; but this mode had been chosen out of regard to the more delicate members of our party, and those of us who were endowed with more strength were nothing loth to exchange the saddle for a comfortable seat in an Occidental carriage. Nor did we enjoy the magnificent scenery any less for the change.

We were to start for Damascus at four o'clock in the morning, nearly two hours before daylight. As the diligence would not come to our hotel, Mohammed like we concluded to go to the diligence. On retiring, we had given special and repeated charge to landlord and porter to call us by two o'clock, that we might have every thing in readiness for our night walk of nearly a mile to the office; but I had learned that the proverb has double force in the East: "If you wish a thing done, do it yourself," and accordingly I attended to my own waking. If I had not risen and called myself, we should have spent the day in Beyrout instead of crossing Mount Lebanon. Not very cheerful was that walk through the streets of Beyrout under a cloudy, moonless sky, with a single lantern dimly burning, nor was the first hour or two of our journey much more inspiriting. In the darkness our thoughts were all the while turning to the easy couches we had left more than to the scenery around us, which we could not see, or the views of Damascus, its rivers and its plains, which were yet before us. But when the morning fairly dawned, as we were ascending those lofty heights from which Hiram had cut the cedars to build and adorn the Temple of Solomon, and when, in the frequent windings of the road, as we made our zigzag way upward, we looked back upon the plain and the city of Beyrout far down below, and then out upon the sea, the thermometer of our hearts rose as many degrees as did the thermometer of Fahrenheit. And all day long we were catching new glimpses of the sublime heights and sublime depths, until, as we were drawing near to Damascus, the hoary head of Mount Hermon appeared in the distance.

The valley of Cœlo-Syria is a beautiful episode in the journey. The mountains have little verdure or foliage. Occasionally a garden spot or a vineyard appeared, but the mountains are usually masses of rock, on which no vegetation can take root. After traversing those wild ranges for hours, all of a sudden an emerald valley was seen several thousand feet below, the mountains rising again on the opposite side. The descent was long, and we went down into the valley only to climb the anti-Lebanon range which lies beyond. About four o'clock, in the afternoon we commenced the descent. In the course of an hour we were in a deep gorge, and suddenly came upon a swift-flowing stream, which we traversed for many miles, its banks shaded with groves and diversified with gardens, the River Abana, of the story of Naaman and the Syrian maid. Following the course of the stream, we were presently at the entrance to the city, and soon found quarters at the excellent hotel of Dimitri Cara.

It was Saturday night when we reached Damascus. In the morning we went out into "the street *called* Straight" (some traveler has remarked very truly that it could have been called so only out of courtesy), and after a long walk we found, at the other extremity of the city, the American Mission, and heard an excellent sermon in Arabic from the Rev. Mr. Crawford. I call it excellent; I am sure, from my subsequent acquaintance with him, it was so, and his manner was at once so easy, earnest, and eloquent, that I heartily enjoyed his discourse without understanding a word of it. We had a sermon from a stranger, in English, at 11 o'clock; and in the afternoon went out to visit the cemetery of the martyrs of 1860—the Christian population who, in the fearful massacre set on foot by the Mohammedans and shared by the Druses, were slain in this city to the number of 2500 men, besides women and children. Far greater would have been the slaughter of the Christians had not the hero of Algiers, Abd el Kader, espoused the cause of the persecuted. More by his valor than his eloquence he saved the lives of at least 15,000 whom the Mohammedans had sworn to put to the sword. We regretted much that this noble but unfortunate chieftain was not in Damascus during our stay. We desired to pay our respects to the hero who had not only won the admiration of the world by his valor in the wars of Algiers, and its sympathy by the treacherous treatment he received from his French conquerors, but who, though a Mohammedan, had stood forth as the defender of the Christians when those of his own faith were fanatically putting them to the sword. We sent him our cards, but he was on the Plains.

Damascus is the oldest city now in existence. It is mentioned in the time of Abraham, the steward of whose house was "this Eliezer of Damascus," and its interesting record reaches down all along the ages to the present time. The city covers a wide extent, and with its suburbs, which are well watered and green, is an oasis in the desert in which it lies. It is a lovely picture as seen from the mountains, the water-courses and the irrigated portion of the plain being thickly studded with trees, and shading off into green fields of grain that at length are lost in the arid desert. We explored its quaint old streets, which have more of magnificence than one could imagine from the distant view. The bazars are busy marts of trade, well supplied with the productions and fabrics of the East. The khans, the warehouses of the merchants, are many of them solid and magnificent stone structures, surrounding open courts, in which the ships of the desert—camels—were discharging and receiving their freights of silk and other goods. The khan of Esaad Pasha was truly gorgeous in its architecture. After going through the bazars and khans, we climbed the mountain overlooking the great plain to see the city from above, and from the lonely kiosk upon its summit had the view which arrested the Prophet Mohammed when he exclaimed, "Man can have only one paradise; I shall not enter this below lest I should have none above," and turned back without ever entering Damascus. Such is the legend.

DAMASCUS.

Fresh snow had fallen upon the brow of Hermon the morning that we left Damascus on our way back to Beyrout, and when the sun rose it shone first with golden and then with silver light, reflecting the glory of the East which was poured upon it. There it stands as it has stood for thousands of years, one of the great landmarks on which the patriarchs and prophets looked long before it was trod by Him who was greater than them all. Mount Hermon, in the opinion of many Biblical scholars, was the scene of the Transfiguration. Even now it shines with an ineffable brightness, as if still in the light of that glorious One whose raiment, when on the mount, "became shining exceeding white as snow, so as no fuller on earth can white them."

At Sturza, in the vale of Cœlo-Syria, a portion of our party struck off to the north to the ruins of Baalbec, while we returned to Beyrout, reaching the outlook upon the Mediterranean early in the afternoon of a charming day, and enjoying in a wonderfully clear atmosphere, during the long zigzag descent, one of the most glorious sights of mountain, and plain, and sea that can be found on any of the heights of this world. In descending the mountain I heard an uproar and a din that gathered strength as we proceeded, and presently we were in the midst of one of those clouds of locusts that in all ages have infested Syria. A public order had been issued requiring the inhabitants to turn out and drive the locusts into the sea. The people had formed an extensive line, and with horns, and drums, and pans, and any thing that would make a hideous noise, were pursuing the invaders, which were fleeing before them. The music reminded me of a scene I had witnessed in Bombay on the occasion of an eclipse of the moon, when the Hindoos swarmed in the streets armed with the same weapons, hoping by their insufferable jargon to drive away the monster that was swallowing the queen of night. They were both successful. The Hindoo monster was compelled to disgorge—the moon came out as bright as before; and on the mountains of Lebanon the locusts that had been destroying all the greenness of the earth, unable to endure the music, moved on in a vast cloud toward the Mediterranean. Whether they reached the sea and were drowned I do not know.

Once more we were afloat. We had again said the farewell, which we have so often found it hard to say; the anchor was lifted, and we were steaming onward through the waves; the city at the foot of Lebanon grew dim in the distance—the city of which the author of the "Crescent and the Cross," in his unrivaled sketches of Eastern travel, wrote: "Beautiful Beyrout! I yield to thee the palm over all the cities of the earth;" the mountains grew darker and dimmer in the twilight, and night at length settled down over the sea.

In the morning we touched at the island of Cyprus, the scene of a strange mixture of myths and traditions, and history, reaching down from the days of fable, when Venus rose from the foam of the sea in all her beauty, to the days of Richard Cœur de Lion, when the island passed into the hands of the Templars, and until it was at last captured by the Turks. The third day we anchored off the harbor of Rhodes, where once stood the famed Colossus, one of the seven wonders of the world. The same evening we sailed along the shores of "the isle that is called Patmos," to which the beloved disciple of Jesus, the Apostle John, was banished in the persecution under Domitian, the scene of the apocalyptic vision. On the fourth day, as the sun was lifting its face above the hills that overhang

PATMOS.

the city of Smyrna, we entered the deep harbor and anchored off the town. The country around was greener and fresher than any we had seen since leaving the shores of Japan, always excepting the tropical shores near the equator. The city was smiling in the morning light as if conscious of its surroundings, and of its own beauty as seen from the sea. It had other attractions for one of our number, and a few hours were most agreeably spent in the society of friends, and in an excursion to the hill on which stand the ruins of the ancient castle. Here we received the usual welcome from a score of Mohammedan boys, a general stoning, which greeting was returned until they dispersed over the hill.

Smyrna is memorable as one of the many cities in which Homer was born, and still more sacred in the eyes of the Christian as the scene of the martyrdom of Polycarp, to whom, as "the Angel of the Church in Smyrna," according to Archbishop Usher, one of the seven epistles of the Apocalypse was addressed. He had been bishop of this church more than eighty years, when, in one of the Roman persecutions, he was summoned to judgment. As he was led out to the place of execution, the proconsul, ashamed to put to death so venerable a man, besought him to blaspheme Christ and save his life. It was then that he uttered those heroic words: "Eighty-six years have I served him; during all this time he never did me any injury; how then can I blaspheme my King and Saviour?"

Leaving Smyrna toward evening, we stopped at Mytilene, touched the next day at Tenedos, Dardanelles, and Gallipoli, and on the following morning at sunrise were in sight of the domes and minarets of Stamboul.

## XXXI.

### STAMBOUL TO NAPLES.

Almost the only place in all the world where the smile of heaven through pleasant skies forsook us was at Constantinople. Circumstances had shortened my stay in Palestine and Syria so that I reached this stage of the journey a month earlier than I had arranged on leaving home, and a month too soon to enjoy the beauties of Stamboul and the Golden Horn of the Bosphorus. We sailed up the Sea of Marmora and rounded Seraglio Point in the midst of a drizzling rain, which changed to snow soon after we landed; the snow continued to fall, or rather to drive impetuously for two whole days; and for nearly three weeks it was almost incessant rain. Not for a day, no, not for an hour in all this time did the sun come out and shine upon us as it had shone for nearly a year. Those were dismal days in which to see the glories of the Orient, although very conducive to enjoyment in the many circles of friends which we found in Stamboul and scattered along the Bosphorus. One can appreciate friends five or six thousand miles away from home, when the heavens are weeping over him, and there were many associations that made the society at this place peculiarly agreeable to some of us.

Of all the cities that I have visited, Constantinople proper is the last to be chosen for a season of rain and mud; but, despite all difficulties, we made the tour of the mosques, palaces, bazars, and other places of renown, and, after waiting in vain for the skies to clear, we saw the Bosphorus and the Golden Horn under a cloud. If I do not celebrate the beauties of this part of the Orient, it must be because I saw them only in deep shadows, and other pens will more than supply all that may be lacking in these sketches. The next time that we go to Constantinople it shall be on the first of May.

The political condition of this part of the world remains unchanged, while progress is the order of the day East and West. Turkey is still Turkey. Its government is the most effete, inefficient, irresponsible, and at the same time despotic, with which civilized nations have any thing to do, and Constantinople, in one way or another, is a centre of interest to nearly all the nations of the West. In the provinces the government is even worse than at the capital. In the vocabulary of Turkish officials *Justice* has no name, excepting as it is represented by the Turkish synonyms of *bribery* or *influence*. What is to be the future of Turkey is still one of the problems over which philanthropists and diplomatists, and especially the powers of Europe, are exercised. Almost any change would be for the better; it could scarcely be for the worse. A radical change of some kind is needed to bring Turkey into sympathy with the rest of the world, but the present government is past reform.

There are some signs of a waking up among the different nationalities which compose the population of the capital. The press, and steam, and the telegraph are doing their work. I noticed, in passing up and down the Bosphorus from day to day, that nearly every man on the steamer had his morning or evening paper. There are now published at Constantinople four daily papers in Turkish, one of which has a weekly illustrated edition for ladies, printed on embossed paper, and another for children. There are three dailies in Greek and three in Armenian. Besides, there are numerous weekly papers in Turkish, Armenian, Bulgarian, Arabic, etc.; the most of which are owned and conducted by natives.

The revival of evangelical religion among the Armenian population has been a part of the history of the times, and one of the most remarkable movements in connection with missionary labor in any part of the East. Forty years ago the Rev. William Goodell and his wife landed at Constantinople, the first Christian missionaries to this place from America. Others joined them and took up the work, men and women whose names will not be forgotten so long as the sun and moon endure — Schauffler, Riggs, Hamlin, Dwight, Bliss, with many younger. Some of the early laborers I found toiling on in the field, but others have gone to their reward, having finished their labors. The workmen die, but the work goes on here as elsewhere. Twenty-five years ago there were only about a hundred Armenians who had embraced the evangelical faith. There are now in Turkey seventy churches, with 3200 members, and the movement has extended all over the empire. Two thirds of the churches which are the fruit of missionary labor have native pastors, and nearly half of these are self-supporting. In 1847 there were only about 500 recognized as Protestants; there are now from fifteen to twenty thousand.

Scarcely any other city has such a cosmopolitan population. This is indicated by the number of languages in which the Holy Scriptures are circulated. I learned from the Rev. Mr. Bliss, the Secretary of the American Bible Society for Turkey, that there had been circulated within the last twelve years 333,415 copies of the Scriptures, including the whole Bible in Arabic, Armenian, Armeno-Turkish, Osmanlee-Turkish, Greco-Turkish, Hebrew, Wallachian, Hungarian, Servian, Judæo-Spanish, English, French, German, Italian, Latin, Swedish, Portuguese, and Dutch, with the New Testament in Russian, Bulgarian, Albanian, Syriac, Slavic, Ancient Greek, and Ancient Armenian, with the Gospels in Koordish — thirty languages in all. These are not all the languages spoken at this cosmopolitan city.

While I was at the hotel at Pera an American gentleman arrived who had been in Constantinople before. In speaking of his former visit, he said to me very enthusiastically, "There is one thing in this city that you must not fail to see. Of course you have been to the Mosque of St. Sophia, and up and down the Bosphorus and the Golden

Horn, and have seen the Sultan and all that, but there is one thing that you must not fail to see." Before he concluded his impressive injunction I had become rather impatient to know what it was, when he added, "It is Dr. Hamlin." He then gave me an account of the circumstances in which he made the acquaintance of this remarkable man. He came there a stranger, fell sick, and, having heard the name of Dr. Hamlin, sent for him, and was speedily cured. Dr. Hamlin happens to be a Doctor of Divinity, but there is scarcely any science or art in which he is not worthy of the highest degree. I assured my friend that I had long enjoyed his acquaintance.

Robert College, so liberally endowed by Christopher R. Robert, Esq., of New York, and now established on its beautiful site upon the Bosphorus, owes its existence in a great measure to Dr. Hamlin, the president, by whose perseverance it secured a local habitation. Year after year the Turkish government, in its usual dilatory way, withheld its sanction for the location and erection of the building. Dr. Hamlin neglected no opportunity to press his application. Once, after a longer interval than usual, he applied through some intercessor, when Ali Pasha, the late Grand Vizier, gave vent to his desires in the impatient inquiry, "Will that Dr. Hamlin never die?" And so, to get rid of him, seeing he would not die, he gave him permission to build.

After once deferring our departure another week in hope of brighter skies, we at length went on board the steamer bound for Athens in the midst of a storm of snow, and hail, and rain, one of the most forbidding days of our sojourn. We had scarcely reached the Sea of Marmora before the sun burst forth from the clouds to cheer us on our voyage, and to tantalize us with the remembrance of all the days of gloom in which his face had been hid. But we had the satisfaction to learn that we had escaped a perilous voyage on the steamer by which I had engaged passage the week previous. She was overtaken by a storm on the Sea of Marmora, and lay all night in the lee of an island waiting for the morning, all on board having no little apprehension in regard to the result.

We did not trust ourselves to the Turkish or Greek steamers, which are to be avoided by all who seek either comfort or safety in sailing on the Mediterranean. Those belonging to the Sultan's navy are splendid specimens of naval architecture, and, as they ride at anchor in line on the Bosphorus, make a formidable appearance, but I heard many stories not at all to the credit of the men who commanded them. A Turkish naval officer, once sent with his ship to Malta, was gone about three weeks, at the expiration of which time he turned up at Constantinople, and reported that he had searched diligently, and there was no such place in the Mediterranean Sea. Another was sent to Jaffa, and, after cruising up and down the Syrian coast, returned with the report that he could not find it. It is to be hoped that those who have command of the passenger steamers have a better knowledge of the sea, but I never felt disposed to test their nautical skill. On the Mediterranean I invariably took either the French or the Austrian steamers, between which there was little to choose; they are both good, well officered, and well managed.

We left Constantinople at four o'clock in the afternoon, and had fine weather through the Sea of Marmora and the Archipelago to the shores of Greece. The second night out we retired not expecting to be on shore before morning, but about half past one we were roused with the cry that the lights of the Piræus were in sight, and that we must be prepared to land within a few minutes.

Far worse than starting off by night in a stage-coach is being roused from sleep to be set ashore in a small boat, on some strange coast, in a dark night. But the same familiar stars on which we had looked at home from early childhood, and which were as familiar as the faces of sisters and brothers, were looking down and smiling upon us, and silently whispering to our hearts that above them was an eye that never sleeps. We dropped anchor about a mile from the landing. As we were rowed ashore in the quiet starlight I heard the sound of approaching oars, and, knowing that friends who were some days in advance of us would probably take the steamer that we were leaving, I called a name, and heard over the waters an answering voice—"All's well!"—and so we passed; the boatmen not even resting on their oars, we were able only to exchange this transient salutation in the darkness. We found a carriage in waiting on the shore, and within an hour were at the hotel in Athens, about six miles distant, and had a pleasant sleep before the morning appeared.

Our steps were first directed to the Acropolis, the centre of Athens and of all Greece. We climbed the heights crowned with the ruins of the most perfect structure of antiquity, and looked out upon the theatre of so many grand events in the history of the classic age; upon the ruins of temples, and arches, and amphitheatres, and down upon Mars Hill, where Paul stood before an assembly of Athenian philosophers and preached Jesus and the resurrection; and upon the Pnyx, where Demosthenes enchained with his eloquence the crowds who gathered round the rostrum; and out over the grand panorama of Lower Greece to the same old mountains on which the eyes of sages and orators, poets, and sculptors, and warriors had looked centuries ago, when Greece was in her glory. The Acropolis,

FRIEZE OF THE PARTHENON.

with its commanding height, its magnificent temples, its peerless sculpture, and its crowning feature, the colossal statue of Minerva, of ivory and gold, a landmark to the mariner at sea as well as to the dweller on the Plains, might well be called "the eye of all Greece."

We were strongly urged to make an excursion to the Plains of Marathon, but I declined for prudential reasons, which soon after had melancholy force. I had escaped the Bedouins in the valley of the Jordan, while others were compelled to pay tribute, and not without risk to their lives. I was well aware, and so was every traveler at the time, that the Greek brigands were no more scrupulous in regard to the rights of property, and that they were on the alert for prey. They have a very unhappy way of detaining for ransom those who happen to fall into their hands, and occasionally sending back an ear or a finger if the ransom is delayed. I assured my urgent friends that I was not willing to run one risk in fifty of paying a heavy ransom, or of losing my ears for the satisfaction of seeing a little more of the classic soil of Greece, and I was somewhat laughed at for my prudence.

At the same hotel where we were staying was a party who determined to make the excursion. Their fate soon after shocked the whole civilized world. They left in the morning for Marathon in high spirits, but before night they were all in the hands of the brigands. The ladies of the party were released and sent back to Athens. Lord Moncaster was subsequently sent to negotiate the ransom of his companions, and escaped. The rest were murdered and horribly mutilated.

Returning to the Piræus by carriage in preference to the rail, we crossed in the night to the island of Syra, and took the Austrian steamer for Corfu. The next day we rounded Cape Matapan, usually a stormy point with a turbulent sea, but on this occasion the elements were enjoying a holiday, the winds were off duty, and the waves asleep. In the afternoon we were off the Bay of Navarino, where the decisive battle was fought in 1827 between the Turkish and Egyptian navies on the one side, and the allied British, French, and Russian fleets on the other. It was the destruction of the Turkish power on the sea and the liberation of Greece. In the course of the day we passed Cephalonia, the Samos of Homer, and, later in the day, Zante, "the Flower of the Levant," of which some writer extravagantly says, "Zante is especially delightful in spring, when the fragrance of the flowering vineyards, orange-trees and gardens, floats for miles over the surrounding sea."

The next morning we were entering the Gulf of Corfu, and one of the most beautiful scenes that we had looked upon in all our travels, reminding us of the Inland Sea of Japan, was before us. The day was perfectly serene. The sun rose in great splendor, and poured upon land and sea a flood of gorgeous light. Not a ripple, not even a dimple, was on the face of the water to break the reflection of the shores. As we rounded the point of the citadel, a rocky height of great strength and greater beauty, overgrown with vines of the richest green, the picturesqueness of the scene was such as the pen will not describe. The day we spent in driving about the charming island was one of the days to be recalled when we are looking into the memories of the past for some lovely nook in which to find rest from the weariness of toil and care.

We could have tarried much longer with great delight, but, finding a steamer that was to sail in the evening, and uncertain when we should be able to leave again, we went on board, and the next morning were landed at Brindisi, a place that has acquired new importance. It is the Brundusium of the ancient Romans, and was once their chief naval station. It was also the southeastern terminus of the ancient Appian Way, and, in the completion of one of those remarkable cycles which not unfrequently occur in the history of nations and countries, has become the terminus of the great railway from London and Paris to the East. The most direct route to Egypt and India, and the most speedy, is now through the Mont Cenis Tunnel to Brindisi, whence the steamer leaves for Alexandria.

Brindisi is a good place to stop at, provided one is not detained. We tarried just twelve hours longer than was desirable, landing at seven in the morning, and leaving at the same hour in the evening. With nothing to see, and nothing to do but to wait for the evening train, the hours passed on leaden wheels. It was rainy without and damp within; the new *Grand Hotel des Indes Orientales*, then scarcely completed, was dripping with wet, and we sat and meditated on fevers and rheumatism until the cars kindly bore us away, bound for Naples.

In crossing the mountain range between the eastern and western shores of Italy, we were transferred, for a few miles, from the cars to the diligence, the tunnel not being completed. We were here reminded once more of banditti—the Italian brigands, who belong to the same fraternity with the Greeks and Bedouins, whose hands we had escaped. They have the same habit of picking off stragglers and picking up baggage. The conductor prepared for them by placing the baggage-wagons under the protection of the passenger train of carriages, and we crossed the mountain without having a sight of their muskets.

I know of no other part of Italy, unless it be the plain of Sardinia, that bears the marks of such fertility or of such careful cultivation as the region north of Naples. It is a vast plain, the soil is rich and easily tilled, and every rood is improved. The trees are trimmed far up, destroying their beauty to a great degree, but letting in the sun and air upon the fields; while the vines are festooned from tree to tree above the growing crops, giving the country a holiday aspect. The peasantry of Italy belong to a different race from the dwellers in the towns. They are more industrious in their habits, and large sections of the country, devoted to corn and the vine, attest their thrift.

In entering Naples one is struck with the vagabond, and, at the same time, lively character of the mass of the people. They swarm every where, like bees that are just ready to desert a hive that has become too close to contain them. They live in the open air, not only seeking their amusements and attending to their ordinary business out of doors, but cooking and eating in the very thoroughfares of the city. All seem bent on catching the pleasures of the day as if there were no to-morrow. Formerly the beggars constituted one of the most striking features of Neapolitan street life. They were your escort in entering the city, coming out in crowds, sometimes for miles, to meet the public conveyances. They were unremitting in their attentions as long as you staid, never failing to take off their hats to you whenever you made your appearance in the streets, and when you were leaving they followed you out of town, wishing you every blessing by all the saints if you answered their demands, and cursing you by the whole calendar if you did not. Many of them had a merry way of begging, throwing somersaults, or playing a tune upon their chins, or cutting antics to attract attention, like the merriest creatures alive, when they would tell you, as the next thing, that they were dying of hunger, and ask for a little money for the love of the Madonna. The whole kingdom of Naples, and, for aught I know, adjacent kingdoms, had been raked and scraped to gather in the halt, the maimed, the lame, the blind, and all the miserable and disgusting objects that could be found, as so much capital on which to drive the thriving trade of begging, one of the principal branches of business in Naples, and not the least profitable either. But that is now changed, and one can go into and out of Naples, and stay there, with comparatively little annoyance from this source.

The Bay of Naples I regard as, beyond comparison, the finest single view in the world. It has a combination of beautiful features and of interesting associations that cluster around no other spot. The bay itself has a graceful sweep of thirty or forty miles within the islands placed at its mouth as sentinels to ward off the towering waves that come rolling in from the sea. Its waters are almost as blue as the vault of the sky above it. At the centre of its broad sweep stands the genius of the scene, the beautiful, majestic, living mountain, that has no equal; graceful in its outlines, and standing alone in its grandeur, like Fusiyama, the glory and pride of Japan. No other mountain has, for my eye, such a power of fascination. I have never looked upon it, from whatever point, or how often soever, that it has not had the same strange, fresh interest, as if I had never seen it before. It seems to be a living thing. There it stands, year after year, gently breathing out its vapor, like breath upon the frosty air, that floats away and is soon dissipated. When in a state of eruption the signs of life are far more striking.

The top of Vesuvius is the best point from which to take in the beauties of the bay and its surroundings. To the west lie the islands that form an important element in the perfection of the view. To the south are Sorrento and other sunny towns, with the blue mountains towering up behind them. The bright, gay city of Naples stretches for miles along the shore to the north. In the distance stands the tomb of Virgil, and farther on the town of Pozzuoli, the ancient Puteoli, the terminus of the Appian Way, at which Paul landed on his memorable journey to Rome, when he appealed to Cæsar's judgment. Farther on are Baiæ and Cumæ, the summer resorts of the Roman emperors and men of wealth, the Newport of those days, where they erected splendid palaces, and reveled in luxury and display. The ruins of their magnificent summer palaces, which were built out into the sea, and overhung the heights, stretch for miles along the shores. From these same shores and their surroundings Virgil took the scenery of his Æneid. Here are Lake Avernus, and the River Styx, and the Elysian Fields. Here, too, are the Sibyl's caves. No part of Italy, not even Rome itself, with its suburbs, was more consecrated by the homes and writings of her emperors, and orators, and bards.

At the foot of Vesuvius lie the long-buried cities of Herculaneum and Pompeii, revealed to-day after slumbering forgotten for eighteen centuries. A world of interest gathers around them as we look down into the silent, deserted streets, that so long ago were filled with a bustling crowd, and then in one dark storm were overwhelmed.

In what part of the world can so much that is beautiful in scenery, so much that is fraught with classic interest, and so much that stirs the heart with tragic recollection, be seen at a single glance as from the heights of this burning mountain? And this is an indication of what the traveler has to occupy his time and his attention in his sojourn at the sunny city of Naples. It requires many days to make the various excursions, but I shall not attempt to conduct the reader through them all.

Vesuvius was a burning mountain two thousand years before the Christian era. Its fires were extinguished and slumbered for a while, but just about the time that Paul landed at Puteoli it was seized with convulsions; the whole region was shaken, and several towns were laid in ruins. The memorable eruption in which Herculaneum and Pompeii were overwhelmed, the former by lava, and the latter by the shower of ashes, occurred in the year 79. The younger Pliny, who witnessed it, states that about one o'clock in the day he saw a strange cloud overhanging the plain of Naples, like a huge pine-tree shooting up to a great height and stretching out its branches. This singular cloud, which seemed to be composed of earth and cinders, excited his curiosity, and he embarked in a boat to cross the bay and examine into it. As he approached the coast, the red-hot cinders and stones fell into the boat, and he was obliged to retreat. He proceeded to Stabiæ to spend the night with a friend, but before morning they were driven to the fields by the shaking of the house.

The morning came, but it brought no relief. One shock of earthquake succeeded another, as if the foundations of the world were giving way. The sea receded from the shore. The mountain poured forth a mass of flame and burning rock, and the cloud of cinders spread over the bay and over the land. They attempted again to escape to a safer distance, and joined the crowd that was surging onward. Pliny's father had already perished. He led his mother by the hand, and fearing she would be pressed to death, proposed to step aside and suffer the crowd to pass by. He says: "We had scarce stepped out of the path when darkness overspread us—not like that of a cloudy night, or when there is no moon, but of a room when it is shut up and all the lights are extinguished. Nothing was to be heard but the shrieks of women, the screams of children, and the cries of men; some calling for their children, others for their parents, others for their husbands, and only distinguishing each other by their voices; one lamenting his own fate, another that of his family; some wishing to die from the very fear of dying; some lifting their hands to the gods; but the greater part imagining that the last and eternal night was come which was to destroy the gods and the world together."

This was the most fearful eruption on record. Many of less account have since occurred, the most remarkable in 1779, in which, according to Sir William Hamilton, the molten lava was thrown in jets to the height of 10,000 feet. More than once have the sides of the mountain broken in while the melted lava poured out of its sides, and ran in streams toward the plain below. In 1855 I made the ascent of the mountain, reaching the top of the cone, and looking down into the abyss. It was then comparatively quiet; only the presage of a coming explosion was noticeable. Soon after I had left the pent-up fires broke forth; the lava came rushing down in broad streams, filling up the ravines, and moving onward toward the sea. At night the mountain cast up a fiery mass, and flames marked the course of the burning tide. The green trees, encircled by the red-hot lava, generated steam, and then exploded with terrific noise, scattering the lava in all directions, and making the scene still more brilliant by setting fire to the trees, which, with the mountain itself, illuminated the whole Bay of Naples, and the surrounding cities and country.

Herculaneum was buried too deep in solid lava ever to be excavated to any great extent, but the larger part of Pompeii has been reclaimed, and one may now walk for miles through its streets and among its buildings. He need not lose his way; many of the streets still have the names upon the corners, as in modern cities. The ancient pavement, rutted deep by the carriage-wheels, remains intact, not equal, it is true, to the Belgian, but as firm as when it was laid eighteen centuries ago.

Entering the homes of the Pompeians as they were discovered, we find in them bracelets and jewels, some of exquisite workmanship, gold and precious stones. Here are writing materials; ink-stands and pens; lamps, as they went out when Pompeii was extinguished; thimbles, and distaffs, and spinning-wheels—in short, the whole catalogue of a woman's domestic life, together with all the paraphernalia of the toilet, even to the rouge and false hair. (The apothecaries' shops have on hand a large quantity of cosmetics, showing that they were in great demand.)

The cellars were stored with wine, and, although the old Falernian has long since evaporated, the amphoræ, or earthen jars which contained the wine, stand in rows along the walls. In the house of Diomede, one of the most extensive and elaborately ornamented villas, situated near one of the gates of the city, were large numbers of wine-jars of great size. This house, being remote from the centre of the town, was evidently resorted to by the friends of the owner as a place of comparative safety; but more persons probably lost their lives in it than in any other. The skeletons or forms of seventeen persons were found in the cellars. On the women were found gold necklaces, and bracelets, and other ornaments. Two were little children, whose heads were still covered with beautiful hair. In one of the houses in Pompeii two of the bodies are kept in a glass case, the attitudes and posture of the limbs expressing the mortal agony which came upon them. Diomede himself (or one who is supposed to have been the owner of the villa bearing his name) was found near the garden gate with a purse of gold and other valuables in his hand, while an attendant stood by his side grasping the key to the gate. Some of the houses have the names of the owners inscribed on the outer wall, especially those of a more imposing character. Among the familiar names is that of " C. Sallust." The house of Pansa, thus marked, one of the largest in the city, contained five skeletons when it was opened.

The shops, with their contents, are as great a curiosity as the homes. Some of them are extensive, the property of wealthy citizens, from which they derived their incomes. There are several bakeries, or cook-shops, in perfect preservation, from which large quantities of viands have been taken. In some the bread was found standing in the ovens. The notices around the doors and in the interior show that the art of advertising is not a modern invention. In one of the villas was found the following poster:

"JULIA HAS TO LET FOR FIVE YEARS,
A BATH, A VENERIUM, NINETY SHOPS,
WITH TERRACES AND UPPER CHAMBERS."

They are still without tenants, although they have been advertised 1800 years.

Nearly every thing found in the houses and shops at Pompeii is preserved in the National Museum at Naples, one of the most interesting collections of antiquities in the world. By its help we can readily refurnish the luxurious but now deserted homes, see how their inmates lived, and learn more of their domestic history than from any other source. One can study and muse for days over this extraordinary collection, and find his interest growing deeper every hour that he lingers.

Before leaving Naples we drove to the cities of its own dead, among the characteristic features of the place. The Protestant cemetery is a neat church-yard in the outskirts of the town. The cypress here waves over the grave of many a stranger who has died far away from the friends and scenes of home, but flowers also bloom profusely in this sweet resting-place of those who have no more seas to cross, and no farther journey in life to make. After lingering to note, by the various inscriptions, from how many lands the sleepers had come, we drove to the *Campo Santo Vecchio*, the great charnel-house of Naples. It contains three hundred and sixty-five pits, under a wide, paved square. Every evening the stone which covers one of these pits is removed, and the common dead of the city for the day are thrown into it, without even a winding-sheet to cover them. The old man and the child, the rough lazzaroni and the tender maiden, are dropped in together, and lie in one indiscriminate mass; quick-lime is thrown in to consume the bodies, and the pit is sealed for another year, to be opened at its close. We did not wait to witness the revolting scene, although the city carts were arriving with the dead, but drove to the Campo Santo Nuovo, the cemetery for the aristocratic dead, and here I was surprised to find a burial-ground laid out with refined taste, shaded with the cypress and other trees, and adorned with tombs of the most costly description. Many of them were in the form of chapels built of fine Italian marble, elaborately finished. After what I had heard of the burial of the dead at Naples, and after what I had seen at the Campo Vecchio, it was a relief to enter one that indicated so much refinement of feeling.

## XXXII.

### ROME TO FLORENCE.

The old route from Naples to Rome along the sea, through Terracina and Mola di Gaeta, was far more picturesque than the present route by rail, and one could fully enjoy it when traveling leisurely by vettura. I was once several days on the way, spending a night at Terracina in a storm, when the wild waves came rolling in from the sea, dashing against the walls of the hotel, and threatening to wash away its very foundations. It was quite equal to being rocked in the cradle of the deep. The true way to see Italy is not to whirl through it by the rail-car, but to take the old modes of conveyance. But every mode has its advantages, although no gain in time can compensate for the loss of the charming Italian scenery, and glimpses of Italian country life which were once enjoyed in traveling through the interior and along the shores.

On reaching the Roman frontier, for the first time, and, I may add also, the last time in all our journey around the world, a demand was made for passports. We had traveled from one end of Asia to the other, through Egypt and Syria, European Turkey and Greece, and thus far in Italy, without being called upon to declare our nationality, or obtain permission to go or come. But now, as we were entering the estate of his holiness the Pope, we must needs go through the old investigation. In no respect has a greater change come over the countries of Europe, and especially those having Roman Catholic rulers, than in the abolition of the passport system, and it is one of the many significant indications of the progress of religious freedom, as well as of the principles of free government. Several years since I had traveled over the route I was now taking, and, upon reaching home, found that my passport had on it eighty-seven *visés*, or official seals and signatures, as evidence of my having been permitted to enter and leave different countries and cities, and in nearly every instance it was where Roman Catholic influence was predominant. In going even from Rome to Naples and returning, fifteen or twenty examinations were required. The fact that in my recent journey, of which I am now writing, my passport was only once exhibited in the entire circuit of the earth, is a volume of testimony in regard to the progress which the world has been making, and also in regard to the waning power of popery as a political element. Passports are no longer required even at the gates of Rome. They belong to an order of things that has passed away even at Rome.

It was night when we reached the Alban Hills and came out upon the heights that overlook the Campagna and the city of the Cæsars, and we could study the scene only in imagination, peopling it with the multitudes of the past instead of the present. As we entered Rome we found it illuminated in commemoration of the anniversary of the return of Pius IX. from his long but voluntary exile after the occurrence and success of the Revolution of 1848. I call it voluntary because he was in no sense compelled, excepting by his fears, to flee or to remain in exile. When he was chosen pope in 1846, he entered upon a course of reform, and corrected many of the abuses which had become hoary with the lapse of time. He established his temporal government on a sort of popular basis, and gave the people a taste of liberty, which led to their taking the government into their own hands. Pius IX. was personally popular, nor was there at any time the least disposition to interfere with his position or power as head of the Church. On the assassination of his minister, Count Rossi, the pope became alarmed, and fled in disguise to Mola di Gaeta, within the territory of King Ferdinand of Naples. As soon as his departure from Rome became known, a deputation of eminent citizens was appointed to wait on him and urge his return, with the assurance that there would be no interference with his dignity or his functions as the head of the Church. But the reactionary cardinals had him in their hands, and would allow no interview, and under their advice he remained in exile until the French army had suppressed the rising liberties of the people and re-established the temporal tyranny of a spiritual power. The freedom which the city of Rome is now enjoying is that which its people won for themselves by their own right arms in 1848, and which was subsequently wrested from them by French bayonets alone. Never were claims to temporal power more false than those which are now urged in behalf of the pope.

A somewhat striking coincidence marked my coming to Rome. I had reached the city in 1854 while the council was in session that adopted the dogma of the Immaculate Conception as an article of the faith of the Church. I stood at that time near the high altar in St. Peter's on the day of its public announcement, and heard the pope read it from beginning to end. His heart had been set on making this declaration, and cardinals, and bishops, and dignitaries of all degrees were called from all parts of the earth to bow to his will and say that it was the will of God. He read the Latin with a feeble voice, weeping as he read it, and it was generally thought at the time that this would be the expiring act of his pontificate. I reached Rome again in season to be present in St. Peter's at the first public session of the Council of 1870, and heard the same pope announce the dogma *De Fide* preliminary to the impious claim of infallibility. He was feebler than before, with more than fifteen years added to his age, but there was the same iron will before which all inferior ecclesiastics have been made to bow. The utterance of this impious assumption of divine prerogatives was the signal for the providential destruction of his temporal as well as spiritual power.

Once, as we learn from sacred writ, another ruler, "Herod, arrayed in royal apparel, sat upon his throne and made an oration. And the people gave a shout, saying, It is the voice of a god, and not of a man. And immediately the angel of the Lord smote him because he gave not God the glory, and he was eaten of worms, and gave up the ghost." Pius IX. survives, but almost immediately upon the utterance of his dogma, and the shout of the people, "It is the voice of a god, and not of a man," his throne crumbled and fell, and his spiritual power over those who acknowledged his supremacy is fast passing away.

With modern Rome and with the remains of the ancient city every intelligent reader is familiar, and I should not attempt any general description even did my space permit. I shall refer only to one or two of its innumerable objects of interest.

The first point to which I bent my steps on entering Rome was not the Church of St. Peter, nor the Vatican, nor the Coliseum, but a monument that stands on the ancient *Via Sacra*, in some respects the most interesting object in the ancient or modern city. It is the smallest of the triumphal arches, and is known as the Arch of Titus. It bears the following inscription:

SENATVS.
POPVLVSQVE ROMANVS.
DIVO. TITO. DIVIA. VESPASIANA.
VESPASIANO. AVGVSTO.

This arch was erected to commemorate the conquest of Jerusalem. While at the head of the army before the walls of the Holy City, Vespasian, upon the death of Nero, was proclaimed emperor. He hastened back to Rome, leaving Titus in command, who, upon the fall of the city and the destruction of the Temple, made a triumphal march into Rome, bringing with him a long train of captive Jews, together with the spoils, among which were the sacred vessels of the Temple. It is this procession which is commemorated in the beautiful arch. The great interest of the bas-relief is in the fact that it supplies a place in the illustration of the Bible which can be filled from no other source. It is the only visible representation that exists of those sacred vessels, the patterns of which were received from heaven.

The frieze of the arch is ornamented with sculpture—a procession of warriors leading oxen to sacrifice. Upon a side panel of the interior is a group representing Titus in the act of celebrating his triumph over the Jews. He stands in a chariot drawn by four horses abreast, accompanied by the senators of Rome, and officers bearing the fasces. The sculptured form of Victory holds a wreath of laurel, with which she is about to crown the conqueror. Upon the opposite side, on a similar panel, is the celebrated group bearing the sacred vessels of the Jewish Temple. First comes a standard-bearer leading the way, with a canopy or arch supported above his head. The table of shewbread, with a cup and the silver trumpets used by the priests of the Temple to proclaim the year of jubilee, is borne on staves. Other bearers follow, carrying chaplets of laurel, and the golden candlestick with its seven branches. In size and form these bas-reliefs correspond precisely with the descriptions of the sacred record and the minute descriptions of Josephus. Little did those ancient pagans—the Roman senate and the Roman people—when decreeing and erecting this monument to a deified warrior, imagine that they were erecting a monument to the true God in the verification of prophecy and divine history, and little did they suppose that, after nearly two thousand years, the disciples of that faith which they had already begun to persecute even unto cruel death would come from distant lands to read the record and to be confirmed in their faith. The Jews of modern Rome are said to be the descendants of the captives which Titus brought from Jerusalem to grace his triumph. Not one of them, even at this day, will pass under the Arch of Titus, although it spans one of the thoroughfares of the city. They shun it as a memorial of the subjugation of their nation, a fall which has never yet been retrieved.

One of the most perfect and most striking of the relics of pagan Rome is the Pantheon. It has lost its external beauty in the covering of marble, but its massive walls and the form of the building remain just as when erected several years before the Christian era. It is still a wonder of architecture, faultless in its beautiful and grand proportions, and, notwithstanding its simplicity, it is to me the most impressive of the ancient or modern buildings of Rome. It stands in what was formerly the Campus Martius, where it was surrounded by the buildings belonging to the Thermæ of Agrippa, and was reached by a flight of steps, all of which must have added greatly to its effect. Now it is in one of the meanest corners of the city, and is scarcely on a level with the adjacent streets. The portico, which is regarded as a model, is 110 feet long, forty-four in depth, and is composed of sixteen Corinthian columns of Oriental granite, each one of which is a single block or shaft. They are forty-six and a half feet in height, and fifteen in circumference. The entablature and pediment are still perfect, and the frieze bears the following inscription, extending along the entire front:

M. AGRIPPA. L. F. COS. TERTIVM FECIT.

The massive bronze doors are acknowledged by the best authorities to be those set up by Agrippa. Although nearly forty feet in height, and having swung upon their hinges for nineteen centuries, they may still be moved by the hand of a child. The building is circular, 143 feet in diameter, or more than 400 feet in circumference. The walls, which are twenty feet in thickness, rise to the height of seventy feet, when they pass into one vast dome, the centre of which is 143 feet above the pavement. The dome is more impressive than that of St. Peter's, and one peculiarity adds a charm to that impression such as I have never found in any other building. The dome is open at its centre, the aperture being twenty-seven feet in diameter. It was never closed, even by glass, and the storms of nearly two thousand years have beaten through it and fallen upon the pavement below. This might seem a defect, but it constitutes, in reality, its most beautiful, if not its grandest feature. The circular walls are unbroken by windows, and, when the massive bronze doors are closed, this aperture in the dome is the only source of light, and communicates directly with the heavens above. One can look up and see the clouds floating by, or gaze into the blue ether, while the lower world is shut out by walls which no earthly sounds can penetrate. The poetry and sublimity of this conception for a temple may be imagined. It excludes all things terrestrial—opens heaven alone to the worshiper, and that, too, without any intervening medium.

An anecdote characteristic of Roman morals is related in a manuscript narrative of the sack of Rome, preserved at the Vatican. When Charles V. visited Rome in 1536, he ascended the roof of the Pantheon, and looked down through the aperture from above. A young Roman who had been ordered to accompany him afterward confessed to his father that he was strongly tempted to push the monarch over on the pavement below, a depth of nearly 150 feet, in revenge for the sack of the city a few years before. The wily old Italian said, "My son, such things should be done, and not talked about."

The Pantheon has been stripped of all its costly ornaments, leaving only its simple grandeur to delight the eye. Formerly the outer walls were faced with marble, which is now all gone. The vast dome was covered with gilded bronze, and its interior either lined or profusely ornamented with silver. The plates of bronze that covered the roof, and the silver, were removed by Constans II., A.D. 655, and afterward taken to Alexandria. Pope Urban VIII. completed the plunder of the building by taking the bronze beams of the portico to form the baldachino of the high altar of St. Peter's, and to cast cannon for the castle of St.

Angelo. This pope belonged to the Barberini family, and used a part of the plunder to ornament the Barberini palace. Pasquin, the mediæval oracle of Rome, made the following record of its final desecration: *Quod non fecerunt Barbari Romæ, fecerunt Barberini.* (What the Barbarians left of Rome, the Barberini destroyed.) The prince of painters, Raphael, who was a great admirer of the sublime structure, requested that he might be buried within its walls. When he died, his body, together with his last and noblest work, the Transfiguration, was exposed for three days in the Pantheon, and visited by crowds, who gazed upon both with equal interest, but with different emotions. His remains were afterward deposited in a niche formed in the walls, and the spot is now marked by a simple slab with an inscription in Latin. For many years the Academy of St. Luke, an association of artists, had a skull in their possession, said to be Raphael's. As doubts had arisen in regard to the actual resting-place of the immortal master of the pencil, it was determined in 1833 to settle the question by an examination of his tomb. It was accordingly opened in the presence of several ecclesiastical dignitaries and artists, and the skeleton was found entire just as it had been entombed. The relics were replaced, inclosed in an antique marble sarcophagus from the Vatican Museum. Of course the skull in the possession of the Academy of St. Luke lost its value, notwithstanding it had often awakened the admiration of phrenologists, who had found the painter's bump strikingly developed. But perhaps it did belong to a great artist. Who knows?

The ardent student of classical poetry and history (which in ancient times were often identical) is greatly scandalized in coming to the banks of the Tiber. Instead of a mighty river commensurate with its fame, he finds a small, muddy stream, scarcely any where two hundred yards wide. The mud, the narrowness, the very swiftness of its current, as if it were hurrying away to the sea to escape observation, are too much for him at the first glance. But as he gazes, the events which ages ago crowded around its banks, and which were known and felt the world over, come up before him like a grand procession, and it is no longer the insignificant stream, but the river of ancient Rome. That is distinction enough. It matters little to an ordinary traveler whether the stories of Æneas, and of Romulus and Remus, are myths or veritable history. Very few who come to Italy have any purpose or desire to settle the questions of fancy and of fact with which the early days of Rome are environed. This is left for the Niebuhrs whose tastes incline them in that direction. It is far more pleasant (and, for all practical purposes at the present day, it is just as well) to do as we did when school-boys—accept as history the story of the founder of Rome cast by the waters of the Tiber upon the spot where he afterward built the city.

The river is always turbid. Virgil is the only author who calls it cœrulean, and this was a stretch of poetic license quite beyond the mark. Upon what the fancy was founded it would be difficult to tell. It often overflows its banks as in ancient times, and the Campus Martius, on which the modern city is chiefly built, becomes inundated. The height of the water is marked upon columns standing on the river bank in the Via Ripetta, and also upon the façade of the Church of Santa Maria Sopra Minerva, in the very heart of the city, where the marks are some ten or twelve feet above the pavement. I have seen the pavement of the Pantheon several feet under water, so that the building could be entered only by boats. Treasures of art have often found their way into the river, which, if they could be recovered, would bring in the art markets of the world immense prices. Statuary more perfect, and perhaps more beautiful than any of the works of the ancient masters that are now preserved in the Vatican, doubtless lie imbedded in groups in the muddy bottom. The famous banker of the time of Leo X., Agostino Chigi, gave to the pope and his cardinals a splendid and costly entertainment, at which the dishes were all of the precious metals. It is said that when the feast was over they were thrown into the Tiber by the order of the rich banker, that no less illustrious guests might use them. There is a tradition that the sacred vessels of the Jewish Temple, brought from Jerusalem, among them the golden candlestick, were lost or thrown from the Milvian Bridge and never recovered.

There is nothing connected with the antiquities of Rome that Christian travelers visit with deeper interest than the Catacombs, although few venture far into their dark and intricate recesses. These narrow passages, some of which are sixty or seventy feet below the surface of the ground, run in all directions under the city and under the Campagna. The whole country is honey-combed by them, and it is said that in ancient times there was communication through them from Rome to the sea, fifteen or twenty miles distant. The openings or entrances are few, but it is not uncommon for riders over the Campagna to break through into those that are nearer the surface.

Their origin is not absolutely known—at least there are no authentic records of their excavation; but it is altogether probable they were formed in the early days of Rome by digging for the volcanic sand called *pozzulana*, which was used extensively in making the Roman cement for the erection of buildings—that mortar which has resisted the action of the elements more than two thousand years, and which bids fair to last as long as the stones themselves. The pozzulana was removed in the same way that coal is dug—in long avenues crossing each other at various angles, leaving enough of the earth or rock to sustain the superincumbent mass. They have fallen in at many places, completely blocking up the way, and, as there is always danger of such an occurrence, visitors are usually taken only a short distance, just to show how they were formed, and for what purpose they were subsequently used. Sad indeed would be the fate of those who should be buried beneath the falling mass, and sadder yet of those whose retreat should be cut off, while they were left to

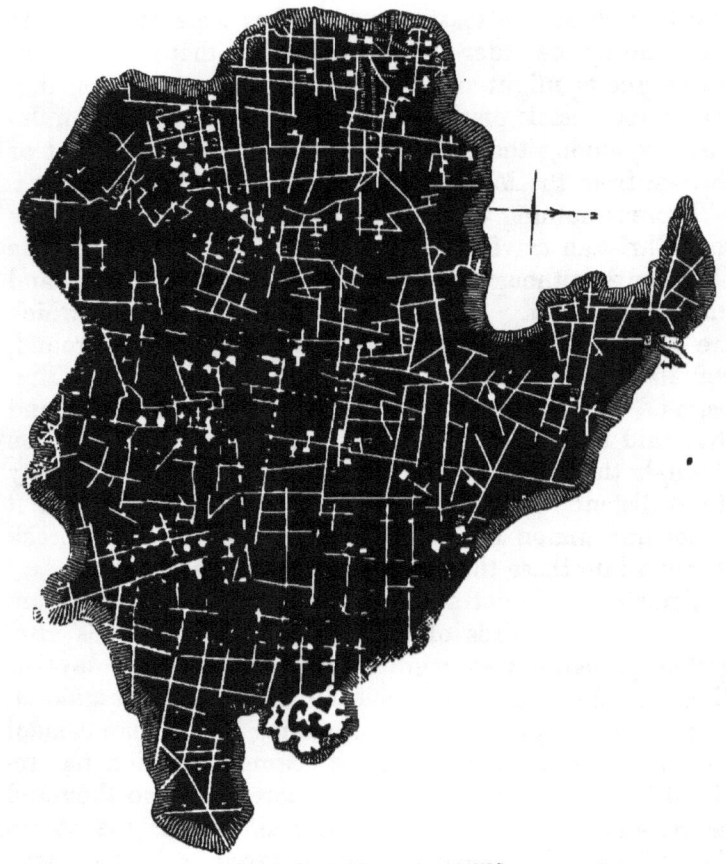

GROUND PLAN OF THE CATACOMBS.

wander hopelessly until compelled by weariness and weakness to lie down and die. Some thrilling incidents are related as warnings to those who enter, and to repress the curiosity of such as might wish to exceed the limits which prudence has assigned to the exploration of these subterranean passages. Several years since, fifteen or twenty youth, connected with one of the colleges of Rome, accompanied by a teacher, descended with candles, taking the usual precautions to secure their safe return to the light of day, but not one of them ever came out to tell the fate of the rest. They either lost their way, and wandered on in hope of finding the path that would lead them back until compelled by exhaustion to lie down and die, or the fall of the earth on the path they had taken cut off their escape. Long and diligent search was made, but to this day nothing is known of how or where in the vast labyrinth they were overtaken by death. The imaginations of those who go down into those dark recesses picture many a fearful scene which no words have power to express.

Later still, an artist entered the Catacombs alone, providing himself with a ball of twine, which he unwound as he wandered on, until he became absorbed with the records and recollections of other days. When he came to himself, the slender thread that bound him to the outer world was missing; with his dim taper he searched for it in vain; at last the light grew dim, and was then extinguished. In the horror of despair, he groped from one passage to another, until at last he stumbled in the darkness, and, in his struggles, his hand caught the thread which brought him back to the world.

The peculiar interest attaching to these Catacombs is, that during the early ages of Christianity, in the times of persecutions by the Roman emperors, they were the resort of Christians for safety, and probably, to some extent, for worship. They formed a secure refuge for those who were familiar with their windings, and it is probable that great numbers fled to them to escape the cruel death to which they were devoted by their persecutors. Either at the time they were thus used, or subsequently, they became sepulchres for the Christian dead. Niches were cut longitudinally in the sides of the long corridors, sometimes five or six one above another, in which the dead were deposited; they were then closed with a slab of marble or terra cotta, and sealed with cement. In this way they became populous cities of the dead. Not thousands, but hundreds of thousands, were here laid to sleep their last sleep. When they were first opened the bodies were in all states of preservation or decay. Some retained their form, in other cases the skeletons only remained, while the great multitude had crumbled into dust or had entirely disappeared.

The entrances to the Catacombs, which have all been under the strict supervision of the ecclesiastical authorities, are chiefly through or in connection with the churches, and are few in number, notwithstanding the limitless extent of the excavations. The one most accessible and most frequently visited by strangers is at the Church of St. Sebastian, a mile or more on the Appian Way, outside of the walls of the city. I had several times been into this as far as the old monk in charge consented to act as guide, and as far, probably, as he was familiar with the windings of the way, beyond which it certainly was not safe to venture alone, as a single turn might bewilder any one, and lead him into an endless labyrinth. An ecclesiastic who was visiting Rome to be present at the council entered at one time with our party, but he soon became alarmed, and entreated us not to go farther, as we must needs keep together to have the services of the guide. Having seen all that was to be seen of this, I was desirous to make a more extensive examination of those which had not been so completely rifled of their contents, and learning that the Catacombs in connection with the Church of St. Agnese, in another part of the Campagna, were far more interesting on this account, a party was made up, application was made to the cardinal vicar, and, through the intercession of an American lady, permission to enter was obtained. An intelligent gentleman who was well acquainted with the place and with its history was deputed to accompany us. We spent a large part of the morning appointed for the visit in wandering through the silent vaults, which, unlike the others, are still filled with the crumbling remains of the early confessors of the Christian faith. The excavations are much more regular, and on a larger scale than those which we had previously seen. Instead of being more unsafe, as is generally supposed, they are less liable to crumble and fall. The rock in which the excavations are made is more solid, allowing the passages to be cut with more exactness, and they run often to a great distance in a right line. The roofs are vaulted with regularity, and the sides cut perfectly square. The same niches occur as in the other Catacombs, and rise one above another to the number of five or six, but they have not been touched excepting to remove the slabs and inscriptions. The bones of the dead by hundreds, and even thousands, were lying where they were deposited sixteen or eighteen centuries ago. Occasionally they were in a state of preservation, and not unfrequently were covered with a mineral deposit from the drippings of the rock above, which had assisted in keeping them entire; in many cases it seemed to have produced a sort of petrification, but generally, where the form of a body, or even of a bone appeared, it would sink and almost vanish under the touch, all substance having gone. The teeth were occasionally undecayed, and, as I took one from its socket, the bone to which it had been attached sank immediately away.

The bodies had been laid in their narrow couches uncoffined, and, as the slabs had been removed, all that remained of the sleepers was exposed to view; but there was nothing repulsive in the sight, as there would be in an ordinary charnel-house, nor any thing melancholy in the place itself. The sacred, Christian associations dispelled such thoughts. These bodies, which had been slumbering quietly for nearly two thousand years, had been laid away in the hope of a coming morning—the morning of the resurrection, when the dust into which they would crumble should be gathered again and reanimated, to meet at his coming Him who is the resurrection and the life. Many trembling hearts had been driven by the persecutors into these recesses to escape the sword or the jaws of wild beasts; but when they ceased to beat, whether through violence or by a natural death, they were all and forever at rest. The storms of centuries had raged above their heads, armies had met in deadly conflict on the soil above them, but they slept on undisturbed. Instead of being oppressed with sad or mournful thoughts, a feeling of triumph—of actual joy, came over me in the remembrance of the glorious victories over death and every other foe that had been gained by the host around me. After fighting the good fight of faith, and resisting unto blood, they had gone up to receive the reward and the crown of the martyrs.

When the Catacombs were first opened inscriptions were found on the slabs, some of them rudely cut, and not unfrequently they were accompanied with emblematical devices expressive of Christian hope or sentiment. The slabs were removed and set in the wall of the long corridor leading to the Museum of the Vatican, where they may now be seen. Among the most common emblems were the Three Children in the Fiery Furnace, and Daniel in the Lions' Den, doubtless used as emblems of martyrdom; the Good Shepherd, with a Lamb on his shoulders; Noah at the window of the Ark; the Dove; an Anchor; a Fish, the significance of which as an early Christian emblem is well known; with representations of the miracles of Christ, etc.

I give but a few specimens of the multitude of inscriptions: "Valeria dormit in pace" (Valeria sleeps in peace). "In pace Domini dormit" (He sleeps in the peace of the Lord). "In pace" and "In Christo" occur frequently. The constant occurrence of the word "sleep" as a synonym for death is striking. The following are mere translations of inscriptions:

"Lannes, the martyr of Christ, rests here. He suffered under Diocletian."

"In the time of the Emperor Adrian, Marius, a young military leader, who had lived long enough: with his blood he gave up his life for Christ. At length he rested in peace. The well-deserving, with tears and fears, erected this in the Ides of December, VI."

"Here lies Gordianus, deputy of Gaul, murdered with all his family for his faith. They rest in peace. Theophila, his maid, erected this."

I can not attempt even the briefest enumeration of the places and objects of interest, ancient and modern, which are in and around Rome; it is a world in itself, and I have found by experiment that months would not exhaust the study. The Vatican, the Capitol, the ancient and modern palaces, the Coliseum, the churches, which are also repositories of art; the Seven Hills, the Appian Way, the suburbs, Albano, Frascati, and a thousand ruins, each one of which has its classic history, all claim the attention of the traveler, but can not have their record here. There is no other city in Europe where an intelligent traveler can tarry so long with so much interest. But we must pass on. I can not do so, however, without expressing my own pleasure in the thought that Rome, which I had seen only under a dark shadow—the shadow of spiritual despotism, is now in the light. The sun is shining on Rome as it has not shone for many long centuries, save in the brief period after the Revolution of 1848. Its people walk the streets breathing the air of freedom—freedom to think their own thoughts and speak their own words, enjoying the protection of a liberal government, even though it be a kingly. Long live Victor Emanuel, and long may he reign over United Italy—at least so long as he pursues the enlightened policy which he has been carrying out since he came to the throne. And ever may the people of Rome rejoice in freedom from ghostly tyranny, the most oppressive of all forms of despotism. The temporal power of the pope will assuredly never be re-established with "the consent of the governed."

As a matter of necessity, owing to the arrangement of the trains, we made a night journey to Florence, entering it in the morning, and greatly enjoying the views of river, and mountain, and vale as we approached the city. Victor Emanuel can not have set his heart upon making Rome the capital of the new kingdom of Italy on account of its greater beauty. There is no inland city in Europe more superbly located than Florence. If not a gem in itself, the setting makes it one. The surrounding heights, with the numerous villas, and vineyards, and monasteries that crown the hills, make the sight one to be enjoyed and never forgotten. The view from San Miniato, which is reached by one of the most beautiful drives in the suburbs of any city in the world, can scarcely be surpassed by any mere inland view.

FLORENCE, FROM SAN MINIATO.

And Florence is as attractive as ever in its works of art. The Uffizi and Pitti Palaces, the treasure-houses of painting, have witnessed revolutions raging around them, but their pictures and other treasures remain where they were. It is a marvel as well as a pleasure, after reading of the many changes in the government of these lands, to find its galleries of art and all that they contain untouched. The first Napoleon ruthlessly despoiled Italy, but the sentiment of the world, as well as his own changing fortunes, compelled him to restore what others have not dared to touch. The removal of the court to Rome will make no change in the art treasures of Florence; they will remain undisturbed, and future travelers will find them just where they were found before Victor Emanuel was welcomed to Florence.

The days passed quickly away in visiting and revisiting the galleries, where one can linger for weeks; the Duomo, with its Campanile and Baptistery; Santa Croce, and San Lorenzo, and the many places and objects of interest which have so long attracted crowds of travelers to the beautiful city, made more attractive than ever before. An excursion to Pisa, distant about an hour, afforded a sight of the Leaning Tower, and of the Cathedral in which still hangs the bronze chandelier, the swinging of which suggested to the philosophical mind of Galileo the theory of the pendulum, the first step toward his demonstration of the nature and order of the solar system, for which he came near suffering martyrdom at the hands of the Church of Rome. I greatly scandalized the priest who attended us when I gently touched the chandelier and gave it a swing, that I might be brought more into communication with the heretic Galileo by seeing it in motion.

Florence, since it has passed from under the dominion of the Grand-duke, has become a centre of light and true religious influence for all Italy. There is something truly sublime and almost inexplicable in the stand which Victor Emanuel has taken in regard to religious liberty. He is not reputed to be a man of religious sentiment or feeling; quite otherwise; and yet, since he first came to his father's throne, he has pursued a steady course in securing to his subjects the right to worship God, and in granting to his people equal privileges without regard to their religious opinions. The Waldenses, who for ages suffered oppression even when they were not suffering persecution, are now represented in the Italian Parliament, and enjoy full ecclesiastical privileges. It was said in Turin many years ago, when Victor Emanuel was king of that corner of Italy, that he received the principles of religious toleration as a sacred legacy from Charles Albert; if so, he has been a faithful executor of his father's will. Not all the threats of excommunication, nor excommunication itself, which has been hurled at his head more than once, has had any effect to turn him from his course.

## XXXIII.

### VENICE HOMEWARD.

IN the journey from Florence to Venice, where once the traveler passed over the Apennines, we passed directly through them, piercing the mountains by more than forty tunnels within the space of two or three hours. We scarcely emerged from one before we dived into the gloom and darkness of another, until it really seemed as if the eye of day was simply winking at us—now shut, now open, and now shut again. Night came on, and the stars came out long before we reached "The City of the Sea;" but near midnight we *landed* (if leaving *terra firma* and taking to the water can be called landing), and glided quietly to our quarters at the hotel a mile or more distant.

There are only two cities in the world that I have found just what I expected. When I first caught sight of Jerusalem in crossing the hills of Judea, and when I looked down upon it from the Mount of Olives, it was the Jerusalem of my thoughts; I had been there often before. When I reached the railway terminus on the lagoon at Venice, and took a gondola instead of an omnibus, and was rowed by moonlight through one street after another, and at length landed at the door of the hotel, into which I stepped from the gondola; and when, on the following days, I floated through the liquid streets, into and along the Grand Canal, past the old and now deserted palaces, beneath the Rialto, and under the Bridge of Sighs; and as I stood in the grand square of San Marco, and entered the Doge's Palace, and walked through its great historic halls, and descended into its subterranean and subaqueous dungeons, I found myself just where I had been a hundred times. It was not the realization of a dream—it was the dream prolonged; every thing was as I had fancied it. Venice is a city so peculiar, so unlike all other cities we have ever known, that we do not base our conceptions of it upon what we have seen of other places, but upon actual descriptions.

In this singular city travelers must needs become amphibious. They sleep in houses, not upon the land, but anchored in the sea. If they step into the street they step upon the water. If they wish to make a call upon a friend, they order, not a carriage, but a gondola. There is not a carriage in all Venice, and only one horse, which is kept on an adjacent island as a curiosity. He would have been, in truth, *rara avis* if he had not been a horse. Over the streets, which are water, a stillness reigns throughout the year which to many becomes oppressive, absolutely painful; but to me it is a positive luxury. Here the noise and bustle of life are suspended, the days float along as still as the flight of a bird in the air, or as smoothly as one of the gondolas in which we glide over the surface of the water.

Thoroughly to enjoy Venice, one must come at the right season, and have plenty of time. In midwinter the air is too cool to enter into the spirit of the place. In midsummer, and all through the warm season, the canals are offensive, reminding one of the streets of Cologne; and if one has been in China, they will slightly remind him of the cities of the Celestial Empire. The month of May, when the air is balmy, and just warm enough to enjoy the open air without exercise (for exercise here is almost out of the question), is, perhaps, the best time of the year.

And then to take a gondola in front of the Doge's Palace, and allow your gondolier to row you gently into the Grand Canal, and through its whole extent, and give you—as he will, if you secure an intelligent gondolier—the name and the story of each one of the old marble palaces as you glide by it, or pause to read up its history; to enter these ancient halls of the Venetian princes, as you may by a suitable introduction; to bring up the days of the Old Republic, when these water streets were resplendent with naval displays, with gorgeous regattas, and with the magnificence of Oriental sights—all this bewilders and delights the imagination, until one can scarcely do any thing but give way to the intoxicating influence of the scenes and associations by which he is surrounded. Even visiting and studying the works of art which abound in Venice seem almost too much like servile labor for the atmosphere of the place. Venice itself is the work of art which each one will most delight to contemplate.

The evening before leaving Venice, after making a call on some friends on the Grand Canal, we took a gondola to return to our own hotel. The night was enchanting, and, instead of going directly to our quarters, I told the gondolier to row down the bay toward the Lido. The skies were perfectly clear, the stars were out in hosts, looking down upon the placid scene; the water of the bay was literally like glass, and, as we returned, the whole city, with its brilliant lights, was reflected from its surface, making two perfect cities, one above and one below the sea. Not a sound came from the city itself, in which no rumbling wheels are ever heard. All was perfect stillness. I directed the gondolier to rest upon his oars, and leave us to float. Just then the great historic bell of San Marco, swinging in the lofty Campanile, with its deep-toned voice rung out the hour of midnight, and the bells all over the city echoed the sound. Was it all a dream? It was not like the common realities of earth. We returned to our hotel to dream in truth, and to bring away with us the remembrance of this last evening as the most appropriate of all our pleasant memories of the Queen of the Adriatic.

Going from Venice to Vienna, we chose the route by rail, around the head of the Adriatic, having had enough of the sea to satisfy our most earnest longings. From Trieste the road leads over the Semmering Pass by one of the grandest pieces of engineering, and through some of the grandest scenery on any railroad in the world. We ascended many lofty heights, now passing through dark, rocky galleries, now rushing along the mountain side, from which we had charming views of the valleys beneath us, and anon winding down until we were in the very depths of the valleys preparing to ascend other heights beyond.

Vienna, the splendid capital of the Austrian Empire, is becoming more and more magnificent. The internal fortifications were razed in 1858 to furnish room for the growing city, and piles of buildings have been and are still in course of erection. Paris, taken as a whole, is more beautiful, but there is no city in all Central or Southern Europe that is more magnificent. In the old town the streets are narrow; but the new, broad avenues, which stretch for miles and encircle the city, are lined with splendid blocks of buildings, giving it the aspect of a city of palaces.

A great change has come over this capital, and over the whole empire within the last few years. The Austrian government is now carrying out the principle which I saw inscribed as a motto on one of the arches leading to the imperial palace—an inscription which was long a dead letter—JUSTITIA REGNORUM FUNDAMENTUM. The contrast between Austria as it was and Austria as it is I have had occasion to test. A few years since, in crossing the frontier, I was taken by the police into a private room, and subjected to a long and rigid examination in regard to my birthplace, my family, my destination, my purposes of travel, and many other particulars; the answers were all committed to writing and forwarded to Vienna. But now I entered Austria without a question being asked, and traveled from one end of it to the other without a challenge. When I first entered it, Austria was in complete subjection to Rome. The Concordat was in force. The educational system of the country was, by treaty, in the hands of Romish priests, whose persons were inviolate, and whose power was almost supreme. Austria is now ruled by its own government. The Concordat with Rome has been dissolved. The education of the country has been taken out of the hands of the priests, and is directed by the government. Romish priests and bishops are now required to obey the laws like other citizens, and are sent to prison when they violate them. I know not why the priests should decline to show themselves, since they enjoy equal protection and privileges with others, but I did not see a single one in priestly garb in the streets of Vienna during my stay. It is not the least of the signs of change that the prime minister of Austria, whose emperor is a Roman Catholic, is himself a thorough Protestant.

Among all that was to be seen in this splendid capital, there was nothing of deeper interest than the crypt of the Capucin Church, in which lie the remains of a long line of emperors and princes. Descending a staircase, we entered a long hall, and walked by the side of coffined dust once animated by ambitious spirits struggling for empire, but now sleeping their long sleep, the turmoil of the battle of life all ended with them. The sarcophagi stand in regular order upon the pavement of the long corridor like so many cots spread for repose at night. The Emperor Mathias Corvinus, who died at Vienna two years before the discovery of the Western Continent by Columbus, was the first buried. After him a succession of kings wrapped their imperial robes around them, and were laid in this royal mausoleum. It is a treasure-house of history, and the stories of some of the royal occupants are romantic and tragic to the last degree. Here lies the Duke of Reichstadt, only son of the first Napoleon, who received from his father, at his birth, the title of King of Rome, that proved but an empty name. He closed his melancholy life at the palace of Schonbrunn, in the suburbs of Vienna, at the age of twenty-one, attended by his mother, Marie Louise. His last words were a wail of despair: "I am sinking, oh my mother, my mother!"

But far more tragic was the end of one of the royal sleepers in this hall of kings. The last deposited coffin, still covered from day to day with fresh flowers, is that of the Emperor Maximilian, the tool of Napoleon in the attempted conquest of Mexico. Sad as was his fate, it is to be envied before that of Carlotta, who still lingers in hopeless insanity. There are more than eighty coffins in this corridor of illustrious dead, one of them—that of Joseph I.—of solid silver. It is said that the Empress Maria Theresa, mother of the illustrious Joseph II., descended every day, for thirteen years, into the crypt to mourn for her husband Francis I., until at length she was laid by his side.

A singular precaution against the premature resurrection of any of these departed monarchs has been adopted. The bodies lie in the crypt of the Church of the Capucins, their hearts are deposited in urns in the Church of St. Augustine not far distant, and their bowels are buried in St. Stephen's Cathedral in another part of the city.

From Vienna we made our way by rail across the battlefields of Austria to one of the most curious cities in Europe, and one of the most interesting in its historical incidents, the ancient capital of Bohemia. Prague is charmingly situated on both sides of the River Moldan, and the variegated surface of the ground on which it is built, especially the bluff on which the old palace stands, gives to it an exceedingly picturesque appearance. A portion of the town is very ancient, and the whole has a more antique and unique aspect than any other European city that I can recall. I was attracted to Prague by its association with the early martyrs of the Reformation—John Huss and his associate, Jerome of Prague; but I found that I had entered a city that was filled with curious old buildings and monuments, and with records of stirring events that occurred all along through the centuries. The Rathaus or Town-hall, which has in one of its towers a famous clock that rivals the celebrated clock of the Strasbourg Cathedral, was the scene of some of these events. As the Hussites, under Ziska, were marching through the city in 1419, they were assaulted with stones from the Rathaus, when they rushed into the council-chamber and threw the councillors, to the number of thirteen, out of the windows. They were caught upon the pikes of the people.

This throwing of people out of the windows became so common as to acquire the name of "The Bohemian Fashion." In 1483, the people, dissatisfied with the course of the magistrates, entered the Rathaus, pitched the burgomaster out of the window, and then threw several of the senate down upon the spears of the expectant crowd.

The Rathaus in the Neustadt was the scene of a similar occurrence, the magistrates, on two separate occasions, having been ejected from the windows. Two members of the imperial government were thrown from the windows of the palace, a height of nearly eighty feet from the ground, but, falling on a dung-heap, their lives were saved. Their secretary, thrown after them, of course came down atop, and is said to have made a humble apology to his superiors for coming into their presence in this unceremonious manner.

Prague was the seat of the observations of the celebrated Danish astronomer, Tycho Brahe, who was invited by the Emperor Rudolph II. to make the city his home. His observatory was on the castle hill, near the ancient palace, where his nocturnal study of the heavens was greatly disturbed by the monks of a neighboring convent; in consequence of which, an imperial order was issued that the monks should finish their prayers and cease the tolling of the bells before the rising of the stars which the astronomer was intending to watch.

The palace of Count Wallenstein, the hero of the Thirty Years' War, though now neglected, was once a princely seat, and is said to have been, during the life of that distinguished and eccentric warrior, the scene of splendors such as have been rarely seen in any regal court. He lived in great state; barons and knights were his attendants, and sixty pages of noble families waited on his orders.

But of all the memories connected with this ancient city, none stand out upon the pages of history like those associated with John Huss, and his faithful friend and coadjutor, Jerome of Prague. Huss was born in the south of Bohemia in the year 1373. He came to Prague to pursue his studies in what was then the first university in Europe. At that time, it is estimated that as many as 20,000 students were present from all parts of Europe. Here, too, he became acquainted with the writings of Wickliffe, and began at once to preach against the errors and iniquities of the Church of Rome, and though threatened, and placed under interdict, and excommunicated, he went on with his work, appealing from the pope to a General Council of the Church, and to Christ, its only Head. Summoned to appear before the Council of Constance in 1414 on a charge of heresy, he obeyed the summons, protected, as he had a right to believe, by a safe-conduct from the Emperor Sigismund. The emperor was told that a promise made to a heretic was not binding, and gave him up into the hands of the Council, which condemned him and his writings to be burned together. His friend Jerome, who braved all perils, and came to Constance to defend him, was cast into prison, where, after being reduced to utter weakness and the verge of despair by six months of solitary confinement, he recanted, but not long after retracted his recantation, and died heroically at the stake.

On the 6th of July, 1413, Huss, then forty-two years of age, having boldly avowed his firm belief in the Gospel of Christ as revealed in the inspired Scriptures, was condemned by the Council to be burned alive. He was stripped of his priestly garments, and arrayed in fantastic robes on which devils were painted, emblematical of the companionship to which his persecutors would fain consign him. While the fagots were piled around him he remained perfectly calm, and as the torch was applied, and the flames sprang up, he broke forth in a hymn of praise which was heard above the noise of the multitude, and, commending his soul to the Saviour in words of prayer, his spirit went aloft in the chariot of fire. His ashes were collected and cast into the Rhine, as those of Wickliffe, "the morning star" of the Reformation that had guided him to Christ, were cast into the Severn.

Stirring scenes occurred within the city of Prague after this noble martyr had given his dying testimony to the truth, and his spirit still animates the Bohemian people. His name is yet used as a watchword—a sort of synonym for liberty, even by those who reject the doctrines of the Reformation. I searched out the spot where he lived, and found it occupied by a Roman Catholic; but the house is conspicuously marked with a large medallion likeness of the great reformer in front, while over the door is the following inscription, cut into the stone and gilt: "Here lived Master John Huss." The house has been rebuilt, but a stone window-frame taken from the former building is inserted in the corridor leading to the court-yard, and incloses a stone tablet with the words,

A Relic of the House where lived<br>
MASTER JOHN HUSS,<br>
Who preached at Betlemske Chapel.

All clerical titles are denied him—he is simply Master John Huss. I found the ancient chapel where he preached occupied as a carriage-maker's shop.

By another stage of our journey we were, in the course of a few hours, in the former capital of Saxony, a capital only in name, since the kingdom has been swallowed up in Prussia, and, still later, in the German Empire of to-day. Dresden, although charmingly situated on the Elbe, and in the midst of a beautiful champaign, has its chief attractions in the right royal gallery of paintings, celebrated the world over, and in its collections of antiquities and arts, many of which are associated with the history of Saxony. Not the gem, but the diadem of the collection, is Raphael's Madonna del Sisto—an exception to nearly all the Madonnas of fame in the deep thoughtfulness, the almost superwomanly look into futurity which marks her countenance. Artists, in giving us their ideals of the mother and child, have seldom done more than paint the portraits of comely women and expressionless infants. But one who looks upon this masterpiece of Raphael may well imagine the mother to be pondering in her heart the deep meaning of those prophetic words of Simeon: "Yea, a sword shall pierce through thy own soul also." It is a majestic creation of the pencil—the queen of the Madonnas.

It was only two months before the breaking out of hostilities between France and Prussia when we reached Berlin. There was not then a whisper of war, not a breath in the atmosphere which made one apprehend that such scenes of strife were at hand, and yet the whole aspect of things was martial. There was military display in the streets. There was a grand military review at Potsdam, and at evening the capital was like a military camp. The people themselves were talking over the old scores with France which had never been settled. As we rode out to Charlottenberg to see the exquisite statuary, by Rauch, which adorns the tomb of Frederick William III. and his lovely wife, the Queen Louise, whose memory is almost adored by the Prussians, a German who was with us gave expression to the national hatred of the first Napoleon, and the desire to redress the insults and injuries which had been heaped upon the Prussian royal family and upon the kingdom and capital. But little did we imagine that another Napoleon would so soon afford the opportunity for avenging these wrongs.

We devoted a day to Wittenberg, long the home of Luther, and the scene of some of the most important events of the Reformation. It is about sixty miles from Berlin. We first went to the Schlosskirche, upon the doors of which Luther nailed the ninety-five theses, his protest against the doctrines of Rome, and a confession of the faith of one who had been taught by the Holy Spirit out of the Bible. The doors of the church were burned by the French when they ravaged Prussia, but they have been replaced by gates of bronze, on which are engraved the whole of the ninety-five theses in the original Latin text. With much difficulty we obtained the keys, and entered the church to stand within the walls which had resounded with the thunders of that voice that stirred all Europe, the echoes of which have rolled over the earth, and will roll onward until time shall be no more. Luther and Melancthon were both buried in this church. The spot where Luther burned the pope's bull of excommunication before an assembly of doctors, students, and citizens, just outside of the Elster Gate, has been inclosed, and is carefully kept as an ornamental garden. An oak-tree marks the spot where tradition says the bull was consumed. The monastery in which the great reformer lived and taught while yet a monk is now a college for educating Protestant ministers, and the houses occupied by Luther and Melancthon are schools. The statues of the two reformers — costly and noble works of art — stand in the market-place, the former bearing the well-known words, in German, "If it be God's work, it will endure; if man's, it will perish." The University building, in which Luther lived with his wife Catharine, contains many memorials of the reformer, including his chair, the table on which he wrote, and the capacious mug from which he drank his German beer. Kings and nobles many have stood within this room to pay homage to the memory of one who was mightier than kings and princes. The sign-manual of Peter the Great rudely adorns the wall.

Another day we devoted to Potsdam, the home of Frederick the Great, and in his time the real capital of Prussia.

It is a cluster of royal palaces, the grounds of which are laid out with royal taste and on a magnificent scale. Founded by Frederick Wilhelm, Elector of Brandenburg, its chief glory was imparted to it by the great Frederick, who erected its finest buildings and enlarged its parks. Here he indulged to the utmost his peculiar tastes. The room at the chateau of Sans Souci in which he died is preserved in the same state as when his spirit departed from it nearly a hundred years ago. The clock, which stopped the moment at which he breathed his last, remains undisturbed, the hands pointing to the memorable hour and minute.

One of the monuments of the place is the famous windmill. Adjoining the royal grounds was a field, in which stood a wind-mill, a sort of vineyard of Naboth to the great Frederick, who wished to add it to his own parks. The miller refused to sell, on which the king brought an action in the courts to dispossess him. It was decided against the king, who regarded the decision of the judges as so honorable to the nation that he built for the miller a fine stone mill that is still standing, although the grounds have been added to the royal domain by purchase. Such triumphs are worthy of commemoration by kings and people.

From Berlin we crossed the country to Cologne. The city, within the last few years, has been greatly improved, the "two-and-seventy stenches" of Coleridge being reduced in number and power, while the perfumery establishments have multiplied. Progress has been made in the renovation of the Cathedral, which is the grandest ecclesiastical structure in the world. St. Peter's, at Rome, is larger and more highly adorned with works of art; the Cathedral at Milan is in some respects more beautiful; but, take it all in all, in appropriateness and purity of architecture, in simplicity and grandeur of effect, in its power of appeal to the heart, it is without a rival among all the structures erected for Christian worship.

Disdaining the railway as a profanation of the romance of the Rhine, we took the steamer at Cologne to ascend the river, the beauties of which, with the historic tales that are written on its rocky heights, and castle walls, and crumbling ruins, have been sung for ages, but not exaggerated.

BINGEN ON THE RHINE.

The sun had set and the moon had risen as we passed Bingen on the Rhine, and for two or three hours we enjoyed the perfection of the romance of this river, which is more thickly crowded with legendary interest than any other that pours its waters into the sea. As we sat in the soft moonlight on the deck of the steamer, tracing the outlines of the lofty heights and catching shadowy glimpses of the shores, the nightingales on either bank regaled us with their melody, displaying alike their marvelous power of song and their exquisite taste in preferring moonlight.

to sunlight for song. We thought of good Izaak Walton's pious ejaculation as he listened to their melody, "Lord, what music hast thou provided for the saints in heaven, when thou affordest bad men such music on earth!"

After spending the Sabbath at Mayence, we went to Worms, recalling, as we entered the city, the time when Luther, summoned to appear before the Diet to answer to the charge of being a heretic, and to show cause why he should not be burned, like Huss and Jerome of Prague, made answer to his friends, who dissuaded him from trusting himself in the hands of his perfidious enemies, "Though there were as many devils in Worms as there are tiles on the roofs of the houses, I would go on," and boldly entered, chanting the Marseillaise of the Reformation, "*Ein feste Burg ist unser Gott.*" Here it was that, standing up before the Emperor Charles V. and his nobles, and a multitude of Romish prelates, who were eager to light the fagots around his body, he boldly defended his doctrine, and ended with the declaration, "Let me, then, be refuted and convinced by the testimony of the Scripture, or by the clearest argument; otherwise I can not and will not recant, for it is neither safe nor expedient to act against conscience. Here I stand; I can not do otherwise; God help me."

Never, since the Lord Jesus was arraigned before Pontius Pilate, has there been witnessed on earth a sublimer judicial spectacle, or one in which the example of the Master was more nobly illustrated in the bravery of the disciple, than Luther before the Diet of Worms avowing, in the face of all his enemies, the truth of Jesus as revealed in his Word. The Episcopal palace in which the Diet was held, near the great Cathedral, has disappeared; but the memory of that scene is now preserved in a group of monumental bronze statuary, erected at great cost, representing Luther surrounded by the early reformers of many lands—Wickliffe, Huss, Savonarola, etc.—and the faithful electors who stood by him while alive. The group stands upon an elevated stone terrace in the open air, at the entrance to a park or garden, embracing a secluded ravine, in the deep shade of which, even at noonday, the nightingales were pouring forth their sweetest lays.

From Worms we reached French territory at the town of Weissenberg, where our baggage was overhauled by the officials. This little town, a few weeks later, took its place in history as the spot where the French and Prussian armies first met in deadly conflict, but as we halted on our way it had no presage of its coming distinction. All was smiling and peaceful. An hour later we were at Strasbourg. By a singular but undesigned coincidence, I found it was fifteen years to a day, and almost to an hour, since I had entered it once before. The town was not a little changed in the mean while, having lost a measure of its quaintness; but no amount of polish or paint could make a French city of·it. It was German still, and will be more at home in Germany than in France, whether the inhabitatants are at home or not.

We tarried at Strasbourg over a day to see the grand Cathedral, with its wondrous clock. The Cathedral, as a specimen of Gothic architecture, is not far behind that of Cologne. It is melancholy to know that this monument of many centuries suffered so much in the siege. That it did not suffer more was marvelous. The famous clock, a wonder of mechanism, was but slightly injured. We paid a visit to the Protestant Church of St. Thomas to see the group of statuary erected by Louis XV. in memory of Marshal Saxe — a noble monument to a noble Protestant by a Catholic king. The marshal was represented as descending into the tomb; Death, in the form of a skeleton, stood lifting the lid of the coffin for his reception; while France, in the form of a beautiful female weeping, was holding the hero back dissuasively. Other emblematical devices completed the group. The church and its monuments were reported as destroyed in the siege.

The afternoon before we left Strasbourg we took a walk

outside of the fortifications on the north, and, seating ourselves in the fine old park which stretched out into the country, we speculated more in a sentimental than a serious way upon the effects of war. The great fortress which incloses the city very naturally suggested such thoughts; but, in the total absence of every thing intimating the possibility of war as near, our sympathy was mainly expended upon the venerable trees under the shade of which we were resting. They looked as if they might have been standing there for centuries. We lamented that, if war should ever come into these parts, one of the first measures of defence would be the leveling of every one of those majestic monarchs of the soil, all which was done very shortly after we had left the city.

It was but a few weeks before the French army came into the region throwing down the gage, and then commenced that series of disasters to their arms that has seldom, if ever, had a parallel in the history of European wars. Strasbourg was surrounded by a besieging force, and one after another of its buildings and monuments disappeared in the long and fierce bombardment. The hotel at which we had lodged was demolished, and the faithful porter who waited on us, and attended us to the cars as we were leaving, I afterward learned, had his head carried off by a cannon ball as he was going his nightly round of inspection, lantern in hand.

Our way to Paris was through Nancy, Bar le Duc, Chalons, and other places that became famous in the progress of the war, and through the beautiful champaign that was soon devastated by the opposing armies. It was then covered with luxuriant crops that were smiling in the summer's sun, but they were not gathered before the iron heel pressed them into the soil. As the terrific conflict went on, and the forces of both armies drew all the while nearer to the French capital, we read the accounts with deeper interest and more intense sympathy from having so lately seen the fields smiling with the promise of a peaceful harvest, and the cities rejoicing in the quiet and plenty which were to pass away and be succeeded by scenes of blood.

Paris was more gay and beautiful than ever. Twenty years of rebuilding under Louis Napoleon, with the purse of the nation at command, had made it the most splendid city in the world. Its palaces and boulevards, its parks and public buildings, its residences and shops, were never so attractive, nor was the city ever thronged with so gay a crowd. There were no signs of the coming storm; all was the luxury, the intoxication of peace. The wickedness of the city was more unrestrained than I had ever seen it— less garnished with the outward covering of propriety, but no one dreamed that its doom was so close at hand, or that the empire was about to commit suicide by plunging into war. Much sooner should I have predicted revolution in Paris than war on the frontier. In the shops, on the streets, and in social circles, curses deep, but not loud, were heard against the emperor whose ambition and extravagance had run their race with the French nation, notwithstanding he had done so much to gratify French vanity. Louis Napoleon never had the hearts of the people; they never really believed in him, and they were becoming weary of his iron though brilliant rule. The change in popular feeling was strikingly perceptible—it was scarcely concealed, and was the subject of general remark among foreigners who had been familiar with Paris in the former years of his reign.

Weeks passed quickly away in recovering from the fatigues of nearly a year's journeying; in the society of friends who were gathering from the Continent and from home; in excursions here and there in and around Paris; and in doing nothing; and then we crossed the Channel to sojourn for a little season in merry England, and to enjoy the scenery of Scotland and Ireland.

An excursion of two days in the Isle of Wight, made from London, I shall ever recall among the most pleasing memories of British soil. The island is a beautiful garden; some of its scenery, especially the cliffs upon the sea-shore, in the highest degree picturesque and striking; the ruins of Carisbrooke Castle furnish the romance and history; and the scenes which have been recorded by the pen of Legh Richmond are invested with a sacred interest scarcely equaled in any other localities outside of the Holy Land. No one who has read his Annals of the Poor—among the most touching and instructive of human biographies, simple though they are—can fail to appreciate a visit to the cottage of the Dairyman's Daughter, and to the home and the grave of Little Jane.

Taking it leisurely through the interior of England, going here and there as inclination led us, and stopping now and then as attraction held us, at Oxford, Stratford-on-Avon, Kenilworth, Chatsworth, and many other places of interest, we at length reached the Tweed, and made another pilgrimage to the home and the haunts of Sir Walter Scott. We paused again at Edinburg, appropriately styled the modern Athens. Its location, in regard to land and sea, is strikingly like that of the Grecian capital, its monuments are not unworthy of the ancient city, and it has long embodied much of the learning of Britain.

Fresh in our hearts shall we ever keep the memory of the days we spent in the hospitable homes of the ancient kingdom of Fife, among the associations of the early days of Chalmers, where our time for sojourning was so short that we almost wished we had there begun instead of ending our travels. But the days would not wait upon us, and leaving reluctantly those delightful circles of friends, we made the tour of the Trosachs and the Lakes. From Glasgow we crossed the Irish Channel, ended our wanderings on land by journeying through the Emerald Isle, and took the steamer for home.

Gladly would we have avoided the Atlantic had there been any other way of reaching home. Long ago did I come to be of the same opinion with one of the Catos of ancient Rome. As he was drawing near his end, he said there were three regrets still lying on his mind. The first was, that he had spent a day without bringing any thing good to pass; the second, that he had once intrusted a secret to a woman (in which I differ from him *toto cœlo*); but the third regret was one that has always commanded my profound respect for the old Roman since first I was rocked in the cradle of the deep—that once in his lifetime he had made a journey by sea when he could have gone by land. Had there been any way to make the journey around the world by land, I should have avoided all the seas. Not that I have any fear of the ocean; nor am I called upon, like most voyagers, to pay tribute to Neptune; but I greatly prefer the solid earth.

With the exception of the China Seas, we found the winds and the waves nowhere so inhospitable as on the Atlantic. It was the month of July—the month and year of the extremest heat recorded on our shores, but, between northerly winds and the icebergs, we suffered intensely with the cold. Not until we had crossed the Banks was there a day on which it was mild enough to enjoy the deck. The voyage was boisterous and protracted, a perfect contrast to our experience on the Pacific.

But every voyage, not excepting that of life, must have its close. The familiar shores at length appeared, and we hailed Columbia, the sight of which was never so dear as when, after having tossed upon so many seas, and wandered in so many lands, the highlands of the coast, and then the green shores of the harbor, and then the spires of the city of New York rose into view.

And here we are at home again. Thanks to the kind Providence which has been over us in all the perils of the land and of the sea. And more thankful than ever shall we be that this land is our home. Each country that we have seen has its own peculiar features and its own attractions, but nowhere have we found such a combination of all that makes a country attractive in scenery and desirable as a life-long residence: majestic mountains and broad prairies, wide-spreading lakes and rivers navigable for thousands of miles, grand old forests and magnificent waterfalls, boundless mineral resources of every kind, all the varieties of climate, and the fruits of the earth poured out with a profusion scarcely imagined in any other part of the world. If we have learned nothing more in our wanderings, we have learned to appreciate our own country, and to be thankful to Him who "hath made of one blood all nations for to dwell on all the face of the earth, and hath determined the bounds of their habitation," for the goodly heritage he hath given us. The American who can travel abroad and not have his admiration for his own land increased can have seen but little of it, and is equally to be pitied with him who can see nothing good or beautiful in other lands.

Here evermore may our home be, until our journeyings on earth shall come to an end, and we take our departure to "a better country—that is, an heavenly."

THE END.

# VALUABLE STANDARD WORKS

## FOR PUBLIC AND PRIVATE LIBRARIES,

### PUBLISHED BY HARPER & BROTHERS, NEW YORK.

---

☞ *For a full List of Books suitable for Libraries, see* HARPER & BROTHERS' TRADE-LIST *and* CATALOGUE, *which may be had gratuitously on application to the Publishers personally, or by letter enclosing Five Cents.*

☞ HARPER & BROTHERS *will send any of the following works by mail, postage prepaid, to any part of the United States, on receipt of the price.*

MOTLEY'S DUTCH REPUBLIC. The Rise of the Dutch Republic. By JOHN LOTHROP MOTLEY, LL.D., D.C.L. With a Portrait of William of Orange. 3 vols., 8vo, Cloth, $10 50.

MOTLEY'S UNITED NETHERLANDS. History of the United Netherlands: from the Death of William the Silent to the Twelve Years' Truce—1609. With a full View of the English-Dutch Struggle against Spain, and of the Origin and Destruction of the Spanish Armada. By JOHN LOTHROP MOTLEY, LL.D., D.C.L. Portraits. 4 vols., 8vo, Cloth, $14 00.

NAPOLEON'S LIFE OF CÆSAR. The History of Julius Cæsar. By His Imperial Majesty NAPOLEON III. Two Volumes ready. Library Edition, 8vo, Cloth, $3 50 per vol.

*Maps to Vols. I. and II. sold separately. Price $1 50 each,* NET.

HAYDN'S DICTIONARY OF DATES, relating to all Ages and Nations. For Universal Reference. Edited by BENJAMIN VINCENT, Assistant Secretary and Keeper of the Library of the Royal Institution of Great Britain; and Revised for the Use of American Readers. 8vo, Cloth, $5 00; Sheep, $6 00.

MACGREGOR'S ROB ROY ON THE JORDAN. The Rob Roy on the Jordan, Nile, Red Sea, and Gennesareth, &c. A Canoe Cruise in Palestine and Egypt, and the Waters of Damascus. By J. MACGREGOR, M.A. With Maps and Illustrations. Crown 8vo, Cloth, $2 50.

WALLACE'S MALAY ARCHIPELAGO. The Malay Archipelago: the Land of the Orang-Utan and the Bird of Paradise. A Narrative of Travel, 1854–1862. With Studies of Man and Nature. By ALFRED RUSSEL WALLACE. With Ten Maps and Fifty-one Elegant Illustrations. Crown 8vo, Cloth, $3 50.

WHYMPER'S ALASKA. Travel and Adventure in the Territory of Alaska, formerly Russian America—now Ceded to the United States—and in various other parts of the North Pacific. By FREDERICK WHYMPER. With Map and Illustrations. Crown 8vo, Cloth, $2 50.

ORTON'S ANDES AND THE AMAZON. The Andes and the Amazon; or, Across the Continent of South America. By JAMES ORTON, M.A., Professor of Natural History in Vassar College, Poughkeepsie, N. Y., and Corresponding Member of the Academy of Natural Sciences, Philadelphia. With a New Map of Equatorial America and numerous Illustrations. Crown 8vo, Cloth, $2 00.

WINCHELL'S SKETCHES OF CREATION. Sketches of Creation: a Popular View of some of the Grand Conclusions of the Sciences in reference to the History of Matter and of Life. Together with a Statement of the Intimations of Science respecting the Primordial Condition and the Ultimate Destiny of the Earth and the Solar System. By ALEXANDER WINCHELL, LL.D., Professor of Geology, Zoology, and Botany in the University of Michigan, and Director of the State Geological Survey. With Illustrations. 12mo, Cloth, $2 00.

WHITE'S MASSACRE OF ST. BARTHOLOMEW. The Massacre of St. Bartholomew: Preceded by a History of the Religious Wars in the Reign of Charles IX. By HENRY WHITE, M.A. With Illustrations. 8vo, Cloth, $1 75.

2    *Harper & Brothers' Valuable Standard Works.*

LOSSING'S FIELD-BOOK OF THE REVOLUTION. Pictorial Field-Book of the Revolution; or, Illustrations, by Pen and Pencil, of the History, Biography, Scenery, Relics, and Traditions of the War for Independence. By BENSON J. LOSSING. 2 vols., 8vo, Cloth, $14 00; Sheep, $15 00; Half Calf, $18 00; Full Turkey Morocco, $22 00.

LOSSING'S FIELD-BOOK OF THE WAR OF 1812. Pictorial Field-Book of the War of 1812; or, Illustrations, by Pen and Pencil, of the History, Biography, Scenery, Relics, and Traditions of the Last War for American Independence. By BENSON J. LOSSING. With several hundred Engravings on Wood, by Lossing and Barritt, chiefly from Original Sketches by the Author. 1088 pages, 8vo, Cloth, $7 00; Sheep, $8 50; Half Calf, $10 00.

ALFORD'S GREEK TESTAMENT. The Greek Testament: with a critically revised Text; a Digest of Various Readings; Marginal References to Verbal and Idiomatic Usage; Prolegomena; and a Critical and Exegetical Commentary. For the Use of Theological Students and Ministers. By HENRY ALFORD, D.D., Dean of Canterbury. Vol. I., containing the Four Gospels. 944 pages, 8vo, Cloth, $6 00; Sheep, $6 50.

ABBOTT'S FREDERICK THE GREAT. The History of Frederick the Second, called Frederick the Great. By JOHN S. C. ABBOTT. Elegantly Illustrated. 8vo, Cloth, $5 00.

ABBOTT'S HISTORY OF THE FRENCH REVOLUTION. The French Revolution of 1789, as viewed in the Light of Republican Institutions. By JOHN S. C. ABBOTT. With 100 Engravings. 8vo, Cloth, $5 00.

ABBOTT'S NAPOLEON BONAPARTE. The History of Napoleon Bonaparte. By JOHN S. C. ABBOTT. With Maps, Woodcuts, and Portraits on Steel. 2 vols., 8vo, Cloth, $10 00.

ABBOTT'S NAPOLEON AT ST. HELENA; or, Interesting Anecdotes and Remarkable Conversations of the Emperor during the Five and a Half Years of his Captivity. Collected from the Memorials of Las Casas, O'Meara, Montholon, Antommarchi, and others. By JOHN S. C. ABBOTT. With Illustrations. 8vo, Cloth, $5 00.

ADDISON'S COMPLETE WORKS. The Works of Joseph Addison, embracing the whole of the "Spectator." Complete in 3 vols., 8vo, Cloth, $6 00.

ALCOCK'S JAPAN. The Capital of the Tycoon: a Narrative of a Three Years' Residence in Japan. By Sir RUTHERFORD ALCOCK, K.C.B., Her Majesty's Envoy Extraordinary and Minister Plenipotentiary in Japan. With Maps and Engravings. 2 vols., 12mo, Cloth, $3 50.

ALISON'S HISTORY OF EUROPE. FIRST SERIES: From the Commencement of the French Revolution, in 1789, to the Restoration of the Bourbons, in 1815. [In addition to the Notes on Chapter LXXVI., which correct the errors of the original work concerning the United States, a copious Analytical Index has been appended to this American edition.] SECOND SERIES: From the Fall of Napoleon, in 1815, to the Accession of Louis Napoleon, in 1852. 8 vols., 8vo, Cloth, $16 00.

BALDWIN'S PRE-HISTORIC NATIONS. Pre-Historic Nations; or, Inquiries concerning some of the Great Peoples and Civilizations of Antiquity, and their Probable Relation to a still Older Civilization of the Ethiopians or Cushites of Arabia. By JOHN D. BALDWIN, Member of the American Oriental Society. 12mo, Cloth, $1 75.

BARTH'S NORTH AND CENTRAL AFRICA. Travels and Discoveries in North and Central Africa: being a Journal of an Expedition undertaken under the Auspices of H. B. M.'s Government, in the Years 1849–1855. By HENRY BARTH, Ph.D., D.C.L. Illustrated. 3 vols., 8vo, Cloth, $12 00.

HENRY WARD BEECHER'S SERMONS. Sermons by HENRY WARD BEECHER, Plymouth Church, Brooklyn. Selected from Published and Unpublished Discourses, and Revised by their Author. With Steel Portrait. Complete in 2 vols., 8vo, Cloth, $5 00.

LYMAN BEECHER'S AUTOBIOGRAPHY, &c. Autobiography, Correspondence, &c., of Lyman Beecher, D.D. Edited by his Son, CHARLES BEECHER. With Three Steel Portraits, and Engravings on Wood. In 2 vols., 12mo, Cloth, $5 00.

BOSWELL'S JOHNSON. The Life of Samuel Johnson, LL.D. Including a Journey to the Hebrides. By JAMES BOSWELL, Esq. A New Edition, with numerous Additions and Notes. By JOHN WILSON CROKER, LL.D., F.R.S. Portrait of Boswell. 2 vols., 8vo, Cloth, $4 00.

**DRAPER'S CIVIL WAR.** History of the American Civil War. By JOHN W. DRAPER, M.D., LL.D., Professor of Chemistry and Physiology in the University of New York. In Three Vols. 8vo, Cloth, $3 50 per vol.

**DRAPER'S INTELLECTUAL DEVELOPMENT OF EUROPE.** A History of the Intellectual Development of Europe. By JOHN W. DRAPER, M.D., LL.D., Professor of Chemistry and Physiology in the University of New York. 8vo, Cloth, $5 00.

**DRAPER'S AMERICAN CIVIL POLICY.** Thoughts on the Future Civil Policy of America. By JOHN W. DRAPER, M.D., LL.D., Professor of Chemistry and Physiology in the University of New York. Crown 8vo, Cloth, $2 50.

**DU CHAILLU'S AFRICA.** Explorations and Adventures in Equatorial Africa: with Accounts of the Manners and Customs of the People, and of the Chase of the Gorilla, the Crocodile, Leopard, Elephant, Hippopotamus, and other Animals. By PAUL B. DU CHAILLU. Numerous Illustrations. 8vo, Cloth; $5 00.

**BELLOWS'S OLD WORLD.** The Old World in its New Face: Impressions of Europe in 1867–1868. By HENRY W. BELLOWS. 2 vols., 12mo, Cloth, $3 50.

**BRODHEAD'S HISTORY OF NEW YORK.** History of the State of New York. By JOHN ROMEYN BRODHEAD. 1609–1691. 2 vols. 8vo, Cloth, $3 00 per vol.

**BROUGHAM'S AUTOBIOGRAPHY.** Life and Times of HENRY, LORD BROUGHAM. Written by Himself. In Three Volumes. 12mo, Cloth, $2 00 per vol.

**BULWER'S PROSE WORKS.** Miscellaneous Prose Works of Edward Bulwer. Lord Lytton. 2 vols., 12mo, Cloth, $3 50.

**BULWER'S HORACE.** The Odes and Epodes of Horace. A Metrical Translation into English. With Introduction and Commentaries. By LORD LYTTON. With Latin Text from the Editions of Orelli, Macleane, and Yonge. 12mo, Cloth, $1 75.

**BULWER'S KING ARTHUR.** A Poem. By EARL LYTTON. New Edition. 12mo, Cloth, $1 75.

**BURNS'S LIFE AND WORKS.** The Life and Works of Robert Burns. Edited by ROBERT CHAMBERS. 4 vols., 12mo, Cloth, $6 00.

**REINDEER, DOGS, AND SNOW-SHOES.** A Journal of Siberian Travel and Explorations made in the years 1865–'67. By RICHARD J. BUSH, late of the Russo-American Telegraph Expedition. Illustrated. Crown 8vo, Cloth, $3 00.

**CARLYLE'S FREDERICK THE GREAT.** History of Friedrich II., called Frederick the Great. By THOMAS CARLYLE. Portraits, Maps, Plans, &c. 6 vols., 12mo, Cloth, $12 00.

**CARLYLE'S FRENCH REVOLUTION.** History of the French Revolution. Newly Revised by the Author, with Index, &c. 2 vols., 12mo, Cloth, $3 50.

**CARLYLE'S OLIVER CROMWELL.** Letters and Speeches of Oliver Cromwell. With Elucidations and Connecting Narrative. 2 vols., 12mo, Cloth, $3 50.

**CHALMERS'S POSTHUMOUS WORKS.** The Posthumous Works of Dr. Chalmers. Edited by his Son-in-Law, Rev. WILLIAM HANNA, LL.D. Complete in 9 vols., 12mo, Cloth, $13 50.

**COLERIDGE'S COMPLETE WORKS.** The Complete Works of Samuel Taylor Coleridge. With an Introductory Essay upon his Philosophical and Theological Opinions. Edited by Professor SHEDD. Complete in Seven Vols. With a fine Portrait. Small 8vo, Cloth, $10 50.

**CURTIS'S HISTORY OF THE CONSTITUTION.** History of the Origin, Formation, and Adoption of the Constitution of the United States. By GEORGE TICKNOR CURTIS. 2 vols., 8vo, Cloth, $6 00.

**DOOLITTLE'S CHINA.** Social Life of the Chinese: with some Account of their Religious, Governmental, Educational, and Business Customs and Opinions. With special but not exclusive Reference to Fuhchau. By Rev. JUSTUS DOOLITTLE, Fourteen Years Member of the Fuhchan Mission of the American Board. Illustrated with more than 150 characteristic Engravings on Wood. 2 vols., 12mo, Cloth, $5 00.

**GIBBON'S ROME.** History of the Decline and Fall of the Roman Empire. By EDWARD GIBBON. With Notes by Rev. H. H. MILMAN and M. GUIZOT. A new cheap Edition. To which is added a complete Index of the whole Work, and a Portrait of the Author. 6 vols., 12mo, Cloth, $9 00.

**HARPER'S NEW CLASSICAL LIBRARY.** Literal Translations. The following Volumes are now ready. Portraits. 12mo, Cloth, $1 50 each. CÆSAR.—VIRGIL.—SALLUST.—HORACE.—CICERO'S ORATIONS.—CICERO'S OFFICES, &c.—CICERO ON ORATORY AND ORATORS.—TACITUS (2 vols.).—TERENCE.—SOPHOCLES.—JUVENAL.—XENOPHON.—HOMER'S ILIAD.—HOMER'S ODYSSEY.—HERODOTUS.—DEMOSTHENES.—THUCYDIDES.—ÆSCHYLUS.—EURIPIDES (2 vols.).—LIVY (2 vols.).

**DAVIS'S CARTHAGE.** Carthage and her Remains: being an Account of the Excavations and Researches on the Site of the Phœnician Metropolis in Africa and other adjacent Places. Conducted under the Auspices of Her Majesty's Government. By Dr. DAVIS, F.R.G.S. Profusely Illustrated with Maps, Woodcuts, Chromo-Lithographs, &c. 8vo, Cloth, $4 00.

**EDGEWORTH'S (MISS) NOVELS.** With Engravings. 10 vols., 12mo, Cloth, $15 00.

**GROTE'S HISTORY OF GREECE.** 12 vols., 12mo, Cloth, $18 00.

**HELPS'S SPANISH CONQUEST.** The Spanish Conquest in America, and its Relation to the History of Slavery and to the Government of Colonies. By ARTHUR HELPS. 4 vols., 12mo, Cloth, $6 00.

**HALE'S (MRS.) WOMAN'S RECORD.** Woman's Record; or, Biographical Sketches of all Distinguished Women, from the Creation to the Present Time. Arranged in Four Eras, with Selections from Female Writers of each Era. By Mrs. SARAH JOSEPHA HALE. Illustrated with more than 200 Portraits. 8vo, Cloth, $5 00.

**HALL'S ARCTIC RESEARCHES.** Arctic Researches and Life among the Esquimaux: being the Narrative of an Expedition in Search of Sir John Franklin, in the Years 1860, 1861, and 1862. By CHARLES FRANCIS HALL. With Maps and 100 Illustrations. The Illustrations are from Original Drawings by Charles Parsons, Henry L. Stephens, Solomon Eytinge, W. S. L. Jewett, and Granville Perkins, after Sketches by Captain Hall. 8vo, Cloth, $5 00.

**HALLAM'S CONSTITUTIONAL HISTORY OF ENGLAND,** from the Accession of Henry VII. to the Death of George II. 8vo, Cloth, $2 00.

**HALLAM'S LITERATURE.** Introduction to the Literature of Europe during the Fifteenth, Sixteenth, and Seventeenth Centuries. By HENRY HALLAM. 2 vols., 8vo, Cloth, $4 00.

**HALLAM'S MIDDLE AGES.** State of Europe during the Middle Ages. By HENRY HALLAM. 8vo, Cloth, $2 00.

**HILDRETH'S HISTORY OF THE UNITED STATES.** FIRST SERIES: From the First Settlement of the Country to the Adoption of the Federal Constitution. SECOND SERIES: From the Adoption of the Federal Constitution to the End of the Sixteenth Congress. 6 vols., 8vo, Cloth, $18 00.

**HUME'S HISTORY OF ENGLAND.** History of England, from the Invasion of Julius Cæsar to the Abdication of James II., 1688. By DAVID HUME. A new Edition, with the Author's last Corrections and Improvements. To which is Prefixed a short Account of his Life, written by Himself. With a Portrait of the Author. 6 vols., 12mo, Cloth, $9 00.

**JAY'S WORKS.** Complete Works of Rev. William Jay: comprising his Sermons, Family Discourses, Morning and Evening Exercises for every Day in the Year, Family Prayers, &c. Author's enlarged Edition, revised. 3 vols., 8vo, Cloth, $6 00.

**JEFFERSON'S DOMESTIC LIFE.** The Domestic Life of Thomas Jefferson: compiled from Family Letters and Reminiscences by his Great-Granddaughter, SARAH N. RANDOLPH. With Illustrations. Crown 8vo, Illuminated Cloth, Beveled Edges, $2 50.

**JOHNSON'S COMPLETE WORKS.** The Works of Samuel Johnson, LL.D. With an Essay on his Life and Genius, by ARTHUR MURPHY, Esq. Portrait of Johnson. 2 vols., 8vo, Cloth, $4 00.

**KINGLAKE'S CRIMEAN WAR.** The Invasion of the Crimea, and an Account of its Progress down to the Death of Lord Raglan. By ALEXANDER WILLIAM KINGLAKE. With Maps and Plans. Two Vols. ready. 12mo, Cloth, $2 00 per vol.

**KINGSLEY'S WEST INDIES.** At Last: A Christmas in the West Indies. By CHARLES KINGSLEY. Illustrated. 12mo, Cloth, $1 50.

KRUMMACHER'S DAVID, KING OF ISRAEL. David, the King of Israel: a Portrait drawn from Bible History and the Book of Psalms. By FREDERICK WILLIAM KRUMMACHER, D.D., Author of "Elijah the Tishbite," &c. Translated under the express Sanction of the Author by the Rev. M. G. EASTON, M.A. With a Letter from Dr. Krummacher to his American Readers, and a Portrait. 12mo, Cloth, $1 75.

LAMB'S COMPLETE WORKS. The Works of Charles Lamb. Comprising his Letters, Poems, Essays of Elia, Essays upon Shakspeare, Hogarth, &c., and a Sketch of his Life, with the Final Memorials, by T. NOON TALFOURD. Portrait. 2 vols., 12mo, Cloth, $3 00.

LIVINGSTONE'S SOUTH AFRICA. Missionary Travels and Researches in South Africa; including a Sketch of Sixteen Years' Residence in the Interior of Africa, and a Journey from the Cape of Good Hope to Loando on the West Coast; thence across the Continent, down the River Zambesi, to the Eastern Ocean. By DAVID LIVINGSTONE, LL.D., D.C.L. With Portrait, Maps by Arrowsmith, and numerous Illustrations. 8vo, Cloth, $4 50.

LIVINGSTONES' ZAMBESI. Narrative of an Expedition to the Zambesi and its Tributaries, and of the Discovery of the Lakes Shirwa and Nyassa. 1858–1864. By DAVID and CHARLES LIVINGSTONE. With Map and Illustrations. 8vo, Cloth, $5 00.

M'CLINTOCK & STRONG'S CYCLOPÆDIA. Cyclopædia of Biblical, Theological, and Ecclesiastical Literature. Prepared by the Rev. JOHN M'CLINTOCK, D.D., and JAMES STRONG, S.T.D. 3 vols. now ready. Royal 8vo. Price per vol., Cloth, $5 00; Sheep, $6 00; Half Morocco, $8 00.

MARCY'S ARMY LIFE ON THE BORDER. Thirty Years of Army Life on the Border. Comprising Descriptions of the Indian Nomads of the Plains; Explorations of New Territory; a Trip across the Rocky Mountains in the Winter; Descriptions of the Habits of Different Animals found in the West, and the Methods of Hunting them; with Incidents in the Life of Different Frontier Men, &c., &c. By Brevet Brigadier-General R. B. MARCY, U.S.A., Author of "The Prairie Traveller." With numerous Illustrations. 8vo, Cloth, Beveled Edges, $3 00.

MACAULAY'S HISTORY OF ENGLAND. The History of England from the Accession of James II. By THOMAS BABINGTON MACAULAY. With an Original Portrait of the Author. 5 vols., 8vo, Cloth, $10 00; 12mo, Cloth, $7 50.

MOSHEIM'S ECCLESIASTICAL HISTORY, Ancient and Modern; in which the Rise, Progress, and Variation of Church Power are considered in their Connection with the State of Learning and Philosophy, and the Political History of Europe during that Period. Translated, with Notes, &c., by A. MACLAINE, D.D. A new Edition, continued to 1826, by C. COOTE, LL.D. 2 vols., 8vo, Cloth, $4 00.

NEVIUS'S CHINA. China and the Chinese: a General Description of the Country and its Inhabitants; its Civilization and Form of Government; its Religious and Social Institutions; its Intercourse with other Nations; and its Present Condition and Prospects. By the Rev. JOHN L. NEVIUS, Ten Years a Missionary in China. With a Map and Illustrations. 12mo, Cloth, $1 75.

OLIN'S (DR.) LIFE AND LETTERS. 2 vols., 12mo, Cloth, $3 00.

OLIN'S (DR.) TRAVELS. Travels in Egypt, Arabia Petræa, and the Holy Land. Engravings. 2 vols., 8vo, Cloth, $3 00.

OLIN'S (DR.) WORKS. The Works of Stephen Olin, D.D., late President of the Wesleyan University. 2 vols., 12mo, Cloth, $3 00.

OLIPHANT'S CHINA AND JAPAN. Narrative of the Earl of Elgin's Mission to China and Japan, in the Years 1857, '58, '59. By LAURENCE OLIPHANT, Private Secretary to Lord Elgin. Illustrations. 8vo, Cloth, $3 50.

OLIPHANT'S (MRS.) LIFE OF EDWARD IRVING. The Life of Edward Irving, Minister of the National Scotch Church, London. Illustrated by his Journals and Correspondence. By Mrs. OLIPHANT. Portrait. 8vo, Cloth, $3 50.

RAWLINSON'S MANUAL OF ANCIENT HISTORY. A Manual of Ancient History, from the Earliest Times to the Fall of the Western Empire. Comprising the History of Chaldæa, Assyria, Media, Babylonia, Lydia, Phœnicia, Syria, Judæa, Egypt, Carthage, Persia, Greece, Macedonia, Parthia, and Rome. By GEORGE RAWLINSON, M.A., Camden Professor of Ancient History in the University of Oxford. 12mo, Cloth, $2 50.

RECLUS'S THE EARTH. The Earth: a Descriptive History of the Phenomena and Life of the Globe. By ELISÉE RECLUS. Translated by the late B. B. Woodward, and Edited by Henry Woodward. With 234 Maps and Illustrations, and 23 Page Maps printed in Colors. 8vo, Cloth, $5 00.

POETS OF THE NINETEENTH CENTURY. The Poets of the Nineteenth Century. Selected and Edited by the Rev. ROBERT ARIS WILLMOTT. With English and American Additions, arranged by EVERT A. DUYCKINCK, Editor of "Cyclopædia of American Literature." Comprising Selections from the Greatest Authors of the Age. Superbly Illustrated with 132 Engravings from Designs by the most Eminent Artists. In elegant small 4to form, printed on Superfine Tinted Paper, richly bound in extra Cloth, Beveled, Gilt Edges, $6 00; Half Calf, $6 00; Full Turkey Morocco, $10 00.

SHAKSPEARE. The Dramatic Works of William Shakspeare, with the Corrections and Illustrations of Dr. JOHNSON, G. STEEVENS, and others. Revised by ISAAC REED. Engravings. 6 vols., Royal 12mo, Cloth, $9 00.

SMILES'S LIFE OF THE STEPHENSONS. The Life of George Stephenson, and of his Son, Robert Stephenson; comprising, also, a History of the Invention and Introduction of the Railway Locomotive. By SAMUEL SMILES, Author of "Self-Help," &c. With Steel Portraits and numerous Illustrations. 8vo, Cloth, $3 00.

SMILES'S HISTORY OF THE HUGUENOTS. The Huguenots: their Settlements, Churches, and Industries in England and Ireland. By SAMUEL SMILES. With an Appendix relating to the Huguenots in America. Crown 8vo, Cloth, $1 75.

SPEKE'S AFRICA. Journal of the Discovery of the Source of the Nile. By Captain JOHN HANNING SPEKE, Captain H. M. Indian Army, Fellow and Gold Medalist of the Royal Geographical Society, Hon. Corresponding Member and Gold Medalist of the French Geographical Society, &c. With Maps and Portraits and numerous Illustrations, chiefly from Drawings by Captain GRANT. 8vo, Cloth, uniform with Livingstone, Barth, Burton, &c., $4 00.

STRICKLAND'S (Miss) QUEENS OF SCOTLAND. Lives of the Queens of Scotland and English Princesses connected with the Regal Succession of Great Britain. By AGNES STRICKLAND. 8 vols., 12mo, Cloth, $12 00.

THE STUDENT'S SERIES.
France. Engravings. 12mo, Cloth, $2 00.
Gibbon. Engravings. 12mo, Cloth, $2 00.
Greece. Engravings. 12mo, Cloth, $2 00.
Hume. Engravings. 12mo, Cloth, $2 00.
Rome. By Liddell. Engravings. 12mo, Cloth, $2 00.
Old Testament History. Engravings. 12mo, Cloth, $2 00.
New Testament History. Engravings. 12mo, Cloth, $2 00.
Strickland's Queens of England. Abridged. Engravings. 12mo, Cloth, $2 00.
Ancient History of the East. 12mo, Cloth, $2 00.
Hallam's Middle Ages. 12mo, Cloth, $2 00.
Lyell's Elements of Geology. 12mo, Cloth, $2 00.

TENNYSON'S COMPLETE POEMS. The Complete Poems of Alfred Tennyson, Poet Laureate. With numerous Illustrations by Eminent Artists, and Three Characteristic Portraits. 8vo, Paper, 75 cents; Cloth, $1 25.

THOMSON'S LAND AND THE BOOK. The Land and the Book; or, Biblical Illustrations drawn from the Manners and Customs, the Scenes and the Scenery of the Holy Land. By W. M. THOMSON, D.D., Twenty-five Years a Missionary of the A.B.C.F.M. in Syria and Palestine. With two elaborate Maps of Palestine, an accurate Plan of Jerusalem, and several hundred Engravings, representing the Scenery, Topography, and Productions of the Holy Land, and the Costumes, Manners, and Habits of the People. 2 large 12mo vols., Cloth, $5 00.

TYERMAN'S WESLEY. The Life and Times of the Rev. John Wesley, M.A., Founder of the Methodists. By the Rev. LUKE TYERMAN, Author of "The Life of Rev. Samuel Wesley." Portraits. 3 vols., Crown 8vo.

VÁMBÉRY'S CENTRAL ASIA. Travels in Central Asia. Being the Account of a Journey from Teheran across the Turkoman Desert, on the Eastern Shore of the Caspian, to Khiva, Bokhara, and Samarcand, performed in the Year 1863. By ARMINIUS VÁMBÉRY, Member of the Hungarian Academy of Pesth, by whom he was sent on this Scientific Mission. With Map and Woodcuts. 8vo, Cloth, $4 50.

WOOD'S HOMES WITHOUT HANDS. Homes Without Hands: being a Description of the Habitations of Animals, classed according to their Principle of Construction. By J. G. WOOD, M.A., F.L.S. With about 140 Illustrations. 8vo, Cloth, Beveled Edges, $4 50.

www.ingramcontent.com/pod-product-compliance
Lightning Source LLC
Chambersburg PA
CBHW031956300426
44117CB00008B/792